Annual Editions: Aging, 27/e

Edited by Elaina F. Osterbur

http://create.mcgraw-hill.com

This McGraw-Hill Create text may include materials submitted to
McGraw-Hill for publication by the instructor of this course.
The instructor is solely responsible for the editorial content of such
materials. Instructors retain copyright of these additional materials.

ISBN-10: 1259161161   ISBN-13: 9781259161162

Contents

Preface

The decline of the crude birth rate in the United States and other nations, combined with improving food supplies, sanitation, and medical technology, has resulted in an ever-increasing number and percentage of people remaining alive and healthy well into their retirement years. The result is a shifting age composition of the populations in these nations—a population composed of fewer people under age 20 and more people 65 and older.

In 1900 in the United States, approximately 3 million Americans were 65 years old and older, and they composed 4 percent of the population. In 2000, 36 million persons were 65 years old and older, and they represented 13 percent of the total population. The most rapid increase in the number of older persons is expected between 2010 and 2030 when the baby boom generation reaches the age of 65. Demographers predict that by 2030, there will be 66 million older persons representing approximately 22 percent of the total population. [The increasing number of older people has made many of the problems of aging immediately visible to the average American. These problems have become widespread topics of concern for political leaders, government planners, and average citizens. Moreover, the aging of the population has become perceived as a phenomenon of the United States and the industrialized countries of Western Europe—it is also occurring in the underdeveloped countries of the world. An increasing percentage of the world's population is now defined as aged.] Today, almost all middle-aged people expect to live to retirement age and beyond. Both the middle-aged and the elderly have pushed for solutions to the problems confronting older Americans. Everyone seems to agree that granting the elderly a secure and comfortable status is desirable. Voluntary associations, communities, and state and federal governments have committed themselves to improving the lives of older people. Many programs for senior citizens, both public and private, have emerged in the last 50 years.

The change in the age composition of the population has not gone unnoticed by the media or the academic community. The number of articles appearing in the popular press and professional journals has increased dramatically over the last several years. Although scientists have been concerned with the aging process for some time, the volume of research and writing on this subject have expanded in the last three decades.

This volume represents the field of gerontology in that it is interdisciplinary in its approach, including articles from the biological sciences, medicine, nursing, psychology, sociology, and social work. The articles are taken from the popular press, government publications, and scientific journals. They represent a wide cross-section of authors, perspectives, and issues related to the aging process. They were chosen because they address the most relevant and current problems in the field of aging and present divergent views on the appropriate solutions to these problems. The topics covered include demographic trends; the aging process; longevity; the quality of later life; social attitudes toward old age; problems and potentials of aging; retirement; death; living environments in later life; and social policies, programs, and services for older Americans.

The articles are organized into an anthology that is useful for both the student and the teacher. *Learning Outcomes* outline the key concepts that students should focus on as they read the material. *Critical Thinking* questions allow students to test their understanding of the key concepts, and a list of recommended *Internet References* guides them to the best sources of additional information on a topic. A *Topic Guide* assists students in finding other articles on a given subject within this edition. The goal of *Annual Editions: Aging* is to choose articles that are pertinent, well written, and helpful to those concerned with the field of gerontology. Comments, suggestions, and constructive criticism are welcome to help improve future editions of this book.

Editor

Dr. Elaina F. Osterbur is an assistant professor at Saint Louis University in St. Louis, Missouri. After receiving a Master's Degree in Gerontology, Elaina received her PhD in Epidemiology at the University of Illinois Urbana-Champaign. Her research interests include gynecological cancer screening in older women and family caregiving.

Academic Advisory Board

Members of the Academic Advisory Board are instrumental in the final selection of articles for the *Annual Editions* series. Their review of the articles for content, level, and appropriateness provides critical direction to the editor(s) and staff. We think that you will find their careful consideration reflected in this book.

James Blackburn
Hunter College

Ric Ferraro
University of North Dakota

Stephen M. Golant
University of Florida

Lisa Hollis-Sawyer
Northeastern Illinois University

William Hoyer
Syracuse University

Robert C. Intrieri
Western Illinois University

Correlation Guide

The *Annual Editions* series provides students with convenient, inexpensive access to current, carefully selected articles from the public press. **Annual Editions: Aging, 27/e** is an easy-to-use reader that presents articles on important topics such as *living longer, retirement, health care, dying,* and many more. For more information on other McGraw-Hill Create™ titles and collections, visit www.mcgrawhillcreate.com.

This convenient guide matches the articles in **Annual Editions: Aging 27/e** with **Aging and the Life Course: An Introduction to Social Gerontology** by Quadagno.

Aging and the Life Course: An Introduction to Social Gerontology, 6/e By Quadagno	Annual Editions: Aging 27/e
Chapter 1: The Field of Social Gerontology	Attitudes towards Older People: Findings and Recommendation for Practice Friendships, Family Relationships Get Better with Age Thanks to Forgiveness, Stereotypes A Longitudinal Analysis of Social Engagement in Late-Life Widowhood Social Security: Fears vs Facts: What Social Security Critics Keep Getting Wrong The U-bend of Life: Why, Beyond Middle Age, People Get Happier as They Get Older
Chapter 2: Life Course Transitions	City Governments and Aging in Place: Community Design, Transportation, and Housing Innovation Adoption End-of-Life Concerns and Care Preferences: Congruence among Terminally Ill Elders and Their Family Caregivers The Myriad Strategies for Seeking Control in the Dying Process Time Trends of Incidence of Age-Associated Disease in the U.S. Elderly Population: Medicare-Based Analysis Will Baby Boomers Phase into Retirement?
Chapter 3: Theories of Aging	Age and Gender Effects on the Assessment of Spirituality and Religious Sentiments (ASPIRES) Scale: A Cross-Sectional Analysis Cognitive Assessment in the Practice of Medicine: Dealing with the Aging Physician The Effect of Exercise on Affective and Self-Efficacy Responses in Older and Younger Women Treatment of Alzheimer's Disease The U-bend of Life: Why, Beyond Middle Age, People Get Happier as They Get Older
Chapter 4: Demography of Aging	Demography Is Not Destiny: The Challenges and Opportunities of Global Population Aging End-of-Life Care in the United States: Current Reality and Future Promise: A Policy Review Social Security: Fears vs. Facts: What Social Security Critics Keep Getting Wrong Social Security Heading for Insolvency Even Faster: Trust Funds Could Run Dry in about 2 Decades Time for a Tune-Up
Chapter 5: Old Age and the Welfare State	Medicare May Soon Take New Shape Retooling Medicare? Social Security: Fears vs. Facts: What Social Security Critics Keep Getting Wrong Social Security Heading for Insolvency Even Faster: Trust Funds Could Run Dry in about 2 Decades Top 25 Social Security Questions
Chapter 6: Biological Perspectives on Aging	America's Old Getting Older: 90-Somethings Triple in Number since 1980 Healthy Aging in the 22nd Century Poll: Obesity Hits More Boomers in U.S. Poll: Upbeat Baby Boomers Say They're Not Old Yet The U-bend of Life: Why, Beyond Middle Age, People Get Happier as They Get Older Will You Live to Be 100?
Chapter 7: Psychological Perspectives on Aging	Age and Gender Effects on the Assessment of Spirituality and Religious Sentiments (ASPIRES) Scale: A Cross-Sectional Analysis Cognitive Assessment in the Practice of Medicine: Dealing with the Aging Physician The Effect of Exercise on Affective and Self-Efficacy Responses in Older and Younger Women How Old Do You Feel Inside? The Key to Staying Healthy and Living Longer Is Deciding You're Not Old and Decrepit Poll: Upbeat Baby Boomers Say They're Not Old Yet
Chapter 8: Family Relationships and Social Support Systems	"Affordable" Death in the United States: An Action Plan Based on Lessons Learned from the *Nursing Economic$* Special Issue Attitudes towards Caring for Older People: Findings and Recommendation for Practice City Governments and Aging in Place: Community Design, Transportation, and Housing Innovation Adoption End-of-Life Concerns and Care Preferences: Congruence among Terminally Ill Elders and Their Family Caregivers Friendships, Family Relationships Get Better with Age Thanks to Forgiveness, Stereotypes
Chapter 9: Living Arrangements	City Governments and Aging in Place: Community Design, Transportation, and Housing Innovation Adoption Happy Together A Little Help Can Go a Long Way: "Aging in Place" Requires Good Luck, Support Network The Real Social Network

(continued)

(concluded)

Aging and the Life Course: An Introduction to Social Gerontology, 6/e By Quadagno	Annual Editions: Aging 27/e
Chapter 10: Work and Retirement	Do-It-Yourself Financial Freedom Live for Today, Save for Tomorrow Top 25 Social Security Questions Will Baby Boomers Phase into Retirement?
Chapter 11: Health and Health Care	Health Disparities among Lesbian, Gay, and Bisexual Older Adults: Results from a Population-Based Study Healthy Aging in the 22nd Century How Do You Feel Inside?: The Key to Staying Healthy and Living Longer Is Deciding You're Not Old and Decrepit Palliative Care: A Paradigm of Care Responsive to the Demands for Health Care Reform in America Time Trends of Incidence of Age-Associated Diseases in the U.S. Elderly Population: Medicare-Based Analysis Treatment of Alzheimer's Disease
Chapter 12: Caring for the Frail Elderly	"Affordable" Death in the United States: An Action Plan Based on Lessons Learned from the *Nursing Economic$* Special Issue Attitudes towards Caring for Older People: Findings and Recommendations for Practice End-of-Life Concerns and Care Preferences: Congruence among Terminally Ill Elders and Their Family Caregivers Palliative Care: A Paradigm of Care Responsive to the Demands for Health Care Reform in America Six Steps to Help Seniors Make the CPR/DNR Decision
Chapter 13: Death, Dying, and Bereavement	"Affordable" Death in the United States: An Action Plan Based on Lessons Learned from the *Nursing Economic$* Special Issue End-of-Life Care in the United States: Current Reality and Future Promise: A Policy Review End-of-Life Concerns and Care Preferences: Congruence among Terminally Ill Elders and Their Family Caregivers Palliative Care: Impact on Quality and Cost
Chapter 14: The Economics of Aging	Do-It-Yourself Financial Freedom Let's Restore the Middle Class Palliative Care: A Paradigm of Care Responsive to the Demands for Health Care Reform in America Palliative Care: Impact on Quality and Cost Will Baby Boomers Phase into Retirement?
Chapter 15: Poverty and Inequality	City Governments and Aging in Place: Community Design, Transportation, and Housing Innovation Adoption Medicare May Soon Take New Shape Protect Social Security Social Security Heading for Insolvency Even Faster: Trust Funds Could Run Dry in about 2 Decades The Real Social Network
Chapter 16: The Politics of Aging	Medicare May Soon Take New Shape Protect Social Security Retooling Medicare? Social Security: Fears vs. Facts: What Social Security Critics Keep Getting Wrong Social Security Heading for Insolvency Even Faster: Trust Funds Could Run Dry in about 2 Decades

Topic Guide

This topic guide suggests how the selections in this book relate to the subjects covered in your course.

All the articles that relate to each topic are listed below the bold-faced term.

Adulthood, late

America's Getting Older: 90-Somethings Triple in Number since 1980
Healthy Aging in the 22nd Century
Let's Restore the Middle Class
Poll: Upbeat Baby Boomers Say They're Not Old Yet
Protect Social Security
Retooling Medicare?
Time for a Tune-Up

Age discrimination

Attitudes towards Caring for Older People: Findings and Recommendation for Practice
We Need to Fight Age Bias

Alternative lifestyles

America's Old Getting Older: 90-Somethings Triple in Number since 1980
City Governments and Aging in Place: Community Design,Transportation, and Housing Innovation Adoption
How to Live to 100
The Effect of Exercise on Affective and Self-Efficacy Responses in Older and Younger Women

Assisted living

A Little Help Can Go a Long Way: "Aging in Place" Requires Good Luck, Support Network
City Governments and Aging in Place: Community Design, Transportation, and Housing Innovation Adoption
Happy Together

Attitudes toward aging

How Old Do You Feel Inside?: The Key to Staying Healthy and Living Longer Is Deciding You're Not Old and Decrepit
Poll: Upbeat Baby Boomers Say They're Not Old Yet
We Need to Fight Age Bias

Biology of aging

Age-Proof Your Brain: 10 Easy Ways to Stay Sharp Forever
America's Old Getting Older: 90-Somethings Triple in Number since 1980
End-of-Life Concerns and Care Preferences: Congruence among Terminally Ill Elders and Their Family Caregivers
How Old Do You Feel Inside?: The Key to Staying Healthy and Living Longer Is Deciding You're Not Old and Decrepit
How to Live to 100
Long Live . . . Us
Never Have a Heart Attack
Poll: Obesity Hits More Boomers in U.S.
The Effect of Exercise on Affective and Self-Efficacy Responses in Older and Younger Women
The Myriad Strategies for Seeking Control in the Dying Process
The U-bend of Life: Why, Beyond Middle Age, People Get Happier as They Get Older
The Worst Place to Be If You're Sick

Centenarians

America's Old Getting Older: 90-Somethings Triple in Number since 1980
How to Live to 100
Will You Live to Be 100?

Death

"Affordable" Death in the United States: An Action Plan Based on Lessons Learned from the Nursing Economic$ Special Issue
A Longitudinal Analysis of Social Engagement in Late-Life Widowhood
End-of-Life Concerns and Care Preferences: Congruence among Terminally Ill Elders and Their Family Caregivers
End-of-Life Care in the United States: Current Reality and Future Promise: A Policy Review
Palliative Care: A Paradigm of Care Responsive to the Demands for Health Care Reform in America
Palliative Care: Impact on Quality and Cost
Six Steps to Help Seniors Make the CPR/DNR Decision
The Myriad Strategies for Seeking Control in the Dying Process
The Worst Place to Be If You're Sick

Demography

America's Old Getting Older: 90-Somethings Triple in Number since 1980
Demography Is Not Destiny: The Challenges and Opportunities of Global Population Aging
Long Live . . . Us
Retooling Medicare?

Diet

Will You Live to Be 100?

Economic status

Do-It-Yourself Financial Freedom
Let's Restore the Middle Class
Live for Today, Save for Tomorrow
Medicare May Soon Take New Shape
Protect Social Security
Retooling Medicare?
Social Security: Fears vs. Facts: What Social Security Critics Keep Getting Wrong
Social Security Heading for Insolvency Even Faster: Trust Funds Could Run Dry in about 2 Decades
Time for a Tune-Up
Top 25 Social Security Questions
We Need to Fight Age Bias
Will Baby Boomers Phase into Retirement?

Education

Age-Proof Your Brain: 10 Easy Ways to Stay Sharp Forever
America's Old Getting Older: 90-Somethings Triple in Number since 1980
Demography Is Not Destiny: The Challenges and Opportunities of Global Population Aging
Healthy Aging in the 22nd Century
Retooling Medicare?
Time for a Tune-Up
Top 25 Social Security Questions
We Need to Fight Age Bias

Elder care

A Little Help Can Go a Long Way: "Aging in Place" Requires Good Luck, Support Network
Attitudes towards Caring for Older People: Findings and Recommendation for Practice
City Governments and Aging in Place: Community Design, Transportation, and Housing Innovation Adoption
Happy Together

Unit 1

UNIT

Prepared by: Elaina F. Osterbur, *Saint Louis University*

The Phenomenon of Aging

The process of aging is complex and includes biological, psychological, sociological, and behavioral changes. Biologically, the body gradually loses the ability to renew itself. Various body functions begin to slow, and the vital senses become less acute. Psychologically, aging persons experience changing sensory processes; perception, motor skills, problem-solving ability, and drives and emotions are frequently altered. Sociologically, this group must cope with the changing roles and definitions of self that society imposes on individuals. For instance, the role expectations and the status of grandparents differ from those of parents, and the roles of retirees are quite different from those of employed persons. Being defined as "old" may be desirable or undesirable, depending on the particular culture and its values. Behaviorally, aging individuals may move more slowly and with less dexterity. Because they are assuming new roles and are viewed differently by others, their attitudes about themselves, their emotions, and, ultimately, their behavior can be expected to change.

Those studying the process of aging often use developmental theories of the lifecycle—a sequence of predictable phases that begins with birth and ends with death—to explain individuals' behavior at various stages of their lives. An individual's age, therefore, is important because it provides clues about his or her behavior at a particular phase of the lifecycle—be it childhood, adolescence, adulthood, middle age, or old age. There is, however, the greatest variation in terms of health and human development among older people than among any other age group.

Although every 3-year-old child can be predicted to have certain developmental experiences, there is a wide variation in the behavior of 65-year-old people. We find that by age 65, some people are in good health, employed, and performing important work tasks. Others of this cohort are retired but in good health or are retired and in poor health. Still others have died prior to the age of 65. The articles in this section are written from biological, psychological, and sociological perspectives. These disciplines attempt to explain the effects of aging and the resulting choices in lifestyle as well as the wider, cultural implications of an older population.

Article   Prepared by: Elaina F. Osterbur, *Saint Louis University*

Healthy Aging in the 22nd Century

Marta M. Keane

Learning Outcomes

After reading this article, you will be able to:

- Identify the four major components of health.

- Discuss the future technologies and how they affect the four components of health.

- Understand how societal views on aging will evolve in the future.

What will the term *elder* mean in the future? And at what age will someone be considered an elder in 2100?

To be born in 2012 and only be 88 years old in 2100 will probably mean middle age rather than elderhood. Elders will be those who have lived triple-digit years and have been through several careers and cycles of education, career, and leisure. These elders will have exponentially more knowledge and experience, and they will continue to be contributing to society. Technology will be a key element allowing individuals to age with more independence and more choice.

Here, we examine each component of health (as defined by the World Health Organization) and how each will be manifested in 2100.

- **Physical health.** People's physical health will be monitored daily in their homes. The smart home will be outfitted with readers to take vital signs and send them directly to a medical professional to review, and provide feedback on any medications or supplements that need to be altered that day. Rather than prescriptions as we have known them, medications will all be personalized to individuals' DNA, keeping all healthier for longer.

Elders will be able to live in their own homes longer. With driverless cars, limitations on transportation will be a thing of the past. And the smart home will adapt to people's changing needs so that they will not need to move from their current home to maintain a safe environment.

- **Social-emotional health.** As elders continue to work longer and cycle through more periods of leisure during their lifetimes, they will have more friends and engage in more activities that will allow them to stay involved. Twenty-second-century elders will see their generation continue to be involved in social-action projects, coming together for the specific project and meeting new people, and continuing some relationships and letting others end with the project.

As with work, there will be cycles with marriage and family dynamics. It will be unlikely that there will be marriages that will last 100 years, so there will be multiple groupings of families that will have a fresh approach to embracing each addition to the family and expanding the definition of the extended family.

- **Spiritual health.** Views of a "divine power" will be transformed by advances in science and technological power. As scientific breakthroughs increase longevity, the fear of mortality and what follows will disappear. Spiritual practices and beliefs will become more individualized; many elders, for instance, will continue to be concerned for the environment, and in so doing, get back in touch with nature and the earth.

- **Intellectual health.** Elders will be honored for their knowledge and experience. The many cycles of work and relationships will enrich their lives and be an inspiration to others. The ability to live longer will focus importance on lifelong learning and continuing to experience the world through all the senses.

The year 2100 will be an exciting time to be "old." Technology and societal views will encourage a new attitude about aging. Elderhood will be viewed as the period in one's life with the most opportunity for independence and quality choices about one's own life.

Critical Thinking

1. This article discusses the evolution of societal thoughts on aging. Describe this evolution.
2. Envision the types of resources needed in communities and in institutions to provide the technology that the article describes.

Create Central

www.mhhe.com/createcentral

Internet References

CDC Healthy Aging
www.cdc.gov/aging

Medline Plus: Healthy Aging
www.nlm.nih.gov/medlineplus/healthyaging.html

Article

Prepared by: Elaina F. Osterbur, *Saint Louis University*

Demography Is Not Destiny: The Challenges and Opportunities of Global Population Aging

The world's population is aging: eventually there will be more older people than younger. Population patterns in three countries offer a projected, diverse view of the possibilities that await.

PETER UHLENBERG

Learning Outcomes

After reading this article, you will be able to:

- Identify the challenges of an aging population.

- Identify the reasons for an aging world.

- Discuss the social changes necessary to appreciate an aging population.

The world is undergoing a major demographic restructuring of its population: in nearly every country around the globe, the proportion of children is declining and the proportion of old people is increasing.

Population aging began in Sweden and France in the nineteenth century as a consequence of their declining fertility rates, and was pervasive across all developed countries by 1950. Nevertheless, as recently as 1950, only 5 percent of the world's population was older than age 65, and 34 percent were children under age 15. (Unless otherwise noted, all population statistics are taken from the United Nations Department of Economic and Social Affairs, 2011).

Population projections suggest that by 2060, the proportion of people older than age 65 will almost equal the proportion younger than age 15 (18 percent versus 20 percent). And in the more developed regions of the world in 2060, there will be 156 people older than age 65 for every 100 children younger than age 15.

Demographers thoroughly understand the reasons for global population aging and the patterns of population aging across countries. The more interesting and complex questions concern the social, political, and economic implications of this phenomenon. This article offers a brief explanation of why populations

around the world are growing older, compares patterns of population aging in three countries to illustrate the diversity that exists, and provides a foundation for thinking about a future where older people are more numerous than children.

Why Populations Age

The age composition of a population is determined by its past patterns of fertility, mortality, and international migration. Of these three variables, fertility decline is by far the most important factor leading to population aging. As women have fewer children, the proportion of children in the population declines and the proportion of older people increases. The reason developed countries have older populations than do developing countries is because fertility decline occurred far earlier in developed countries than it did in developing countries. In Western Europe, where low fertility rates persisted over most of the twentieth century, 20 percent of the population will be older than age 65 in 2015. In Eastern Africa, where fertility rates remained high until recently, only 3 percent of the population will be older than age 65 in 2015. Looking ahead, fertility rates are falling in Eastern Africa, and projections indicate that by 2060, the proportion of older adults in the population will increase to 7 percent. But because very low fertility is expected to persist in Western Europe, that region of the world is expected to have more than 27 percent elders by 2060. In Japan, where there is extremely low fertility, 35 percent of the population is projected to be older than age 65 in 2060.

The effect of declining mortality on population aging is more complex than declining fertility. Declining mortality among infants and children actually works to make populations younger. On the other hand, decreasing death rates at older ages increases the proportion of older adults in a population. Historically, declining mortality among the young caused gains in life expectancy as countries moved from high to moderate levels of mortality. But as most people survive to old age, declining death rates in later life become the primary reason for increased levels of life expectancy; future improvements in life expectancy in low-mortality countries will contribute to further aging of their populations. But the impact of declining mortality on population age composition is small compared with that of fertility change.

The effect of declining mortality on population aging is more complex than declining fertility.

Contrary to some popular thinking, international migration has only a small effect on population aging. Net positive immigration of young adults has an immediate effect of making a population younger, but in the long run, these immigrants age. A steady flow of in-migrants will lead to a slightly younger population over time, but demographers agree that immigration at any reasonable level will not significantly affect population aging in countries with low fertility (Keely, 2009). The relatively small effect of even large-scale immigration on population aging can be illustrated by comparing two projections of what percent of the U.S. populace will be older than age 65 in 2050. Assuming a steady stream of 820,000 immigrants annually produces a projection of 20 percent of the populace being older than age 65; assuming zero immigration yields a projection of 22 percent (United States Census Bureau, 1996). Without immigration, the population would be older, but only slightly.

Variability of Global Population Aging

In discussing global population aging, it is important to recognize the large demographic and social variability across regions and countries. The demographic contrast between Western Europe and Eastern Africa was mentioned above. Equally important are the large differences that exist across societies regarding the role of the state versus the family in caring for dependent elders. Because of this, population aging may have different implications for different societies. A comparison of population aging in three countries (Sweden, China, and the United States) illustrates the importance of examining aging within a social and historical context.

Sweden

Sweden was one of the first countries to experience population aging—8 percent of its population was older than age 65 in 1900. Across the twentieth century, the percentage of elders in Sweden more than doubled (to 17 percent in 2000), and this trend will continue in the coming decades, reaching a level of 26 percent of the populace older than age 65 in 2060. Although

Sweden no longer has the oldest population (Japan tops the list), what is occurring there is of interest because of Sweden's long history of population aging, combined with its generous welfare state. One goal of the Swedish welfare state has been to allow elders to maintain a high standard of living and to keep their independence in old age by providing them with state pensions, healthcare, housing, and access to social services. Providing these benefits requires a high tax rate on the working population. How viable this welfare-state model is—as the older population expands significantly relative to the working population-is a major question being asked in more developed countries at this time.

Population aging may have different implications for different societies.

While future adjustments to the welfare state in Sweden are uncertain, the choices made thus far suggest that changes can be made without abandoning popular welfare policies. The pension system was redesigned in the late 1990s to provide strong incentives for delaying retirement age and continuing to work past age 60, and average age at exit from the labor force increased by two years between 2001 and 2010. Greater restrictions on public financing of homecare and institutional care have increased the importance of family care for older people needing assistance. Survey evidence shows that only 5 percent of older Swedes in need of assistance with activities of daily living depend exclusively on in-home help if they are married and have a child, while 80 percent depend exclusively on family help (Sundstrom, 2009).

The tax base supporting the welfare state is being expanded by policies that increase the percentage of the population in the workforce and increase the hours worked by those who are employed. Sweden provides an example of a country that, in the face of aging, has made adjustments to welfare polices while continuing to provide a high level of support for its older population (and its younger populations).

Critics of a generous welfare state model have argued that as the state assumes more responsibility for the welfare of its population, the role of the family in providing care is undermined. However, a growing body of evidence suggests this has not been the case in Sweden. Not only does the family continue to be responsive to its older members, but elders continue to be involved in caring for their grandchildren. Given the high level of welfare support for children and working parents in Sweden, few Swedish grandparents co-reside with their grandchildren or provide regular childcare. But most Swedish grandparents care for grandchildren on an occasional basis, and they overwhelmingly agree that grandparents should help their grandchildren when needed (Albertini, Kohli, and Vogel, 2007). All evidence suggests that intergenerational bonds remain strong in Sweden.

China

Population aging in China stands out—and merits special attention—because of its magnitude, the speed with which it will occur, and the timing of its occurrence relative to China's economic development. One-fifth of the older people in the world now live in China, and by 2060, the older population of China will exceed the total older population living in developed countries (357 million versus 343 million). While most discussions of population aging focus on aging in wealthy countries such as Japan and those in Europe and North America, a global perspective calls attention to the fact that two-thirds of all older people live in developing countries. That fraction will increase to four-fifths by 2060.

The proportion of China's population that is older than age 65 doubled (or soon will) between 1950 and 2015 (from 5 percent to 10 percent), but between 2015 and 2060, that proportion will triple again, to 30 percent. The rapidity of this aging is unprecedented in world history—to go from a 10 percent elderly population up to 28 percent is taking 100 years in Western Europe (from 1950 to 2050), but this phenomenon will occur in merely forty years in China (from 2015 to 2055). This accelerated pace is because of the dramatic decline in fertility that occurred after institutionalization of the one-child policy in 1979. Some authors have warned of the devastating economic and social consequences that China will face as it encounters this so-called old age tsunami, but alarmist prophecies about the future consequences of demographic change tend to miss the mark because they fail to appreciate how social institutions adapt to changing conditions.

There is no question that rapid population aging will present challenges to China over the next several decades. China will become old before becoming rich. In contrast to most developed countries, China's state pension system does not cover most of the workforce, and it is largely unfunded. The availability of working-age people to support the older population is now favorable in China, but that will change dramatically. In 2015, there will be 7.7 people of ages 15 to 64 for every person older than age 65; by 2060, there will be only 1.9. Traditionally older people in China have depended upon their children for support, but in the future, older adults will have relatively few children (Chen and Liu, 2009).

Another factor to consider is China's unbalanced sex ratio from selective abortion under the one-child policy; this means that daughters to provide care to elderly parents and other family members will be in short supply. Healthcare for the aging population also presents challenges because the cost of providing healthcare for the old greatly exceeds that of caring for the young. Despite these challenges, demography is not destiny. The failure of economists to foresee the economic growth that occurred in China in recent decades should be a caution for those who think that the challenges of population aging cannot be overcome.

The United States

Between 1900 and 2010 there was a gradual aging of the U.S. population as the percentage of those older than age 65 increased from 4 percent to 13 percent. However, a much more rapid aging of the population will occur between 2010 and 2030 as the baby boomer cohort enters old age. By 2030, 20 percent of the population will be older than age 65. After 2030,

population aging will again be gradual, with those older than 65 reaching 22 percent by 2060. The aging of baby boomers in the United States has stimulated a great deal of discussion about the challenges of population aging. Most attention has been directed at issues facing Social Security, Medicare, and Medicaid—although both experts and average citizens disagree about what changes should be made to these programs. Equally important, but less discussed, is a question about how population aging might impact the supply of informal care for older people by spouses, children, and siblings. Data from the 2004 National Long-Term Care Survey shows that 79 percent of the care received by older people with disabilities who lived in the community was provided by family members (Houser, Gibson, and Redfoot, 2010). But the declining fertility that leads to population aging also leads to a decrease in the number of adult children and siblings available to provide informal care. How serious are these concerns? The following four observations provide some perspective.

Compared to other developed countries, the United States is exceptional in having a low level of population aging. Projections show 26 percent of the population in the more developed regions of the world, and 33 percent in Spain, will be older than age 65 in 2050, compared to only 21 percent in the United States. Why? Because fertility in the United States remains relatively high.

Other countries already have populations as old as the United States' population will be in 2030, after the baby boomer cohort passes age 65. But reaching this level of population aging has not inevitably resulted in significant social and economic upheaval. For example, Sweden now has an age composition similar to that expected in the United States in 2030. While no one knows how the United States will respond to population aging over the next several decades, other countries can provide insight into what is possible.

Alarmist writing on implications of population aging tends to exclude considerations of elders as resources. If reaching age 65 meant dependency and an end to productive activity, one might have cause for deep concern. But viewing old age as a long stage of life marked by dependency and unproductivity is a negative stereotype unsupported by empirical evidence. Along with growing labor force participation among those older than age 65, findings show high levels of volunteer work and engagement in family caregiving. Furthermore, aging is malleable and there is potential for greatly increasing the productivity of older people through greater opportunities and incentives, such as reducing age discrimination toward older workers, increasing recruitment of older volunteers, and providing them with more support and training and recognition.

Concerns have also been raised about the effects of population aging on the well-being of children (Uhlenberg, 2009). As the proportion of the populace that is older than age 65 increases from 15 percent to 21 percent between 2015 and 2050, the proportion that is younger than age 15 declines only from 20 percent to 19 percent. In other words, the demands on the working population to support children will not decrease as the demands of supporting the older population increase. The potential tension between supporting the old and supporting the young, sometimes referred to as the intergenerational equity issue, could be further complicated by the changing racial-ethnic composition of age groups. In 2050, it is expected that a majority of elders (66 percent) will be non-Hispanic whites, but only 43 percent of children will be in this category (United States Census Bureau, 1996). While conflict across generational lines has not yet been revealed in survey data on attitudes toward old-age entitlements, attention should be given to possible growing competition for scarce resources.

Thinking Clearly about Population Aging

In response to population aging, all societies face a number of common issues. The following points may provide a starting place for future discussions of global population aging.

There is no viable demographic way to avoid population aging. Countries with very low fertility might try to slow aging by encouraging women to have more babies, but efforts to implement pronatalist policies have not succeeded. No country is likely to adopt a policy of increasing death rates for the older population. And the level of immigration required to make a significant difference is politically infeasible. In a world with low fertility, low mortality, and restricted immigration, countries must deal with the reality of having 20 percent or 30 percent of their populations older than age 65.

As a country experiences the transition from high to low birth rates, shifts in its age composition are dynamic. In the early phase, which lasts at least three or four decades, the proportion of children in the population drops, while the proportion of elders hardly changes. Consequently, the ratio of the working-age population to the dependent age groups (children and older adults) grows substantially. This growth in the support ratio (number in the working ages divided by number in dependent ages) is referred to as the "demographic dividend," because it provides an opportunity for less spending on dependents and more savings to foster economic growth (Lee and Mason, 2006).

China provides a clear example of how the support ratio changes with a decline in fertility. Between 1950 and 2015, the ratio of the population ages 15 to 64 to the population younger than age 15 and older than age 65 increased from 1.6 to 2.7. But moving forward, this demographic dividend will disappear as the proportion of elders grows at the expense of the working-age population. By 2060, the support ratio will be only 1.3. All countries can expect this pattern of growth, followed by a decline of the support ratio, during the demographic transition, although the speed of change is variable and depends on how rapidly the fertility decline occurs.

The hope is that countries will take advantage of the demographic dividend to make investments that accelerate economic growth and establish an infrastructure that will provide long-term economic benefits. In the long run, countries must be prepared for much older populations and lower support ratios.

Business will need to adapt to the new demographic reality of older populations. Up to now, ageism in the business sector has presented an obstacle to constructive response to aging populations. Such ageism has led both to discrimination against older workers and to the neglect of older adults as a market. But change in the business sector is happening and will likely accelerate in coming decades.

The challenge for the global community is to champion social change that capitalizes on the worth of an increasing older population.

Business must re-evaluate the potential for older workers to make productive contributions. Empirical research challenges the stereotype that older workers are unhealthy, unable to learn, and too expensive (Biggs, Carstensen, and Hogan, 2012; Seiko, Biggs, and Sargent, 2012). In developed countries, cohorts reaching age 65 are increasingly composed of individuals who are well-educated and healthy, and who expect to live for another twenty to thirty years. To take advantage of older workers' potential, several straightforward responses by business are needed. The workplace can be made friendlier to older workers by increasing flexibility—offering gradual retirement, part-time work, and flexible hours. Employers can help workers avoid becoming obsolete by providing lifelong education and physical fitness programs. The linear career plan can be replaced with one that allows the transfer of older workers into less demanding jobs at lower salaries. Such adaptation by organizations can both improve the quality of life for older people and reduce the economic burden of population aging.

Recognition of the older population as a major market for business is beginning, as evidenced by an increasing number of articles about the "silver market." Because a great deal of wealth is held by the older population and the number of elders is increasing relative to other age groups, it makes sense for business to design products appealing to the older market, and to direct advertising to them. Consumption by the older population can stimulate the economy. The economic power of older adults also can act as a force to change the ageist stereotypes often perpetuated by advertising.

Finally, the way in which people age and the cultural meaning of old age can change. As sociologists put it, aging is to a large extent socially constructed. Social institutions can (and do) change over time, so the implications of a large portion of the population cresting age 65 are not static. As noted above, the way work is organized can change to take advantage of older workers' potential. Education can change to foster lifelong learning. Healthcare can move toward an emphasis on preserving good health and promoting healthy lifestyles that reduce disabilities and dependency in later life. New technology can be developed that enables people in later life to experience fewer limitations. Public policy can change to provide incentives for volunteering in later life. Religious organizations can move beyond seeing older people merely as a group in need of help to seeing them as a resource for ministry.

Little good comes from viewing population aging as the "gray peril." Large-scale population aging will inevitably occur in all countries around the world, and the challenge for the global community is to champion social change that capitalizes on the worth of an increasing older population. There is vast potential for improving and enhancing opportunity and incentive structures for people in later life. If we do this, we can help forge a future that includes a more balanced view of aging—one in which we collectively view older people more as a valuable resource than as a burden.

References

Albertini, M., Kohli, M., and Vogel, C. 2007. "Intergenerational Transfers of Time and Money in European Families: Common Patterns—Different Regimes?" *Journal of European Social Policy* 17(4): 319–34.

Biggs, S., Carstensen, L., and Hogan, P. 2012. "Social Capital, Lifelong Learning and Social Innovation." In Beard, J. R., et al., eds. *Global Population Ageing: Peril or Promise?* (pp. 39–41). Geneva, Switzerland: World Economic Forum. www3.weforum .org/docs/WEF_GAC_GlobalPopulationAgeing_Report_2012. pdf. Retrieved January 8, 2013.

Chen, F., and Liu, G. 2009. "Population Aging in China." In Uhlenberg, P., ed. *International Handbook of Population Aging* (pp. 157–72). Dordrecht, the Netherlands: Springer.

Houser, A., Gibson, M. J., and Redfoot, D. L. 2010. *Trends in Family Caregiving and Paid Home Care for Older People with Disabilities in the Community: Data from the National Long-Term Care Survey.* AARP Public Policy Institute Research Report 2010-09. Washington, DC: AARP Public Policy Institute.

Keely, C. B. 2009. "Replacement Migration." In Uhlenberg, P., ed. *International Handbook of Population Aging* (pp. 395–405). Dordrecht, the Netherlands: Springer.

Lee, R., and Mason, A. 2006. "What Is the Demographic Dividend?" *Finance and Development* 43(3). www.imf.org/external/pubs/ft/ fandd/2006/09/basics.htm#author. Retrieved September 12, 2012.

Seiko, A., Biggs, S., and Sargent, L. 2012. "Organizational, Adaptation and Human Resource Needs for an Aging Population." In Beard, J. R., et al., eds. *Global Population Ageing: Peril or Promise* (pp. 46–50). Geneva, Switzerland:

World Economic Forum.www3.weforum.org/docs/WEF_GAC_ GlobalPopulationAgeing_Report_2012.pdf.

Sundstrom, G. 2009. "Demography of Aging in the Nordic Countries." In Uhlenberg, P., ed. *International Handbook of Population Aging* (pp. 91–111). Dordrecht, the Netherlands: Springer.

Uhlenberg, P. 2009. "Children in an Aging Society." *The Journals of Gerontology: Social Sciences* 64B (4): 489–96.

United Nations Department of Economic and Social Affairs (UN DESA), Population Division. 2011. *World Population Prospects: The 2010 Revision, Volume I: Comprehensive Tables.* ST/ESA/ SER.A/313.esa.un.org/unpd/wpp/unpp/panel_indicators.htm. Retrieved September 12, 2012.

United States Census Bureau. 1996. *Population Projections of the United States by Age, Sex, Race, and Hispanic Origin: 1995 to 2050.* Current Population Reports P25–1130. census.gov/prod/1/ pop/p25-1130.pdf. Retrieved September 12, 2012.

Critical Thinking

1. What are the global effects of an aging population?
2. How does an aging population affect healthcare resources globally?

Create Central

www.mhhe.com/createcentral

Internet References

National Council on Aging
　www.ncoa.org
World Health Organization: Aging and Life Course
　www.who.int/ageing/en

PETER UHLENBERG, PH.D., is professor of sociology and a Fellow of the Carolina Population Center at the University of North Carolina at Chapel Hill, North Carolina.

Article   Prepared by: Elaina F. Osterbur, *Saint Louis University*

America's Old Getting Older

90-Somethings Triple in Number since 1980

Learning Outcomes

After reading this article, you will be able to:

- Identify two major problems that confront the population aged 90 and over.
- Identify what makes the age composition of the current U.S. population different from previous generations.

The rolls of America's oldest old are surging: Nearly 2 million now are 90 or over, nearly triple their numbers of just three decades ago.

It's not all good news. They're more likely than the merely elderly to live in poverty and to have disabilities, creating a new challenge to already strained retiree income and health care programs.

First-ever census data on the 90-plus population highlight America's ever-increasing life spans, which are redefining what it means to be old.

Demographers attribute the increases mostly to better nutrition and advances in medical care. Still, the longer life spans present additional risks for disabilities and chronic conditions such as arthritis, diabetes and Alzheimer's disease.

Richard Suzman, director of behavioral and social research at the National Institute on Aging, which commissioned the report, said personal savings for retirement can sometimes be a problem if people don't anticipate a longer life or one with some form of disability.

An Associated Press-LifeGoesStrong.com poll in June found that more than one in four adults expect to live to at least 90, including nearly half of those currently 65 or older. A majority of adults also said they expected people in their generation to live longer than those in their parents' generation, with about 46 percent saying they expected a better quality of life in later years as well.

"A key issue for this population will be whether disability rates can be reduced," Suzman said. "We've seen to some extent that disabilities can be reduced with lifestyle improvements, diet and exercise. But it becomes more important to find ways to delay, prevent or treat conditions such as Alzheimer's disease."

According to the report, the share of people 90–94 who report having some kind of impairment such as inability to do errands, visit a doctor's office, climb stairs or bathe is 13 percentage points higher than those 85–89—82 percent versus 69 percent.

Among those 95 and older, the disability rate climbs to 91 percent.

Census figures show that smaller states had the highest shares of their older Americans who were at least 90.

North Dakota led the list, with about 7 percent of its 65-plus population over 90. It was followed by Connecticut, Iowa and South Dakota.

In absolute numbers, California, Florida and Texas led the nation in the 90-plus population, each with more than 130,000.

Traditionally, the Census Bureau has followed established norms in breaking down age groups, such as under-18 to signify children or 65-plus to indicate seniors.

Since the mid-1980s, the bureau often has released data on the 85-plus population, describing them as the "oldest old"—a term coined by Suzman.

But some of those norms, at least culturally, may be shifting. Young people 18–29 more than ever are delaying their transition to work in the poor job market by pursuing advanced degrees or moving in with Mom and Dad. Older Americans, who are living longer and staying healthier than prior generations, are now more likely to work past 65.

As America ages . . .

- The oldest of the old are projected to increase from 1.9 million to 8.7 million by midcentury—making up 2 percent of the total U.S. population and one in 10 older Americans.
- A century ago, fewer than 100,000 people reached 90.
- Among the 90-plus population, women outnumber men by a ratio of nearly 3 to 1.
- Broken down by race and ethnicity, non-Hispanic whites made up the vast majority of the 90-plus population, at 88.1 percent. That's compared to 7.6 percent who were black, 4 percent Hispanic, 2.2 percent Asian.
- Most people who were 90 or older lived in households alone, about 37.3 percent. Some 37.1 percent lived in households with family or others, about 23 percent in nursing homes.

On Thursday, the Census Bureau said it was putting out its study of the 90-plus age group at NIA's request in recognition of longer life expectancies, which are just over 78 for babies now being born.

By the time a person reaches 65, Americans are generally expected to live close to 20 years longer, up from 12 years in 1930. At age 90, their expectancy is another five years.

Critical Thinking

1. Do older Americans expect to live longer than their parents did?
2. Do older Americans expect to have a better quality of life than their parents did in their later years?
3. What are the key health issues that the 85 and older population are confronted with?

Create Central

www.mhhe.com/createcentral

Internet References

The Aging Research Centre
www.arclab.org

National Center for Health Statistics
www.cdc.gov/nchs/agingact.htm

Article   Prepared by: Elaina F. Osterbur, *Saint Louis University*

Will You Live to Be 100?

THOMAS PERLS AND MARGERY HUTTER SILVER

Learning Outcomes

After reading this article, you will be able to:

- Describe the effect of caloric restriction on the body's free radicals.

- Describe the advantages that older people seem to have in dealing with health problems.

After completing a study of 150 centenarians, Harvard Medical School researchers Thomas Perls, MD, and Margery Hutter Silver, EdD, developed a quiz to help you calculate your estimated life expectancy.

Longevity Quiz

Score

1. Do you smoke or chew tobacco, or are you around a lot of secondhand smoke? Yes (−20) No (0)
2. Do you cook your fish, poultry, or meat until it is charred? Yes (−2) No (0)
3. Do you avoid butter, cream, pastries, and other saturated fats as well as fried foods (e.g., French Fries)? Yes (+3) No (−7)
4. Do you minimize meat in your diet, preferably making a point to eat plenty of fruits, vegetables, and bran instead? Yes (+5) No (−4)
5. Do you consume more than two drinks of beer, wine, and/or liquor a day? (A standard drink is one 12-ounce bottle of beer, one wine cooler, one five-ounce glass of wine, or one and a half ounces of 80-proof distilled spirits.) Yes (−10) No (0)
6. Do you drink beer, wine, and/or liquor in moderate amounts (one or two drinks/day)? Yes (+3) No (0)
7. Do air pollution warnings occur where you live? Yes (−4) No (+1)
8. **a.** Do you drink more than 16 ounces of coffee a day? Yes (−3) No (0) **b.** Do you drink tea daily? Yes (+3) No (0)
9. Do you take an aspirin a day? Yes (+4) No (0)
10. Do you floss your teeth every day? Yes (+2) No (−4)
11. Do you have a bowel movement less than once every two days? Yes (−4) No (0)
12. Have you had a stroke or heart attack? Yes (−10) No (0)
13. Do you try to get a sun tan? Yes (−4) No (+3)
14. Are you more than 20 pounds overweight? Yes (−10) No (0)
15. Do you live near enough to other family members (other than your spouse and dependent children) that you can and want to drop by spontaneously? Yes (+5) No (−4)
16. Which statement is applicable to you? **a.** "Stress eats away at me. I can't seem to shake it off." Yes (−7) **b.** "I can shed stress." This might be by praying, exercising, meditating, finding humor in everyday life, or other means. Yes (+7)
17. Did both of your parents either die before age 75 of nonaccidental causes or require daily assistance by the time they reached age 75? Yes (−10) No (0) Don't know (0)
18. Did more than one of the following relatives live to at least age 90 in excellent health: parents, aunts/uncles, grandparents? Yes (+24) No (0) Don't know (0)
19. **a.** Are you a couch potato (do no regular aerobic or resistance exercise)? Yes (−7) **b.** Do you exercise at least three times a week? Yes (+7)
20. Do you take vitamin E (400–800 IU) and selenium (100–200 mcg) every day? Yes (+5) No (−3)

Score

STEP 1: Add the negative and positive scores together. Example: −45 *plus* +30 = −15. Divide the preceding score by 5 (−15 divided by 5 = −3).

STEP 2: Add the negative or positive number to age 84 if you are a man or age 88 if you are a woman (example: −3 + 88 = 85) to get your estimated life span.

The Science behind the Quiz

Question 1 Cigarette smoke contains toxins that directly damage DNA, causing cancer and other diseases and accelerating aging.

Question 2 Charring food changes its proteins and amino acids into heterocyclic amines, which are potent mutagens that can alter your DNA.

Questions 3, 4 A high-fat diet, and especially a high-fat, high-protein diet, may increase your risk of cancer of the breast, uterus, prostate, colon, pancreas, and kidney. A diet rich in fruits and vegetables may lower the risk of heart disease and cancer.

Questions 5, 6 Excessive alcohol consumption can damage the liver and other organs, leading to accelerated aging and increased susceptibility to disease. Moderate consumption may lower the risk of heart disease.

Question 7 Certain air pollutants may cause cancer; many also contain oxidants that accelerate aging.

Question 8 Too much coffee predisposes the stomach to ulcers and chronic inflammation, which in turn raise the risk of heart disease. High coffee consumption may also indicate and exacerbate stress. Tea, on the other hand, is noted for its significant antioxidant content.

Question 9 Taking 81 milligrams of aspirin a day (the amount in one baby aspirin) has been shown to decrease the risk of heart disease, possibly because of its anticlotting effects.

Question 10 Research now shows that chronic gum disease can lead to the release of bacteria into the bloodstream, contributing to heart disease.

Question 11 Scientists believe that having at least one bowel movement every 20 hours decreases the incidence of colon cancer.

Question 12 A previous history of stroke and heart attack makes you more susceptible to future attacks.

Question 13 The ultraviolet rays in sunlight directly damage DNA, causing wrinkles and increasing the risk of skin cancer.

Question 14 Being obese increases the risk of various cancers, heart disease, and diabetes. The more overweight you are, the higher your risk of disease and death.

Questions 15, 16 People who do not belong to cohesive families have fewer coping resources and therefore have increased levels of social and psychological stress. Stress is associated with heart disease and some cancers.

Questions 17, 18 Studies show that genetics plays a significant role in the ability to reach extreme old age.

Question 19 Exercise leads to more efficient energy production in the cells and overall, less oxygen radical formation. Oxygen (or free) radicals are highly reactive molecules or atoms that damage cells and DNA, ultimately leading to aging.

Question 20 Vitamin E is a powerful antioxidant and has been shown to retard the progression of Alzheimer's, heart disease, and stroke. Selenium may prevent some types of cancer.

Critical Thinking

1. What stomach problems can be the result of too much coffee consumption?
2. What are the advantages in terms of one's health to being a member of a stable family?
3. What are the health problems associated with smoking?

Create Central

www.mhhe.com/createcentral

Internet References

The Aging Research Centre
    www.arclab.org
Centenarians
    www.hcoa.org/centenarians/centenarians.htm

Adapted from *Living to 100: Lessons in Living to Your Maximum Potential at Any Age* (Basic Books, 1999) by **Thomas Perls, MD**, and **Margery Hutter Silver, EdD**, with **John F. Lauerman**.

Article   Prepared by: Elaina F. Osterbur, *Saint Louis University*

Long Live . . . Us

In never-say-die America, life expectancy is longer than ever.

MARK BENNETT

Learning Outcomes

After reading this article, you will be able to:

- Identify the life expectancy in the United States for all persons, regardless of sex, in 2009.
- Identify the life expectancy of men and women in the United States in 2009.

Six members of the Class of '74 sit around a restaurant table.

They sip red wine and munch on a trail-mix-style bowl filled with fish oil, flaxseed oil and DHEA gel tabs. A joke about a classmate's spring break photo with her great-grandson's frat brothers on Facebook sparks hysterical laughter. As the chuckles subside, they check their iPhone clocks, realize the abs-crunch marathon fundraiser for the Macrobiotic Diet Consortium starts in an hour, and get busy planning their 85th reunion.

A retro "Dancing with the Stars" theme wins unanimous approval. One guy tweets his mother-in-law about next week's library tax protest, the class president picks up the tab, and they scatter out the door.

Sure, the ages of the folks in that futuristic dinner party would be around 103, but in never-say-die America, life expectancy is longer than ever, according to a report issued this month by the U.S. Centers for Disease Control and Prevention.

A baby born in 2009 will live an average of 78 years and two months. If that kid is a girl, she will likely linger on Earth for 80.6 years, compared to 75.7 for a boy. Back in 1930, a man's life expectancy was 58 and a woman's 62.

The CDC won't say why Americans live longer until the second half of its life expectancy report is released later this year, but the agency has a pretty good guess. Improved medical treatment, vaccinations and anti-smoking campaigns have helped drop the death rate to a record low as deaths from strokes, Alzheimer's, diabetes, heart disease and cancer decreased during the past 12 months.

Plus, our ancestors had no idea that red wine contained antioxidants and resveratol that protect blood vessels and reduce "bad" cholesterol. Or that DHEA supposedly repairs damage to cells in our bodies. Or that fish oil and flaxseed oil fight free radicals, which are cell-damaging molecules, not 1960s fugitives.

So, with almonds stashed in our shirt pockets instead of Marlboros, we've nearly tacked an extra decade onto our lives since 1970, when life expectancy in the U.S. was 70.8 years.

"It does go up every year, little by little," CDC statistician Ken Kochanek said by telephone from Washington, D.C., last week.

Seemingly, this age-defying trend could extend and create bizarre cultural dynamics, not unlike the aforementioned class reunion committee meeting. In Britain, for example, government researchers estimate that by 2014—just a little more than two years from now—the number of Brits ages 65 and older will surpass that of the under-16 population. Think of the implications—there are more people sitting around the UK who look like Keith Richards than fresh-faced kids. Actually, the Stones guitarist (now 67) would be considered a mere pup, if a BBC report is true. That story quoted a *Science* magazine analysis that concluded there is no natural limit to human life. The greeting card companies may be printing a new "Happy 200th" line someday.

Mel Brooks' 2,000-year-old man comes to mind. When asked if he knew Joan of Arc, Mel's character responded, "Know her? I went with her, dummy."

Reality continues to apply, though. Humans are managing to live longer, but not indefinitely. Though 36,000 fewer Americans died in 2009 than the year before, a total of 2.4 million still passed on in '09. The leading causes were, in order, heart disease, malignant neoplasms, chronic lower respiratory diseases, cerebrovascular diseases, accidents, Alzheimer's, diabetes, flu and pneumonia and nephritis. "In general, you have the same problems that have existed for a long time," said Kochanek.

Men show up in those statistics sooner than women, apparently because we do dumb stuff more often, such as smoking and exceeding the speed limit. "Men take more risks, and that affects life expectancy," Kochanek said. Both genders eat less wisely, too, even if we're popping those Omega-3 pills. Americans in the sixtysomething age range are, on average, 10 pounds heavier than folks of a similar vintage a decade earlier, according to FDA statistics cited by *U.S. News & World Report*.

The impact of poor choices in our lifetimes can be tabulated. For those dying to know how much time they've got, Northwestern Mutual Life Insurance Co. provides an online calculator. Just punch in your age, height, weight, then answer 11 other questions about your lifestyle, family history and habits and—voilà!—your final number appears. If you want something handy enough to stick onto the front of the fridge, the U.S. Census Bureau offers a less detailed chart subtitled "Average Number of Years of Life Remaining."

Of course, those are national figures. Averages. They vary by location. According to a nationwide study by the Robert Wood Johnson Foundation of the University of Wisconsin Population Health Institute, Vigo County's mortality rate ranks 69th out of 92 counties in Indiana, which isn't good. The mortality rate is a measure of premature death—the years of potential life lost prior to age 75.

Why do Vigo Countians die so young?

Well, in terms of health behaviors (smoking, binge drinking, car crashes, diet and exercise, STDs and teen birth rates), Vigo County rates an abysmal 80th out of 92 counties. (Apparently, very few of the wine-drinking, fish-oil-eating, fitness-crazed baby boomers described earlier call Vigo County home.) When calculating mortality rates, health behaviors account for nearly one-third of the influencing factors, along with clinical care, socioeconomics and physical environment, the Population Health Institute study said.

Given those real numbers, the secret of long life may not be such a secret after all. Author and psychologist Howard Friedman's new book, *The Longevity Project*, explores the topic. In a *Time* magazine interview this month, he explained that "conscientiousness" was a primary enhancer of life expectancy.

"The most intriguing reason why conscientious people live longer is that having a conscientious personality leads you into healthier situations and relationships," Friedman told *Time*. "In other words, conscientious people find their way to happier marriages, better friendships and healthier work situations. They help create healthy, long-life pathways for themselves. This is a new way of thinking about health."

That should give Keith Richards something to consider every time the Stones play "Time Is On My Side."

Critical Thinking

1. Why is the life expectancy of men lower than the life expectancy of women?
2. What were the leading causes of death in the United States in 2009?
3. How has the weight of persons over 60 changed in the last ten years?
4. Why does Howard Friedman believe that conscientious people live longer?

Create Central

www.mhhe.com/createcentral

Internet References

The Aging Research Centre
    www.arclab.org
National Center for Health Statistics
    www.cdc.gov/mchs/agingact.htm

As seen in *Terre Haute Tribune-Star*, March 27, 2011. Copyright © 2011 by Terre Haute Tribune Star. Reprinted by permission of Mark Bennett, columnist, on behalf of the Terre Haute (Indiana) Tribune-Star.

Article   Prepared by: Elaina F. Osterbur, *Saint Louis University*

How to Live to 100

The latest research suggests the key to longevity lies in changing daily habits.

KIMBERLY PALMER

Learning Outcomes

After reading this article, you will be able to:

- Identify the elements of longevity.
- Discuss the positive behaviors associated with long life.
- Discuss the behaviors that do not contribute to longevity.

Why do some people live long, healthy, and happy lives, while others struggle with dementia, heart disease, and depression? Are there steps we can take to protect ourselves from those outcomes, or is it all a matter of luck (and good genes)? What do the latest scientific advancements say about helping us get the most out of our lifespans, and how can we afford our longer lives?

Those are the questions *U.S. News* sought to answer with this project, *How to Live to 100*. Promises of magic elixirs abound: in television ads for skin-care products, in doctor's offices, and even at the grocery store. Every day, new research seems to suggest something new: Drink red wine, skip red meat, take vitamin C, drink coffee. We sought to find out the truth about steps we can all take to increase our chances of staying healthy, happy, and affording it.

The financial side of longevity is playing an increasingly visible role as people begin to routinely live 10, 20, and even 30 years after retirement. "People have many more years to worry about and take care of, and we're living at a time when a lot of their resources have been diminished. The drop in the value of homes has probably wiped out an average of two-thirds of home equity for American homeowners. And your job might not be there as long as you had hoped," says Mort Zuckerman, editor-in-chief of *U.S. News*.

In addition to interviewing the country's top researchers on health, longevity, happiness, and finances, we sought out people who seem to have discovered the answer to successful aging. They often echoed each other's thoughts about consciously choosing healthier diets, opting to spend more time with family over work, and finding meaning by giving back to communities and connecting with others long past retirement. As actress

Betty White, perhaps the nation's most famous nonagenarian, recently put it to CNN's Piers Morgan, "Old age is all up here," gesturing to her head.

That's certainly the case for 77-year-old marathoner Ruth Heidrich, a breast cancer survivor who changed her diet and exercise habits after her diagnosis in 1982. "That's what started me on this whole road," she says, referring to her all-raw diet and extreme exercise habits, including triathlons and Iron Man competitions.

Heidrich, who lives in Honolulu, eats a large bowl of leafy greens for breakfast, mixed with a banana, a mango, and raw steel-cut oats. She sprinkles cinnamon and ginger on top, and drinks green tea mixed with a tablespoon of pure unsweetened cocoa, along with some Stevia to sweeten the drink. A typical dinner includes more leafy greens and fruit along with broccoli and salsa. For dessert and snacks, she munches on blueberries, walnuts, prunes, apples, and popcorn. "I started eating at least a cup of blueberries a day after I read that blueberries are good for the brain," she says. She doesn't drink coffee or alcohol.

Today, she no longer competes in Iron Man competitions but continues to work out for three hours daily, typically running, biking, or swimming before breakfast, and plans to continue doing so, albeit at a slower pace. "I will keep exercising forever," she says. "My energy levels are through the roof and I'm having fun. I feel like I've got to tell everybody, 'You've got to eat right and exercise right . . . Walking is not exercise. You've gotta sweat, you've gotta breathe hard.'"

Robert Kuhns, 69, found fulfillment in retirement through a second career: The retired IBM executive works as a forest ranger in Virginia's Shenandoah National Park during part of the year, leading hikes, giving talks on animal habits, and taking photographs for park brochures. From the end of March through the end of November, he works 40 hours a week, which includes plenty of exercise, hiking up and down trails as he shares information about native species of insects and trees with visitors. "It's one of the most rewarding things I've done in my life," he says. He plans to continue for as long as he can, perhaps another 10 years.

Kuhns earns extra cash from the gig, too. "[My wife and I] have more available funds when I'm working than during the months when I'm not," he says, and this year he got promoted to a higher pay grade.

Doreen Orion, 52, and her husband, Tim Justice, 54, decided to scale back work and hit the road in their 340 square-foot RV, so they could focus on adventure, each other, and reducing their dependence on material goods. She documented their trip in her 2008 memoir, *Queen of the Road*. As psychiatrists who work for insurance companies, they can do much of their work remotely. "We had a really good marriage before, but being thrust into new situations all the time and having to problem-solve, it can't help but bring you closer together," she says. Orion and her husband recently decided to put their Colorado home on the market and live in their RV full-time.

While still in her twenties, Nicole Mladic, a communications director in Chicago, realized she was never going to save enough for retirement if she continued on her current trajectory of little or no savings each month. So she started slowly by saving 2 percent of her salary each month. A few months later, she raised it to 3 percent, then 4 percent, and eventually reached her goal of 10 percent. Today, Mladic is in her early thirties and her net worth is over $100,000. "The thought of saving 10 percent of my salary for retirement each month seemed impossible when I first started working," says Mladic. "But by starting small, it was easy to get to 10 percent, and far less of a shock to my budget."

George Vaillant, a professor of psychiatry at Harvard Medical School, has overseen the longest-running longitudinal study of health and happiness. His study has tracked the lives of more than 500 Harvard students and men from inner-city Boston since the 1930s, and has drawn some intriguing conclusions, including that stable relationships are one key to a long and happy life. Divorce, he says, "is very bad for your health."

Vaillant says what makes him happiest now, at age 77, are his grandchildren. His advice is sometimes at odds with what one usually hears: He urges people to take money out of their retirement accounts to go on vacation, because learning how to relax and spend time with loved ones is essential to one's happiness later in life. "Just remember, if you get nothing else out of talking to me, to put some of your IRA money into vacations," he says.

As for what brings happiness to that retirement, he says it almost always comes down to relationships. "There were three things that correlated with a fun retirement: 1) whether your marriage was good, 2) whether you took fun vacations before you retired, and 3) whether you have always liked doing things for other people. So it's being more interested in others than yourself that leads to a happy retirement, and having somebody you enjoy being with. And it's having learned before you retire how to play." That's why he suggests investing in vacations long before retirement—to practice.

Love of grandchildren, he found, can trump even disease. "People in poor health with 13 grandchildren are happy . . . I'm 77, and what I enjoy most are my grandchildren."

There are seemingly endless findings about what you can do now to increase your odds of being a healthy and happy 77-year-old, 90-year-old, and beyond. Getting your heart rate up by exercising at least 150 minutes a week, for example, can cut your chances of heart disease and cancer. Eating a Mediterranean diet, which is heavy on olive oil and fish, capping red meat at 18 ounces per week, flossing daily, sleeping at least six hours a night, and having no more than two drinks a day for men and one for women also appear to promote good health.

To boost your chances of happiness, build a long and loving marriage, cultivate gratitude and optimism, and commit to constant self-improvement. To afford your long life, start a vigorous savings plan as early as your twenties, make frugal lifestyle choices, such as living in a smaller home and cooking more meals at home, and work as long as possible, well past age 65.

Changing ingrained habits, of course, isn't easy. Sometimes it takes a major life event, such as a cancer diagnosis, as it did for Ruth Heidrich. But habits can also be changed with conscious effort. *New York Times* reporter Charles Duhigg, author of *The Power of Habit,* found that changing a habit requires first identifying a cue, such as putting your running shoes on before breakfast, that your brain connects to going for a run. Then, he suggests rewarding yourself after the run, with a piece of chocolate or a long shower.

"There has to be some sort of reward at the end of the routine to make it a habit," he says. Exercise does contain its own reward, because people feel good after running, but he says it can take a few weeks for the brain to pick up on those internal rewards, which is why he suggests supplementing with a more obvious, external reward. "That's how the neurology learns to encode that behavior," he adds.

One worthy new habit might be earning supplemental income, even before retirement, to help fund those decades. Says Zuckerman: "Understand that there is no point in your life when you have to stop learning. Continue to read, try and learn and understand what is going in the world, and hopefully train yourself for other work."

Critical Thinking

1. How will increased longevity impact the U.S. healthcare system?
2. Why do positive health behaviors contribute to long life and quality of life?

Create Central

www.mhhe.com/createcentral

Internet References

The Aging Research Centre
    www.arclab.org

Harvard Health Publications
    www.wifle.org/pdf/Living_to_100.pd

Unit 2

UNIT

Prepared by: Elaina F. Osterbur, *Saint Louis University*

The Quality of Later Life

Although it is true that one ages from the moment of conception to the moment of death, children are usually considered to be "growing and developing," but adults are often thought of as "aging." Having accepted this assumption, most biologists concerned with the problems of aging focus their attention on what happens to individuals after they reach maturity. Moreover, most of the biological and medical research dealing with the aging process focuses on the later part of the mature adult's life cycle. A commonly used definition of *senescence* is "the changes that occur generally in the postreproductive period and that result in decreased survival capacity on the part of the individual organism" (B. L. Shrehler, *Time, Cells and Aging,* New York: Academic Press, 1977).

As a person ages, physiological changes take place. The skin loses its elasticity, becomes more pigmented, and bruises more easily. Joints stiffen, and the bone structure becomes less firm. Muscles lose their strength. The respiratory system becomes less efficient. The individual's metabolism changes, resulting in different dietary demands. Bowel and bladder movements are more difficult to regulate. Visual acuity diminishes, hearing declines, and the entire system is less able to resist environmental stresses and strains.

Increases in life expectancy have resulted largely from decreased mortality rates among younger people rather than from increased longevity after age 65. In 1900, the average life expectancy at birth was 47.3 years; in 2000, it was 76.9 years. Thus, in the last century, the average life expectancy rose by 29.6 years. However, those who now live to the age of 65 do not have an appreciably different life expectancy than did their 1900 cohorts. In 1900, 65-year-olds could expect to live approximately 11.9 years longer, and in 2000, they could expect to live approximately 17.9 years longer, an increase of six years.

Although more people survive to age 65 today, the chances of being afflicted by one of the major killers of older persons is still about as great for this generation as it was for its grandparents. Medical science has had considerable success in controlling the acute diseases of the young—such as measles, chicken pox, and scarlet fever—but it has not been as successful in controlling the chronic conditions of old age, such as heart disease, cancer, and emphysema. Organ transplants, increased knowledge of the immune system, and undiscovered medical technologies will probably increase the life expectancy for the 65-and-over population, resulting in longer life for the next generation. Although people 65 years of age today are living only slightly longer than 65-year-olds did in 1900, the quality of their later years has greatly improved. Economically, Social Security and a multitude of private retirement programs have given most older persons a more secure retirement. Physically, many people remain active, mobile, and independent throughout their retirement years. Socially, most older persons are married, involved in community activities, and leading productive lives. Although they may experience some chronic ailments, most people 65 or older are able to live in their own homes, direct their own lives, and involve themselves in activities they enjoy.

Article   Prepared by: Elaina F. Osterbur, *Saint Louis University*

Age-Proof Your Brain

10 Easy Ways to Stay Sharp Forever

BETH HOWARD

Learning Outcomes

After reading this article, you will be able to:

- Name the foods a person can eat that would reduce the risk of developing Alzheimer's disease.
- Identify the chronic health problems that are often associated with dementia.

Alzheimer's isn't inevitable. Many experts now believe you can prevent or at least delay dementia—even if you have a genetic predisposition. Reducing Alzheimer's risk factors like obesity, diabetes, smoking and low physical activity by just 25 percent could prevent up to half a million cases of the disease in the United States, according to a recent analysis from the University of California, San Francisco.

"The goal is to stave it off long enough so that you can live life without ever suffering from symptoms," says Gary Small, M.D., director of the UCLA Longevity Center and coauthor of *The Alzheimer's Prevention Program: Keep Your Brain Healthy for the Rest of Your Life*. Read on for new ways to boost your brain.

1 Get Moving

"If you do only one thing to keep your brain young, exercise," says Art Kramer, Ph.D., professor of psychology and neuroscience at the University of Illinois. Higher exercise levels can reduce dementia risk by 30 to 40 percent compared with low activity levels, and physically active people tend to maintain better cognition and memory than inactive people. "They also have substantially lower rates of different forms of dementia, including Alzheimer's disease," Kramer says.

Working out helps your hippocampus, the region of the brain involved in memory formation. As you age, your hippocampus shrinks, leading to memory loss. Exercise can reverse this process, research suggests. Physical activity can also trigger the growth of new nerve cells and promote nerve growth.

How you work up a sweat is up to you, but most experts recommend 150 minutes a week of moderate activity. Even a little bit can help: "In our research as little as 15 minutes of regular exercise three times per week helped maintain the brain," says Eric B. Larson, M.D., executive director of Group Health Research Institute in Seattle.

2 Pump Some Iron

Older women who participated in a yearlong weight-training program at the University of British Columbia at Vancouver did 13 percent better on tests of cognitive function than a group of women who did balance and toning exercises. "Resistance training may increase the levels of growth factors in the brain such as IGF1, which nourish and protect nerve cells," says Teresa Liu-Ambrose, Ph.D., head of the university's Aging, Mobility, and Cognitive Neuroscience Laboratory.

3 Seek Out New Skills

Learning is like Rogaine for your brain: lt spurs the growth of new brain cells. "When you challenge the brain, you increase the number of brain cells and the number of connections between those cells," says Keith L. Black, M.D., chair of neurosurgery at Cedars-Sinai Medical Center in Los Angeles. "But it's not enough to do the things you routinely do—like the daily crossword. You have to learn new things, like sudoku or a new form of bridge."

UCLA researchers using MRI scans found that middle-aged and older adults with little Internet experience could trigger brain centers that control decision-making and complex reasoning after a week of surfing the net. "Engaging the mind can help older brains maintain healthy functioning," says Cynthia R. Green, Ph.D., author of *30 Days to Total Brain Health*.

4 Say *"Omm"*

Chronic stress floods your brain with cortisol, which leads to impaired memory. To better understand if easing tension changes your brain, Harvard researchers studied men and women trained in a technique called mindfulness-based stress reduction (MBSR). This form of meditation—which involves focusing one's attention on sensations, feelings and state of mind—has been shown to reduce harmful stress hormones. After eight weeks, researchers took MRI scans of participants' brains. The density of gray matter in the hippocampus increased significantly in the MBSR group, compared with a control group.

5 Eat Like a Greek

A heart-friendly Mediterranean diet—fish, vegetables, fruit, nuts and beans—reduced Alzheimer's risk by 34 to 48 percent in studies conducted by Columbia University.

"We know that omega-3 fatty acids in fish are very important for maintaining heart health," says Keith Black of Cedars-Sinai. "We suspect these fats may be equally important for maintaining a healthy brain." Data from several large studies suggest that seniors who eat the most fruits and vegetables, especially the leafy-green variety, may experience a slower rate of cognitive decline and a lower risk for dementia than meat lovers.

And it may not matter if you get your produce from a bottle instead of a bin. A study from Vanderbilt University found that people who downed three or more servings of fruit or vegetable juice a week had a 76 percent lower risk for developing Alzheimer's disease than those who drank less than a serving weekly.

6 Spice It Up

Your brain enjoys spices as much as your taste buds do. Herbs and spices like black pepper, cinnamon, oregano, basil, parsley, ginger and vanilla are high in antioxidants, which may help build brainpower. Scientists are particularly intrigued by curcumin, the active ingredient in turmeric, common in Indian curries. "Indians have lower incidence of Alzheimer's, and one theory is it's the curcumin," says Black. "It bonds to amyloid plaques that accumulate in the brains of people with the disease." Animal research shows curcumin reduces amyloid plaques and lowers inflammation levels. A study in humans also found those who ate curried foods frequently had higher scores on standard cognition tests.

7 Find Your Purpose

Discovering your mission in life can help you stay sharp, according to a Rush University Medical Center study of more than 950 older adults. Participants who approached life with clear intentions and goals at the start of the study were less likely to develop Alzheimer's disease over the following seven years, researchers found.

8 Get a (Social) Life

Who needs friends? You do! Having multiple social networks helps lower dementia risk, a 15-year study of older people from Sweden's Karolinska Institute shows. A rich social life may protect against dementia by providing emotional and mental stimulation, says Laura Fratiglioni, M.D., Ph.D., director of the institute's Aging Research Center. Other studies yield similar conclusions: Subjects in a University of Michigan study did better on tests of short-term memory after just 10 minutes of conversation with another person.

9 Reduce Your Risks

Chronic health conditions like diabetes, obesity and hypertension are often associated with dementia. Diabetes, for example, roughly doubles the risk for Alzheimer's and other forms of dementia. Controlling these risk factors can slow the tide.

"We've estimated that in people with mild cognitive impairment—an intermediate state between normal cognitive aging and dementia—good control of diabetes can delay the onset of dementia by several years," says Fratiglioni. That means following doctor's orders regarding diet and exercise and taking prescribed medications on schedule.

10 Check Vitamin Deficiencies

Older adults don't always get all the nutrients they need from foods, due to declines in digestive acids or because their medications interfere with absorption. That vitamin deficit—particularly vitamin B_{12}—can also affect brain vitality, research from Rush University Medical Center shows. Older adults at risk of vitamin B_{12} deficiencies had smaller brains and scored lowest on tests measuring thinking, reasoning and memory, researchers found.

Critical Thinking

1. What food that a person consumes seems to reduce the risk of Alzheimer's disease?
2. What is the advantage of an active social life for reducing the person's chances of developing dementia?
3. How does learning new skills reduce the risk of dementia?

Create Central

www.mhhe.com/createcentral

Internet References

Aging with Dignity
www.aging with dignity.org
The National Council on Aging
www.ncoa.org

Article

Prepared by: Elaina F. Osterbur, *Saint Louis University*

The U-bend of Life

Why, Beyond Middle Age, People Get Happier as They Get Older

THE ECONOMIST

Learning Outcomes

After reading this article, you will be able to:

- Explain why life is happier for people in their older years.

- Explain why older people have fewer arguments and are better at resolving conflict.

Ask people how they feel about getting older, and they will probably reply in the same vein as Maurice Chevalier: "Old age isn't so bad when you consider the alternative." Stiffening joints, weakening muscles, fading eyesight and the clouding of memory, coupled with the modern world's careless contempt for the old, seem a fearful prospect—better than death, perhaps, but not much. Yet mankind is wrong to dread ageing. Life is not a long slow decline from sunlit uplands towards the valley of death. It is, rather, a U-bend.

When people start out on adult life, they are, on average, pretty cheerful. Things go downhill from youth to middle age until they reach a nadir commonly known as the mid-life crisis. So far, so familiar. The surprising part happens after that. Although as people move towards old age they lose things they treasure—vitality, mental sharpness and looks—they also gain what people spend their lives pursuing: happiness.

This curious finding has emerged from a new branch of economics that seeks a more satisfactory measure than money of human well-being. Conventional economics uses money as a proxy for utility—the dismal way in which the discipline talks about happiness. But some economists, unconvinced that there is a direct relationship between money and well-being, have decided to go to the nub of the matter and measure happiness itself.

These ideas have penetrated the policy arena, starting in Bhutan, where the concept of Gross National Happiness shapes the planning process. All new policies have to have a GNH assessment, similar to the environmental-impact assessment common in other countries. In 2008 France's president, Nicolas

The U-bend

Self-reported well-being, on a scale of 1–10

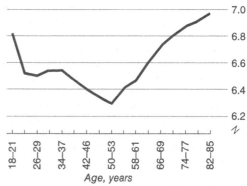

Age, years

Source: PNAS Paper: "A snapshot of the age distribution of Psychological well-being in the United States" by Arthur Stone

Sarkozy, asked two Nobel-prize-winning economists, Amartya Sen and Joseph Stiglitz, to come up with a broader measure of national contentedness than GDP. Then last month, in a touchy-feely gesture not typical of Britain, David Cameron announced that the British government would start collecting figures on well-being.

There are already a lot of data on the subject collected by, for instance, America's General Social Survey, Eurobarometer and Gallup. Surveys ask two main sorts of question. One concerns people's assessment of their lives, and the other how they feel at any particular time. The first goes along the lines of: thinking about your life as a whole, how do you feel? The second is something like: yesterday, did you feel happy/contented/angry/anxious? The first sort of question is said to measure global well-being, and the second hedonic or emotional well-being. They do not always elicit the same response: having children, for instance, tends to make people feel better about their life as a whole, but also increases the chance that they felt angry or anxious yesterday.

Statisticians trawl through the vast quantities of data these surveys produce rather as miners panning for gold. They are trying to find the answer to the perennial question: what makes people happy?

Four main factors, it seems: gender, personality, external circumstances and age. Women, by and large, are slightly happier than men. But they are also more susceptible to depression: a fifth to a quarter of women experience depression at some point in their lives, compared with around a tenth of men. Which suggests either that women are more likely to experience more extreme emotions, or that a few women are more miserable than men, while most are more cheerful.

Two personality traits shine through the complexity of economists' regression analyses: neuroticism and extroversion. Neurotic people—those who are prone to guilt, anger and anxiety—tend to be unhappy. This is more than a tautological observation about people's mood when asked about their feelings by pollsters or economists. Studies following people over many years have shown that neuroticism is a stable personality trait and a good predictor of levels of happiness. Neurotic people are not just prone to negative feelings: they also tend to have low emotional intelligence, which makes them bad at forming or managing relationships, and that in turn makes them unhappy.

Whereas neuroticism tends to make for gloomy types, extroversion does the opposite. Those who like working in teams and who relish parties tend to be happier than those who shut their office doors in the daytime and hole up at home in the evenings. This personality trait may help explain some cross-cultural differences: a study comparing similar groups of British, Chinese and Japanese people found that the British were, on average, both more extrovert and happier than the Chinese and Japanese.

Then there is the role of circumstance. All sorts of things in people's lives, such as relationships, education, income and health, shape the way they feel. Being married gives people a considerable uplift, but not as big as the gloom that springs from being unemployed. In America, being black used to be associated with lower levels of happiness—though the most recent figures suggest that being black or Hispanic is nowadays associated with greater happiness. People with children in the house are less happy than those without. More educated people are happier, but that effect disappears once income is controlled for. Education, in other words, seems to make people happy because it makes them richer. And richer people are happier than poor ones—though just how much is a source of argument.

The View from Winter

Lastly, there is age. Ask a bunch of 30-year-olds and another of 70-year-olds (as Peter Ubel, of the Sanford School of Public Policy at Duke University, did with two colleagues, Heather Lacey and Dylan Smith, in 2006) which group they think is likely to be happier, and both lots point to the 30-year-olds. Ask them to rate their own well-being, and the 70-year-olds are the happier bunch. The academics quoted lyrics written by Pete Townshend of The Who when he was 20: "Things they do look awful cold / Hope I die before I get old." They pointed out that Mr Townshend, having passed his 60th birthday, was writing a blog that glowed with good humour.

Mr Townshend may have thought of himself as a youthful radical, but this view is ancient and conventional. The "seven ages of man"—the dominant image of the life-course in the 16th and 17th centuries—was almost invariably conceived as a rise in stature and contentedness to middle age, followed by a sharp decline towards the grave. Inverting the rise and fall is a recent idea. "A few of us noticed the U-bend in the early 1990s," says Andrew Oswald, professor of economics at Warwick Business School. "We ran a conference about it, but nobody came."

Since then, interest in the U-bend has been growing. Its effect on happiness is significant—about half as much, from the nadir of middle age to the elderly peak, as that of unemployment. It appears all over the world. David Blanchflower, professor of economics at Dartmouth College, and Mr Oswald looked at the figures for 72 countries. The nadir varies among countries—Ukrainians, at the top of the range, are at their most miserable at 62, and Swiss, at the bottom, at 35—but in the great majority of countries people are at their unhappiest in their 40s and early 50s. The global average is 46.

The U-bend shows up in studies not just of global well-being but also of hedonic or emotional well-being. One paper, published this year by Arthur Stone, Joseph Schwartz and Joan Broderick of Stony Brook University, and Angus Deaton of Princeton, breaks well-being down into positive and negative feelings and looks at how the experience of those emotions varies through life. Enjoyment and happiness dip in middle age, then pick up; stress rises during the early 20s, then falls sharply; worry peaks in middle age, and falls sharply thereafter; anger declines throughout life; sadness rises slightly in middle age, and falls thereafter.

Turn the question upside down, and the pattern still appears. When the British Labour Force Survey asks people whether they are depressed, the U-bend becomes an arc, peaking at 46.

Happier, No Matter What

There is always a possibility that variations are the result not of changes during the life-course, but of differences between cohorts. A 70-year-old European may feel different to a 30-year-old not because he is older, but because he grew up during the second world war and was thus formed by different experiences. But the accumulation of data undermines the idea of a cohort effect. Americans and Zimbabweans have not been formed by similar experiences, yet the U-bend appears in both their countries. And if a cohort effect were responsible, the U-bend would not show up consistently in 40 years' worth of data.

Another possible explanation is that unhappy people die early. It is hard to establish whether that is true or not; but, given that death in middle age is fairly rare, it would explain only a little of the phenomenon. Perhaps the U-bend is merely an expression of the effect of external circumstances. After all, common factors affect people at different stages of the life-cycle. People in their 40s, for instance, often have teenage children. Could the misery of the middle-aged be the consequence of sharing space with angry adolescents? And older people tend to be richer. Could their relative contentment be the result of their piles of cash?

The answer, it turns out, is no: control for cash, employment status and children, and the U-bend is still there. So the growing happiness that follows middle-aged misery must be the result not of external circumstances but of internal changes.

People, studies show, behave differently at different ages. Older people have fewer rows and come up with better solutions to conflict. They are better at controlling their emotions, better at accepting misfortune and less prone to anger. In one study, for instance, subjects were asked to listen to recordings of people supposedly saying disparaging things about them. Older and younger people were similarly saddened, but older people less angry and less inclined to pass judgment, taking the view, as one put it, that "you can't please all the people all the time."

There are various theories as to why this might be so. Laura Carstensen, professor of psychology at Stanford University, talks of "the uniquely human ability to recognise our own mortality and monitor our own time horizons." Because the old know they are closer to death, she argues, they grow better at living for the present. They come to focus on things that matter now—such as feelings—and less on long-term goals. "When young people look at older people, they think how terrifying it must be to be nearing the end of your life. But older people know what matters most." For instance, she says, "young people will go to cocktail parties because they might meet somebody who will be useful to them in the future, even though nobody I know actually likes going to cocktail parties."

Death of Ambition, Birth of Acceptance

There are other possible explanations. Maybe the sight of contemporaries keeling over infuses survivors with a determination to make the most of their remaining years. Maybe people come to accept their strengths and weaknesses, give up hoping to become chief executive or have a picture shown in the Royal Academy, and learn to be satisfied as assistant branch manager, with their watercolour on display at the church fete. "Being an old maid", says one of the characters in a story by Edna Ferber, an (unmarried) American novelist, was "like death by drowning—a really delightful sensation when you ceased struggling." Perhaps acceptance of ageing itself is a source of relief. "How pleasant is the day," observed William James, an American philosopher, "when we give up striving to be young—or slender."

Whatever the causes of the U-bend, it has consequences beyond the emotional. Happiness doesn't just make people happy—it also makes them healthier. John Weinman, professor of psychiatry at King's College London, monitored the stress levels of a group of volunteers and then inflicted small wounds on them. The wounds of the least stressed healed twice as fast as those of the most stressed. At Carnegie Mellon University in Pittsburgh, Sheldon Cohen infected people with cold and flu viruses. He found that happier types were less likely to catch the virus, and showed fewer symptoms of illness when they did. So although old people tend to be less healthy than younger ones, their cheerfulness may help counteract their crumbliness.

Happier people are more productive, too. Mr Oswald and two colleagues, Eugenio Proto and Daniel Sgroi, cheered up a bunch of volunteers by showing them a funny film, then set them mental tests and compared their performance to groups that had seen a neutral film, or no film at all. The ones who had seen the funny film performed 12% better. This leads to two conclusions. First, if you are going to volunteer for a study, choose the economists' experiment rather than the psychologists' or psychiatrists'. Second, the cheerfulness of the old should help counteract their loss of productivity through declining cognitive skills—a point worth remembering as the world works out how to deal with an ageing workforce.

The ageing of the rich world is normally seen as a burden on the economy and a problem to be solved. The U-bend argues for a more positive view of the matter. The greyer the world gets, the brighter it becomes—a prospect which should be especially encouraging to *Economist* readers (average age 47).

Critical Thinking

1. How did the stress level in people affect how they responded to wounds and health problems?
2. Why are older people believed to be better at living for the present?
3. What are the human emotions that rise or dip in the middle years?

Create Central

www.mhhe.com/createcentral

Internet References

Aging with Dignity
    www.agingwithdignity.org
The Gerontological Society of America
    www.geron.org
The National Council on the Aging
    www.ncoa.org

Article   Prepared by: Elaina F. Osterbur, *Saint Louis University*

Poll: Obesity Hits More Boomers in U.S.

Learning Outcomes

After reading this article, you will be able to:

- Compare the percentage of the current baby-boomer population that is obese with that of people who are younger and older.

- Cite how much more Medicare pays for an obese senior than for one who is at a healthy weight.

Baby boomers say their biggest health fear is cancer. Given their waistlines, heart disease and diabetes should be atop that list, too.

Boomers are more obese than other generations, a new poll finds, setting them up for unhealthy senior years.

And for all the talk of "60 is the new 50" and active aging, even those who aren't obese need to do more to stay fit, according to the Associated Press-LifeGoesStrong.com poll.

Most baby boomers say they get some aerobic exercise, the kind that revs up your heart rate, at least once a week. But most adults are supposed to get 2½ hours a week of moderate-intensity aerobic activity—things like a brisk walk, a dance class, pushing a lawn mower. Only about a quarter of boomers polled report working up a sweat four or five times a week, what the average person needs to reach that goal.

Worse, 37 percent never do any of the strength training so crucial to fighting the muscle loss that comes with aging.

Walking is their most frequent form of exercise. The good news: Walk enough and the benefits add up.

"I have more energy, and my knees don't hurt anymore," says Maggie Sanders, 61, of Abbeville, S.C. She has lost 15 pounds by walking four miles, three times a week, over the past few months, and eating better.

More boomers need to heed that feel-good benefit. Based on calculation of body mass index from self-reported height and weight, roughly a third of the baby boomers polled are obese, compared with about a quarter of both older and younger responders. Only half of the obese boomers say they are regularly exercising.

An additional 36 percent of boomers are overweight, though not obese.

The nation has been bracing for a surge in Medicare costs as the 77 million baby boomers, the post-war generation born from 1946 to 1964, begin turning 65. Obesity—with its extra risk of heart disease, diabetes, high blood pressure and arthritis—will further fuel those bills.

"They're going to be expensive if they don't get their act together," says Jeff Levi of the nonprofit Trust for America's Health. He points to a study that found Medicare pays 34 percent more on an obese senior than one who's a healthy weight.

About 60 percent of boomers polled say they're dieting to lose weight, and slightly more are eating more fruits and vegetables or cutting cholesterol and salt.

But it takes physical activity, not just dieting, to shed pounds. That's especially important as people start to age and dieting alone could cost them precious muscle in addition to fat, says Jack Rejeski of Wake Forest University, a specialist in exercise and aging.

Whether you're overweight or just the right size, physical activity can help stave off the mobility problems that too often sneak up on the sedentary as they age. Muscles gradually become flabbier until people can find themselves on the verge of disability and loss of independence, like a canoe that floats peacefully until it gets too near a waterfall to pull back, Rejeski says.

He led a study that found a modest weight loss plus walking 2½ hours a week helped people 60 and older significantly improve their mobility. Even those who didn't walk that much got some benefit. Try walking 10 minutes at a time two or three times a day, he suggests, and don't wait to start.

"I don't think there's any question the earlier you get started, the better," says Rejeski, who at 63 has given up running in favor of walking, and gets in 30 miles a week. "If you allow your mobility to decline, you pay for it in terms of the quality of your own life."

When it comes to diseases, nearly half of boomers polled worry most about cancer. The second-leading killer, cancer does become more common with aging.

"It's the unknown nature, that it can come up without warning," says Harry Forsha, 64, of Clearwater, Fla., and Mill Spring, N.C.

Heart disease is the nation's No. 1 killer, but it's third in line on the boomers' worry list. Memory loss is a bigger concern.

In fact, more than half of boomers polled say they regularly do mental exercises such as crossword puzzles.

After Harding retires, he plans to take classes to keep mentally active. For now, he's doing the physical exercise that's important for brain health, too. He also takes fish oil, a type of fatty acid that some studies suggest might help prevent mental decline.

Sanders, the South Carolina woman, says it was hard to make fitness a priority in her younger years.

"When you're younger, you just don't see how important it is," says Sanders, whose weight began creeping up when breast cancer in her 40s sapped her energy. Now, "I just know that my lifestyle had to change."

Critical Thinking

1. Why is dieting alone not the most efficient way to lose weight?

2. What is the most efficient way to stave off mobility problems in later life?

3. What is the biggest health problem on the worry list of the baby boomers?

Create Central

www.mhhe.com/createcentral

Internet References

Aging with Dignity
www.agingwithdignity.org

The Gerontological Society of America
www.geron.org

The National Council on the Aging
www.ncoa.org

Article

Prepared by: Elaina F. Osterbur, *Saint Louis University*

Age and Gender Effects on the Assessment of Spirituality and Religious Sentiments (ASPIRES) Scale: A Cross-Sectional Analysis

I. TUCKER BROWN ET AL.

Learning Outcomes

After reading this article, you will be able to:

- Discuss the Assessment of Spirituality and Religious Sentiments (ASPIRES) Scale.
- Identify the age and gender effects suggested by the ASPIRES Scale.
- Discuss the differing religious styles among younger and older generations.

A substantive and growing body of empirical research demonstrates the salience of spirituality and religiousness as stand-alone psychological constructs (Hill & Pargament, 2008; Hill et al., 2000; Kapuscinski & Masters, 2010; McCullough, Enders, Brion, & Jain, 2005; Piedmont, Ciarrocchi, Dy-Liacco, & Williams, 2009; Slater, Hall, & Edwards, 2001). In the early debate on the relevance and application of these numinous dimensions, some researchers posited that they were better accounted for by already existent, underlying psychological processes (Buss, 2002; Van Wicklin, 1990). In an effort to validate the empirical and practical significance, if not existence, of these constructs (e.g., that they are causal inputs as opposed to outcomes), research in the psychology of religion and spirituality has centered on their construct validity. For example, Piedmont (2004, 2005) has focused on establishing spirituality's unique predictive power over and above the Five-Factor Model of personality (FFM), as well as showing statistically significant correlations with a variety of psychosocial markers (Piedmont et al., 2009).

Studies of this sort, although necessary, are only as robust as the sound psychometric properties of the instruments used to measure the targeted spiritual and religious variables. There is clearly a need for more rigorously developed and conceptually anchored measures in the field (e.g., Kapuscinski & Masters, 2010). The Assessment of Spirituality and Religious Sentiments (ASPIRES; Piedmont, 2010) scale was developed to meet the need for an empirically sound instrument, based on a psychological model of personality, that articulates relevant and robust numinous qualities. Indeed, studies employing the ASPIRES—a 35-item scale measuring two independent though correlated psychological dimensions, Spiritual Transcendence and Religious Sentiments—showed that spirituality and religiousness: (a) function as motivational variables; (b) are both independent of established models of personality; (c) reflect different, yet interrelated, psychological systems; (d) exhibit potential causal influences on a variety of significant psychosocial outcomes; and (e) demonstrate conceptual and structural invariance across religious denominations and cultures (see Chen, 2011; Piedmont, 1999, 2004, 2005, 2007; Piedmont et al., 2009; Piedmont & Leach, 2002; Rican & Janosova, 2010).

Although interest in scale development garners much attention in the research literature (cf. Hill & Pargament, 2008; Hill et al., 2000; Kapuscinski & Masters, 2010), evaluation of how these numinous constructs evolve over the life span, and between genders, represent areas requiring further empirical investigation (Seifert, 2002). Though there are theoretical and empirical models based on the hypothesis that individuals experience systematic changes in levels of spirituality and religiousness over the course of their lives (e.g., Argue, Johnson, & White, 1999; Dalby, 2006; Dillon, Wink, & Fay, 2003; Ingersoll-Dayton, Krause, & Morgan, 2002; Koenig, McGue, & Iacono, 2008; Wink & Dillon, 2002, 2008), relatively few empirical studies have used standardized and cross-culturally validated measures, such as the ASPIRES.

Studies examining changes in spirituality and religiousness over time and between genders have been, for the most part, grounded in personality theory and research. This rigorous background of psychological inquiry has established a sound foundation upon which to advance emergent theory and social scientific investigation (cf. Piedmont, 2005). The vast majority of age and gender effects designs are based on data taken from single-item responses (e.g., "Are you spiritual" and "How often do you pray") and recoded interview segments contained within much broader sets of self-report measures primarily intended to assess other aspects of psychological functioning (e.g., Argue et al., 1999; Dillon et al., 2003; Good, Willoughby, & Busseri, 2011; McCullough et al., 2005; McCullough & Laurenceau, 2005; McCullough, Tsang, & Brion, 2003; Wink & Dillon, 2002, 2003).

Wink and Dillon (2002, 2008) collated longitudinal data evaluating the role of spirituality and religiousness across a life span of over 60 years. Drawing from a sample of more than 200 participants born in the 1920s, Wink and Dillon examined the development and expression of these numinous dimensions from young adulthood through old age. Their findings suggested that levels of spirituality increased significantly over the course of the life span, especially from middle to late adulthood, with women evidencing a higher level of spirituality than men. Men's spirituality, however, showed a more significant increase than women's from early to middle adulthood. For women, a high level of spirituality in late adulthood was related to the number of negative life events experienced in middle adulthood, most notably financial strain and spousal and parental conflicts.

Drawing from data collected in the Terman Longitudinal Study of high ability children, McCullough, Enders, Brion, and Jain (2005) identified three reliable models of religious experience, each with a unique arc or trajectory over time. There were individuals who scored low on religiousness in youth and remained low throughout their lives (i.e., homeostatic). A second group scored high on religiousness in youth and remained high longitudinally. Finally, there was a group that expressed a moderate level of religiousness in youth with an increase into middle adulthood and then a decrease in late life (i.e., nonlinear relationship).

These longitudinal studies were all limited in that they did not use standardized measures of spirituality and religiousness. Rather, they relied on an amalgam of available surveys and interview data. Without clear validity for scores on these indices, regardless of the sophistication of the statistical analyses used in the design, the meaning of the purported relationships across time and between genders cannot be reliably substantiated (cf. Brennan & Mroczek, 2003).

Despite these limitations, the longitudinal designs reviewed here suggest three plausible theoretical perspectives by which to approach potential age effects on spirituality and religiousness across the life span: (a) homeostasis, (b) increasing relevance, and (c) nonlinear relationship. According to the homeostatic model, levels of spirituality and religiousness stay the same from early to late life. In the increasing relevance approach, spirituality and religiousness rise steadily, in a linear fashion, throughout human development. From the perspective of a nonlinear relationship, it is hypothesized that levels of spirituality

and religiousness change by some combination of increase, decrease, and period of plateau, although the sequencing of these changes is not clearly identified. Taken as a whole, these longitudinal data demonstrate that levels of spirituality and religiousness may not be static across the life span.

Although the research literature suggests age- and gender-related effects for numinous constructs, little is known about the *content* that evolves in spirituality and religiousness over time and between genders. In other words, as people age and their experiences of their world evolve, does their understanding of what spirituality and religiousness mean also change? Is spirituality defined and understood differently for older and younger individuals? Answers to these questions have important implications for the assessment of numinous constructs. If peoples' understanding of the numinous changes, or if men and women experience the numinous differently, then there would be a need to develop instruments that capture these differences. It may be possible that scale scores that are valid for one age group, or one gender, may not be valid in another age group or for a different gender. Spirituality would need to be considered an evolving characteristic adaptation that works out of the changing life experiences of people. However, if it can be established that despite mean level changes in scores the underlying structure of the scale remains unchanged over time, then a strong case can be made for the numinous as a cohesive, common, dispositional aspect of human functioning.

The purpose of this study was twofold. First, the study intended to determine whether the observed gender and age effects noted in numerous longitudinal studies would be evidenced on the ASPIRES, a psychometrically sound, cross-culturally validated measure of spirituality and religiousness. As noted above, many longitudinal studies have relied on post hoc-developed indices of religiousness and spirituality that often differed across the assessment intervals. The lack of a single standardized measure suggests that the observed age effects may have been due to differences in instrumentation across the assessment intervals and not to real changes in the construct. Finding age and gender effects in the ASPIRES would add more confidence to the findings of the longitudinal studies. Second, this study sought to determine whether the underlying factor structure of the ASPIRES was consistent across both age and gender groups. Do people of different ages come to understand the numinous in significantly different ways? Or, is there an underlying understanding of the numinous that is constant across the life span? Thus, do mean level changes in scores reflect the varying salience of the numinous over time or fundamental changes in how the transcendent is understood and experienced?

This study offers a first step in evaluating the effects of age and gender on a *standardized* measure of spirituality and religiousness, in a cross-sectional sample. Furthermore, it allows for a first look at the structural nature (i.e., intrinsic meaning and factorial integrity) of the ASPIRES scales among age and gender groups. In so doing it sheds light on how spirituality and religiousness may operate in similar or different ways, both broadly and with respect to age and gender.

Method

Participants

Participants consisted of 1,539 women and 698 men, ranging in age from 17 to 94 (M = 30 years). Of these, 47% were Caucasian, 22% Asian, 6% Hispanic, 2% African American, 1% Middle Eastern, and 11% indicated other. Concerning faith tradition, 90% indicated a Christian tradition, 4% were Jewish, 2% were atheist/agnostic, 2% were Muslim, Buddhist, or Hindu, and 2% indicated "other." Concerning age, 1,603 individuals were between 17 and 29, 357 between 30 and 60, and 277 were between 61 and 94. These individuals represented a sample of convenience obtained from one of four locations: Maryland/Washington, DC area, Massachusetts/New Hampshire, Mississippi, and Illinois. All subjects volunteered. This sample consists of approximately 75% of the current normative sample (N = 2,999) for the ASPIRES. For more information about the normative sample see Piedmont (2010).

Measures

Assessment of Spirituality and Religious Sentiments (ASPIRES)

Developed by Piedmont (2010), this 35-item scale measures two major numinous dimensions: Spiritual Transcendence, the motivational capacity to create a broad sense of personal meaning for one's life; and Religious Sentiments, the extent to which an individual is involved in and committed to the precepts, teachings, and practices of a specific religious tradition. Spiritual Transcendence is measured by three correlated facet scales: Prayer Fulfillment (PF), the ability to create a personal space that enables one to feel a positive connection to some larger reality; Universality (UN), the belief in a larger meaning and purpose to life; and Connectedness (CN), feelings of belonging and responsibility to a larger human reality that cuts across generations and groups. Religious Sentiments consists of two correlated dimensions, Religious Involvement (RI), which reflects how actively involved a person is in performing various religious rituals and activities; and Religious Crisis (RC) which examines whether a person may be experiencing problems, difficulties, or conflicts with the God of their understanding.

Piedmont (2010) presented information on the reliability and validity of this scale. Alpha reliabilities for the self-report scales ranged from .60 (CN) to .95 (PF) with a mean alpha of .82. Structurally, the Spiritual Transcendence Scale (STS) consists of three correlated dimensions respectively defined by the items of the PF, UN, and CN subscales. The Religious Sentiments dimension was shown to have two subscales, which consisted of the items of the RI and RC scales. Scores on these scales were shown to predict significantly a range of psychosocial outcomes (e.g., well-being, self-esteem, prosocial behavior, social support, and sexual attitudes), even after the predictive effects of personality were removed. Support for the structural, predictive, and incremental validity of the ASPIRES has been demonstrated across religious faiths, cultures, and languages (Piedmont, 2007; Piedmont & Leach, 2002; Piedmont, Werdel, & Fernando, 2009; Rican & Janosova, 2010).

Procedure

The subjects in this study were the extant normative sample of the ASPIRES as of June, 2009. The ASPIRES manual contains all relevant descriptive information about this sample (Piedmont, 2010). Although overall gender and age effects have been conducted on the ASPIRES scales (and reflects why scores on the scale are normed on the basis of age and gender), no effort has been made to systematically study how scores change over time and whether the factor structures of the scales remain unchanged across these different demographic groups.

Results

A one-way MANOVA was conducted using gender as the independent variable and total STS, Religious Involvement, and Religious Crisis scores as the outcome criteria. A significant multivariate effect was found [Wilks Λ = .975, multivariate $F(3, 2225)$ = 19.30, $p < .001$]. Univariate analyses indicated that women scored significantly higher (M = 84.05) than men (M = 80.48) on overall Spiritual Transcendence [$F(1, 2229)$ = 34.16, $p < .001$, η^2 = .02], and men scored significantly higher (M = 7.70) than women (M = 7.21) on Religious Crisis [$F(1, 2229)$ = 13.13, $p < .001$, η^2 = .01]. No difference was found for Religious Involvement scores.

Testing for Nonlinear Age Effects

A polynomial regression analysis was performed to examine the presence of nonlinear age effects on these three outcome variables. Three polynomial multiple regression analyses were conducted using each of the ASPIRES scale scores as the dependent variable. Using a hierarchical entry approach, age, its square, and cube were entered (which evaluate the presence of linear, quadratic, and cubic associations, respectively). Results indicated a significant quadratic effect for age on Total STS [ΔR^2 = .05, $F(1, 2234)$ = 120.50, $p < .001$, partial η^2 = .13], Religious Involvement [ΔR^2 = .04, $F(1, 2234)$ = 93.62, $p < .001$, partial η^2 = .21], and Religious Crisis [ΔR^2 = .01, $F(1, 2233)$ = 22.22, $p < .001$, partial η^2 = .03]. Based on theory drawn from life span and personality development, age was partitioned into three groupings (i.e., 17–29, 30–60, 61–94). Figure 1 presents how scores on the ASPIRES scales vary across these age groupings.[1]

To examine these mean level differences among the age groups, a one-way ANOVA was performed using age category as the independent variable and the ASPIRES scale scores as the outcomes. A significant age effect was noted on total STS scores [$F(2, 2234)$ = 148.87, $p < .001$, η^2 = .12] and the LSD post hoc test indicated that STS scores were significantly higher in the middle adulthood group (i.e., 46–55) than in the early adulthood or old age cohorts. However, STS scores for the eldest group still were significantly higher than for the

---

[1] In examining the facet scales for the STS domain, significant quadratic effects were found for age on the Prayer Fulfillment [ΔR^2 = .04, $F(1, 2234)$ = 91.94, $p < .001$, partial η^2 = .09] and Universality [ΔR^2 = .06, $F(1, 2234)$ = 164.85, $p < .001$, partial η^2 = .17] facet scales. The patterns of effect mirrored that presented for the overall STS score. No age effects, linear or otherwise, were found for Connectedness.

Age and Gender Effects on the Assessment of Spirituality and Religious Sentiments (ASPIRES) Scale by I. Tucker Brown et al.

39

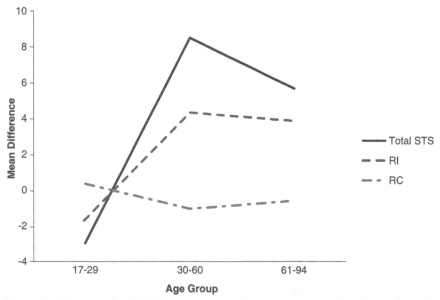

Figure 1   Differences in ASPIRES scores across three age groups.   Note: Scores for each scale are portrayed as each age group's difference from its respective overall group mean.

youngest group (see Figure 1). Concerning Religious Involvement scores, a significant age effect was also noted, $F(2, 2234) = 239.39$, $p < .001$, $\eta^2 = .18$. A post hoc analysis indicated that scores were significantly higher in the middle adulthood group and then stabilized in the old age cohort. Scores for the eldest group were not significantly different from the middle aged group, but they were significantly higher than the youngest group. A significant age effect was also found for Religious Crisis, $F(2, 2233) = 37.39$, $p < .001$, $\eta^2 = .03$. Scores were high in the early adulthood group and were significantly lower for the other two age cohorts, with the middle-aged and eldest groups being significantly lower than the youngest group, although these two groups did not differ between themselves.

To examine whether gender and age interact, a 2 (men vs. women) $\times$ 3 (age grouping) MANOVA was conducted using total STS, Religious Involvement, and Religious Crisis scores as the dependent variables. No significant interactions were found. Thus, age and gender operated as additive effects in influencing scores on the ASPIRES. The effects of gender and age were examined separately in this report.

Structural Invariance

A series of structural equation models (SEM) were conducted to determine the extent to which the putative factor structure of the STS and Religious Sentiments scales were recoverable across the different age and gender groups. LISREL 8.72 was used for these analyses. The STS scale was hypothesized to consist of three positively correlated facet scales, constituting the PF, UN, and CN dimensions. With regards to the Religious Sentiments domain, the RI and RC scales should represent two distinct, negatively correlated scales. These structures were

examined within each age and gender group. The results of these analyses are presented in Table 1. As can be seen, the putative normative structure was clearly obtained in each instance. The weakest findings were obtained for the middle-aged and elderly groups on the Religious Sentiments domain. The overall structure of the scale remained consistent across age and gender groups.

In order to determine whether each dimension was similarly defined by its respective items, a series of confirmatory factor analyses (CFA) were conducted for each numinous domain across the gender and age groups. For the STS domain, three correlated factors were extracted and rotated, Although for the RS domain two correlated factors were extracted and rotated. The resulting pattern loadings from each analysis were then compared both to normative pattern loadings presented in Piedmont (2010) and among the various age and gender groups using congruence coefficients (CC). CCs determine the extent to which two sets of factor loadings on the same items across two groups are identical. Unlike a simple correlation coefficient which evaluates pattern similarity, CCs evaluate similarity in terms of both pattern and magnitude of loadings and are thus, the preferred method for examining profile similarity (see Gorsuch, 1983, pp. 284–288 for a fuller discussion of this index). The null distribution of CCs was determined by conducting a series of Monte Carlo studies that generated random loadings which were then compared with the normative values for both the STS and RS domains. A set of 10,000 iterations was conducted and the 95th, 99th, and 99.9th percentiles in each distribution of CCs were identified. An observed CC was determined to be significant if its value exceeded these cut-off values produced in the null distribution.

Table 1   SEM Results Testing the Factor Structure of the ASPIRES Scales across the Age and Gender Groups

	χ^2	df	RMSEA	SRMR	NFI	CFI	GFI
Spiritual transcendence							
Age group							
Young[a]	184.21	104	.02	.04	.99	1.00	.99
Middle[b]	339.60	207	.04	.05	.96	.98	.92
Elder[c]	224.42	207	.02	.06	.94	.98	.89
Gender							
Men[d]	698.61	196	.06	.05	.96	.97	.92
Women[e]	1,161.86	185	.06	.04	.98	.98	.94
Religious sentiments							
Age group							
Young[a]	100.86	35	.03	.02	.99	1.00	.99
Middle[b]	94.05	41	.08	.06	.95	.97	.93
Elder[c]	165.64	45	.10	.09	.96	.97	.90
Gender							
Men[d]	76.68	39	.04	.02	.99	1.00	.98
Women[e]	115.90	36	.04	.02	.99	1.00	.99
Desired values			<.10	<.10	>.90	>.90	>.90

Note. RMSEA = Root Mean Square Error of Approximation; SRMR = Standardized Root Mean Residual; NFI = Normed Fit Index; CFI = Comparative Fit Index; GFI = Goodness of Fit Index.

[a] $n = 1,608$. [b] $n = 359$. [c] $n = 270$. [d] $n = 1,534$. [e] $n = 697$.

Table 2 presents the results of these analyses. Each age group was compared with the normative factor loadings as well as to each other. Similar analyses were done for gender. All resulting CCs were statistically significant indicating that the factor structure of the ASPIRES was identical across both age and gender groups. Table 3 presents the actual pattern loadings for each ASPIRES item on its respective factor across the identified age and gender groups. For comparison, normative values are also presented. As can be seen, each item on the ASPIRES loaded on its respective domain similarly across the age and gender groups. Although there are some anomalous loadings (e.g., the loading for item CN6 for the "young" group; the loadings for UN1, UN4, and UN5 for the "middle age" group), the values are quite consistent and compare very

Table 2   Congruence Coefficients for Age and Gender Comparisons for all ASPIRES Scales

	ASPIRES Scale				
Comparison	PF	UN	CN	RI	RC
Young[a]	.99	.95	.87	.99	.95
Middle[b]	.97	.76	.83	.99	.92
Elder[c]	.99	.85	.80	.97	.93
Female[d]	.99	.99	.99	.99	.95
Male[e]	.97	.97	.97	.99	.97
Gender	.95	.95	.95	1.00	1.00
Age 1	.97	.67	.59	.99	.98
Age 2	.98	.84	.78	.98	.99
Age 3	.97	.82	.65	.98	.97

Note. Each of these groups were compared with normative data (Piedmont, 2010); Gender = the congruence coefficients between men ($n = 698$) and women ($n = 1,533$); Age 1 = the congruence coefficients between young ($n = 1,603$) and middle age ($n = 357$) groups; Age 2 = congruence between young and elder ($n = 277$) groups; Age 3 = congruence between middle aged and elder groups. PF = Prayer Fulfillment, UN = Universality; CN = Connectedness; RI = Religious Involvement; RC = Religious Crisis. All coefficients are significant at $p < .001$.

[a] $N = 1,608$. [b] $N = 359$. [c] $N = 270$. [d] $N = 1,534$. [e] $N = 697$.

Age and Gender Effects on the Assessment of Spirituality and Religious Sentiments (ASPIRES) Scale by I. Tucker Brown et al.

41

Table 3 Pattern Loadings for Each ASPIRES Item on its Respective Factor for Each Age and Gender Group

ASPIRES item	Young	Middle age	Elderly	Men	Women	Norms
PF1	.67	.75	.81	.63	.72	.73
PF2	.63	.74	.62	.64	.63	.61
PF3	.72	.57	.57	.78	.69	.78
PF4	.78	.73	.76	.77	.83	.81
PF5	.75	.77	.80	.73	.76	.76
PF6	.87	.77	.77	.83	.88	.86
PF7	.86	.72	.75	.86	.83	.86
PF8	.84	.84	.85	.82	.86	.81
PF8	.84	.64	.81	.80	.86	.83
PF10	.72	.70	.78	.76	.75	.73
UN1	.57	.26	.61	.54	.59	.66
UN2	.69	.76	.75	.45	.84	.75
UN3	.58	.61	.50	.30	.76	.59
UN4	.43	.28	.43	.66	.40	.69
UN5	.61	.27	.38	.50	.59	.66
UN6	.40	.56	.59	.25	.64	.57
UN7	.52	.60	.58	.40	.64	.62
CN1	−.12	.00	.01	−.15	−.06	.00
CN2	.79	.63	.61	.74	.82	.82
CN3	.78	.63	.67	.77	.82	.75
CN4	.49	.72	.32	.40	.59	.57
CN5	.26	.27	.63	.33	.24	.34
CN6	.01	.52	.57	.06	.22	.31
RC1	.80	.85	.81	.85	.83	.84
RC2	.70	.80	.76	.76	.78	.77
RC3	.77	.77	.84	.84	.77	.79
RC4	.80	.80	.83	.82	.84	.83
RC5	.83	.70	.86	.85	.83	.83
RC6	.83	.62	.76	.84	.80	.83
RC7	.75	.87	.80	.80	.78	.79
RC8	.43	.39	.55	.54	.46	.53
RS1	.85	.75	.93	.83	.84	.84
RS2	.85	.85	.90	.84	.87	.86
RS3	.81	.71	.71	.81	.80	.80
RS4	.55	.60	.33	.47	.54	.50

Note. PF = Prayer Fulfillment; UN = Universality; CN = Connectedness; RI = Religious Involvement; RC = Religious Crisis.

well to normative values. The items for the two Religious Sentiments and the Prayer Fulfillment scales evidenced the greatest levels of consistency. Despite significant mean level differences in scores across the different age cohorts and between genders, the underlying factor structure was invariant.

Discussion

These data clearly demonstrate that there are significant age and gender effects on the ASPIRES scales. Concerning gender, women scored significantly higher than men on all scales except Religious Crisis, where men scored higher. These observed differences parallel findings in the research literature, where women consistently score higher than men on measures of spirituality and religious involvement (e.g., Maselko & Kubzansky, 2006; Wink & Dillon, 2002). Fortunately, these gender differences do not impact the underlying factor structure of the scale; men and women appear to understand and experience spirituality in a similar manner (e.g., Gomez & Fisher, 2005).

Age effects were also found, which are consistent with longitudinal research that documents changes across the life span in spirituality and religiousness (e.g., Wink & Dillon, 2002). Levels of spirituality and religiousness appear to rise over the late adolescent and adult life course. Levels of Religious

Crisis begin high but decline over time. Again, Although mean levels may vary, the underlying factor structure of the scales remains unchanged. Thus, Although the outward expression of religious sentiments and spiritual motivations may change over time, and across genders, the nature of these constructs is constant. Spirituality and religiousness represent unitary qualities that are common to men and women, young and old. These data suggest that there are not different types of spiritualities and religious understandings (e.g., women's spirituality or an elderly spirituality; see Reich, 1997). Numinous qualities can be understood as cohesive, common dimensions that can be used to describe the human experience. These findings are also consistent with other measures of spirituality that have been found to be independent of the FFM, such as the Faith Maturity Scale (FMS; Benson, Donahue, & Erickson, 1993; Piedmont & Nelson, 2001). The FMS evidenced a common factor structure despite mean level differences between genders and across age groups and religious denominations.

However, the presence of mean-level differences underscores the need for users of spiritual/religious scales to control for age and gender effects in their work. Because most measures of spirituality and religiousness do not have normative data (the ASPIRES does have normative data that adjusts scores by age and gender), users will need to provide their own adjustments to obtained raw scores in order to control for these influences.

Interpreting the Age Effects
Cohort Interpretation

As a cross-sectional study the most direct, and simplest, interpretation of these findings would be to view them as cohort effects. The observed differences across the three age groups represent the unique developmental, cultural, and social experiences that shaped the values for each generation's world view. In the current study, on average, subjects in the three age groups were born in 1936 (the Silent Generation), 1960 (the Baby Boomers), and 1989 (the Millennial Generation), respectively; coming of age in the 1950s, 1980s, and now. The groupings and the related generational interpretations are based on data from the Pew Research Center (2010).

The Baby Boomers and Silent Generation share much in common in terms of religious involvements, both scoring high on this scale. Over 85% in each group are affiliated with religious denominations (Pew Research Center, 2010). Both groups came of age in times of social and political conservatism, periods in which group membership and conformity were more salient (Gitlin, 2011; Strauss & Howe, 1992). In the 1950s, society tried to settle into a uniform, comfortable reality as the chaos and social tumult of World War II began to recede (Strauss & Howe, 1992). The 1980s saw a similar increase in conventionality as the social and political upheavals of the late 1960s and early 1970s, along with the strong focus on the individual, began to fade away (Gitlin, 2011). However, the Baby Boomers seemed to develop a higher need for meaning and purpose along with their religious involvements. Perhaps this was a carry-over from the 1960s where there was an eschewal of material values and an emphasis on finding humanity's higher nature and purpose (Isserman & Kazin, 2011).

In the present study, the youngest group evidences a pattern quite different from the other two groups. The Millennial Generation is low on both spirituality and religious involvement. The Pew Research Center (2010) noted this group to exhibit lower levels of religious intensity than their elders today. The need for conformity and group membership in larger social/religious organizations is less than the other cohort groups. Fully 25% of those in this generational group are "unaffiliated" with any religious group and are more likely to define themselves as "atheist" or "agnostic." For those who do attend services, they do so at lower rates than the other two cohort groups did when they were the same age. With the arrival of the Internet and social media, the youngest generation may be finding their social needs gratified in connectivity through these electronic portals that provide a global community rather than in membership in static physical organizations (Jones, Cox, & Banchoff, 2012). The concomitant rise in both materialism and secularism during the past 20 years may explain the lower scores on spirituality, where the ethos focuses on consumption, acquisition, and upward financial mobility (Fischer, 2010; Pew Research Center, 2007).

Interestingly, though, the higher scores on Religious Crisis suggest that the Millennials are not just ignoring religion and spirituality, finding them irrelevant to their current world-view. Instead, there is a sense in this generation that they feel alienated, isolated, and punished by the God of their understanding. They may avoid religious and spiritual issues because that whole aspect of life is perceived as hostile and threatening. High scores on Religious Crisis have been linked to increased levels of Axis II pathology (Piedmont et al., 2007). Identifying the factors contributing to this process would be an important insight into the social mechanisms that give rise to spiritual isolation and its related psychological implications. Nonetheless, these data may be identifying important motivational and attitudinal shifts that are occurring in our society. Given that high scores on numinous constructs are related to higher levels of well-being, life satisfaction, emotional maturity, and prosocial attitudes, these shifts may carry with them important implications for how the American lifestyle may be evolving over the next half century.

Longitudinal Interpretation

Although the viewing of discontinuities in spiritual and religious styles between the younger and older generations may seem jarring, it may not be reasonable to expect that these mean level scores will remain constant over the life span of this younger group. As our initial review of the longitudinal literature indicated, spirituality and religiousness change in nonlinear ways over the life span. Thus, it may be more appropriate to view these intercohort scores as "snapshots" taken at discrete points in an ongoing, continuous developmental process. Although a cross-sectional study cannot speak to issues of process, it can be pointed out that the different patterns of scores are consistent with several longitudinal studies that have noted increasing levels of spirituality and religiousness over the life span (e.g., Wink & Dillon, 2002, 2008).

In fact, many theories of spiritual development expect individuals to increase in spiritual awareness, maturity, and commitment (e.g., Mattes, 2005). Piedmont (1999) explicitly stated that scores on spirituality should increase as one gets older. He argued that the increasing salience of mortality would be a powerful stimulator of spiritual motivations and religious involvements. When viewed through the lens of ongoing development, these findings offer another set of hypotheses for understanding spiritual and religious maturation that can be tested in future longitudinal work.

The lower scores on religiousness and spirituality for the Millennial cohort may be a consequence of several factors. Late adolescence is a time of great emotional exuberance, where young adults revel in feelings of infallibility, infertility, and immortality. The processes of self-exploration and self-understanding focus on the immediate sense of personhood and may overwhelm any concerns about ultimate personal meaning or issues of teleological significance. Further, religious and spiritual issues may also be perceived as remnants of parental control that young adults may move against as the process of individuation unfolds. The higher scores on Religious Crisis may be a reflection of the more general feelings of emotional dysphoria that characterize this age group (Costa & McCrae, 1994). Young adults feel insecure and emotionally vulnerable as they interact with others and strive to find personal and social adequacy in their peer groups. These feelings of alienation and inadequacy begin to melt away as the person finds his or her place in the world.

Moving into middle adulthood is a time characterized by many firsts. People find love and marriage, begin a family, and undertake a vocational trajectory in the hope of building a life. Here the issues of meaning and community involvement become important. Building a future entails having a blueprint to follow. As such, the need to create ultimate meaning becomes more salient now because it helps to create an interpretive context for understanding the self. Having a broad sense of personal meaning provides emotional stability, which in turn enables one to make long-term commitments. It also helps one to find and develop a sense of community, within which social support and amity provide a focus and venue for ones identity and generativity needs. Thus, the middle adulthood group had higher levels of religious involvement and spiritual transcendence than the youngest age group.

Curiously, for those in the older adulthood group, their levels of spirituality were lower than those in the middle age group Although religious involvement remained at a comparable level. It seems odd that issues of meaning appear to be less salient at a time when many developmental theories claim that individuals are motivated to pull together a final, integrative sense of meaning that describes and characterizes the life that was led (e.g., Erikson, 1959). Thus, the findings for the older aged cohort appear incongruous with theory. From a cross-sectional perspective, this finding may just represent a cohort-specific effect: People of this generation always have been more focused on religious activities and involvements than on spiritual relationships. From a developmental perspective, lower scores on spirituality may represent a shifting focus toward the numinous as death becomes more salient. The greater emphasis on religious rituals and involvements may be providing individuals with greater confidence that they will find ultimate spiritual security in the next life. Marrow (1986) captured this motivation when explaining why St. Paul's ideas of salvation through faith have not been as persuasive as the need for good works, "... working to prescribed rules and earning quantifiable merit is more reassuring than belief ... especially when the required faith remains refractory to our preferred methods of verification" (p. 106).

Thus, behavioral expressions of one's faith provide external "evidence" that one is committed to God and is actively working to perfect that relationship in concrete ways. Involvement in religious ritual may provide more psychological comfort to the elderly as they attempt to create the final synthesis of their lives. However, with age comes decreasing mobility and social contact, and therefore greater attention may need to be directed toward insuring the elderly's continued participation in social/religious activities.

Conclusions

Longitudinal research on spirituality and religiousness has clearly demonstrated that the numinous is an important part of most peoples' lives across their life span. These studies further demonstrated that the nature of peoples' involvements in the numinous do change over their life span, in that how it becomes expressed does vary over time, although no consistencies have yet been found across studies. Further, the spiritual experiences of men and women also vary. The results of this study provide support for these fundamental findings: Mean levels of spirituality and religiousness, as measured by the ASPIRES, do vary across age groups in nonlinear ways. In addition, mean levels on these dimensions are different for men and women, although these differences appear constant across age group. This study's significant contribution is that although the expression of spirituality and religious sentiments may vary across age and gender, the fundamental meaning of the construct remains constant. How people come to understand and experience the numinous, regardless of age and gender, is a unitary reality. Despite how it may be differently expressed by men and women, or by young and old, its underlying meaning is the same.

This finding explains why strong cross-observer validity is found with the ASPIRES scales both in the U.S. (Piedmont, 2010) and abroad (Piedmont, 2007). It also explains why the ASPIRES has been found both structurally and predictively valid across religious denominations, cultures, and languages (e.g., Chen, 2011; Piedmont & Leach, 2002; Rican & Janosova, 2010). The value of this finding is the parsimony it suggests to exist within the numinous domain. There is no need for a measure of spirituality for the elderly or one for the young nor is there a need for a female versus male measure of spirituality. The unitive nature of the construct provides additional evidence that religious and spiritual dynamics represent a cohesive, definable, and robust aspect of individual differences, qualities worthy of scientific examination.

Certainly more longitudinal research is needed in this area. Including standardized, validated measures of spiritual and religious qualities, such as the ASPIRES, that are relevant for all faith denominations and cultural contexts, is highly recommended. Use of such measures across time will provide better assessments of how numinous qualities may, or may not, be changing across the life span. The findings of this study represent one set of hypotheses that can be tested longitudinally. Replicating these findings within groups over time will provide a great foundation for constructing empirically informed developmental theories about how individuals create personal meaning and how aspects of the numinous become differentially salient as one deals with evolving life tasks.

References

Argue, A., Johnson, D. R., & White, L. K. (1999). Age and religiosity: Evidence from a three-wave panel analysis. *Journal for the Social Scientific Study of Religion, 38,* 423–435. doi:10.2307/1387762

Benson, P. L., Donahue, M. J., & Erickson, J. A. (1993). The Faith Maturity Scale: Conceptualization, measurement, and empirical validation. *Research in the Social Scientific Study of Religion, 5,* 1–26.

Brennan, M., & Mroczek, D. K. (2002). Examining spirituality over time: Latent growth curve and individual growth curve analyses. *Journal of Religious Gerontology, 14,* 11–29. doi:10.1300/J078v14n01_02

Buss, D. M. (2002). Sex, marriage, and religion: What adaptive problems do religious phenomena solve? *Psychological Inquiry, 13,* 201–203.

Chen, T. P. (2011). *A cross-cultural psychometric evaluation of the Assessment of Spirituality and Religious Sentiments Scale in Mainland China* (Unpublished doctoral dissertation). Loyola University Maryland, Baltimore, MD.

Costa, P. T., Jr., & McCrae, R. R. (1994). Stability and change in personality from adolescence through adulthood. In C. F. Halverson, G. A. Kohnstamm, & R. P. Martin (Eds.), *The developing structure of temperament and personality from infancy to adulthood* (pp. 139–150). Hillsdale, NJ: Lawrence Erlbaum Associates.

Dalby, P. (2006). Is there a process of spiritual change or development associated with ageing? A critical review of research. *Aging & Mental Health, 10,* 4–12. doi:10.1080/13607860500307969

Dillon, M., Wink, P., & Fay, K. (2003). Is spirituality detrimental to generativity? *Journal for the Scientific Study of Religion, 42,* 427–442. doi:10.1111/1468-5906.00192

Erikson, E. H. (1959). *Identity and the life cycle.* New York, NY: International Universities Press.

Fischer, C. S. (2010). *Made in America: A social history of American culture and character.* Chicago, IL: University of Chicago Press.

Gitlin, M. (2011). *The Baby Boomer encyclopedia.* Santa Barbara, CA: ABC-CLIO.

Gomez, R., & Fisher, J. W. (2005). The spiritual well-being questionnaire: Testing for model applicability, measurement and structural equivalencies, and latent mean differences across gender. *Personality and Individual Differences, 39,* 1383–1393. doi:10.1016/j.paid.2005.03.023

Good, M., Willoughby, T., & Busseri, M. A. (2011). Stability and change in adolescent spirituality/religiosity: A person-centered approach. *Developmental Psychology, 47,* 538–550. doi:10.1037/a0021270

Gorsuch, R. L. (1983). *Factor analysis* (2nd ed.). Hillsdale, NJ: Lawrence Erlbaum Associates.

Hill, P. C., & Pargament, K. I. (2008). Advances in the conceptualization and measurement of religion and spirituality: Implications for physical and mental health research. *Psychology of Religion and Spirituality, 5,* 3–17. doi:10.1037/1941-1022.S.1.3

Hill, P. C., Pargament, K. I., Hood, R. W., McCullough, M. E., Sawyers, J. P., Larson, D. B., & Zinnbauer, B. J. (2000). Conceptualizing religion and spirituality: Points of commonality, point of departure. *Journal for the Theory of Social Behavior, 30,* 51–77. doi:10.1111/1468-5914.00119

Ingersoll-Dayton, B., Krause, N., & Morgan, D. (2002). Religious trajectories and transitions over the life course. *International Journal of Aging & Human Development, 55,* 51–70. doi:10.2190/297Q-MRMV-27TE-VLFK

Isserman, M., & Kazin, M. (2011). *America divided: The civil war of the 1960s.* New York, NY: Oxford University Press.

Jones, R. P., Cox, D., & Banchoff, T. (2012). *A generation in transition: Religion, values, and politics among college-age Millennials. Finding from the 2012 Millennial Values Survey.* Washington, DC: Public Religion Research Institute, Inc. and Georgetown University's Berkley Center for Religion, Peace, and World Affairs.

Kapuscinski, A. N., & Masters, K. S. (2010). The current status of measures of spirituality: A critical review of scale development. *Psychology of Religion and Spirituality, 2,* 191–205. doi:10.1037/a0020498

Koenig, L. B., McGue, M., & Iacono, W. G. (2008). Stability and change in religiousness during emerging adulthood. *Developmental Psychology, 44,* 532–543. doi:10.1037/0012-1649.44.2.532

Marrow, S. B. (1986). *Paul: His letters and his theology: An introduction to Paul's epistles.* Mahwah, NJ: Paulist Press.

Maselko, J., & Kubzansky, L. D. (2006). Gender differences in religious practices, spiritual experiences and health: Results from the U.S. General Social Survey. *Social Science & Medicine, 62,* 2848–2860. doi:10.1016/j.socscimed.2005.11.008

Mattes, R. (2005). Spiritual need one: Spiritual development: The aging process: A journal of lifelong spiritual formation. *Journal of Religion, Spirituality, & Aging, 17,* 55–72. doi:10.1300/J496v17n03_06

McCullough, M. E., Enders, C. K., Brion, S. L., & Jain, A. R. (2005). The varieties of religious development in adulthood: A longitudinal investigation of religion and rational choice. *Journal of Personality and Social Psychology, 89,* 78–89. doi:10.1037/0022-3514.89.1.78

McCullough, M. E., & Laurenceau, J. P. (2005). Religiousness and the trajectory of self-rated health across adulthood. *Personality and Social Psychology Bulletin, 31,* 560–573. doi:10.1177/0146167204271657

McCullough, M. E., Tsang, J., & Brion, S. (2003). Personality traits in adolescence as predictors of religiousness in early adulthood: Findings from the Terman Longitudinal study. *Personality and Social Psychology Bulletin, 29,* 980–991. doi:10.1177/0146167203253210

Pew Research Center. (2007). *Trends in attitudes toward religion and social issues: 1987–2007.* Retrieved from http://pewresearch.org/pubs/614/religion-social-issues

Pew Research Center. (2010). *Millennials: A portrait of generation next.* Washington, DC: Author. Retrieved from http://

pewsocialtrends.org/files/2010/10/millennials-confident-connected-open-to-change.pdf

Piedmont, R. L. (1999). Does spirituality represent the sixth factor of personality? Spiritual transcendence and the five-factor model. *Journal of Personality, 67,* 985–1013. doi:10.1111/1467-6494.00080

Piedmont, R. L. (2004). Spiritual transcendence as a predictor of psychological outcome from an outpatient substance abuse program. *Psychology of Addictive Behaviors, 18,* 213–222. doi:10.1037/0893-164X.18.3.213

Piedmont, R. L. (2005). The role of personality in understanding religious and spiritual constructs. In R. F. Paloutzian & C. L. Park (Eds.), *Handbook of the psychology of religion and spirituality* (pp. 253–273). New York, NY: The Guilford Press.

Piedmont, R. L. (2007). Cross-cultural generalizability of the Spiritual Transcendence Scale to the Philippines: Spirituality as a human universal. *Mental Health, Religion, & Culture, 10,* 89–107. doi:10.1080/13694670500275494

Piedmont, R. L. (2010). *Assessment of Spirituality and Religious Sentiments (ASPIRES): Technical manual* (2nd ed.). Timonium, MD: Author.

Piedmont, R. L., Ciarrocchi, J. W., Dy-Liacco, G. S., & Williams, J. E. G. (2009). The empirical and conceptual value of the spiritual transcendence and religious involvement scales for personality research. *Psychology of Religion and Spirituality, 1,* 162–179. doi:10.1037/a0015883

Piedmont, R. L., Hassinger, C. J., Rhorer, J., Sherman, M. F., Sherman, N. C., & Williams, J. E. G. (2007). The relations among spirituality and religiosity and Axis II functioning in two college samples. *Research in the Social Scientific Study of Religion, 18,* 53–74. doi:10.1163/ej.9789004158511.i-301.24

Piedmont, R. L., & Leach, M. M. (2002). Cross-cultural generalizability of the Spiritual Transcendence Scale in India: Spirituality as a universal aspect of human experience. *American Behavioral Scientist, 45,* 1886–1899. doi:10.1177/0002764202045012011

Piedmont, R. L., & Nelson, R. (2001). A psychometric evaluation of the short form of the Faith Maturity Scale. *Research in the Social Scientific Study of Religion, 12,* 165–183.

Piedmont, R. L., Werdel, M. B., & Fernando, M. (2009). The utility of the Assessment of Spirituality and Religious Sentiments (ASPIRES) scale with Christians and Buddhists in Sri Lanka. *Research in the Social Scientific Study of Religion, 20,* 131–143. doi:10.1163/ej.9789004175624.i-334.42

Reich, K. H. (1997). Do we need a theory for the religiousness development of women? *International Journal for the Psychology of Religion, 7,* 67–86. doi:10.1207/s15327582ijpr0702_1

Rican, P., & Janosova, P. (2010). Spirituality as a basic aspect of personality: A cross-cultural verification of Piedmont's model. *The International Journal for the Psychology of Religion, 20,* 2–13. doi:10.1080/10508610903418053

Seifert, L. S. (2002). Toward a psychology of religion, spirituality, meaning-search, and aging: Past research and a practical application. *Journal of Adult Development, 9,* 61–70. doi:1068-0667/02/0100-0061/0

Slater, W., Hall, T. D., & Edwards, K. J. (2001). Measuring spirituality and religion: Where are we and where are we going? *Journal of Psychology and Theology, 29,* 4–21.

Strauss, W., & Howe, N. (1992). *Generations: The history of America's future, 1584 to 2069.* New York, NY: HarperCollins.

Van Wicklin, J. F. (1990). Conceiving and measuring ways of being religious. *Journal of Psychology and Christianity, 9,* 27–40.

Wink, P., & Dillon, M. (2002). Spiritual development across the adult life course: Findings from a longitudinal study. *Journal of Adult Development, 9,* 79–94. doi:10.1023/A:1013833419122

Wink, P., & Dillon, M. (2003). Religiousness, spirituality, and psychosocial functioning in late adulthood: Findings from a longitudinal study. *Psychology and Aging, 18,* 916–924. doi:1037/0882-7974.18.4.916

Wink, P., & Dillon, M. (2008). Religiousness, spirituality, and psychosocial functioning in late adulthood: Findings from a longitudinal study. *Psychology of Religion and Spirituality, 1,* 102–115. doi:10.1037/1941-1022.S.1.102

Critical Thinking

1. How has the concept of spirituality and religiosity evolved over the past 25 years in medicine?

2. How does spirituality and religiosity affect the resources provided by the health-care system?

3. Does the community play a role in the development and nurturing of spirituality and religion?

Create Central

www.mhhe.com/createcentral

Internet References

American Society on Aging: Forum on Religion, Spirituality and Aging (FORSA)
www.asaging.org/forum-religion-spirituality-and-aging-forsa

National Council on Aging
www.ncoa.org

Unit 3

UNIT

Prepared by: Elaina F. Osterbur, *Saint Louis University*

Societal Attitudes toward Old Age

There is a wide range of beliefs regarding the social position and status of the aged in U.S. society today. Some people believe that the best way to understand the problems of the elderly is to regard them as a minority group faced with difficulties similar to those of other minority groups. Discrimination against older people, like racial discrimination, is believed to be based on a bias against visible physical traits. Because the aging process is viewed negatively, it is natural that the elderly try to appear and act younger. Some spend a tremendous amount of money trying to make themselves look and feel younger.

The theory that old people are a weak minority group is questionable because too many circumstances prove otherwise. The U.S. Congress, for example, favors its senior members and delegates power to them by bestowing considerable prestige on them. The leadership roles in most religious organizations are held by older persons. Many older Americans are in good health, have comfortable incomes, and are treated with respect by friends and associates.

Perhaps the most realistic way to view people who are aged is as a status group, like other status groups in society. Every society has some method of "age grading" by which it groups together individuals of roughly similar age. ("Preteens" and "senior citizens" are some of the age-grade labels in U.S society.) Because it is a labeling process, age grading causes members of the age group to be perceived by themselves as well as others in terms of the connotations of the label. Unfortunately, the tag "old age" often has negative connotations in U.S. society. The readings included in this section illustrate the wide range of stereotypical attitudes toward older Americans. Many of society's typical assumptions about the limitations of old age have been refuted. A major force behind this reassessment of the elderly is that so many people are living longer and healthier lives, and in consequence, playing more of a role in all aspects of our society. Older people can remain productive members of society for many more years than has been traditionally assumed.

Such standard stereotypes of the elderly as frail, senile, childish, and sexually inactive are topics discussed in this unit.

Article   Prepared by: Elaina F. Osterbur, *Saint Louis University*

We Need to Fight Age Bias

Congress should act where the courts failed.

JACK GROSS

Learning Outcomes

After reading this article, you will be able to:

- Explain why younger adults often avoid spending time around older people.

- Describe how the media stereotype the image of older people.

- Discuss the different decisions that were made by the lower courts and the Supreme Court in the Jack Gross age discrimination in employment case.

- Explain how the Supreme Court's ruling in the Jack Gross case—that age had to be the exclusive factor in the business decision rather than just a motivating factor for age discrimination to have occurred—made it more difficult for demoted older workers to win their cases in court.

I never, never imagined when I was demoted seven years ago and then filed an age discrimination suit that I would end up in the U.S. Supreme Court, that I would testify before five congressional committees, or that my name would become associated with the future of age discrimination laws in our country. I do believe, however, that it happened for a reason.

This all began in January 2003. When my employer, Farm Bureau Financial Group (FBL) in Iowa, merged with the Kansas Farm Bureau, the company apparently wanted to purge claims employees who were over age 50. All the Kansas claims employees over 50 with a certain number of years of employment were offered a buyout, which most accepted. In Iowa, virtually every claims supervisor over 50 was demoted.

Being 54, I was included in that sweep, despite 13 consecutive years of top performance reviews. The company claimed this was not discrimination but simply a reorganization. In 2005, a federal jury spent a week hearing testimony and seeing the evidence. The jurors agreed with me, and determined that age was a motivating factor in my demotion. Since then, the case has taken on a life of its own, including an appeal to

the 8th Circuit Court and a U.S. Supreme Court hearing and decision.

Since the Age Discrimination in Employment Act was passed in 1967, courts had ruled consistently that the law protected individuals if their age was a factor in any employment decision. But in my case, the Supreme Court unexpectedly changed course and ruled that age had to be the exclusive reason for my demotion, even though that wasn't the question before them. They simply hijacked my case and used it as a vehicle to water down the workplace discrimination laws passed by Congress.

This new and much higher standard of proof is clearly inconsistent with the intent of the ADEA and four decades of precedent, and will affect millions of workers. A new trial was ordered and is scheduled for November, nearly eight years after my demotion.

I did not pursue this case just for myself. From my observation, discrimination victims are usually the most vulnerable among us, those who simply cannot fight back. Thanks to my attorneys, who believed in me, my case, and now our cause, I was able to take a stand against my unjust and unlawful treatment. Many of my friends are also farm or small-town "kids" who feel like they are the forgotten minority. Many have been forcibly retired or laid off. Some have been looking for work for months, only to find doors closed when they reveal the year they graduated. Others are working as janitors despite good careers and college degrees. They all know that age discrimination is very real and pervasive.

We now look to Congress to pass the Protecting Older Workers Against Discrimination Act (H.R. 3721), to provide the same protection for older people as protection given to people of color, women or people of different faiths.

While this ordeal has been stressful, observing all levels of our judicial and congressional processes "up close and personal" has been a real education. My faith in our judicial system was shattered by the Supreme Court's errant 5–4 decision. I believe Congress, as representatives of we, the people, will rectify it. You can help by contacting your own senators and representatives to encourage their support.

I am sincerely grateful for the assistance of people and groups truly dedicated to ending workplace discrimination of any kind in our great nation.

Critical Thinking

1. How did the Supreme Court's decision in the Jack Gross age discrimination case change the rules that determined if the employers had violated the Age Discrimination in Employment Act of 1967?
2. What bill now before Congress would give older workers the same protection as are given to people of color, women, or people of different faiths?
3. Does Jack Gross believe that the U.S. Congress will pass the new Protecting Older Workers Against Discrimination Act (H.R. 3721) which would re-establish the previous rules for judging age discrimination in employment which were established in 1967?

Create Central

www.mhhe.com/createcentral

Internet References

Adult Development and Aging: Division 20 of the American Psychological Association
www.iog.wayne.edu/APADIV20/APADIV20.HTM

American Society on Aging
www.asaging.org/index.cfm

Canadian Psychological Association
www.cpa.ca

JACK GROSS was aided by AARP in the U.S. Supreme Court's precedent-setting age discrimination case.

Article   Prepared by: Elaina F. Osterbur, *Saint Louis University*

Friendships, Family Relationships Get Better with Age Thanks to Forgiveness, Stereotypes

Amy Patterson Neubert

Learning Outcomes

After reading this article, you will be able to:

- Explain why older adults are inclined to be less confrontational in dealing with others with whom they interact.

- Explain why older adults report better interpersonal relationships than younger age groups do.

Part of what makes those relationships so golden during the golden years is that people of all ages are more likely to forgive and respect one's elders, according to research from Purdue University.

"Older adults report better marriages, more supportive friendships and less conflict with children and siblings," said Karen Fingerman, the Berner-Hanley Professor in Gerontology, Developmental and Family Studies. "While physical and cognitive abilities decline with age, relationships improve. So what is so special about old age? We found that the perception of limited time, willingness to forgive, aging stereotypes and attitudes of respect all play a part. But it's more than just about how younger people treat an older person, it's about how people interact."

Fingerman and Susan T. Charles, an associate professor of psychology and social behavior at the University of California in Irvine, published their research in this month's *Current Directions in Psychological Science.*

This article is based on their earlier work, including research showing that older adults are less confrontational than younger adults when they are upset. The article also builds on studies published in 2009 in the *Journal of Gerontology: Psychological Sciences* and in 2008 in the journal *Psychology and Aging.*

One study compared young adults, ages 22–35, and older adults, ages 65–77, by asking the participants to respond to several stories about personal interactions. The study participants heard stories about how an adult committed a social transgression, such as rudeness towards a waitress or ignoring property boundaries. Half the subjects read the story with the offending character portrayed as an older adult and the other half read the same story, but the offending character was portrayed as a younger adult. When the offending character was elderly, participants of all ages indicated that the person who was offended would avoid conflict and not react, but the opposite was found if the offending character was younger. When participants read a story in which a young adult committed a social faux pas, they thought other characters should confront that person and tell them they were upset.

These assumptions play out in daily interactions that Fingerman compares to a dance.

"Each person is acting and reacting in response to his or her partner, and, in this case, each partner is anticipating the next person's move, and that determination is often based on age," she said. "People vary their behavior with social partners depending on their age. When there is a negative interaction, younger people are generally more aggressive and confrontational than older people are. But younger people often are more accommodating to older people when there is a negative interaction."

For example, an older adult may be more cordial because of the assumption that a younger person may be confrontational. At the same time, the younger adult may conform to age stereotypes that indicate they should be more patient with an older person or they may hold stereotypes that older adults cannot change and do not attempt to change this person.

"Also, with age, people get better at regulating their emotions when something upsets them," Fingerman said. "The other advantage is that older people often have more opportunity to select who they want to associate with because they are retired and do not go to work."

Other reasons for better treatment of older adults reflect care, concern and cherishing the moment. No matter the age, people are going to be more pleasant if they perceive that there is little time left in a relationship, Fingerman said. That applies not just to people who are elderly, but even young people who may not see each other because of life changes such as moving out of state or serving in the military. When time is limited, people want to make the most of their remaining interactions and enjoy the other person rather than spending time fighting.

"We've also seen this in studies when adult daughters don't want to confront their elderly mothers or discuss negative things with them because they feel there is little time left with them," Fingerman said.

Fingerman plans to study how the "need to respect one's elders" plays a role in other cultures. Her work is supported by the Department of Child Development and Family Studies.

Critical Thinking

1. Are younger people generally more or less aggressive in dealing with the negative reactions of other people with whom they interact?
2. In general do older persons' relationships with others improve or decline with age?

3. How does the perception that there is little time left in a relationship affect the quality of the interaction between people?

Create Central

www.mhhe.com/createcentral

Internet References

Adult Development and Aging: Division 20 of the American Psychological Association
www.iog.wayne.edu/APADIV20/APADIV20.HTM
American Society on Aging
www.asaging.org/index.cfm
Canadian Psychological Association
www.cpa.ca

As seen in *Terre Haute Tribune-Star*, July 20, 2010. Copyright © 2010 by Purdue University News Service. Reprinted by permission of the author and Purdue University News Service. www.purdue.edu/newsroom/research/2010/100624FingermanRelationsh.html

Article   Prepared by: Elaina F. Osterbur, *Saint Louis University*

How Old Do You Feel Inside?

The Key to Staying Healthy and Living Longer Is Deciding You're Not Old and Decrepit

ALEXIA ELEJALDE-RUIZ

Learning Outcomes

After reading this article, you will be able to:

- Describe the advantages and disadvantages that one's attitude on aging can have on his or her behavior.
- Cite the advantages of feeling younger for older people.

Those of us lucky enough to grow old must contend with the miserable stereotypes of what it's like: the frailty, the forgetfulness, the early bird specials.

But in aging, as in many things, attitude can make all the difference. Research has shown that how people feel inside, and their expectations of their capabilities, can have a greater impact on health, happiness and even longevity than the date on their birth certificates.

In her seminal "counterclockwise" study, in 1979, Harvard University psychologist Ellen Langer brought men in their 70s and 80s to a weeklong retreat that was retrofitted, from the music to the newspapers, to look and feel like 1959. One group of men was told to reminisce about the era. The other group was told to let themselves be who they were 20 years earlier.

By the end of experiment, both groups of men, who upon entering had been highly reliant on relatives to do things for them, were functioning independently, actively completing chores, and showed significant improvements in hearing, memory, strength and intelligence tests. The group told to behave like they were 20 years younger also showed better dexterity, flexibility and looked younger, according to outside observers who judged photos of the participants taken before and after the retreat.

Expectation, not biology, leads many elderly people to set physical limits on themselves, Langer concluded; they assume they'll fall apart, so they let it happen.

"What we want to do is not get older people to think of themselves as young, but to change their mindsets about what it means to be older," Langer said. And being older doesn't have to equal decay.

Take memory. Thirty-year-olds forget lots of things, but they don't blame dementia. Older people jump to the conclusion that memory failures are part of their inevitable decline, when in fact it could be that their values change about what's meaningful enough to remember, Langer said.

Rather than declare failure when they aren't as nimble on the tennis court or spry on the stairs as they used to be, older people should recognize that anything is still possible; they just may have to try a few different strategies, Langer says.

Internalizing negative stereotypes about aging can have dire health consequences, even among the young, some studies suggest.

Men and women over 50 with more positive self-perceptions of aging lived 7.6 years longer than those with negative perceptions, according to a 2002 study led by Yale University epidemiology and psychology professor Becca Levy. Young, healthy people under 50 who held negative attitudes toward the elderly were more likely to experience a cardiovascular disorder over the next four decades than their peers who had more positive view of the elderly, a 2006 study by Levy found.

Pessimism about elderly decline, the researchers suggest, becomes a self-fulfilling prophecy.

Other studies that look at age identity—also known as subjective, or felt, age—have found that feeling younger than you really are is linked to better health, life satisfaction and cognitive abilities.

It's not clear what comes first: If identifying as younger makes you vital and sharp, or if people who feel vital and sharp associate that with feeling younger, said Markus Schafer, assistant professor of sociology at the University of Toronto, who last year published a study on age identity while a graduate student at Purdue University.

His study, in which people on average felt 12 years younger than their actual age, found subjective age was more important than chronological age in predicting performance on memorization and other mental tasks 10 years later. The cognitive benefits of feeling young were slightly more pronounced among women, he said, perhaps because of greater pressure on women to maintain youthfulness.

Regardless of what causes the correlation, he said, there's benefit to staying engaged.

"Learning new things, reading in a new area, at least trying to become connected with new technologies and platforms: Those are ways people can feel connected with the ebb and flow of the world," Schafer said.

The concept of "feeling younger" can be misleading: People usually mean that they feel healthier than they expected to feel at a particular age, not that they're denying their age or yearning for youth, said Laura Carstensen, founding director of the Stanford Center on Longevity. When asked in studies how old they'd like to be, most people say they wish to be 10 years younger— 70-year-olds want to be 60, 60-year-olds wish to be 50—because they'd be healthier. No one wants to be 20, she said.

More important than reversing the clock is to be optimistic about it, she said. And aging does have its upsides.

Emotional satisfaction and stability tend to improve as people get older, despite sad events like losing friends or social status, Carstensen said. Because time seems short, elderly people focus on what matters most to them, such as personal relationships, rather than flailing about in the uncertain what-ifs of youth, she said. It's not a happy-go-lucky happiness, but a deeper sense of gratitude.

"The misery myth is one of the most pernicious myths, because when you think the future is really bleak if you don't plan," Carstensen said. "When you think, 'I'm going to be the coolest 80-year-old and will start a line of clothing for old people,' there is so much possibility."

Critical Thinking

1. In terms of performance on mental tasks, which was the more important: the individual's subjective age or chronological age?

2. When asked how old they would like to be, how do most older people respond?

3. How is the person's stability and emotional satisfaction affected by getting older?

Create Central

www.mhhe.com/createcentral

Internet References

Adult Development and Aging: Division 20 of the American Psychological Association
www.iog.wayne.edu/APADIV20/APADIV20.HTM

American Society on Aging
www.asaging.org/index.cfm

Canadian Psychological Association
www.cpa.ca

Attitudes towards Caring for Older People: Findings and Recommendations for Practice by Angela Kydd, Deidre Wild, and Sara Nelson

55

Article

Prepared by: Elaina F. Osterbur, *Saint Louis University*

Attitudes towards Caring for Older People: Findings and Recommendations for Practice

Angela Kydd, Deidre Wild, and Sara Nelson

Learning Outcomes

After reading this article, you will be able to:

- Discuss professional health-care staff's attitudes toward working and caring for older adults.

- Identify proactive approaches to caring for older adults.

- Identify gerontology as a speciality.

The developed world continues to be challenged by the care required for an increasing and aged population, with the frailest of older people requiring care in institutional settings. In providing such care, nurses and healthcare assistants (HCAs) in particular need to have a range of essential and remedial specialist skills. However, evidence suggests that nursing older people is not an attractive career choice (Brown *et al* 2008, Stevens 2011). There have been many theories about the positive and negative attitudes of healthcare professionals working with older people, some of which were discussed in part one of this article (Kydd and Wild 2013).

Gerontology, as a specialty, is evolving in response to changes in demographics, health, socioeconomic and environmental factors (Kneale *et al* 2012). Where possible, older people are being cared for in the community, with the most vulnerable being cared for in residential or nursing homes. The expertise of research-aware and evidence-based practitioners has never been more necessary, especially in the care home sector, yet a career in gerontology is still viewed by many to be at the low end of the professional status in nursing and care home work carries little professional kudos. Furthermore, and perhaps as a consequence, gerontology is an unpopular choice for students in the health and social care professions (Happell 2002, Henderson *et al* 2008).

Although many individuals do choose to work with older people and value their roles and the skills they possess, there is a general feeling that health and social care workers in other areas do not respect the knowledge and skills of those who work with this group of patients. This perception is strengthened in Scotland, where newly qualified nurses are having difficulty getting hospital posts and many seek work in care homes. Therefore the stance that 'any job is better than no job' serves to fuel the notion that working with older people is work that could be done by anyone (Firth-Cozens and Cornwell 2009).

Method

The literature review, aim and method were provided in part 1 of this article (Kydd and Wild 2013). In summary, a 20-item Multifactorial Attitudes Questionnaire (MAQ) was developed by one of the authors (AK) in 1999 (Kydd *et al* 1999). A second study was initiated in 2009 with the aim of replicating the unpublished findings of the 1999 study. The MAQ reflected five broad themes identified from the literature review as having the potential to influence healthcare professionals' attitudes towards older people: ageism; learning environment; working environment; professional esteem; and specialist status. Each theme had four related statements in the MAQ designed to collect respondents' attitudes towards themselves as professionals working with older people and their perceptions of other professionals' attitudes towards staff working with older people.

For each statement, a response was required on a five-point Likert scale: 1 = strongly agree; 2 = agree; 3 = unsure; 4 = disagree; 5 = strongly disagree. Although minor changes were made to the MAQ statements for use in the 2009 study, mainly to reflect the change in terminology over time such as changing 'elderly care' to 'care of older people', the meaning of the statements and the use of an ordinal response format (Likert scale) remained unchanged.

Study Participants

The MAQ was distributed to staff in healthcare services dedicated to the care of older people and also in adult healthcare services because older people use adult services as well. The detailed MAQ is provided in part 1 of the article (Kydd and Wild 2013). The professional groups targeted were nurses, HCAs, doctors, allied health professionals (AHPs), nursing students and students of other healthcare professions.

Data Analysis

MAQ data collected in 2009 were compared with data collected in 1999 using the SPSS statistical analysis package to identify change, if any, over the intervening decade. The data are presented in five tables, each showing the ordinal responses to the four statements relating to each of the five themes of the MAQ. The scores from the 1999 study and the 2009 study were compared using the Mann-Whitney U test. This test explores the significance of difference between two data sets. When a significant difference was found, that is, one that is unlikely to have occurred by chance, the P value obtained from the test is given as equal to ($=$) or less than ($<$) 0.05, or 0.01 or 0.001, depending on the level of chance calculated. When the P value from this test is greater than ($>$) 0.05, the difference is regarded as not significant (Brace *et al* 2012).

Ethical Considerations

The University of the West of Scotland ethics committee deemed that a further ethical approval process was not required for either study. As participation was voluntary and anonymous, there was no harmful intervention, and the questionnaire's content was not regarded as sensitive.

Results

The number of respondents completing the MAQ in 1999 was 376, with 546 respondents in 2009. Where data were missing, these have been reported as such in the tables and missing data are reflected in the totals.

In 1999, 373 of the total respondents ($n = 376$) provided information about their professional status, and three were excluded because data were missing. In this study, the majority of respondents were nurses ($n = 204$; 55 per cent) and HCAs ($n = 117$; 31 per cent), with the remainder comprising other health professions, such as AHPs ($n = 35$; 9 per cent), nursing students ($n = 11$; 3 per cent) or 'other' ($n = 6$; 2 per cent).

In 2009, 544 of the total respondents ($n = 546$) provided information about their professional status, with two excluded due to missing data. The percentage of nurses ($n = 169$; 31 per cent) and HCAs ($n = 140$; 26 per cent) responding was lower; however, the percentage of nursing students responding in 2009 was nearly nine times higher than in 1999 ($n = 154$; 28 per cent). AHPs and 'others' accounted for 5 per cent ($n = 29$) and 10 per cent ($n = 52$) for others, respectively. In 1999, the group of 'others' comprised medical students, ward clerks, nurse lecturers and people who worked as volunteers on the wards. However, in 2009, there was the additional inclusion as 'others' of administrators, secretarial staff and repair staff.

Reasons for the differences between the two studies' occupational group sizes can only be speculative. This could lie in the difference in the method of distribution of the MAQ. In 1999, the MAQ was delivered by hand and post to hospitals and long-term care settings, whereas in 2009, email was also used for its distribution, which widened access for all workers in all health and social care settings.

The reasons for the differences in respondents' occupation between the two studies can also only be speculative, but it is possible that the expansion of nursing education in academic institutions rather than in individual hospitals served to make access to classes of nursing students possible, thereby increasing the numbers of students as respondents. It is also possible that because nursing students in 2009 were more research aware than those in 1999, due to nursing being a degree course, they may have been more willing to participate in a research study.

Ageism

In the theme of ageism, the only change between the 1999 study and the 2009 study was in response to question 1 (Table 1). In 1999, the majority of respondents agreed (49 per cent) and strongly agreed (42 per cent) that 'older people should have access to medical and surgical procedures regardless of their age'. By 2009 fewer respondents (29 per cent) agreed and more strongly agreed (63 per cent). This difference was found to be significant using the Mann-Whitney U test (U = 79024.0; $P < 0.001$).

Responses to the other three statements were consistent between the 1999 and 2009 studies: most respondents disagreed that 'communicating with older people can be very frustrating' (question 2) and that 'as older people become increasingly old they become more irritable, touchy and unpleasant' (question 4). However, despite these non-ageist responses, there was agreement with question 3 that 'the thought of being old worries me', possibly because respondents empathised with the older people they cared for.

Learning Environment

There was no significant change in the response to questions 5 to 8 relating to the learning environment between 1999 and 2009 (Table 2). The majority of respondents in both studies disagreed with the statement that 'working with older people can be very depressing' (question 5) and agreed that 'working in care of older people could be described as both challenging and stimulating' (question 7). The answers to these two questions suggest that respondents held a consistent and positive attitude towards their work with older people. The majority of respondents in both studies agreed that the care of older people should be taught by specialists (question 6) and that 'care of older people as a specialist subject should be given more curriculum time in the training of healthcare professionals' (question 8).

Table 1   Responses to Questions Relating to Ageism

	1999 n (%)		2009 n (%)	
Q1 Older people should have access, if appropriate, to medical and surgical procedures regardless of their age				
Strongly agree	157	(42)	346	(63)
Agree	184	(49)	159	(29)
Unsure	26	(7)	21	(4)
Disagree	7	(2)	10	(2)
Strongly disagree	2	(1)	4	(1)
Missing data	0	(0)	6	(1)
Total	376	(100)	546	(100)
Q2 On the whole, communicating with older people can be very frustrating				
Strongly agree	9	(2)	23	(4)
Agree	87	(23)	98	(18)
Unsure	12	(3)	41	(8)
Disagree	232	(62)	288	(53)
Strongly disagree	36	(10)	91	(17)
Missing data	0	(0)	5	(1)
Total	376	(100)	546	(100)
Q3 The thought of being old worries me				
Strongly agree	57	(15)	74	(14)
Agree	139	(37)	208	(38)
Unsure	60	(16)	92	(17)
Disagree	99	(26)	140	(26)
Strongly disagree	21	(6)	31	(6)
Missing	0	(0)	1	(0)
Total	376	(100)	546	(100)
Q4 As older people become increasingly old they become more irritable, touchy and unpleasant				
Strongly agree	8	(2)	17	(3)
Agree	40	(11)	42	(8)
Unsure	30	(8)	39	(7)
Disagree	234	(62)	320	(59)
Strongly disagree	64	(17)	123	(23)
Missing	0	(0)	5	(1)
Total	376	(100)	546	(100)

Working Environment

In 1999, 64 per cent of respondents agreed (combined values) and 18 per cent were unsure that 'working conditions in care of older people are not conducive to recruiting and retaining staff' (question 9, Table 3). However, in 2009, there was a significant change, with 49 per cent agreeing (combined values) and 27 per cent unsure. The differences between these data were significant (U = 84187.0; $P < 0.001$).

In both studies, respondents were unsure whether older people are cared for in inadequate and depressing settings (question 10). The majority of respondents in 1999 and 2009 agreed that 'if care of older people wards had better resources it would be easier to attract staff' (question 11). However, a significant difference was observed in response to the statement that 'there are too many routine tasks in care of older people' (question 12).

In 1999, respondents were unsure of their response to this question (34 per cent agreed, 36 per cent disagreed, with 16 per cent unsure), but in 2009 the response had moved towards disagreement with 43 per cent disagreeing, 13 per cent who were unsure and 25 per cent agreeing (U = 86352.5; $P < 0.001$). This may reflect positive changes in health and social care provision over the decade.

Professional Esteem

The responses to the statements under the theme of professional esteem (questions 13 to 16, Table 4) were the same between both studies except for the response to question 14. In 1999, the majority of staff agreed or strongly agreed (60 per cent in total) that 'there is a lack of career advancement in care of the older person'. By 2009, fewer staff either agreed or strongly

Table 2   Responses to Questions Relating to Learning Environment

	1999 n (%)		2009 n (%)	
Q5 Working with older people can be very depressing				
Strongly agree	8	(2)	5	(1)
Agree	37	(10)	43	(8)
Unsure	26	(7)	22	(4)
Disagree	212	(56)	296	(54)
Strongly disagree	93	(25)	178	(33)
Missing	0	(0)	2	(0)
Total	376	(100)	546	(100)
Q6 Care of older people should be taught by specialists				
Strongly agree	81	(22)	104	(19)
Agree	183	(49)	226	(41)
Unsure	36	(10)	67	(12)
Disagree	63	(17)	125	(23)
Strongly disagree	13	(4)	20	(4)
Missing	0	(0)	4	(1)
Total	376	(100)	546	(100)
Q7 Working in care of older people could be described as both challenging and stimulating				
Strongly agree	73	(19)	193	(35)
Agree	181	(48)	300	(55)
Unsure	54	(14)	23	(4)
Disagree	56	(15)	15	(3)
Strongly disagree	12	(3)	11	(2)
Missing	0	(0)	4	(1)
Total	376	(100)	546	(100)
Q8 Care of older people as a specialist subject should be given more curriculum time in the training of healthcare professionals				
Strongly agree	96	(26)	176	(32)
Agree	206	(55)	274	(50)
Unsure	48	(13)	59	(11)
Disagree	25	(7)	24	(4)
Strongly disagree	1	(0)	8	(2)
Missing	0	(0)	5	(1)
Total	376	(100)	546	(100)

agreed with this statement (46 per cent in total) with more choosing to disagree (25 per cent versus 16 per cent in 1999) (U = 82780.0; P < 0.001).

In 2009, the majority of staff agreed (41 per cent) and strongly agreed (25 per cent) that 'people working in care of older people are deemed to have a lower professional status than those who work in high technology areas' (question 13). Despite this negative view, 64 per cent in total agreed or strongly agreed that they had 'chosen to/would consider a career in geriatric medicine/nursing' (question 16) and 61 per cent in total disagreed or strongly disagreed that 'the less experienced and most out-of-date doctors and nurses seem to work in care of older people' (question 15).

Specialist Status

There were no significant differences between the responses to the four statements regarding specialist status in the 1999 study and the 2009 study (Table 5). In the 2009 study, the majority (63 per cent in total) agreed or strongly agreed that 'people who work in care of the older person are enthusiastic about their work' (question 18), with only 11 per cent agreeing or strongly agreeing that 'working with older people is more demoralising than working in high technology areas' (question 19). However, 84 per cent of respondents in 1999 and 81 per cent in 2009 agreed or strongly agreed that 'other healthcare professionals do not seem to appreciate that care of the older person is a highly skilled specialty' (question 20). This attitude was supported by the response to question 17; the majority of respondents disagreed or strongly disagreed (58 per cent in 1999, 54 per cent in 2009) that 'a qualified nurse/doctor does not need to have specialist training in order to deliver excellent care for older people'.

Discussion

Some of the study limitations, predominantly related to the use of questionnaires, were discussed in part one of this article (Kydd and Wild 2013). Both studies were unfunded,

Attitudes towards Caring for Older People: Findings and Recommendations for Practice by Angela Kydd, Deidre Wild, and Sara Nelson

59

Table 3   Responses to Questions Relating to Working Environment

Q9 In general, working conditions in care of older people are not conducive to recruiting and retaining staff	1999 n (%)		2009 n (%)	
Strongly agree	72	(19)	63	(12)
Agree	170	(45)	201	(37)
Unsure	66	(18)	145	(27)
Disagree	61	(16)	112	(21)
Strongly disagree	7	(2)	19	(4)
Missing	0	(0)	6	(1)
Total	376	(100)	546	(100)

Q10 I feel that older people are cared for in inadequate and depressing settings				
Strongly agree	62	(17)	49	(9)
Agree	101	(27)	158	(29)
Unsure	55	(15)	77	(14)
Disagree	132	(35)	193	(35)
Strongly disagree	26	(7)	66	(12)
Missing	0	(0)	3	(1)
Total	376	(100)	546	(100)

Q11 If care of older people wards had better resources it would be easier to attract staff				
Strongly agree	144	(38)	140	(26)
Agree	160	(43)	225	(41)
Unsure	34	(9)	101	(19)
Disagree	34	(9)	64	(12)
Strongly disagree	4	(1)	11	(2)
Missing	0	(0)	5	(1)
Total	376	(100)	546	(100)

Q12 There are too many routine tasks in care of older people				
Strongly agree	38	(10)	50	(9)
Agree	128	(34)	135	(25)
Unsure	62	(16)	70	(13)
Disagree	136	(36)	235	(43)
Strongly disagree	12	(3)	50	(9)
Missing	0	(0)	6	(1)
Total	376	(100)	546	(100)

which dictated the choice of method and scope of the research. Respondents were voluntary participants and it was therefore not possible to get an equal number of HCAs, nursing students or nurses. It is also questionable if this method of recruitment is more likely to lead to positive or negative responses about the questions posed. The respondents differed between the 1999 and the 2009 studies, although the areas of work from which they were drawn and in which the questionnaire was circulated were similar in both studies.

It would have been neither practical to have followed up the same respondents given their work mobility and life changes over the decade, nor desirable as this would have probably resulted in a much smaller sample for the second study. In the event, reliance on busy staff to disseminate and collect the questionnaires, and the more personal use of email in 2009, could have had a negative impact on participation in the respective studies but it is not possible to determine if this was the case.

In the 1999 study, 800 questionnaires were distributed by post and hand and 376 returned, giving a response rate of 47 per cent. In the 2009 study, there were 546 respondents.

However, in addition to post and hand delivery, the questionnaires were also sent via email to multiple email addresses, some of which were also forwarded on request to other addresses. This email distribution made it impossible to either calculate the response rate or calculate if the larger number of respondents to the second study represented a percentage increase in the return rate. The questions of the MAQ may have been subject to different interpretation due to each individual's perception of 'old', which may be influenced by the diversity of respondents' working context, their level of familiarity with the needs of older people and their own age.

While taking account of limitations, comparisons drawn between the two studies can be justified by the consistent use of the MAQ, with only minor modification to update key words, and the distribution of questionnaires to staff in similar roles and settings in adult health care and in a comparable geographical area of Scotland. However, caution is recommended in generalising the findings to the wider population.

Overall, the findings from these studies indicate a consistent and long-held desire for the care of older people to be

Table 4 Responses to Questions Relating to Professional Esteem

Q13 People working in care of older people are deemed to have a lower professional status than those who work in high technology areas	1999 n (%)		2009 n (%)	
Strongly agree	97	(26)	134	(25)
Agree	174	(46)	223	(41)
Unsure	34	(9)	48	(9)
Disagree	52	(14)	89	(16)
Strongly disagree	19	(5)	51	(9)
Missing	0	(0)	1	(0)
Total	376	(100)	546	(100)

Q14 On the whole there is a lack of career advancement in care of the older person				
Strongly agree	58	(15)	61	(11)
Agree	171	(45)	189	(35)
Unsure	83	(22)	124	(23)
Disagree	60	(16)	138	(25)
Strongly disagree	4	(1)	26	(5)
Missing	0	(0)	8	(1)
Total	376	(100)	546	(100)

Q15 I feel the less experienced and most out-of-date doctors and nurses seem to work in care of older people				
Strongly agree	14	(4)	17	(3)
Agree	39	(10)	78	(14)
Unsure	52	(14)	114	(21)
Disagree	207	(55)	246	(45)
Strongly disagree	64	(17)	89	(16)
Missing	0	(0)	2	(0)
Total	376	(100)	546	(100)

Q16 I have chosen to/would consider a career in geriatric medicine/nursing				
Strongly agree	56	(15)	117	(21)
Agree	151	(40)	233	(43)
Unsure	81	(22)	90	(16)
Disagree	69	(18)	64	(12)
Strongly disagree	19	(5)	18	(3)
Missing	0	(0)	24	(4)
Total	376	(100)	546	(100)

recognised as a discrete specialism supported by specialist education. Over the past decade, attention has been drawn to the need for specialist roles in the care of older people, particularly in nursing (Masterson and Heath 2001, Heath 2006) but also through multidisciplinary working (Royal College of Physicians 2000) and in medicine (British Geriatrics Society 2007). The positive findings about working with older people suggest that awareness of a more proactive approach to care has developed over the decade between the studies. This could be due to changes in nurse education in Scotland from diploma to degree, with gerontology included in the curriculum. Edelmann (2000) suggested that changes in knowledge and beliefs can influence attitudes and Mellor et al (2007) found a positive relationship between knowledge and attitude. However, it is not only classroom education that is important, but clinical placements, post-registration education (Aoki and Davies 2002, Brown et al 2008) and exposure to examples of best practice (Kydd 2002).

Attitudes toward a specialty have been associated with career choice (Happell and Brooker 2001, Marsland and Hickey 2003, Rognstad et al 2004, Aud et al 2006, Alabaster 2007) and can affect quality of care (Gallagher et al 2006). Although several studies have shown that nursing students were attracted to the 'glamorous' acute and high-tech areas of nursing (Happell 2002, Brown et al 2008, Stevens 2011), the majority of the respondents in the 2009 study stated that they had chosen, or would choose, to work with older people.

In general, respondents were consistent across both studies in their enthusiasm towards the care of older people, even though they viewed working with older people as having a lower professional status than working in other settings. A similar finding was reported by Stevens (2011). One factor that may have affected attitudes in the studies could be the difficulty of nurses, especially those newly qualified, in finding employment in Scotland. However, despite the possibility that the attitude of some staff to caring for older people could have been 'any job may be better than no job', the overall positive attitudes of respondents towards care of older people and an appreciation of the need for specialism exist in tandem with awareness of the issues that could inhibit specialist career prospects and professional status.

Attitudes towards Caring for Older People: Findings and Recommendations for Practice by Angela Kydd, Deidre Wild, and Sara Nelson

61

Table 5   Responses to Questions Relating to Specialist Status

	1999		2009	
Q17 A qualified nurse/doctor does not need to have specialist training in order to deliver excellent care for older people	*n*	(%)	*n*	(%)
Strongly agree	18	(5)	48	(9)
Agree	97	(26)	138	(25)
Unsure	44	(12)	65	(12)
Disagree	161	(43)	223	(41)
Strongly disagree	56	(15)	69	(13)
Missing	0	(0)	3	(1)
Total	376	(100)	546	(100)
Q18 On the whole, people who work in care of the older person are enthusiastic about their work				
Strongly agree	40	(11)	75	(14)
Agree	180	(48)	265	(49)
Unsure	79	(21)	90	(16)
Disagree	67	(18)	101	(18)
Strongly disagree	10	(3)	9	(2)
Missing	0	(0)	6	(1)
Total	376	(100)	546	(100)
Q19 Working with older people is more demoralising than working in high technology areas				
Strongly agree	10	(3)	14	(3)
Agree	52	(14)	46	(8)
Unsure	64	(17)	69	(13)
Disagree	176	(47)	274	(50)
Strongly disagree	74	(20)	140	(26)
Missing	0	(0)	3	(1)
Total	376	(100)	546	(100)
Q20 Other healthcare professionals do not seem to appreciate that care of the older person is a highly skilled specialty				
Strongly agree	122	(32)	182	(33)
Agree	195	(52)	263	(48)
Unsure	31	(8)	54	(10)
Disagree	23	(6)	39	(7)
Strongly disagree	5	(1)	7	(1)
Missing	0	(0)	1	(0)
Total	376	(100)	546	(100)

Better resources and working conditions were perceived as necessary to influence recruitment of staff into gerontology. Sprang *et al* (2007) suggested that resources are needed to protect against burnout in healthcare professionals. Working in poorly resourced environments leads to stress and ultimately to poor morale (Stapleton *et al* 2007). The importance of the working environment was illustrated in the findings of the studies: respondents believed that older people should have equal rights in accessing services, but they were less confident about the quality of care settings. Brown *et al* (2008) and Stevens (2011)

found that nursing students developed negative attitudes towards working with older people only after working in impoverished care environments. This could be why respondents in the studies tended to agree that their own old age could be a cause for worry.

The reason why this vulnerable, but sizeable, part of society has consistently been disregarded in terms of specialist care could lie in the disparate nature of the definition of 'older people' with either health or social care needs. Although several publications have addressed the issue of definition of late life (Department of Health 2001, Blood and Bamford 2010,

Serra *et al* 2011), the focus has tended to be on the social constructs of numeric age with and without consideration of health status, or in numeric age bands. Isaacs (1992) captured the dichotomy in defining late life by age alone by pointing out that 'old age is having been born a long time ago' and 'old age is having lived a long time' are not the same. In terms of specialisation to promote health and social wellbeing, recognising the co-existence of numeric age with life experience would seem a more rounded understanding of what being 'old' means.

Conclusion

In the first of two articles (Kydd and Wild 2013), the development and use of the MAQ were critically described and the literature reviewed. The first study was conducted in 1999, a year before major policy changes reflecting national concern about the standards and organisation of care for older people. Between 1999 and 2009, many pre- and post-registration nursing courses included gerontology as a specialist subject, coincident with an increase in post-graduate gerontology courses.

In light of these initiatives, the expectation was that there would be an improvement in attitudes about and towards the care of older people between 1999 and 2009. However, even after taking the limitations of the study into account, this seems not to be the case. Although there was some change in attitudes in the philosophy of care—a shift towards proactive rather than reactive care, and continued enthusiasm of those working with older people, usually by choice—attitudes became more ambivalent towards the working environment and career opportunities. Therefore, it would seem that, despite external impetus to create change, the more culturally relevant question as to why this area of care is still seen as a clinical backwater compared with other areas of health care remains unanswered.

References

Alabaster E (2007) Involving students in the challenges of caring for older people. *Nursing Older People.* 19, 6, 23–28.

Aoki Y, Davies S (2002) Survey of continuing professional education within nursing homes. *British Journal of Nursing.* 11, 13, 902–912.

Aud M, Bostick J, Marek K *et al* (2006) Introducing baccalaureate student nurses to gerontological nursing. *Journal of Professional Nursing.* 22, 2, 73–78.

Blood I, Bamford S-M (2010) *Equality and Diversity and Older People with High Support Needs.* tiny.cc/5ekmuw (Last accessed: March 27 2013.)

Brace N, Kemp R, Snelgar R (2012) *SPSS for Psychologists.* Fifth edition. Palgrave Macmillan, Basingstoke.

British Geriatrics Society (2007) *Standards of Medical Care for Older People.* tiny.cc/u8pauw (Last accessed: March 27 2013.)

Brown J, Nolan M, Davies S *et al* (2008) Transforming students' views of gerontological nursing: realizing the potential of 'enriched' environments of learning and care: a multi-method longitudinal study. *International Journal of Nursing Studies.* 45, 8, 1214–1232.

Department of Health (2001) *National Service Framework for Older People.* DH, London.

Edelmann R (2000) Attitude measurement. In Cormack D (Ed) *The Research Process in Nursing.* Fourth edition. Blackwell Science, Oxford.

Firth-Cozens J, Cornwell J (2009) *The Point of Care: Enabling Compassionate Care in Acute Hospital Settings.* King's Fund, London.

Gallagher S, Bennett K, Halford J (2006) A comparison of acute and long-term health-care personnel's attitudes towards older adults. *International Journal of Nursing Practice.* 12, 5, 273–279.

Happell B (2002) Nursing home employment for nursing students: valuable experience or a harsh deterrent? *Journal of Advanced Nursing.* 39, 6, 529–536.

Happell B, Brooker J (2001) Who will look after my grandmother? Attitudes of student nurses toward the care of older adults. *Journal of Gerontological Nursing.* 27, 12, 12–17.

Heath H (2006) *Specialist Community Nurses for Older People at Home. A Report on the Feasibility of the Role.* tiny.cc/gkrauw (Last accessed: March 27 2013.)

Henderson J, Xiao L, Siegloff L *et al* (2008) 'Older people have lived their lives': first year nursing students' attitudes towards older people. *Contemporary Nurse.* 30, 1, 32–45.

Isaacs B (1992) *The Challenge of Geriatric Medicine.* Oxford University Press, Oxford.

Kneale D, Mason M, Bamford S-M (2012) *Population Ageing: Pomp or Circumstance.* International Longevity Centre—UK, London.

Kydd A (2002) Sharing good practice in the care of older people. *Nursing Times.* 98, 32, 42–44.

Kydd A, Wild D (2013) Attitudes towards caring for older people: literature review and methodology. *Nursing Older People.* 25, 3, 22–27.

Kydd A, Gilhooly M, Lightbody P *et al* (1999) *Factors Affecting the Professional Esteem of Health Care Professionals Working with Older People. Part One: A Quantitative Study.* Poster presentation, British Society of Gerontology annual conference, Bournemouth, September 18.

Marsland L, Hickey G (2003) Planning a pathway in nursing: do course experiences influence job plans? *Nurse Education Today.* 23, 3, 226–235.

Masterson A, Heath H (2001) Gerontological nurse specialists. *Nursing Standard.* 16, 12, 39–42.

Mellor P, Chew D, Greenhill J (2007) Nurses' attitudes toward elderly people and knowledge of gerontic care in a multi-purpose health service (MPHS). *Australian Journal of Advanced Nursing.* 24, 4, 37–41.

Rognstad M, Aasland O, Granum V (2004) How do nursing students regard their future career? Career preferences in the post-modern society. *Nurse Education Today.* 24, 7, 493–500.

Royal College of Physicians (2000) *The Health and Care of Older People in Care Homes: A Comprehensive Interdisciplinary Approach.* Report of a Joint Working Party of the Royal College of Physicians, the Royal College of Nursing and the British Geriatrics Society. RCP, London.

Attitudes towards Caring for Older People: Findings and Recommendations for Practice by Angela Kydd, Deidre Wild, and Sara Nelson

63

Serra V, Watson J, Sinclair D *et al* (2011) *Living Beyond 100: A Report on Centenarians.* tiny.cc/s1dbuw (Last accessed: March 27 2013.)

Sprang G, Clark J, Whitt-Woosley A (2007) Compassion fatigue, compassion satisfaction, and burnout: factors impacting a professional's quality of life. *Journal of Loss and Trauma.* 12, 3, 259–280.

Stapleton P, Henderson A, Creedy D *et al* (2007) Boosting morale and improving performance in the nursing setting. *Journal of Nursing Management.* 15, 8, 811–816.

Stevens J (2011) Student nurses' career preferences for working with older people: a replicated longitudinal survey. *International Journal of Nursing Studies.* 48, 8, 944–951.

Critical Thinking

1. How do attitudes of Scottish health-care professionals toward older adults translate to the attitudes of the United States and other developed countries?

2. Health-care professionals are offended that they are not given greater recognition for their work with older adults.

Do you think these attitudes will change as our population continues to gray?

Create Central

www.mhhe.com/createcentral

Internet References

American Medical Association
www.ama.org
Royal College of Physicians
www.rcplondon.ac.uk

ANGELA KYDD is a senior lecturer in research, Institute of Older Persons' Health and Wellbeing, School of Health, Nursing and Midwifery, University of the West of Scotland, Hamilton. DEIDRE WILD is a visiting senior research fellow, University of the West of England, Bristol. SARA NELSON is a research fellow, University of the West of England, Bristol.

Article   Prepared by: Elaina F. Osterbur, *Saint Louis University*

Health Disparities among Lesbian, Gay, and Bisexual Older Adults: Results from a Population-Based Study

KAREN I. FREDRIKSEN-GOLDSEN ET AL.

Learning Outcomes

After reading this article, you will be able to:

- Discuss the health outcomes of lesbian, gay, and bisexual older adults.

- Identify the health disparities among lesbian, gay, and bisexual older adults.

- Identify the methods to learn more about the health needs in the lesbian, gay, and bisexual communities.

Changing demographics will make population aging a defining feature of the 21st century. Not only is the population older, it is becoming increasingly diverse.[1] Existing research illustrates that older adults from socially and economically disadvantaged populations are at high risk of poor health and premature death.[2] A commitment of the National Institutes of Health is to reduce and eliminate health disparities,[3] which have been defined as differences in health outcomes for communities that have encountered systematic obstacles to health as a result of social, economic, and environmental disadvantage.[4]

Social determinants of health disparities among older adults include age, race/ethnicity, and socioeconomic status.[5] Centers for Disease Control and Prevention (CDC) and *Healthy People* 2020 identify health disparities related to sexual orientation as one of the main gaps in current health research.[6] The Institute of Medicine identifies lesbian, gay, and bisexual (LGB) older adults as a population whose health needs are understudied.[7] The institute has called for population-based studies to better assess the impact of background characteristics such as age on health outcomes among LGB adults. A review of 25 years of literature on LGB aging found that health research is glaringly sparse for this population and that most aging-related studies have used small, non-population-based samples.[8]

Several important studies have begun to document health disparities by sexual orientation in population-based data and have revealed important differences in health between LGB adults and their heterosexual counterparts, including higher risks of poor mental health, smoking, and limitations in activities.[9,10] Studies have found higher rates of excessive drinking among lesbians and bisexual women[9,10] and higher rates of obesity among lesbians[10,11] than among heterosexual women; bisexual men and women are at higher risk of limited health care access than are heterosexuals. In addition, important subgroup differences in health are beginning to be documented among LGB adults. For example, bisexual women are at higher risk than lesbians for mental distress and poor general health.[12] A primary limitation of most existing population-based research is a failure to identify the specific health needs of LGB older adults. Most studies to date address the health needs of LGB adults aged 18 years and older[9] or those younger than 65 years.[10] This lack of attention to older adult health leaves unclear whether disparities diminish or persist or even become more pronounced in later life.

A few studies have begun to examine health disparities among LGB adults aged 50 years and older.[13,14] Wallace et al. analyzed data from the California Health Interview Survey and found that LGB adults aged 50 to 70 years report higher rates of mental distress, physical limitations, and poor general health than do their heterosexual counterparts. The researchers also found that older gay and bisexual men report higher rates of hypertension and diabetes than do heterosexual men.[14] To better address the needs of an increasingly diverse older adult population and to develop responsive interventions and public health policies, health disparities research is needed for this at-risk group.

Examining to what extent sexual orientation is related to health disparities among LGB older adults is a first step toward developing a more comprehensive understanding of their health and aging needs. We analyzed population-based data from the Washington State Behavioral Risk Factor Surveillance System (WA-BRFSS) to compare lesbians and bisexual women and

Health Disparities among Lesbian, Gay, and Bisexual Older Adults by Karen Fredriksen-Goldsen et al.

65

gay and bisexual men with their heterosexual counterparts aged 50 years and older on key health indicators: outcomes, chronic conditions, access to care, behaviors, and screening. We also compared subgroups to identify differences in health disparities by sexual orientation among LGB older adults.

Methods

The BRFSS is an annual random-digit-dialed telephone survey of noninstitutionalized adults conducted by each US state. Each year, disproportionate stratified random sampling is used to select eligible households, and from each selected household 1 adult is randomly selected as the respondent.[15] Washington State began including a measure of sexual orientation in 2003. We aggregated the WA-BRFSS data collected from 2003 to 2010 for respondents aged 50 years and older (n = 96 992) and stratified by gender for further analyses. We selected 50 years as the lower age limit to be consistent with previous health studies focusing on sexual minority older adults,[13,14] as well as research addressing specific chronic health conditions[16,17] and older adult health and well-being, such as the Health and Retirement Study and other population-based studies.[18–20] Annual response rates to the WA-BRFSS range from 43% to 50%, calculated according to Council of American Survey and Research Organizations methods.[21] To adjust for unequal probabilities of selection resulting from nonresponse, sample design, and households without telephones, we applied sample weights provided by the WA-BRFSS.

According to weighted estimation, among women aged 50 years and older (n = 58 319), 1.03% (n = 562) identified as lesbian and 0.54% (n = 291) as bisexual; among men aged 50 years and older (n = 37 820), 1.28% (n = 463) identified as gay and 0.51% (n = 215) as bisexual. The age range in the sample for LGB older adults was 50 to 98 years (50–94 years for women and 50–98 years for men).

Measures

To measure sexual orientation, survey respondents were asked to select 1 of the following: heterosexual or straight, homosexual (gay or lesbian), bisexual, or something else. About 0.2% (n = 266) of the sample selected something else, and we excluded them from our analyses.

The background characteristics in this study were as follows: age, household income (≤ 200% vs > 200% of the federal poverty level), education (≤ high school vs ≥ some college), employment (part time or full time vs other), race/ethnicity (non-Hispanic White vs other), living arrangement (living alone vs other), and number of children in household. We categorized relationship status as married versus partnered (a member of an unmarried couple) versus other (divorced, widowed, separated, or never married).

Health outcomes (recommended and validated by CDC) in our study were poor physical health, disability, and poor mental health.[22] We defined poor physical health as 14 or more days of poor physical health during the previous 30 days and poor mental health as 14 or more days of poor mental health during the previous 30 days.[22] We defined disability as limitations in any activities because of physical, mental, or emotional problems or any health problem that required the use of special equipment, as recommended by *Healthy People 2020*.[4]

The BRFSS asked respondents whether they had ever been told by a health professional they had arthritis, asthma, diabetes (not included if prediabetes or gestational diabetes alone), high blood pressure (not included if borderline or during pregnancy alone), or high cholesterol. As recommended by other health studies, we designated cardiovascular disease (CVD) as diagnosis by a physician of a heart attack, angina, or stroke.[23,24] We defined obesity as a body mass index score (defined as weight in kilograms divided by height in meters squared) of 30 or higher, as recommended by CDC.[25] The BRFSS measured health care access by asking whether respondents had insurance coverage, a personal doctor or provider, or a financial barrier to seeing a doctor in the past 12 months.

Health behaviors were (1) current smoking (defined, as suggested by CDC, as having ever smoked ≥ 100 cigarettes and currently smoking every day or some days[26]), (2) excessive drinking (defined, as suggested by National Institute of Alcohol Abuse and Alcoholism, as women having ≥ 4 and men having ≥ 5 drinks on 1 occasion during the past month[27]), and (3) physical activity (defined, as suggested by the US Department of Health and Human Services, as ≥ 30 minutes of moderate-intensity activity ≥ 5 days/week or ≥ 20 minutes of vigorous-intensity activity ≥ 3 days/week[28]). The BRFSS measured health screening, according to public health guidelines for older adults, by whether respondents received a flu shot in the past year,[29] an HIV test ever, a mammogram (for women) in the past 2 years,[30] and a prostate-specific antigen test (for men) in the past year.[31]

Statistical Analysis

We conducted analyses separately by gender. First, we described the weighted distribution of background characteristics by sexual orientation, comparing lesbians and bisexual women with heterosexual women aged 50 years and older and gay and bisexual men with heterosexual men aged 50 years and older, applying t tests or χ^2 tests as appropriate. We also tested statistical significance of differences in background characteristics between lesbians and bisexual women and between gay and bisexual men.

We then estimated weighted prevalence rates of health indicators, which were health outcomes, chronic conditions, access to care, behaviors, and screening, by sexual orientation (lesbian and bisexual vs heterosexual women; gay and bisexual vs heterosexual men). We conducted a series of adjusted logistic regressions, with control for sociodemographic characteristics (age, income, and education), to test associations between health-related indicators and sexual orientation. We also conducted adjusted logistic regression analyses to examine health disparities between lesbian and bisexual women and between gay and bisexual men. We used Stata version 11 (StataCorp LP, College Station, TX) for data analyses.

Results

Table 1 illustrates the weighted prevalence of background characteristics by sexual orientation among older adults. Lesbians

Table 1 Background Characteristics of Respondents Aged 50 Years and Older, by Sexual Orientation: Washington State Behavioral Risk Factor Surveillance System, 2003–2010

| | Women | | | | Men | | | |
| | | Lesbian and Bisexual | | | | | Gay and Bisexual | | |
Characteristic	Heterosexual, % or Mean (SD)	Total, % or Mean (SD)	Lesbian, % or Mean (SD)	Bisexual, % or Mean (SD)	Heterosexual, % or Mean (SD)	Total, % or Mean (SD)	Gay, % or Mean (SD)	Bisexual, % or Mean (SD)
Age, y	63.82 (0.06)	58.63*** (0.37)	58.09 (0.40)	59.67 (0.78)	62.35 (0.07)	59.54*** (0.39)	59.26 (0.45)	60.22 (0.75)
≤ 200% poverty level	27.38	27.12	26.47	28.43	20.85	24.79	25.45	23.18
≤ high school	30.18	13.44***	13.83	12.69	24.96	14.57***	12.34	20.09
Employed	39.97	59.31***	63.07	52.08	51.17	55.30	55.25	55.43
Non-Hispanic White	91.79	90.31	89.86	91.23	90.40	93.22*	92.85	94.18
Relationship status								
Married	61.67	20.15***	9.57	40.44	77.60	20.83***	8.16	52.07
Partnered	1.59	27.83	36.96	10.31	1.50	20.27	27.30	2.96
Other	36.74	52.02	53.47	49.25	20.90	58.90	64.55	44.97
Children in household, no.	0.15 (0.00)	0.20 (0.04)	0.18 (0.05)	0.24 (0.06)	0.22 (0.00)	0.07*** (0.02)	0.03 (0.01)	0.15 (0.05)
Living alone	26.24	29.43	29.65	28.99	15.15	38.34***	40.66	32.59

Note. Estimates were weighted; significance tests were conducted to examine the association between background characteristics and sexual orientation (lesbians and bisexual women vs heterosexual women; gay and bisexual men vs heterosexual men).

*$P < .05$; ***$P < .001$.

and bisexual women were younger, had more education, and had higher rates of employment than did heterosexual women; income levels were similar. Lesbians and bisexual women were less likely to be married and more likely to be partnered than were their heterosexual counterparts, but the average number of children in the household and the likelihood of living alone were similar. Lesbians were more likely than bisexual women to be employed ($P = .019$) and less likely to be married, but more likely to be partnered ($P < .001$). We found no differences in other background characteristics.

Gay and bisexual men were significantly younger and more highly educated than were heterosexual men; income levels and employment rates were similar. Gay and bisexual men were less likely than heterosexual men to be married but more likely to be partnered; they also had fewer children in the household, were more likely to live alone, and were more likely to be non-Hispanic Whites. Gay men had more education ($P = .037$), were less likely to be married and more likely to be partnered ($P < .001$), and had fewer children in the household ($P = .017$) than did bisexual men.

Health Outcomes

Lesbians and bisexual women had higher odds than heterosexual women for disability (adjusted odds ratio [AOR] = 1.47) and poor mental health (AOR = 1.40), but not for poor physical health, after adjustment for age, income, and education (Table 2). Lesbians and bisexual women had similar rates of poor physical health, disability, and poor mental health.

In adjusted analyses, gay and bisexual men were more likely than heterosexual men to have poor physical health (AOR = 1.38), disability (AOR = 1.26), and poor mental health (AOR = 1.77). Although the unadjusted prevalence rates of disability were similar between sexual minority and heterosexual men, the analyses with adjustment for sociodemographic characteristics showed that gay and bisexual men were more likely than their heterosexual counterparts to have a disability. We did not observe differences in health outcomes between gay and bisexual men.

Chronic Conditions

Lesbians and bisexual women had greater adjusted odds of obesity (AOR = 1.42) relative to heterosexual women. Unadjusted odds of CVD were similar for sexual minority and heterosexual women, but after adjustment for sociodemographic characteristics, lesbians and bisexual women had significantly greater risk (AOR = 1.37). The unadjusted odds of asthma for lesbians and bisexual women were significantly higher than for heterosexual women, but the difference did not remain significant when the analyses adjusted for sociodemographic differences. We observed no significant differences in chronic conditions between lesbians and bisexual women in the adjusted analyses.

Gay and bisexual men had significantly lower odds of obesity than did heterosexual men (AOR = 0.72), after adjustment for sociodemographic factors. The unadjusted odds of asthma for gay and bisexual men were higher than for heterosexual men (OR = 1.41), but the difference did not remain significant after

Table 2 Weighted Prevalence Rates and Regression Analyses of Health Outcomes and Chronic Conditions among Respondents Aged 50 Years and Older: Washington State Behavioral Risk Factor Surveillance System, 2003–2010

Health Outcomes/ Conditions	Women				Men			
	Heterosexual, %	Lesbian and Bisexual			Heterosexual, %	Gay and Bisexual		
		%	OR (95% CI)	AOR (95% CI)		%	OR (95% CI)	AOR (95% CI)
Frequent poor physical health	15.47	15.79	1.02 (0.81, 1.30)	1.02 (0.80, 1.30)	12.88	16.79	1.36* (1.05, 1.78)	1.38* (1.04, 1.83)
Disability	36.87	44.27	1.36** (1.14, 1.62)	1.47*** (1.22, 1.77)	33.96	38.27	1.21 (0.98, 1.48)	1.26* (1.02, 1.56)
Frequent poor mental health	9.36	15.92	1.83*** (1.42, 2.37)	1.40* (1.07, 1.81)	6.88	13.09	2.04*** (1.51, 2.76)	1.77** (1.28, 2.45)
Obesity	25.93	36.27	1.63*** (1.36, 1.95)	1.42*** (1.18, 1.71)	27.07	22.57	0.79* (0.62, 0.99)	0.72* (0.56, 0.93)
Arthritis[a]	52.24	53.70	1.06 (0.83, 1.36)	1.29 (0.99, 1.67)	39.25	41.85	1.11 (0.84, 1.48)	1.19 (0.89, 1.60)
Asthma	15.89	20.57	1.37** (1.10, 1.70)	1.20 (0.96, 1.49)	11.56	15.52	1.41* (1.07, 1.85)	1.28 (0.95, 1.71)
Diabetes	11.87	13.59	1.17 (0.91, 1.51)	1.25 (0.96, 1.64)	13.96	12.44	0.88 (0.66, 1.17)	0.92 (0.67, 1.25)
High blood pressure[b]	43.33	36.02	0.74 (0.54, 1.00)	0.86 (0.62, 1.20)	44.35	40.59	0.86 (0.61, 1.21)	0.88 (0.61, 1.26)
High cholesterol[a]	47.13	44.10	0.88 (0.69, 1.14)	1.00 (0.77, 1.30)	50.21	51.66	1.06 (0.79, 1.42)	1.08 (0.80, 1.46)
Cardiovascular disease[c]	10.71	10.51	0.98 (0.73, 1.31)	1.37* (1.00, 1.86)	16.49	14.11	0.83 (0.62, 1.12)	1.04 (0.76, 1.43)

Note. AOR = adjusted odds ratio; CI = confidence interval; OR = odds ratio. Adjusted logistic regression models controlled for age, income, and education; heterosexuals were coded as the reference group.
[a]Questions were asked in 2003, 2005, 2007, and 2009.
[b]Question was asked in 2003, 2005, and 2009.
[c]Questions were asked in 2004 through 2010.
*$P < .05$; **$P < .01$; ***$P < .001$.

adjustment. The adjusted odds of diabetes were significantly higher for bisexual men (19.74%) than for gay men (9.50%; AOR = 2.33; $P < .01$). We detected no other significant differences in chronic conditions between gay and bisexual men.

Access to Care

As shown in Table 3, although we found no significant difference in the prevalence of having a health care provider, lesbians and bisexual women were less likely than heterosexual women to have health insurance coverage and more likely to experience financial barriers to health care. These differences, however, did not remain significant after adjustment for sociodemographic characteristics. We detected no significant differences in health care access indicators between lesbians and bisexual women.

In the unadjusted analyses, gay and bisexual men were less likely than heterosexual men to have health insurance coverage, but the difference did not remain significant after adjustment. No significant differences appeared in the indicators of health care access between gay and bisexual men.

Health Behaviors

Prevalence rates of physical activity were similar among all female respondents, but lesbians and bisexual women were more likely than heterosexual women to smoke (AOR = 1.57) and to drink excessively (AOR = 1.43; Table 3). Lesbians (9.95%) were significantly more likely than bisexual women (3.90%; AOR = 0.40) to drink excessively ($P < .05$).

Gay and bisexual men had higher adjusted odds of smoking (AOR = 1.52) and excessive drinking (AOR = 1.47) than did heterosexual men; prevalence rates of physical activities

were similar. We observed no differences in health behaviors between gay and bisexual men.

Health Screening

Sexual minority women were significantly less likely than heterosexual women to have had a mammogram (AOR = 0.71), more likely to have been tested for HIV (AOR = 1.80), and equally likely to have received a flu shot. We observed no significant differences in health screenings between older lesbians and bisexual women.

The adjusted analyses indicated that gay and bisexual men were more likely than heterosexual men to have received a flu shot (AOR = 1.47) and an HIV test (AOR = 7.91). In the initial analyses, sexual minority men were significantly less likely than heterosexual men to receive a prostate-specific antigen test, but the difference was not significant after adjustment for sociodemographic characteristics. Although we found no significant differences between gay and bisexual men in the prevalence of receiving a flu shot or a prostate-specific antigen test, bisexual men (60.33%) were less likely than gay men (82.59%) to have been tested for HIV (AOR = 0.31; $P < .001$).

Discussion

We conducted one of the first studies to comprehensively examine leading CDC-defined health indicators among LGB older adults in population-based data. Contrary to the myth that older adults will not reveal their sexual orientation in public health surveys, in this population-based survey we found that approximately 2% of adults aged 50 years and older self-identified as

Table 3 Weighted Prevalence Rates and Regression Analyses of Health Indicators among Respondents Aged 50 Years and Older: Washington State Behavioral Risk Factor Surveillance System, 2003–2010

	Women				Men			
		Lesbian and Bisexual				Gay and Bisexual		
Health Indicator	Heterosexual, %	%	OR (95% CI)	AOR (95% CI)	Heterosexual, %	%	OR (95% CI)	AOR (95% CI)
Access to care								
Insurance	94.56	91.24	0.60*** (0.44, 0.82)	0.79 (0.55, 1.13)	93.36	89.42	0.60** (0.43, 0.84)	0.71 (0.48, 1.04)
Financial barrier	8.26	13.05	1.67*** (1.29, 2.16)	1.25 (0.97, 1.62)	6.81	8.43	1.26 (0.86, 1.84)	0.97 (0.63, 1.50)
Personal provider	92.41	93.09	1.11 (0.76, 1.60)	1.43 (0.97, 2.11)	88.57	88.41	0.98 (0.73, 1.33)	1.16 (0.84, 1.60)
Behavior								
Smoking	11.61	18.33	1.71*** (1.36, 2.15)	1.57*** (1.22, 2.00)	13.15	20.04	1.66*** (1.30, 2.11)	1.52** (1.18, 1.96)
Excessive drinking	4.61	7.88	1.77** (1.27, 2.47)	1.43* (1.02, 2.00)	11.12	17.13	1.65** (1.24, 2.20)	1.47* (1.09, 1.98)
Physical activity[a]	49.02	51.92	1.12 (0.88, 1.01)	1.01 (0.78, 1.31)	51.23	53.04	1.08 (0.81, 1.43)	1.04 (0.78, 1.40)
Screening								
Flu shot	55.07	52.99	0.92 (0.77, 1.10)	1.20 (1.00, 1.44)	50.40	54.87	1.20 (0.98, 1.46)	1.47*** (1.18, 1.82)
Mammogram[b]	79.77	74.16	0.73* (0.54, 0.98)	0.71* (0.52, 0.97)	...	...	...	...
PSA test[b]	...	...	...	...	49.85	40.67	0.69* (0.51, 0.93)	0.81 (0.59, 1.10)
HIV test[c]	23.89	40.80	2.20*** (1.79, 2.70)	1.80*** (1.46, 2.23)	28.31	76.47	8.23*** (6.22, 10.88)	7.91*** (5.94, 10.54)

Note. AOR = adjusted odds ratio; CI = confidence interval; OR = odds ratio; PSA = prostate-specific antigen. Adjusted logistic regression models controlled for age, income, and education; heterosexuals were coded as the reference group.

[a]Questions were asked in 2003, 2005, 2007, and 2009.

[b]Questions were asked in 2004, 2006, and 2008.

[c]Question was asked only of those younger than 65 years.

*P <.05; **P < .01; ***P <.001.

lesbian, gay, or bisexual. The findings reveal significant health disparities among LGB older adults, with both strengths and gaps across the continuum of health indicators examined. Our results suggest that some health disparity patterns that have been found in LGB adults at younger ages[9,10] persist in later life, including higher likelihoods of disability, poor mental health, and smoking, and, among lesbians and bisexual women, excessive drinking and obesity. We also found some health disparities—heightened risks of CVD among lesbian and bisexual women and of poor physical health and excessive drinking among gay and bisexual men—that may emerge later in the life course. Such health disparities likely have detrimental consequences for the quality of life of these LGB older adults.[14,32,33]

According to the life course perspective, social context, cultural meaning, and structural location (in addition to time, period, and cohort) affect aging processes, including health.[34,35] Situating LGB older adults within the historical and social context of their lives may help us to better understand the health issues they face as they age.[36] LGB older adults came of age during a time when same-sex relationships were criminalized and severely stigmatized and same-sex identities were socially invisible.

Elevated risks of disability and poor mental health among LGB older adults may be linked with experiences of stigmatization[37–39] and victimization,[39;41] especially in light of the profound impact that events at a given stage of life can have on subsequent stages.[42] The social contexts in which they have lived may have exposed LGB older adults to multiple types

of victimization and discrimination related to sexual orientation, disability, age, gender, and race/ethnicity.[41] D'Augelli and Grossman, for example, argue that lifetime experiences of victimization among sexual minority older adults because of their sexual orientation affects mental health in later life.[40] The evidence of physiological impact of chronic stressors on health[43] suggests that lifetime experiences of victimization may partially account for higher rates of disability among LGB older adults. Although our study was designed to identify health disparities among LGB older adults, further research is needed to compare LGB age cohorts and health changes over time.

Heightened risks of disability and poor physical and mental health among older gay and bisexual men may also be related to HIV.[44] Lacking information on HIV status in our data set, we could not explore this issue, but the disparity may be related to the prevalence of HIV among gay and bisexual men. With the advances in antiretroviral therapies, more adults with HIV are living into old age,[45,46] and older adults living with HIV have been found to be at increased risk of disability and poor physical and mental health.

Elevated risks of smoking and excessive drinking are of major concern among LGB older adults. Although smoking and excessive drinking are leading causes of preventable morbidity and mortality,[47] most prevention campaigns target only younger populations.[48,49] Intervention strategies that both identify and address distinctive cultural factors that may promote smoking and drinking among LGB older adults are desperately

Health Disparities among Lesbian, Gay, and Bisexual Older Adults by Karen Fredriksen-Goldsen et al.

69

needed. Previous research has found that LGB adults smoke at much higher rates than their heterosexual counterparts,[9,10,50] and our findings illustrate that such disparities persist among LGB older adults. We also found that older sexual minority women were more likely than older heterosexual women to drink excessively, which has also been documented in studies of younger sexual minority women.[9,10,50]

Existing research documents that drinking rates decline with age among older adults in general.[51] Although the prevalence rates of excessive drinking among younger gay, bisexual, and heterosexual adult men were similar in other population-based studies, we found higher rates among older gay and bisexual than heterosexual men. It may be that the rate of decline in drinking among older gay and bisexual men is slower than among older heterosexual men.[52] In addition, we found that older lesbians had higher rates of excessive drinking than did older bisexual women, which is also inconsistent with reports from population-based studies of younger lesbian and bisexual women.[10,50] A longitudinal study is warranted to better understand such changes in drinking behavior patterns among sexual minorities, and it will be important to examine how earlier experiences, such as frequent attendance at bars, clubs, and private house parties,[53] combined with minority stressors such as discrimination and victimization,[54] influence changes in drinking patterns over time among LGB older adults.

Older lesbians and bisexual women were more likely than their heterosexual counterparts to be obese and to have CVD; older gay and bisexual men were less likely than heterosexuals to be obese. The higher prevalence of obesity among lesbians and bisexual women than heterosexual women is well documented,[55] but increased risk of CVD has rarely been reported.[56] According to Conron et al., lesbian and bisexual adults may have a higher risk of CVD, possibly attributable to higher prevalence of obesity and smoking.[10] It is likely that disparities in obesity and smoking in early life influence disparities in CVD in later life among lesbians and bisexual women.[57,58]

Our subgroup analyses revealed that diabetes was more common in older bisexual than gay men, even though the obesity rates for the 2 groups were similar. The association between type 2 diabetes and obesity is well known.[59] Although previous studies found that among young adults, gay men were less likely to be obese than were heterosexual men, bisexual men were not.[10] Additional research is needed to investigate whether it is the duration of obesity among older bisexual men that increases their risk of diabetes,[60] as well as to further explore weight change and its impact on older gay men.

We observed some positive trends in preventive screenings, such as the higher likelihood of receiving a flu shot and an HIV test for gay and bisexual than for heterosexual men. Lesbians and bisexual women were more likely than their heterosexual peers to receive an HIV test. Yet we also found evidence of gaps and missed opportunities for prevention. For example, among sexual minority older men, bisexual men were less likely than gay men to obtain an HIV test. Older lesbians and bisexual women were less likely than heterosexual women to report having had a mammogram. Efforts to promote mammography screening among older lesbians and bisexual women

is particularly important, because higher risks of breast cancer have been documented among sexual minority women, attributable to elevated prevalence of obesity, substance use, and nulliparity.[61–63] Hart and Bowen suggest that lack of knowledge regarding breast cancer and the benefits of mammography combined with reluctance to use health services because of stigma likely prevent lesbians and bisexual women from receiving mammography in a timely manner.[64]

We observed several important differences in background characteristics by sexual orientation. Contrary to existing stereotypes, despite higher levels of education among LGB older adults, and the higher likelihood of employment among lesbians and bisexual women, LGB older adults do not have higher incomes than do heterosexuals, as observed in other population-based data.[65] In addition, LGB older adults are less likely than heterosexuals to be married but more likely to be partnered, which may have implications for health care advocacy, caregiving, and the availability of financial resources as they age. A recent study found that for gay men, being legally married is associated with mental health benefits.[38] Older gay and bisexual men have significantly fewer children in the household than do heterosexuals and are more likely to live alone, which corroborates findings in other population-based studies.[14] Higher rates of living alone may be related to the increased likelihood of the loss of a partner to AIDS.[66] It is also possible that structural factors do not support committed relationships or legal marriage among same-sex partners. LGB older adults who live alone are likely at risk for social isolation, which has been linked to poor mental and physical health, cognitive impairment, and premature morbidity and mortality in the general elderly population.[67]

Limitations

The cross-sectional nature of BRFSS data limits the ability to disentangle the temporal relationships between variables of interest. Although the purpose of the BRFSS is monitoring overall prevalence of health status, chronic conditions, and behaviors in the United States, and the measures are based on self-report, objective information such as symptoms and severity of health conditions is not available. We analyzed BRFSS data from only 1 state, limiting applicability to other state populations.

Our findings were limited with respect to the response rate of the BRFSS[68,69] and the self-identification of sexual orientation. The proportion of the older population that self-identified as sexual minorities in our data (~ 2%) was less than the 3.5% of adults aged 18 years and older who self-identified as LGB in most other population-based studies.[70] This may reflect the historical context in which today's LGB older adults came of age; these cohorts may be less likely than younger age groups to identify themselves as a sexual minority in a telephone-based survey.

Conclusions

More research with a life-course perspective is needed to examine how age and cohort effects may differentiate the experiences of younger and older LGB adults. Studies that examine the interplay between resilience and the stressors associated with aging and living as a sexual minority would likely help us better understand the mechanisms through which social contexts directly and indirectly affect the health of LGB older adults. Further research, especially a longitudinal study of health among LGB older adults that directly tests the relationships between transitions and trajectories through the life course and investigates the role of human agency in adapting to structural and legal constraints, would provide a greater understanding of how life experiences and shifting social contexts affect health outcomes in later life. Because LGB older adults may rely less on partners, spouses, and children, future research needs to investigate how differing types of social networks, support, and family structures influence health and aging experiences.[71] Although the sample size in our data did not allow for direct comparisons across different birth cohorts of LGB older adults, they are needed. The oldest-old LGB population, for example, may have experienced greater challenges in disclosing their sexual orientation; they may also have faced more barriers to social resources affecting health outcomes.

Our findings document population-based health disparities among LGB older adults. Early detection and identification of factors associated with such at-risk groups will enable public health initiatives to expand the reach of strategies and interventions to promote healthy communities. It is imperative that we understand the health needs of older sexual minorities in general as well as those specific to subgroups in this population to develop effective preventive interventions and services tailored to their unique needs. It is imperative that we begin to address healthy aging in our increasingly diverse society.

Human Participant Protection

The institutional review board of the University of Washington approved this study.

References

1. Vincent GA, Velkoff VA. *The Next Four Decades, The Older Population in the United States: 2010 to 2050.* Washington, DC: US Census Bureau; 2010.

2. Centers for Disease Control and Prevention, Merck Company Foundation. The state of aging and health in America. 2007. Available at: www.cdc.gov/aging/pdf/saha_2007.pdf. Accessed October 26, 2011.

3. *Biennial Report of the Director, National Institutes of Health, Fiscal Years 2008 & 2009.* Washington, DC: National Institutes of Health; 2010.

4. Disparities. HealthyPeople.gov. Available at: www.healthypeople.gov/2020/about/disparitiesAbout.aspx#six. Accessed October 26, 2011.

5. MacArthur Foundation Research Network on an Aging Society. Facts and fictions about an aging America. *Contexts.* 2009;8(4):16–21.

6. Truman BI, Smith KC, Roy K, et al. Rationale for regular reporting on health disparities and inequalities—United States. *MMWR Suveill Summ.* 2011;60(suppl):3–10.

7. Institute of Medicine. *The Health of Lesbian, Gay, Bisexual, and Transgender People: Building a Foundation for Better Understanding.* Washington, DC: National Academies Press; 2011.

8. Fredriksen-Goldsen KI, Muraco A. Aging and sexual orientation: a 25-year review of the literature. *Res Aging.* 2010;32(3):372–413.

9. Dilley JA, Simmons KW, Boysun MJ, Pizacani BA, Stark MJ. Demonstrating the importance and feasibility of including sexual orientation in public health surveys: health disparities in the Pacific Northwest. *Am J Public Health.* 2010;100(3):460–467.

10. Conron KJ, Mimiaga MJ, Landers SJ. A population-based study of sexual orientation identity and gender differences in adult health. *Am J Public Health.* 2010;100(10):1953–1960.

11. Boehmer U, Bowen DJ, Bauer GR. Overweight and obesity in sexual-minority women: evidence from population-based data. *Am J Public Health.* 2007;97(6):1134–1140.

12. Fredriksen-Goldsen KI, Kim H-J, Barkan SE, Balsam KF, Mincer S. Disparities in health-related quality of life: a comparison of lesbian and bisexual women. *Am J Public Health.* 2010;100(11):2255–2261.

13. Valanis BG, Bowen DJ, Bassford T, Whitlock E, Charney P, Carter RA. Sexual orientation and health: comparisons in the Women's Health Initiative sample. *Arch Fam Med.* 2000;9(9):843–853.

14. Wallace SP, Cochran SD, Durazo EM, Ford CL. *The Health of Aging Lesbian, Gay and Bisexual Adults in California.* Los Angeles: University of California, Los Angeles Center for Health Policy Research; 2011.

15. Centers for Disease Control and Prevention. Behavioral Risk Factor Surveillance System operational and user's guide. Available at: ftp://ftp.cdc.gov/pub/Data/Brfss/userguide.pdf. Accessed July 10, 2012.

16. Levin B, Lieberman DA, McFarland B, et al. Screening and surveillance for the early detection of colorectal cancer and adenomatous polyps, 2008: a joint guideline from the American Cancer Society, the US Multi-Society Task Force on Colorectal Cancer, and the American College of Radiology. *CA Cancer J Clin.* 2008;58(3):130–160.

17. AgePage. Menopause. National Institute on Aging. Available at: www.nia.nih.gov/healthinformation/publications/menopause.htm. Accessed June, 24, 2011.

18. Alexander CM, Landsman PB, Teutsch SM, Haffner SM, Third National Health and Nutrition Examination Survey (NHANES III), National Cholesterol Education Program (NCEP). NCEP-defined metabolic syndrome, diabetes, and prevalence of coronary heart disease among NHANES III participants age 50 years and older. *Diabetes.* 2003;52(5):1210–1214.

19. Office of Applied Studies. *The NSDUH Report—Serious Psychological Distress Among Adults Aged 50 or Older: 2005 and 2006.* Rockville, MD: Substance Abuse and Mental Health Services Administration; 2008.

20. Bowen ME, González HM. Racial/ethnic differences in the relationship between the use of health care services and functional disability: the health and retirement study (1992–2004). *Gerontologist.* 2008;48(5):659–667.

21. 2003–2010 Behavioral Risk Factor Surveillance System summary data quality reports. Centers for Disease Control and Prevention. Available at: www.cdc.gov/brfss/annual_data/annual_data.htm#2001. Accessed July 10, 2012.

22. *Measuring Healthy Days.* Atlanta, GA: Centers for Disease Control and Prevention; 2000.

23. Fan AZ, Strine TW, Jiles R, Berry JT, Mokdad AH. Psychological distress, use of rehabilitation services, and disability status among noninstitutionalized US adults aged 35 years and older, who have cardiovascular conditions, 2007. *Int J Public Health. 2009;*54(suppl 1):100–105.

24. Shankar A, Syamala S, Kalidindi S. Insufficient rest or sleep and its relation to cardiovascular disease, diabetes and obesity in a national, multiethnic sample. *PLoS ONE.* 2010;5(11):e14189.

25. Overweight and obesity: defining overweight and obesity. Centers for Disease Control and Prevention. Available at: www.cdc.gov/obesity/defining.html. Accessed April 10, 2012.

26. Centers for Disease Control and Prevention. Vital signs: current cigarette smoking among adults aged ≥ 18 years–United States, 2005–2010. *MMWR Morb Mortal Wkly Rep.* 2011;60(35):1207–1212.

27. National Institute of Alcohol Abuse and Alcoholism. NIAAA council approves definition of binge drinking. *NIAAA Newsletter.* 2004;3:3.

28. Objectives 22-2 and 22-3. *Healthy People 2010* (conference ed, 2 vols). Washington, DC: US Department of Health and Human Services; 2000.

29. Key facts about seasonal flu vaccine. Centers for Disease Control and Prevention. Available at: www.cdc.gov/flu/protect/keyfacts.htm. Accessed December 13, 2011.

30. National Cancer Institute fact sheet: mammograms. National Cancer Institute. Available at: www.cancer.gov/cancertopics/factsheet/detection/mammograms. Accessed December 13, 2011.

31. National Cancer Institute fact sheet: prostate-specific antigen (PSA) test. National Cancer Institute. Available at: www.cancer.gov/cancertopics/factsheet/detection/PSA. Accessed December 13, 2011.

32. Fried LP, Guralnik JM. Disability in older adults: evidence regarding significance, etiology, and risk. *J Am Geriatr Soc.* 1997;45(1):92–100.

33. Fredriksen-Goldsen KI, Kim H-J, Emlet CA, et al. The aging and health report: disparities and resilience among lesbian, gay, bisexual, and transgender older adults. 2011 Available at: http://caringandaging.org. Accessed December 13, 2011.

34. Mayer KU. New directions in life course research. *Annu Rev Sociol.* 2009;35:413–433.

35. Elder GH., Jr. Time, human agency, and social change: perspectives on the life course. *Soc Psychol Q.* 1994;57(1):4–15.

36. Clunis DM, Fredriksen-Goldsen KI, Freeman PA, Nystrom N. *Lives of Lesbian Elders: Looking Back, Looking Forward.* Binghamton, NY: Haworth Press; 2005.

37. Meyer IH. Prejudice, social stress, and mental health in lesbian, gay, and bisexual populations: conceptual issues and research evidence. *Psychol Bull.* 2003;129(5):674–697.

38. Wight RG, LeBlanc AJ, de Vries B, Detels R. Stress and mental health among midlife and older gay-identified men. *Am J Public Health.* 2012;102(3):503–510.

39. Fredriksen-Goldsen KI, Emlet CA, Kim HJ, et al. The physical and mental health of lesbian, gay male, and bisexual (LGB)

older adults: the role of key health indicators and risk and protective factors. *Gerontologist.* Epub ahead of print October 3, 2012.

40. D'Augelli AR, Grossman AH. Disclosure of sexual orientation, victimization, and mental health among lesbian, gay, and bisexual older adults. *J Interpers Violence.* 2001;16(10):1008–1027.

41. Fredriksen-Goldsen KI, Kim H-J, Muraco A, Mincer S. Chronically ill midlife and older lesbians, gay men, and bisexuals and their informal caregivers: the impact of the social context. *Sex Res Social Policy.* 2009;6(4):52–64.

42. Marmot MG, Wilkinson RG. *Social Determinants of Health.* 2nd ed. New York, NY: Oxford University Press; 2006.

43. Juster RP, McEwen BS, Lupien SJ. Allostatic load biomarkers of chronic stress and impact on health and cognition. *Neurosci Biobehav Rev.* 2010;35(1):2–16.

44. Jia H, Uphold CR, Zheng Y, et al. A further investigation of health-related quality of life over time among men with HIV infection in the HAART era. *Qual Life Res.* 2007;16(6):961–968.

45. Justice AC. HIV and aging: time for a new paradigm. *Curr HIV/AIDS Rep.* 2010;7(2):69–76.

46. Brennan DJ, Emlet CA, Eady A. HIV, sexual health, and psychosocial issues among older adults living with HIV in North America. *Ageing Int.* 2011;36(3):313–333.

47. Center for Substance Abuse Treatment. *Substance Abuse Among Older Adults.* Rockville, MD: Substance Abuse and Mental Health Services Administration; 1998. Treatment Improvement Protocol (TIP) Series 26.

48. Backinger CL, Fagan P, Matthews E, Grana R. Adolescent and young adult tobacco prevention and cessation: current status and future directions. *Tob Control.* 2003;12(suppl 4):iv46–iv53.

49. Wakefield MA, Loken B, Hornik RC. Use of mass media campaigns to change health behaviour. *Lancet.* 2010;376(9748): 1261–1271.

50. Burgard SA, Cochran SD, Mays VM. Alcohol and tobacco use patterns among heterosexually and homosexually experienced California women. *Drug Alcohol Depend.* 2005;77(1):61–70.

51. Kanny D, Liu Y, Brewer RD. Centers for Disease Control and Prevention. Binge drinking–United States, 2009. *MMWR Surveill Summ.* 2011;60(suppl):101–104.

52. Green KE, Feinstein BA. Substance use in lesbian, gay, and bisexual populations: an update on empirical research and implications for treatment. *Psychol Addict Behav.* 2012;26(2):265–278.

53. Trocki KF, Drabble L, Midanik L. Use of heavier drinking contexts among heterosexuals, homosexuals and bisexuals: results from a National Household Probability Survey. *J Stud Alcohol.* 2005;66(1):105–110.

54. Brubaker MD, Garrett MT, Dew BJ. Examining the relationship between internalized heterosexism and substance abuse among lesbian, gay, and bisexual individuals: a critical review. *J LGBT Issues Couns.* 2009;3(1):62–89.

55. Bowen DJ, Balsam KF, Ender SR. A review of obesity issues in sexual minority women. *Obesity (Silver Spring)* 2008;16(2):221–228.

56. Roberts SA, Dibble SL, Nussey B, Casey K. Cardiovascular disease risk in lesbian women. *Womens Health Issues.* 2003;13(4):167–174.

57. Hubert HB, Feinleib M, McNamara PM, Castelli WP. Obesity as an independent risk factor for cardiovascular disease: a 26-year follow-up of participants in the Framingham Heart Study. *Circulation.* 1983;67(5):968–977.

58. He J, Ogden LG, Bazzano LA, Vupputuri S, Loria C, Whelton PK. Risk factors for congestive heart failure in US men and women: NHANES I epidemiologic follow-up study. *Arch Intern Med.* 2001;161(7):996–1002.

59. Nguyen NT, Nguyen XM, Lane J, Wang P. Relationship between obesity and diabetes in a US adult population: findings from the National Health and Nutrition Examination Survey, 1999–2006. *Obes Surg.* 2011;21(3):351–355.

60. Lee JM, Gebremariam A, Vijan S, Gurney JG. Excess body mass index-years, a measure of degree and duration of excess weight, and risk for incident diabetes. *Arch Pediatr Adolesc Med.* 2012;166(1):42–48.

61. Case P, Austin SB, Hunter DJ, et al. Sexual orientation, health risk factors, and physical functioning in the Nurses' Health Study II. *J Womens Health (Larchmt)* 2004;13(9):1033–1047.

62. Cochran SD, Mays VM, Bowen D, et al. Cancerrelated risk indicators and preventive screening behaviors among lesbians and bisexual women. *Am J Public Health.* 2001;91(4):591–597.

63. Dibble SL, Roberts SA, Nussey B. Comparing breast cancer risk between lesbians and their heterosexual sisters. *Womens Health Issues.* 2004;14(2):60–68.

64. Hart SL, Bowen DJ. Sexual orientation and intentions to obtain breast cancer screening. *J Womens Health (Larchmt)* 2009;18(2):177–185.

65. Albelda R, Badgett MVL, Schneebaum A, Gates GJ. *Poverty in the Lesbian, Gay, and Bisexual Community.* Los Angeles, CA: Williams Institute; 2009.

66. Cochran SD, Mays V, Corliss H, Smith TW, Turner J. Self-reported altruistic and reciprocal behaviors among homosexually and heterosexually experienced adults: implications for HIV/AIDS service organizations. *AIDS Care.* 2009;21(6):675–682.

67. Cornwell EY, Waite LJ. Measuring social isolation among older adults using multiple indicators from the NSHAP Study. *J Gerontol B Psychol Sci Soc Sci.* 2009;64B(suppl 1):i38–i46.

68. Schneider KL, Clark MA, Rakowski W, Lapane KL. Evaluating the impact of non-response bias in the Behavioral Risk Factor Surveillance System (BRFSS). *J Epidemiol Community Health.* 2012;66(4):290–295.

69. Keeter S, Kennedy C, Dimock M, Best J, Craighill P. Gauging the impact of growing nonresponse on estimates from a national RDD telephone survey. *Public Opin Q.* 2006;70(5):759–779.

70. Gates GJ. *How Many People Are Lesbian, Gay, Bisexual, and Transgender?* Los Angeles, CA: Williams Institute; 2011.

71. Muraco A, Fredriksen-Goldsen K. "That's what friends do": informal caregiving for chronically ill lesbian, gay, and bisexual elders. *J Soc Pers Relat.* 2011;28(8):1073–1092.

Critical Thinking

1. Do you think that the attitudes of professionals and others influence service delivery to the lesbian, gay, and bisexual population?

2. How do you think some of the gaps in health disparities can be closed, or even shortened?

Create Central

www.mhhe.com/createcentral

Internet References

The LGBT Aging Project
www.lgbtagingproject.org

National Resource Center on LGBT Aging
www.lgbtagingcenter.org

KAREN I. FREDRIKSEN-GOLDSEN, HYUN-JUN KIM, SUSAN E. BARKAN, AND CHARLES P. HOY-ELLIS are with the School of Social Work, University of Washington, Seattle. ANNA MURACO is with the Department of Sociology, Loyola Marymount University, Los Angeles.

Fredriksen-Goldsen et al., Karen. From *American Journal of Public Health*, October 2013, pp. 1802–1809. Copyright © 2013 by American Public Health Association. Reprinted by permission via Sheridan Reprints.

Unit 4

UNIT

Prepared by: Elaina F. Osterbur, *Saint Louis University*

Problems and Potentials of Aging

Viewed as part of the life cycle, aging might be considered a period of decline, poor health, increasing dependence, social isolation, and—ultimately—death. It often means retirement, decreased income, chronic health problems, and death of a spouse. In contrast, the first 50 years of life are seen as a period of growth and development.

For a young child, life centers around the home and then the neighborhood. Later, the community and state become a part of the young person's environment. Finally, as an adult, the person is prepared to consider national and international issues—wars, alliances, changing economic cycles, and world problems. During the later years, however, life space narrows. Retirement may distance the individual from national and international concerns, although he or she may remain actively involved in community affairs. Later, even community involvement may decrease, and the person may begin to stay close to home and the neighborhood. For some, the final years of life may once again focus on the confines of home, be it an apartment or a nursing home.

Many older Americans try to remain masters of their own destinies for as long as possible. They fear dependence and try to avoid it. Many are successful at maintaining independence and the right to make their own decisions. Others are less successful and must depend on their families for care and to make critical decisions. However, some older people are able to overcome the difficulties of aging and to lead comfortable and enjoyable lives.

Time Trends of Incidence of Age-Associated Diseases in the U.S. Elderly Population: Medicare-Based Analysis by Igor Akushevich et al.

75

Article

Prepared by: Elaina F. Osterbur, *Saint Louis University*

Time Trends of Incidence of Age-Associated Diseases in the U.S. Elderly Population: Medicare-Based Analysis

IGOR AKUSHEVICH ET AL.

Learning Outcomes

After reading this article, you will be able to:

- Define time trends.
- Identify the importance of time trend estimates.
- Identify the incidence and mortality of common causes of disease among older Americans.

Introduction

The estimates of the time trends in health indicators (e.g. disease incidence rates) provide valuable information for policymakers and governmental institutions working in the area of medical technology and population health. These trends are associated with changes in socio-economic status and demographic structure of population, risk factors prevalence (e.g. smoking, obesity etc.), as well as changes in prevention, screening and diagnostic strategies. The estimates of time trends become especially important in populations with increasing proportions of the elderly for which maintaining good health is an important issue. While mortality trends have been studied more often, studies on morbidity trends are rare. Part of the difficulties in performing analysis of morbidity trends relate to a definition of chronic disease onset. In the elderly population, studies of the time trends of age-associated diseases are not common because these require large population-based data sets that are costly to collect and maintain. Valuable information about morbidity patterns and time trends in the USA can be extracted from the Medicare Files of Service Use (MFSU) and from two data sets linked with it—the National Long Term Care Survey (NLTCS-Medicare) and the Surveillance, Epidemiology, and End Results (SEER-Medicare); they are both capable of providing the estimates of time trends at the national level.

Data and Methods
Data

Both SEER-Medicare and NLTCS-Medicare represent the set of individual Medicare records from each institutional (inpatient, outpatient, skilled nursing facility, hospice or home health agency) and non-institutional (Carrier-Physician-Supplier and durable medical equipment providers) claim types. Enrolment date and the last date of individual follow-up (i.e. the date of death or censoring in the end of 2005) are available for each individual. The SEER-Medicare data set includes the standard 5% sample of Medicare beneficiaries residing in areas covered by SEER. The number of individuals is year-specific: from 230,286 individuals in 1992 to 300,695 individuals in 2005. The sample represents the US general elderly population [1]. The NLTCS-Medicare uses a sample of individuals drawn from the national Medicare enrolment files for an interview and subsequent 5-year follow-up. The cohorts formed in 1994 and 1999 are used in this analysis. In total, 34,077 individuals were followed-up for 5 years. So-called 'screener weights' released with the NLTCS were used in this study to produce the national population estimates (see Akushevich *et al.* [2] for recent discussion). These data sets allow for reconstruction of individual histories of medical service use and, therefore, for modelling of individual follow-up from age 65 to death or the onset of a disease of interest.

Age of Onset Definitions, Calculation of Rates and Evaluation of Time Trends

Nineteen diseases of various systems were selected for analyses: (i) most common (lung, colon, female breast and prostate) or highly prevalent with increasing incidence (skin melanoma) cancers; (ii) highly prevalent diseases of cardio- (MI, angina pectoris, HF) and cerebrovascular (stroke) system, respiratory system (COPD, asthma) and kidney and gastrointestinal tract (chronic renal disease/failure, ulcer); (iii) highly prevalent

(Parkinson's and Alzheimer's) neurodegenerative diseases; (iv) highly prevalent endocrine disease (diabetes) or disorder with growing prevalence and public health concern (goiter); (v) highly prevalent autoimmune disease with high disability (rheumatoid arthritis) and (vi) trauma/injury associated with high medical costs and disabilities (hip fracture). No diseases were initially selected but later excluded from analysis. The ages at their onsets were reconstructed from the MFSU data using the scheme described in Akushevich et al. [2, 3]. In brief, the individual medical histories of the applicable disease were reconstructed from MFSU combining all records with their respective ICD-9 codes, then a special computational procedure was applied for individuals with the history of the considered disease to separate incident and prevalent cases and to identify the age at disease onset. This procedure was based on two conditions applied to each medical history. The first condition allowed for the identification of the first occurrence of disease code, and the second was required for confirmation of disease presence. The individual Medicare history contains all records with respective disease ICD-9 code; however, only records with primary ICD-9 code and only from the so-called base Medicare sources (inpatient care, outpatient care, physician services and skilled nursing facilities) were used for the disease onset identification.

For NLTCS-Medicare, the age adjusted rates were calculated for cohorts formed in 1994 and 1999 years. Five-year follow-up was considered for each cohort. Only individuals with the mean coverage of health maintenance organisation (HMO) not to exceed 5% of all months of individual follow-up were kept for the analysis resulting in 27,607 individuals. For SEER-Medicare, individuals from geographic areas of the SEER Registers observed since 1992 or earlier were selected. The beginning of individual follow-up was estimated as the latest date among (i) date of 66 years old, (ii) date of enrolment into Medicare, and (ii) earliest date of living in one of the areas of the SEER registers. Only individuals with HMO coverage not >1 month/year were kept for the analysis. The final number of selected individuals is year-specific: from 199,418 in 1992 to 241,693 in 2005. The fraction of unselected individuals because of the HMO cut was from 15 to 25% (maximum in 1999), similar for both genders, and higher for ages 66–70 vs. 71 + (e.g. 24 and 22% in 2000).

For both data sets, the empirical time- and age-specific rates ($\lambda_a(t)$) (i.e. cohort-specific rates for NLTCS-Medicare and year-specific rates for SEER-Medicare) were calculated as a ratio of weighted numbers of cases to weighted person-years at risk: $\lambda_a(t) = n_{a,t}/P_{a,t}$; where $n_{a,t} = \Sigma_n W_n$, $P_{a,t} = \Sigma_i W_i$ and w_i is the individual weight (the screener weights for NLTCS-Medicare and unit weights for SEER-Medicare); n runs over all disease onsets detected in the age group, and i runs over all selected individuals at risk in the age group. The standard error (SE) was calculated as $\sigma_E = \sqrt{\lambda_a(t)(1-\lambda_a(t))/P_{0a,t}}$, where P_{0a} is the number of person-years estimated for unit weights. Thus, the SE was calculated based on the number of actually measured individuals. The age-adjusted rates (or directly standardised incidence rates) are calculated for the population aged 66 + as $\lambda(t) = \Sigma_{a=66}^{105+} \lambda_a(t)P_{a,2000} (\Sigma_{a'=66}^{105+} P_{a',2000})^{-1}$, where $P_{a,2000}$ are age-specific counts of US 2000 standard population. The SE for

the age-adjusted rate was estimated using the approach based on the approximation suggested by Keyfitz [4]: $SE = \lambda(t)/\sqrt{n_0}$, where n_0 was unweighted sum of the cases.

Among many measures appropriate for the analysis of time trends, we deal with the average annual percent change in incidence rates (or the annual rate of change of the incidence rate) estimated using the log-linear model in the form $\log(r(t)) = a + bt + \varepsilon_t$, where t is a calendar time, and ε_t is the error term of the regression. The estimate of the average annual percent change is given by $100b$ and expressed in percent [5]. The model estimation is based on weighted least squares where weights are reciprocal of variance estimated for each annual rate. Thus, this approach allows us to take into account the SEs for incidence rates and therefore this approach is preferable rather than simple averaging of empirically estimated annual percent change.

Sensitivity Analysis

One issue often present in analyses of large administrative data sets is the existence of factors which could produce systematic over- or underestimation of the number of diagnosed diseases or of the age at onset. The reasons for such uncertainties could be the incorrect date of disease onset, latent disenrolment and incorrect reporting of date of birth and date of death: while the first affects the age at onset, the latter tends to reduce or increase the number of person-years at risk. To evaluate the effects of these uncertainties, we performed calculations with different definitions of disease onset including: (i) all Medicare sources were used for completion of individual medical histories, (ii) all codes (not only primary) were used in MedPAR (i.e. inpatient) records, (iii) confirmation of the diagnosis was not required if the first record was from inpatient source, (iv) combining definitions (ii) and (iii) and (v–vi) the cut-offs on frequencies of the HMO coverage (i.e. coverage by an alternative insurance) at 6 and 12 months, respectively.

Results

The age-adjusted disease-specific incidence and total mortality rates were calculated using both NLTCS-Medicare and SEER-Medicare. In both data sets, a slow decrease in total mortality was detected; however in SEER-Medicare this trend was observed since 2000. For most of the studied diseases, an excellent agreement was observed for rates between two data sets. For several diseases such as female breast cancer, myocardial infarction, heart failure and hip fracture, a tendency was observed for NLTCS-Medicare rates to be higher and for rheumatoid arthritis—lower than for SEER-Medicare (higher NLTCS-Medicare rates could be due to the partial disagreement detected in our earlier study for age patterns [3]).

As expected three types of time patterns were detected: with increased, decreased and stable (statistically insignificant) time trends. Quantitatively, the time trend is evaluated using the log-linear model as the average annual percent change. The results of these estimates . . . and their confidence intervals confirm the above conclusions of qualitative analyses of time patterns.

Among the diseases with decreasing incidence rates, average annual percent changes were most dramatic for angina pectoris, COPD and ulcer (>5% of annual decline). For colon and prostate carcinomas, as well as for stroke, heart failure, hip fracture and asthma decreases were also significant, but less prominent (between 1.5 and 3.4%). For certain diseases, increasing trends were observed: the highest rise of an incidence rate was for renal diseases, goiter and melanoma (>6% of annual increase), trends of the Alzheimer's disease and diabetes were less dramatic (between 1.7 and 4%), and an increase of lung cancer incidence was <1% annually. Changes in incidence rates of female breast cancer, myocardial infarction, Parkinson's disease and arthritis were non-significant over the studied period.

Sensitivity analysis was performed for the effects of uncertainties described in 'Methods' section. No significant differences between estimates of time trends within the base and multiple alternative scenarios were found.

Discussion and Conclusion

While total mortality and incidence rates of many diseases (such as prostate cancer, stroke and HF) among the US older adults have been reported to decrease over recent several decades, there are still diseases with rising incidence (e.g. chronic kidney disease, skin melanoma, asthma, diabetes) [6–9]. Trends of some diseases such as Alzheimer's, Parkinson's, coronary heart disease and stroke were not straightforward [5, 10–14]. It is important to evaluate time trends of incidence rates of chronic diseases for elderly population—a fast growing group in the USA—using a nationally representative data set, thus making the results valuable for planning of screening, prevention and medical expenditures. In this study, time trends were calculated using Medicare-linked NLTCS-Medicare and SEER-Medicare data which represent the estimates at the national level.

For the majority of diseases, the calculated time trends were in agreement with other studies: e.g. decreasing trends were observed for COPD [15], hip fracture [16] and cancers of prostate, colon and female breast [6]. Observed decline in the incidence of heart disease and stroke also was in agreement with recent studies [11, 14]. It is likely attributable to reduction in smoking prevalence, earlier diagnoses and treatment of hypertension and diabetes, and general improvements of the lifestyle. While the incidence rates of asthma and ulcer decreased significantly in our study, results of other studies varied from trend stabilisation to their decrease [17–20]. These studies were performed in the general population or among children and young adults but not among elderly, thus making it difficult to compare with our results.

While decreasing incidence of some diseases could prove an effectiveness of preventive strategies, rising incidence of certain diseases are of a great concern. Observed increasing rate of melanoma is in agreement with other studies, and could be predominantly related to increased exposure to ultraviolet radiation [21, 22]. Opposed to melanoma, increase of lung cancer incidence in our and other studies recently became less pronounced; this phenomenon could reflect its long (~30 years) latency, making tumour risk—regardless of decreased smoking prevalence—still significant among those who are older than 65 [7]. The reasons for rising incidence of several non-cancer diseases such as Alzheimer's, renal disease, diabetes and goiter among the US elderly are not well understood. In part, it could be due to a methodological factor (case finding); however, increases could be true and be explained by earlier detection of disease and increasing risk factors prevalence. For example, observed in our study dramatic increase in incidence of renal disease also has been showed in recent studies that have associated its rise with an increasing prevalence of diabetes and hypertension [23]. In its turn, the rising rate of diabetes—which cannot be explained by active screening alone—could be due to increased prevalence of obesity in population, and, probably, of several other still unidentified behavioural factors [24, 25]. Studies on trends of goiter incidence in the US elderly are not available; however, its incidence rises among children and in general population, probably, due to iodine deficiency and more frequent diagnoses via screening [26]. Substantial increase (probably, due to increasing prevalence of diabetes, midlife obesity and depression, among other factors [27]) of highly disabling Alzheimer's disease in our study agreed with other studies, including several Medicare claim-based analyses [10, 28, 29]; however, this increase have not been confirmed in several community-based studies [11].

A unifying approach to the identification of disease onset and the calculation of the incidence rates was used for all considered diseases. This assumption does not restrict the generality of our calculation because there is always certain arbitrariness in defining the date of onset. For example, the diagnostic criteria of different heart studies reviewed by the NHI/NHLBI [30] resulted in different incidence rates observed in these studies. This arbitrariness was used for constructing a unified definition of the date of the onset of all diseases of interest. The effects of alternative onset definitions on time trends were not expected because there are no essential time-dependent factors involved in the date-at-onset definition, and were not found in sensitivity studies. Another issue is that times trends of single diseases are considered without relations to the trends in concurrent diseases e.g., increasing survival from CHD contributes to an increase in the cancer incidence rate if survived individuals were initially susceptible to both diseases. And finally changes in billing practices and office procedures may affect records and produce the errors in the estimates of respective rates and trends.

The evaluated time trends represented in the form of the average annual percent change can be used for projections of future incidence rates for selected diseases under the current-tendencies scenario. The results of this study can be used in analysis of trends of Medicare costs associated with a disease including future Medicare cost projection. Further progress in developing forecasting models can be achieved using specific information from the Medicare-linked data sets: e.g., NLTCS-Medicare can provide disability-specific incidence rates allowing for projecting the estimates for the whole US population, and SEER-Medicare allows to investigate comorbidity effects and detailed cancer characteristics such as histotype- and grade-specific cancer rates. Thus, the approach and reported results of this study have a potential of contributing to policy debates about the effects of current prevention strategies, risk factors prevalence and diagnostic algorithms on disease incidence for the elderly—a rapidly growing sector of the US population.

References

1. Warren JL, Klabunde CN, Schrag D, Bach PB, Riley GF. Overview of the SEER-Medicare data: content, research applications, and generalizability to the United States elderly population. Medical Care 2002; 40: IV-3–IV-18.

2. Akushevich I, Kravchenko J, Ukraintseva S, Arbeev K, Yashin AI. Circulatory diseases in the U.S. elderly in the linked National Long Term Care Survey-Medicare database: population-based analysis of incidence, comorbidity, and disability. Res Aging 2012, June 11; doi:10.1177/0164027512446941 (epub ahead of print).

3. Akushevich I, Kravchenko J, Ukraintseva S, Arbeev K, Yashin AI. Age patterns of incidence of geriatric disease in the U.S. Elderly population: medicare-based analysis. J Am Geriatr Soc 2012; 60: 323–7.

4. Keyfitz. Sampling variance of the standardized mortality rates. Hum Biol 1966; 38: 309–17.

5. Truelsen T, Mahonen M, Tolonen H, Asplund K, Bonita R, Vanuzzo D. Trends in stroke and coronary heart disease in the WHO MONICA Project. Stroke 2003; 34: 1346–52 (Research Support, Non-U.S. Gov't Research Support, U.S. Gov't, P.H.S.).

6. Siegel R, Ward E, Brawley O, Jemal A. Cancer statistics, 2011: the impact of eliminating socioeconomic and racial disparities on premature cancer deaths. CA Cancer J Clin 2011; 61: 212–36.

7. Manton K, Akushevich I, Kravchenko J. Cancer Mortality and Morbidity Patterns in the U.S. Population: An Interdisciplinary Approach, 1 edition. Gail M, Krickeberg K, Samet J, Tsiatis AWong W, eds. New York, NY: Springer; 2009.

8. Rudd RA, Moorman JE. Asthma incidence: data from the National Health Interview Survey, 1980–1996. J Asthma 2007; 44: 65–70.

9. Fox CS, Pencina MJ, Meigs JB, Vasan RS, Levitzky YS, D'Agostino RB Sr. Trends in the incidence of type 2 diabetes mellitus from the 1970s to the 1990s: the Framingham Heart Study. Circulation 2006; 113: 2914–8 (Comparative Study Research Support, N.I.H., Extramural Research Support, Non-U.S. Gov't).

10. Ukraintseva S, Sloan F, Arbeev K, Yashin A. Increasing rates of dementia at time of declining mortality from stroke. Stroke 2006; 37: 1155–9 (Research Support, N.I.H., Extramural).

11. Rocca WA, Petersen RC, Knopman DS et al. Trends in the incidence and prevalence of Alzheimer's disease, dementia, and cognitive impairment in the United States. Alzheimer Demen 2011; 7: 80–93 (Research Support, N.I.H., Extramural).

12. Kitamura A, Iso H, Iida M et al. Trends in the incidence of coronary heart disease and stroke and the prevalence of cardiovascular risk factors among Japanese men from 1963 to 1994. Am J Med 2002; 112: 104–9.

13. Rocca WA, Bower JH, McDonnell SK, Peterson BJ, Maraganore DM. Time trends in the incidence of parkinsonism in Olmsted County, Minnesota. Neurology 2001; 57: 462–7 (Research Support, U.S. Gov't, P.H.S.).

14. Ergin A, Muntner P, Sherwin R, He J. Secular trends in cardiovascular disease mortality, incidence, and case fatality rates in adults in the United States. Am J Med 2004; 117: 219–27 (Clinical Trial Comparative Study).

15. Gershon AS, Wang C, Wilton AS, Raut R, To T. Trends in chronic obstructive pulmonary disease prevalence, incidence, and mortality in ontario, Canada, 1996 to 2007: a population-based study. Arch Intern Med 2010; 170: 560–5 (Research Support, Non-U.S. Gov't).

16. Chevalley T, Guilley E, Herrmann FR, Hoffmeyer P, Rapin CH, Rizzoli R. Incidence of hip fracture over a 10-year period (1991–2000): reversal of a secular trend. Bone 2007; 40: 1284–9.

17. von Hertzen L, Haahtela T. Signs of reversing trends in prevalence of asthma. Allergy 2005; 60: 283–92 (Research Support, Non-U.S. Gov't Review).

18. Gershon AS, Guan J, Wang C, To T. Trends in asthma prevalence and incidence in Ontario, Canada, 1996–2005: a population study. Am J Epidemiol 2010; 172: 728–36 (Research Support, Non-U.S. Gov't).

19. Manuel D, Cutler A, Goldstein J, Fennerty MB, Brown K. Decreasing prevalence combined with increasing eradication of *Helicobacter pylori* infection in the United States has not resulted in fewer hospital admissions for peptic ulcer disease-related complications. Aliment Pharmacol Ther 2007; 25: 1423–7 (Multicenter Study).

20. el-Serag HB, Sonnenberg A. Opposing time trends of peptic ulcer and reflux disease. Gut 1998; 43: 327–33 (Comparative Study).

21. Jemal A, Saraiya M, Patel P et al. Recent trends in cutaneous melanoma incidence and death rates in the United States, 1992–2006. J Am Acad Dermatol 2011; 65(5 Suppl. 1): S17–25 e1-3.

22. Purdue MP, Freeman LE, Anderson WF, Tucker MA. Recent trends in incidence of cutaneous melanoma among US Caucasian young adults. J Invest Dermatol 2008; 128: 2905–8 (Letter Research Support, N.I.H., Intramural).

23. Coresh J, Selvin E, Stevens LA et al. Prevalence of chronic kidney disease in the United States. JAMA 2007; 298: 2038–47 (Research Support, N.I.H., Extramural).

24. Lipscombe LL, Hux JE. Trends in diabetes prevalence, incidence, and mortality in Ontario, Canada 1995–2005: a population-based study. Lancet 2007; 369: 750–6 (Research Support, Non-U.S. Gov't).

25. Gonzalez EL, Johansson S, Wallander MA, Rodriguez LA. Trends in the prevalence and incidence of diabetes in the UK: 1996–2005. J Epidemiol Community Health 2009; 63: 332–6 (Research Support, Non-U.S. Gov't).

26. Deladoey J, Ruel J, Giguere Y, Van Vliet G. Is the incidence of congenital hypothyroidism really increasing? A 20-year retrospective population-based study in Quebec. J Clin Endocrinol Metab 2011; 96: 2422–9 (Research Support, Non-U.S. Gov't).

27. Barnes DE, Yaffe K. The projected effect of risk factor reduction on Alzheimer's disease prevalence. Lancet Neurol 2011; 10: 819–28.

28. Taylor DH Jr, Sloan FA, Doraiswamy PM. Marked increase in Alzheimer's disease identified in medicare claims records between 1991 and 1999. J Gerontol A Biol Sci Med Sci 2004; 59: 762–6 (Research Support, U.S. Gov't, P.H.S.).

Time Trends of Incidence of Age-Associated Diseases in the U.S. Elderly Population: Medicare-Based Analysis by Igor Akushevich et al.

79

29. 2009 Alzheimer's disease facts and figures. Alzheimer Dement 2009; 5: 234–70.

30. NIH/NHLBI. Incidence and Prevalence: 2006 Chart Book on Cardiovascular and Lung Diseases. Bethesda, MD: National Institutes of Health, National Heart, Lung, and Blood Institute; 2006 (cited 2010 June); Available at: www.nhlbi.nih.gov/resources/docs/06a_ip_chtbk.pdf.

Critical Thinking

1. In light of increased population growth among older adults, why is it important to define chronic disease onset?

2. Considering the mortality and incidence rates reflected in Figure 1, reflect on the impact of morbidity of these chronic diseases.

Create Central

www.mhhe.com/createcentral

Internet References

Centers for Medicare & Medicaid Services
www.cms.gov

National Center for Health Statistics
www.cdc.gov/nchs

Article   Prepared by: Elaina F. Osterbur, *Saint Louis University*

Never Have a Heart Attack

Reduce your risk to almost zero by following these six proven steps.

GINA KOLATA

Learning Outcomes

After reading this article, you will be able to:

- Cite the risk factors that are most likely to cause a heart attack.

- List the six steps a person could take to appreciably reduce the chance of ever having a heart attack.

TAKE A GUESS:

Which of the following people is likely to suffer a heart attack?

- Chris Conway, 54, is thin, eats a healthy diet, takes a baby aspirin every day, and exercises regularly.
- Howard Wainer, 66, has diabetes. Until recently, his blood pressure and blood sugar were too high.
- Naomi Atrubin, 79, has already had two heart attacks.

So who's at risk? Surprise—it's all three of them.

Wainer and Atrubin have obvious risk factors, but Conway has to contend with family history—his father had a heart attack in his mid-40s, and died of one at 66. All these people, however, share a common concern about their health: about 1.1 million Americans will suffer a heart attack this year, and some 500,000 will not survive it.

Despite the risks, most people don't understand what causes a heart attack. The common view is that it's simply a plumbing problem—cholesterol builds up, clogging arteries like sludge in a pipe. When an artery supplying blood to the heart becomes completely obstructed, portions of the heart, deprived of oxygen, die. The result is a heart attack, right?

Not quite, say heart experts. Heart disease involves the gradual buildup of plaque. And plaque is like a pus-filled pimple that grows within the walls of arteries. If one of those lesions pops open, a blood clot forms over the spot to seal it and the clot blocks the artery. Other things can stop your heart, but *that's* what causes a heart attack.

The bigger issue is how to stop it from happening. There's no way to predict where an artery-blocking clot will originate,

so prying open a section of an artery with a stent will not necessarily prevent a heart attack. Stents relieve chest pain, but people who have no symptoms—such as Howard Wainer—are better off adhering to tried-and-true measures to slow plaque growth and prevent the lesions from bursting. Those measures, says Peter Libby, M.D., chief of cardiovascular medicine at Brigham and Women's Hospital in Boston, "are things no one wants to hear: keep your weight down, make physical activity a part of your life, stop smoking if you smoke." And, of course, keep your blood pressure and cholesterol under control, taking medications if necessary.

About 1.1 million of us will have a heart attack this year.

Few people are following that advice. Twenty-five percent of Americans over age 50 have at least two risk factors, such as high blood pressure or cholesterol levels, or an elevated blood-sugar level. Only 10 percent of Americans have every risk factor under control.

"In the majority of cases when someone has a heart attack, at least two or three risk factors might have been avoided," says Valentin Fuster, M.D., a cardiologist at Mount Sinai School of Medicine in New York City.

In the majority of cases when someone has a heart attack, most risk factors might have been avoided.

In fact, a 50-year-old man with none of the risk factors has only a 5 percent chance over the next 45 years of ever having a heart attack, according to Daniel Levy, M.D., director of the Framingham Heart Study, a federal study of heart disease in Framingham, Massachusetts. But if that man has even one risk factor, such as high cholesterol, his chance of having a heart attack soars to 50 percent. For a woman with no risk factors, the chance of having a heart attack is 8 percent; with just one risk factor, it goes to 38 percent. (Assess your own ten-year risk at hp2010.nhlbihin.net/atpiii/calculator.asp.)

By focusing on a few key risk factors, most people can significantly reduce their odds of ever having a heart attack. "There's a lot we can do," says Libby.

Keep Your Cholesterol in Check

Excess cholesterol gets stuck in artery walls. The walls become inflamed with white blood cells of the immune system, and those cells release chemicals that cause plaque. The normal level of so-called bad cholesterol, or LDL cholesterol, is 60 to 130. But if you are at high risk of a heart attack—because you have diabetes, for example—your level should be below 100 and, ideally, no higher than 70. Diet and weight loss are the preferred way to control your cholesterol, say heart-disease experts. If that doesn't work, statins—a class of cholesterol-lowering drugs—can reduce your LDL enough to help prevent heart attacks. Two decades of large and rigorous studies have shown that statins are safe for almost everyone.

Exercise Regularly

For optimal heart health, heart researchers recommend 30 minutes of moderate exercise—such as brisk walking—most days of the week. Exercise can help you control your weight, and it can also help you avoid diabetes if your blood sugar is inching up.

Lower Your Blood Pressure

High blood pressure can damage artery walls, causing them to become stiff and narrow. Ideally your blood pressure should be below 120/80. If you can get it that low with diet and exercise, great; if not, medications may do the job. Studies have shown that blood-pressure medications can reduce heart attack risk by 27 percent.

Control Your Weight

Obesity increases the likelihood that your cholesterol, blood pressure, and blood sugar will be too high; losing weight can often bring these numbers down. Being even slightly overweight also boosts your risk of heart attack, particularly if you tend to gain weight around your middle.

Stop Smoking

Smokers are two to three times more likely to die from heart disease than nonsmokers, says the American Heart Association. In addition to raising blood pressure and lowering HDL (good) cholesterol, smoking injures blood vessels, boosting your risk of having a heart attack. Even if you've been smoking for years, kicking the habit will help your heart. Studies have found that within one year of quitting, your heart attack risk is cut almost in half; within 15 years, it's like that of a nonsmoker.

Control Your Blood Sugar

High blood sugar can promote the growth of plaque. To be safe, your blood sugar level, tested after fasting, should be from 70 to 130 milligrams per deciliter of blood. Your doctor can order this test as part of a physical exam.

"I witness the cholesterol story time and time again," says Elliott Antman, M.D., director of the cardiac-care unit at Brigham and Women's Hospital. "People come to me for a second opinion after having a heart attack and I ask them, 'Have you ever been told what your cholesterol levels were?' The person will say, 'Yes, I was told they were normal.' That's not good enough anymore," if you've already had a heart attack. If you can get your LDL cholesterol level below 70, he says, you are unlikely to have another heart attack.

An LDL of less than 70 is also a good goal for people who have never had a heart attack, says Daniel Rader, M.D., head of preventive cardiovascular medicine at the University of Pennsylvania. Rader offers extra tests, including one for the blood protein CRP; if this protein is elevated, it indicates an increased heart-disease risk. Rader also offers heart scans to assess the extent of plaque in a person's arteries. If the tests reveal additional risk, he will suggest drugs to drive an LDL level down to 70. With an LDL level that low, Rader says, "your lifetime risk of heart disease will be reduced dramatically." It may not reach zero, he says, but it will be a lot lower.

Naomi Atrubin is counting on it. Her LDL cholesterol level, with medication, is currently 69; she's taking another drug to control her blood pressure, and she exercises. "I feel good," she says, though she's knows what's at stake: that only an aggressive approach on all fronts will help her avoid a third—and potentially fatal—heart attack.

Critical Thinking

1. What is the chance that a 50-year-old man who has none of the risk factors for a heart attack having a heart attack in the next 45 years?

2. If a 50-year-old man has one risk factor for a heart attack, such as high cholesterol, what are his chances of having a heart attack in the next 45 years?

3. What do doctors recommend as the safest level of a person's LDL or bad cholesterol in order to avoid a heart attack?

4. List the risk factors that are identified as problems that can lead to a heart attack.

Create Central

www.mhhe.com/createcentral

Internet References

AARP Health Information
www.aarp.org/bulletin

Alzheimer's Association
www.alz.org

A.P.T.A. Section on Geriatrics
http://geriatricspt.org

Caregiver's Handbook
www.acsu.buffalo.edu/~drstall/hndbk0.html

Caregiver Survival Resources
www.caregiver.com

International Food Information Council
www.ific.org

University of California at Irvine: Institute for Brain Aging and Dementia
www.alz.uci.edu

GINA KOLATA is a science writer for *The New York Times*.

Reprinted from *AARP The Magazine*, January/February 2010, pp. 22–23. Copyright © 2010 by Gina Kolata. Reprinted by permission of Gina Kolata and AARP.

Article   Prepared by: Elaina F. Osterbur, *Saint Louis University*

The Worst Place to Be If You're Sick

Hospital errors cause 100,000 deaths yearly. These are preventable deaths. What's wrong, and can it be made right?

KATHARINE GREIDER

Learning Outcomes

After reading this article, you will be able to:

- Describe the mistakes that were identified as causing serious health problems for patients in hospitals throughout the country.
- Explain how 100 Michigan hospital intensive care units managed to reduce patient infections by two-thirds.

American hospitals are capable of great medical feats, but they also are plagued by daily errors that cost lives. No one knows that better than Ilene Corina. In the 1990's, she saw a medical team rescue her fragile premature newborn, but she also endured the death of another son—a healthy 3-year-old—when, she says, doctors failed to attend to complications from a routine tonsillectomy.

When a family member dies because of a hospital's mistake, "what do we care about the excellence in the system?" says Corina, 51, of Long Island, N.Y., founder and president of a patient safety advocacy group. "We have to voice our anger about the problems we see in the health care system."

Corina had already joined the patient safety movement when, in 1999, the Institute of Medicine's now-famous report, *To Err Is Human,* burst into public consciousness with its startling announcement: Each year as many as 100,000 Americans die in hospitals from preventable medical mistakes.

Today, more than a decade into the fight against medical errors, there's little reason to believe the risks have declined substantially for the 37 million people hospitalized each year. In fact, recent studies suggest a problem that's bigger and more complex than many had imagined. A report released in January on Medicare patients found that hospital staff did not report a whopping 86 percent of harms done to patients. If most errors that harm patients aren't even reported, they can never be tracked or corrected, the Health and Human Services Department report pointed out.

The number of patients who die each year from hospital errors is equal to 4 jumbo jets crashing each week.

This latest study built on an earlier HHS study of Medicare patients that found one in seven suffered serious or long-term injuries, or died, as a result of hospital care. Researchers said about 44 percent of the problems were preventable.

In another key study published last spring in the journal *Health Affairs,* researchers examined patient charts at three of America's leading hospitals and found that an astounding one in three admissions included some type of harm to the patient.

Mistakes run the gamut. The surgeon nicks a healthy blood vessel; a nurse mistakenly administers a toxic dose of medicine; the staff fails to adequately disinfect a room, and a patient contracts a dangerous "superbug."

The number of patients who die each year from preventable hospital errors is equal to four full jumbo jets crashing each week. If airline tragedies of that magnitude were occurring with such frequency, no one would tolerate the loss.

One study of Medicare patients found that 1 in 7 died or were harmed by their hospital care.

"At its deepest level, what we're now having trouble with is the enormous complexity of medicine," says Atul Gawande, a surgeon, Harvard associate professor and author who promotes the use of medical checklists to save lives. "We now have 13,600 diagnoses, 6,000 drugs, 4,000 medical and surgical procedures," he says. And yet "we have not paid attention to the nuts and bolts of what's required to manage complexity." Experts like Gawande say one reason medical errors continue at such high rates is that hospitals have only recently begun to copy aviation's decades-long effort to create safety procedures that take into account human fallibility—often using only simple checklists.

There has been some progress, to be sure. Around the country, safety innovators have introduced promising ways to minimize slipups—from using checklists to reporting hospital infection rates on state websites. Last spring the Obama administration announced it would spend $1 billion to fund safety measures by hospitals, with the ambitious goal of reducing preventable patient injuries by 40 percent by the end of next year.

Still, the question of how close hospitals can ever come to being error-free is controversial. It seems fair to expect them to reduce the number of times—as many as 40 per week—that U.S. surgeons operate on the wrong person or body part. But what about other procedures?

Patient safety advocates have been able to raise the bar on hospitals in some key areas, showing that they *can* prevent harm to even the most vulnerable patients. A case in point: bloodstream infections that result from inserting a tube into a large vein near the heart to deliver medication. For years, these infections, which resulted in some 30,000 deaths annually, were viewed as largely unavoidable.

But then, in a program launched in 2004, more than 100 Michigan intensive care units managed to reduce these infections by two-thirds—and save some 1,500 lives in just 18 months—using a short checklist of practices for handling the catheters, and a culture change aimed at getting all staff on board. Hospitals around the country then took up the challenger, and the results were impressive.

The trouble is, there are plenty of other problems that may not be susceptible to an approach that tests a simple process that can then be used nationwide. A recent program looking at lapses that could lead to surgery on the wrong section of the patient found that errors can creep in just about anywhere, from scheduling to the marking of the surgical site. A couple of hospitals, for example, were using pens those ink washed off during surgical prep, making the marks useless. Flaws in this process vary from one hospital or surgery center to another, says Mark Chassin, M.D., president of the Joint Commission, the major accrediting organization for hospitals.

1,500 lives were saved in 18 months when Michigan ICUs began using a checklist of practices for handling catheters.

Other, apparently straight-forward problems—like health care workers not washing their hands—have proved surprisingly stubborn. Only about half of hospital workers follow hand washing guidelines, despite excellent staff training and ubiquitous hand sanitizer dispensers at many hospitals, says Robert Wachter, M.D., a patient safety expert at the University of California, San Francisco. He points out an airline pilot would be disciplined or fired for ignoring safety rules. But while penalizing careless individuals remains controversial—and largely untried—in health care, activities have made hospitals more accountable.

Public reporting of hospital performance, more or less unheard of a decade ago, has been an important strategy. Twenty-nine states now require public reporting of hospital infection rates, and 28 require some information on medical errors. The HHS website has now added a key catheter infection rate, along with other results.

There are hundreds of ways to measure safety performance, from death rates after heart surgery to whether doctors gave the right antibiotic. What to report has been a major debate. Infection rates, initially resisted by hospitals, are now generally regarded as some of the most reliable data available to the public, since in most cases reports are made through a standard system developed by the U.S. Centers of Disease Control and Prevention.

Money may be another motivator for hospitals. In 2008 Medicare took the small step of restricting payments to hospitals for extra costs associated with 10 hospital-acquired conditions. This year it will begin giving extra money to hospitals that score the highest on a set of standards linked to better results for patients.

Naturally, many patients want to compare the safety records of their local hospitals before checking in. But that's still tough to do. "There are no existing data that can allow you to be confident you've picked the safest, highest-quality place to get care," says Chassin, who helped prepare the seminal *To Err is*

Protect Yourself from Hospital Errors

Advocates agree that patients can minimize their risks by keeping a close eyes on their care. Hospitals are busy places with lots of moving parts. "You cannot assume that people in the hospital have a really clear idea of who you are or why you're there," says Jean Rexford, director of the Connecticut Center for Patient Safety. Here are some tips on how to protect yourself:

- Bring an advocate—a friend or family member—especially for check-in and discharge. Many hospitals have a patient advocate or staff person you can consult. Or you can hire your own advocate, but be aware that the profession lacks licensing requirements, so get referrals and check credentials.
- Bring a notebook. Write down all your medications, why you take them and who prescribed them. Include phone numbers of key personal and medical contacts (and don't forget your cellphone and charger). In the hospital, when questions arise, write them down.
- Bring a big bottle of hand sanitizer. Put it by your bed to remind you and the staff to keep hands clean.

For More:

- Hospitalcompare.hhs.gov
- Agency for Healthcare Research and Quality, ahrq.gov
- Consumers Union, consumerreports.org
- Connecticut Center for Patient Safety ("5 Things to Know"), ctcps.org

Human report "One reason is that safety and quality varies even within health systems. Just because they're great in one area doesn't mean that they're great in another."

Critical Thinking

1. Twenty-nine states now require what kind of public reporting on medical problems?
2. What financial measures has Medicare taken to force hospitals to comply with safer procedures and results?
3. Why is there no data available that allows the patients to be sure they are choosing the best hospital?

Create Central

www.mhhe.com/createcentral

Internet References

AARP Health Information
www.aarp.org/bulletin

Alzheimer's Association
www.alz.org

A.P.T.A. Section on Geriatrics
http://geriatricspt.org

Caregiver's Handbook
www.acsu.buffalo.edu/~drstall/hndbk0.html

Caregiver Survival Resources
www.caregiver.com

International Food Information Council
www.ifi c.org

University of California at Irvine: Institute for Brain Aging and Dementia
www.alz.uci.edu

Article   Prepared by: Elaina F. Osterbur, *Saint Louis University*

Poll: Upbeat Baby Boomers Say They're Not Old Yet

Learning Outcomes

After reading this article, you will be able to:

- Describe how the baby boomers' views of aging differ from those of younger adults.

- Cite what factors baby boomers consider to be the most undesirable aspects of getting older.

Baby boomers say wrinkles aren't so bad and they're not that worried about dying. Just don't call them "old."

The generation that once powered a youth movement isn't ready to symbolize the aging of America, even as its first members are becoming eligible for Medicare. A new poll finds three-quarters of all baby boomers still consider themselves middle-aged or younger, and that includes most of the boomers who are ages 57–65.

Younger adults call 60 the start of old age, but baby boomers are pushing that number back, according to the Associated Press-LifeGoesStrong.com poll. The median age they cite is 70. And a quarter of boomers insist you're not old until you're 80.

"In my 20s, I would have thought the 60s were bad, but they're not so bad at all," says 64-year-old Lynn Brown, a retired legal assistant and grandmother of 11 living near Phoenix in Apache Junction, Ariz.

The 77 million boomers are celebrating their 47th through 65th birthdays this year.

Overall, they're upbeat about their futures. Americans born in the population explosion after World War II are more likely to be excited about the positive aspects of aging, such as retirement, than worried about the negatives, like declining health. A third of those polled feel confident about growing older, almost twice as many as find it frustrating or sad. Sixteen percent report they're happy about aging, about equal to the number who say they're afraid. Most expect to live longer than their parents.

"I still think I've got years to go to do things," says Robert Bechtel, 64, of Virginia Beach, Va. He retired last year after nearly four decades as a retail manager. Now Bechtel has less stress and more time to do what he pleases, including designing a bunk bed for his grandchildren, remodeling a bathroom and teaching Sunday school.

A strong majority of baby boomers are enthusiastic about some perks of aging—watching their children or grandchildren grow up, doing more with friends and family, and getting time for favorite activities. About half say they're highly excited about retirement. Boomers most frequently offered the wisdom accumulated over their lives as the best thing about aging.

"The older you get, the smarter you get," says Glenn Farrand, 62, of Ankeny, Iowa.

But, he adds, "The physical part of it is the pits."

Baby boomers most often brought up failing health or fading physical abilities when asked to name the worst thing about getting older.

Among their top worries: physical ailments that would take away their independence (deeply worrisome to 45 percent), losing their memory (44 percent), and being unable to pay medical bills (43 percent). Many also fret about running out of money (41 percent).

Only 18 percent say they worry about dying. Another 22 percent are "moderately" concerned about it. More than two-thirds expect to live to at least age 76; 1 in 6 expects to make it into the 90s.

About half predict a better quality of life for themselves than their parents experienced as they aged.

"My own parents, by the time they were 65 to 70, were very, very inactive and very much old in their minds," says Brown. So they "sat around the house and didn't go anywhere."

"I have no intentions of sitting around the house," says Brown, whose hobbies include motorcycle rides with her husband. "I'm enjoying being a senior citizen more than my parents did."

But a minority of boomers–about a fourth–worry things will be harder for them than for the previous generation.

"I think we'll have less," said Vicki Mooney, 62, of Dobbs Ferry, N.Y., who fears older people will be pinched by cuts to Social Security and Medicare and rising health care costs. "The main difference in the quality of life is wondering if we will have a safety net."

Baby boomers with higher incomes generally are more optimistic about aging than their poorer peers. Women tend to feel sunnier than men; college graduates are more positive than those without a degree.

A third of baby boomers say their health has declined in the last five years, and that group is more likely to express fear or frustration about aging. Still, most boomers rate themselves in good or even excellent health overall, with less than 1 in 10 doing poorly.

Looking older is seriously bugging just 12 percent of baby boomers. The vast majority say they wouldn't get plastic surgery. That includes Johanna Taisey, 61, of Chandler, Ariz., who says aging is "no problem at all . . . it's just nature."

"Age with dignity," Taisey advises.

Among the 1 in 5 who have had or would consider cosmetic surgery, about half say they might improve their tummy or eyes. A sagging chin is the next biggest worry–nearly 40 percent would consider getting that fixed.

Only 5 percent of baby boomers say they might use the chemical Botox to temporarily smooth away wrinkles; 17 percent would consider laser treatments to fix varicose veins.

But boomers, especially women, are taking some steps to look younger. A majority of the women—55 percent—regularly dye their hair, and they overwhelmingly say it's to cover gray. Only 5 percent of the men admit using hair color.

A quarter of the women have paid more than $25 for an anti-aging skincare product, such as a lotion or night cream. Just 5 percent of the men say they've bought skincare that expensive.

Almost all baby boomers—90 percent—have tried to eat better. Three-quarters say they're motivated more by a desire to improve their health than their appearance. Most boomers—57 percent—say in the past year they've taken up a regular program of exercise. About the same number do mental exercises, such as crossword puzzles or video games, to stay sharp.

Sixty-four-year-old Loretta Davis of Salem, W.Va., reads and plays games on her computer and takes walks. Diabetes and hypertension keep her focused on her diet these days. "I wish I had been more conscious of what I was eating earlier in life," said Davis, who worked in a grocery store, a factory and an ice cream shop before being disabled by polio in the 1980s.

But Davis says getting older doesn't bother her: "I'm just glad to still be here."

The AP-LifeGoesStrong.com poll was conducted from June 3 to June 12 by Knowledge Networks of Menlo Park, Calif., and involved online interviews with 1,416 adults, including 1,078 baby boomers born between 1946 and 1964. The margin of sampling error for results from the full sample is plus or minus 4.4 percentage points; for the boomers, it is plus or minus 3.3 percentage points.

Knowledge Networks used traditional telephone and mail sampling methods to randomly recruit respondents. People selected who had no Internet access were given it free.

Critical Thinking

1. When considering getting older, what are the things that worry the baby boomers the most?

2. What did boomers consider to be the best thing about aging?

3. How do most of the boomers rate their overall health at their current age in life?

Create Central

www.mhhe.com/createcentral

Internet References

AARP Health Information
  www.aarp.org/bulletin
Alzheimer's Association
  www.alz.org
A.P.T.A. Section on Geriatrics
  http://geriatricspt.org
Caregiver's Handbook
  www.acsu.buffalo.edu/~drstall/hndbk0.html
Caregiver Survival Resources
  www.caregiver.com
International Food Information Council
  www.ific.org
University of California at Irvine: Institute for Brain Aging and Dementia
  www.alz.uci.edu

Article   Prepared by: Elaina F. Osterbur, *Saint Louis University*

The Effect of Exercise on Affective and Self-Efficacy Responses in Older and Younger Women

Fiona Barnett

Learning Outcomes

After reading this article, you will be able to:

- Identify the acute exercise bout and its corresponding positive psychological effects.
- Discuss theories associated with self-efficacy.

An extensive body of research exists on the affective states that occur with an acute bout of exercise.[1–4] A core dimension of the affective states experienced by an individual is hedonic tone or pleasure/displeasure. Hedonic theory[5] proposes that these valenced responses to a behavior may influence whether that same behavior will be repeated. Exercise-induced affect focuses on the relationship between affective responses and exercise with the premise that an individual who partakes in an acute exercise bout producing enhanced positive affect and reduced negative affect would be more likely to adopt exercise practices in the future.[6] Psychological outcomes associated with an acute exercise bout may influence exercise behavior through tension release,[7] improvement of mood,[8] enhancement of self-esteem,[9] and a reduction in anxiety and depression.[8,10,11] Additionally, negative affective responses to a single exercise bout may produce barriers to subsequent exercise participation.[12]

Positive and negative affective states during and after exercise have been reported in the literature. Findings have been mixed, with positive[1,2] and negative[3] affective responses being reported.

Much of the research on the psychological responses to a single bout of exercise is conducted on a single age group, such as younger healthy women or older women. For example, decreased negative affective postexercise responses and increased affective positive responses have been found in older women,[1] middle-aged women,[4] and college-aged women[2] following a single bout of aerobic exercise. Less research is available on the effect of age on affective states. One such study comparing sedentary younger and older women found that an acute bout of exercise resulted in decreased positive responses and increased negative affective responses in both groups of women.[3]

Bandura's[13] Social Cognitive Theory of behavior proposes that individuals gain attitudes from various sources, such as an individual's social network and the media. Self-efficacy, or one's beliefs in his/her capabilities to execute a particular course of action to satisfy a situational demand, is the key construct of the Social Cognitive Theory for explaining behavior.[13] Factors said to influence self-efficacy include mastery experiences (behavioral), modeling (cognitive), verbal persuasion (social), and interpretation of emotional or psychological arousal (physiological).[13] Self-efficacy has long been identified as an important predictor of future exercise behavior.[14–16]

Exercise-induced affect is influenced by many factors including the physiological and psychological differences of the individual, the environment, and the perceived attributes and specific demands of the exercise bout.[10] A reciprocal relationship has been found between self-efficacy and the affective responses to an acute exercise bout, whereby individuals with greater self-efficacy demonstrate more positive affective responses following an acute exercise bout[1,17,18] through mastery accomplishment.[13] As self-efficacy is said to be specific to the task being performed, the mastery experience mechanism may increase the likelihood of repeating the exercise task.

Advancing age is associated with a decline in aerobic and strength capacities and an increase in adiposity.[19,20] These deleterious changes can have an effect on an individual's physiological functional capacity (PFC), defined as the ability to perform the physical tasks of daily life.[21] It would appear that in the adoption stages of physical activity, an older sedentary individual with low PFC may have lower exercise-related self efficacy to partake in an acute bout of physical activity, thus providing a real barrier to future exercise participation.[22]

This study examined the self-efficacy and affective responses of nonexercising younger and older women to an acute exercise bout to determine whether aging has an effect on affective responses to exercise. It was hypothesized that older women would experience more negative affective responses and lower self-efficacy responses compared with younger women following an acute bout of exercise.

Methods
Participants
Twenty-five younger [mean age = 19.9 ± .29 yrs; range 18–23 yrs; body mass index (BMI) 21.9 ± 2.43] and 25 older (mean age = 55.7 ± 1.15 yrs; range 50–69 yrs; BMI 29.2 ± 6.16) women participated and gave their written informed consent to participate in this study as approved by a University Human Research Ethics Committee. Participants were recruited via advertisements in regional newspapers, television and radio, and community bulletin board notices throughout North Queensland, Australia. Participants were required to be sedentary, classified as not having performed regular moderate exercise during the preceding 6 months.[23,24] Older participants were required to be 50 years of age or older and younger women between 18–25 years of age.

A physical activity readiness questionnaire (PAR-Q) was used to determine the medical history and physical activity readiness of the participants. The PAR-Q was designed to identify adults for whom physical activity was inappropriate or should seek medical advice concerning suitable types of activity.[25] Thirty-three older women inquired with 8 women excluded due to medication that would affect heart rate or contraindications to the PAR-Q assessment. Thirty younger women inquired of which 5 were excluded due to age.

Measurements
Exercise-specific self-efficacy scales measure a respondent's belief in their capabilities to successfully participate in exercise when faced with potential barriers.[26] Exercise self-efficacy beliefs were assessed via a 4-item questionnaire[27] designed to determine participant's confidence in their ability to cycle at 60% VO2max during an acute exercise bout without stopping for 5, 10, 15, and 20 minutes. Participants respond to each item on a 100-point percentage scale with 10% increments that range from 0% (not at all confident) to 100% (extremely confident). This measure is similar to self-efficacy measures used previously in the literature[1,3] and has been shown to be a valid and reliable method for assessing self-efficacy.[27] Internal consistency for this scale in the current study was .70.

In line with Tellegen, Watson, and Clark's[28] hierarchical structure of affect, valenced responses and more specific affective responses inherent with acute exercise were measured. The valenced and arousal dimensions of basic affect were measured using the Feeling Scale (FS)[29] and the Felt-Arousal Scale (FAS).[30] The FS ranges from −5 (very bad) to +5 (very good) with 0 (neutral) as the midpoint. The FAS is a 6-point scale measuring perceived activation that ranges from 1 (low arousal) to 6 (high arousal). Internal consistencies for the current study were .60 for the FS and .70 for the FAS.

More specific affective responses to an acute exercise bout were assessed using the Exercise-Induced Feeling Inventory (EFI).[6] The EFI is a 12-item multidimensional scale measuring the degree to which participants are experiencing the 4 specific feeling states of revitalization, positive engagement, tranquility, and physical exhaustion. Participants respond to each inventory item on a 5-point scale ranging from 0 (do not feel) to 4 (feel very strongly). The EFI has been used extensively in exercise-affect studies.[3,24,31,32] Internal consistencies for the current study were .86 for positive engagement, .76 for revitalization, .87 for tranquility, and .83 for physical exhaustion.

Perceived exertion measures an individual's perception of overall effort. Borg's[33] 15-point Rating of Perceived Exertion (RPE) scale was used to measure perceived exertion for this study. The scale ranges from 6–20 and contains verbal anchors at every odd integer to assist participants with rating their overall perceived exertion.

Procedure
Participants were required to attend the university on 2 occasions. On the initial visit, participants were given an information sheet and completed the consent form. Participants were then measured for resting heart rate (HR_{rest}) and resting blood pressure (BP_{rest}) as well as measured for height and weight. Height and weight measurements were used to determine BMI. Participants then performed a 6-minute submaximal graded exercise test (GXT) on a cycle ergometer to determine estimated maximum oxygen uptake (VO2max). The GXT was a modification of the Astrand-Rhyming test developed by Siconolfi et al,[34] consisting of a lower initial work rate of 25 W. This lower initial work rate has been previously found to be more appropriate for unconditioned women.[22] The submaximal test required participants to pedal at a rate of 50 rpm and an initial workload of 25 W for 6 minutes. Workload was increased by 25 W after 2 minutes and then 4 minutes if HR was < 70% HR_{max}. The average HR was taken between the 5th and 6th minute once steady state HR was achieved.

Before the second visit, the participants' cycling workload was established for 60% of the estimated VO_{2max}. The VO_{2max} ($l·min^{-1}$) was firstly estimated from the Astrand-Ryhming nomogram[35] using the steady state heart rate and final stage workload and a regression equation for females, as devised by Siconolfi et al,[34] was then applied. Relative VO_{2max} was then determined by dividing VO_{2max} ($l·min^{-1}$) by the participants' weight and 60% of the estimated VO_{2max} calculated. Finally, the cycling workload was established in watts by using the following equation:

$$\frac{VO_{2max}\,(ml.min^{-1})-7}{10.8} \times weight(kgs).$$

Upon arrival for the second visit HR_{rest} was recorded and preexercise affect and self-efficacy determined immediately before exercise. Affective responses were obtained by participants verbally responding to a Likert scale. Instructions for each of the measures were given to participants. For example, instructions for the FS were as follows: "When participating in this exercise you may experience various changes in mood. Some people may find these changes pleasurable while other people may find them unpleasant. You may also find that your feelings fluctuate during the course of the exercise. Feel free to use the 10 points (-5 to $+5$) to describe how best you feel during the exercise period." Instructions for the FAS were as follows: "I want you to estimate how aroused you are feeling. By arousal I mean 'worked up.' You might experience high arousal in a variety of ways such as excitement, anxiety or anger. Low arousal might be experienced by you in a number of different ways such as relaxation, boredom or calmness."

Participants were then instructed to pedal at 50 revs·min^{-1} for a duration of 20 minutes at their predetermined workload. Heart rate (HR) was recorded every minute while RPE was recorded every 5 minutes during the 20 minute exercise bout. HR was also measured immediately following exercise. Affect was again measured at the 10th minute during and immediately following the 20th minute of cycling. Self-efficacy was also determined immediately following the 20-minute exercise bout.

Data Analysis

Physiological characteristics were analyzed using 1-way analysis of variance (ANOVA). Affective and self-efficacy outcomes and RPE ratings were analyzed using separate mixed design repeated-measures ANOVAs. Two levels corresponding to the age of the groups (younger and older) were used for the between-subjects factor. The within-subjects factor of time of measure represented the before, during, and immediately postexercise measures for the affective outcomes. Self efficacy data were analyzed using a 2 (age: younger and older) by 2 (time: before and post) mixed design. RPE responses were analyzed using a 2 (age: younger and older) by 4 (time: 5, 10, 15, 20 minutes during exercise) mixed design. When the assumption of sphericity was violated, the Hunydt-Feldt adjustments were used. Follow-up univariate contrasts were performed on significant effects to determine the significance of pairwise comparisons. Effect sizes (Cohen's d) accompanying the mean changes of the self-efficacy and affective responses were calculated by dividing the mean difference by the pooled standard deviation.[36] Bivariate correlation analysis was also used to determine whether relationships existed between self-efficacy and affective responses. Correlation analysis was also used to determine whether a relationship existed between the feeling scale and RPE responses.

Results

Descriptive statistics for demographic and physiological characteristics are presented in Table 1. ANOVA results revealed that the older women had higher resting systolic blood pressure (SBP$_{rest}$)[$F(1,48) = 7.423$, $P < .01$], resting diastolic blood pressure (DBP$_{rest}$)[$F(1,48) = 7.766$, $P < .01$], BMI [$F(1,48) = 30.029$, $P < .01$], and lower estimated VO$_{2max}$ [$F(1,48) = 74.916$, $P < .01$] compared with the younger women.

RPE Results

Descriptive statistics for RPE responses are summarized in Table 2. Sphericity was not satisfied (Mauchly's W = 0.375; $\chi^2 = 45.79$; df = 5, $P < .01$), therefore the Huynh-Feldt adjustment was used. Repeated-measures ANOVA indicated that age did not significantly differentiate RPE [$F(1,48) = 0.52$, $P < .81$] measures during exercise. This result suggests that an exercise stimulus variation did not exist, thus ensuring that valid comparisons of affective responses could be made. However, a significant main effect for time of measure was found [$F(1,48) = 22.64$, $P < .01$] for RPE responses. Post hoc analysis revealed that ratings reported at 20 minutes were significantly higher than ratings reported at 5 and 10 minutes of exercise, when collapsed across age.

Affective Responses

Descriptive statistics for self-efficacy and affective responses are summarized in Table 3. ANOVA analysis of the EFI responses revealed a significant main effect for time of measure [$F(1,48) = 7.23$, $P < .01$] for positive engagement. Pairwise comparisons revealed that positive engagement increased significantly immediately following exercise compared with before and during exercise, when collapsed across age groups. A significant main effect for age [$F(1,48) = 10.26$, $P < .01$]

Table 1 Demographic and Physiological Characteristics of Participants

	Younger women (n = 25)	Older women (n = 25)
Education %		
≤ 12 years	0	44
> 12 years	100	56
Marital status %		
Single	100	8
Married	0	76
Separated/divorced	0	16
Body Mass Index M ± SD	21.9 ± 2.43	29.2 ± 6.16*
Resting heart rate M ± SD	78.9 ± 7.7	71.5 ± 8.65
Resting SBP M ± SD	115.12 ± 8.17	126.56 ± 19.33*
Resting DBP M ± SD	72.9 ± 7.9	81.32 ± 12.84*
Estimated VO$_{2max}$ M ± SD	32.8 ± 3.74	22.08 ± 4.93*

*$P < .05$.

Table 2 Ratings of Perceived Exertion (RPE) (M ± SD)

RPE	Younger women (n = 25)	Older women (n = 25)
	M ± SD	M ± SD
5 minutes	11.20 ± .30	11.36 ± .40
10 minutes	12.16 ± .28	12.28 ± .42
15 minutes	12.88 ± .26	12.68 ± .42
20 minutes	13.28 ± .34	12.80 ± .45

Table 3 Self-Efficacy and Affective Responses before, during (10 Minutes), and After Exercise

	Younger women (n = 25)		Older women (n = 25)	
	M ± SD	Effect size	M ± SD	Effect size
Self efficacy				
Pre	79.2 ± 16.31	–	59.5 ± 25.26	–
Post	94.4 ± 12.06	−1.06	91.4 ± 14.32	−1.55
Positive engagement				
Pre	6.60 ± 2.16	–	7.92 ± 2.72	–
During	6.64 ± 2.25	−0.02	7.96 ± 1.88	−0.02
Post	7.04 ± 2.39	−0.17	9.48 ± 1.85	−0.81
Revitalization				
Pre	4.76 ± 2.04	–	4.52 ± 2.87	–
During	4.96 ± 1.45	−0.11	5.20 ± 2.45	−0.25
Post	5.68 ± 2.28	−0.37	7.40 ± 2.06	−0.97
Tranquility				
Pre	7.32 ± 2.17	–	6.44 ± 2.88	–
During	5.52 ± 2.40	0.78	7.04 ± 2.89	−0.21
Post	6.16 ± 2.54	−0.26	8.04 ± 2.17	−0.39
Physical exhaustion				
Pre	5.08 ± 2.54	–	3.12 ± 2.68	–
During	5.28 ± 2.54	−0.08	3.68 ± 3.03	−0.19
Post	5.64 ± 2.37	−0.14	2.48 ± 2.94	0.40
Feeling Scale				
Pre	2.76 ± 1.58	–	2.32 ± 2.19	–
During	1.52 ± 1.87	0.71	2.08 ± 1.77	0.12
Post	2.08 ± 1.49	−0.33	3.12 ± 1.59	−0.62
Felt Arousal Scale				
Pre	3.00 ± 0.76	–	3.16 ± 1.40	–
During	3.44 ± 0.87	−0.54	3.24 ± 1.09	−0.06
Post	3.76 ± 1.05	−0.33	3.80 ± 1.19	−0.49

was also found, whereby positive engagement responses were significantly higher in the older age group compared with the younger age group. No significant interaction between age and time of measure $[F(1,48) = 2.36, P < .12]$ was found.

ANOVA analysis of "revitalization" demonstrated a significant main effect for time of measure $[F(1,48) = 12.33, P < .01]$. Pairwise comparisons found that "revitalization" also increased significantly immediately following exercise compared with before and during exercise, when collapsed across age groups.

No significant effect for age $[F(1,48) = 1.76, P < .20]$ or interaction between age and time of measure $[F(1,48) = 3.25, P < .61]$ was found for "revitalization" responses.

Analysis of "tranquility" responses revealed a significant main effect for time $[F(1,48) = 3.43, P < .05]$ whereby "tranquility" significantly increased immediately following exercise compared with during exercise, when collapsed across age groups. A significant interaction was also found between time of measure and age for "tranquility" $[F(1,48) = 10.73, P < .01]$. Pairwise comparisons revealed that the younger age group had significantly lower "tranquility" responses during and postexercise compared with the older age group. There was no significant main effect for age [$F(1,48) = 1.89$, $P < .18$] for "tranquility" responses.

Analysis of "physical exhaustion" responses revealed a significant main effect for age [$F(1,48) = 13.21$, $P < .01$]. The younger age group had significantly higher "physical exhaustion" responses compared with the older age group. No significant main effect for time of measure [$F(1,48) = 0.70$, $P < .49$] or interaction between age and time of measure [$F(1,48) = 2.19$, $P < .13$] was found for "physical exhaustion" responses.

ANOVA analysis of the FS found a significant main effect for time of measure [$F(1,48) = 4.40$, $P < .02$] and a significant interaction between age and time of measure [$F(1,48) = 3.16$, $P < .05$]. When collapsed across age groups, FS responses significantly decreased during exercise compared with before and postexercise. The younger age group also had significantly lower FS responses immediately following exercise compared with the older age group. No significant main effect for age [$F(1,48) = 1.15$, $P < .29$] was found.

The FAS analysis found a significant main effect for time of measure [$F(1,48) = 8.43$, $P < .01$]. FAS responses significantly increased immediately following exercise compared with before and during exercise, when collapsed across age groups. No significant main effect for age [$F(1,48) = 0.00$, $P < 1.10$] or interaction between age and time of measure [$F(1,48) = 0.56$, $P < .56$] was found. Effect sizes for affective responses varied from small to high with the smallest change occurring in positive engagement ($ES = -0.02$) and the greatest change occurring in revitalization ($ES = -0.97$).

Self-Efficacy

ANOVA analysis of self-efficacy responses demonstrated a significant main effect for time of measure [$F(1,48) = 80.72$,

$P < .01$]. Pairwise comparisons revealed self-efficacy significantly increased immediately following exercise compared with before exercise, when collapsed across age groups. A significant main effect for age [$F(1,48) = 7.07$, $P < .02$] was also found. The younger age group had significantly higher overall self-efficacy compared with the older age group. Lastly, a significant interaction between age and time of measure [$F(1,48) = 10.15$, $P < .01$] was found, whereby the younger age group had significantly higher self-efficacy before exercise compared with the older age group. Effect sizes for self-efficacy change were in the high range for younger ($ES = -1.06$) and older ($ES = -1.55$) women.

Correlation Analysis

Bivariate correlations were used to determine whether relationships existed among self-efficacy and affective responses to exercise (Table 4). No significant correlations were found between self-efficacy before exercise and affective responses during exercise. However, a trend was observed between self-efficacy before exercise and "tranquility" ($r = .35$, $P = .08$) and "physical exhaustion" ($r = -.36$, $P = .07$) during exercise, suggesting that the more efficacious participants reported higher tranquility and lower levels of fatigue during exercise.

Significant correlations were found between self-efficacy immediately following exercise and "tranquility" ($r = .49$, $P = .01$), physical exhaustion ($r = -.60$, $P = .00$) and Feeling Scale ($r = .46$, $P = .02$) responses during exercise. These results suggest that participants who reported greater feelings of "tranquility," less fatigue, and more positive feeling states during exercise felt more efficacious immediately following exercise. A trend was also observed between self-efficacy immediately following exercise and "revitalization" during exercise ($r = .38$, $P = .06$), suggesting that participants reporting greater feelings of "revitalization" during exercise felt more efficacious

Table 4 Correlations between Self Efficacy before (Pre) and Immediately Following (Post) Exercise and Affective Responses during (10 Mins) and Immediately Following (Post) Exercise

	Pre self-efficacy	Post self-efficacy
Positive engagement 10 mins	.076	.029
Revitalization 10 mins	.162	.381
Tranquility 10 mins	.355	.486*
Physical exhaustion 10 mins	−.361	−.595**
Feeling Scale 10 mins	.210	.458*
Felt Arousal Scale 10 mins	−.181	−.342
Positive engagement post	−	.347
Revitalization post	−	.587**
Tranquility post	−	.397*
Physical exhaustion post	−	−.604**
Feeling Scale post	−	.294
Felt Arousal Scale post	−	−.026

* $P < .05$;
** $P < .01$.

immediately following exercise. No significant correlations were found between self-efficacy immediately following exercise and Felt Arousal Scale responses during exercise.

Significant correlations were found between exercise self-efficacy immediately following exercise and "revitalization" ($r = .59, P = .00$), tranquility ($r = .40, P = .04$), and "physical exhaustion" ($r = -.60, P = .00$) immediately following exercise. These results suggest that participants with greater postexercise self-efficacy have greater feelings of "revitalization," "tranquility," and less fatigue immediately following exercise.

Finally, correlation analysis was also conducted to determine whether a relationship existed between the RPE response and the FS and FAS responses reported during exercise and the RPE response reported at 20 minutes of exercise and FS and FAS responses immediately following exercise (Table 5). Significant correlations were found between the RPE and FS ($r = -.48, P = .00$) and FAS ($r = .303, P = .05$) responses during exercise, whereby a higher RPE response correlated with a lower FS and higher FAS response. A significant correlation was also found between RPE responses at 20 minutes of exercise and FS responses immediately following exercise ($r = -.525, P = .00$). Therefore, a higher RPE response at 20 minutes of exercise correlated with a lower Feeling Scale response immediately following exercise. No significant correlations were found between RPE responses at 20 minutes of exercise and FAS responses immediately following exercise.

Discussion

This investigation found that an acute bout of moderate-intensity exercise produced more positive and fewer negative affective states in both younger and older women. The results therefore do not support the hypothesis that older women would experience more negative affective states compared with younger women following an acute bout of exercise. In fact, for this group of women, age does not seem to have a deleterious effect on affective states during exercise. These findings are consistent with previous investigations on acute exercise bouts.[1,2]

However, the current findings are in contrast to Focht et al,[3] who found that both younger and older participants experienced more negative and less positive responses to an acute exercise bout. A possible explanation for the differences between the psychological responses may be due to the variation in methodology. Participants in the current study were working at a lower intensity of VO_{2max} compared with participants in Focht et al's study of 65% VO_{2max}. The sedentary individuals

may have perceived the higher intensity as overly challenging. RPE scores support this view. The current study's RPE scores ranged from "fairly light" to "somewhat hard" throughout the exercise bout. In contrast, RPE scores of participants in Focht et al's study ranged between "somewhat hard" and "hard." Negative relationships between exercise intensity and affective responses have been previously reported.[1,24,37] As physiological cues influence exercise-induced affect[10] it would be feasible that sedentary older women who experience physical exertion would have unpleasant affective responses.[22] For sedentary older women, the intensity of 60% VO_{2max} may elicit more favorable responses to an acute bout of exercise and may lead to the increased possibility of future exercise participation.

The finding that the older women experienced more positive than negative affective responses from the exercise bout was unexpected. Age-related physiological changes negatively affect an individual's PFC.[21] A 10% per decade decline in VO_{2max} occurs in sedentary adults from the age of 30 years.[38] In addition to physiological changes, aging also brings about changes in mood disturbance, namely increased negative affect and decreased positive affect.[39] It would therefore be expected that an exercise bout would elicit more negative responses from the older women. A possible explanation for these results is that the older women had a positive experience through mastery accomplishment. Exercise self-efficacy increased for both groups of women immediately following exercise. Self-efficacy is said to be specific to the task being performed.[13] Therefore, exercise self-efficacy levels may have increased for this particular task through a sense of accomplishment at completing 20 minutes of moderate intensity exercise. One exercise barrier for older adults is the perception that exercise will be tiring, causing concerns for their health.[40] However, the women were able to complete the exercise bout feeling no ill effects despite being fatigued during the task. This may have implications for future exercise participation. Giving sedentary older women the opportunity to successfully complete a moderate-intensity exercise activity may promote a sense of accomplishment and the perception that exercise can be an enjoyable experience. Repeated success in the chosen activity will raise mastery expectations through the acquisition of a skill for dealing with stressful situations.[13] This will ultimately increase efficacy beliefs.

However, while exercise self-efficacy increased for both groups of women, preexercise self-efficacy did differ as a function of age. The younger women experienced higher levels of task-specific exercise self-efficacy compared with the older women before the exercise bout. This would be in keeping with

Table 5 Correlations between Ratings of Perceived Exertion (RPE) at 10 and 20 Minutes and Feeling Scale and Felt Arousal Scale Responses during and Immediately Following Exercise

RPE	Feeling Scale during	Feeling Scale post	Felt Arousal Scale pre	Felt Arousal Scale post
10 mins	−.482**	–	.303*	–
20 mins	–	−.525**	–	.270

* $P < .05$;
** $P < .01$.

the idea that generational circumstances may influence exercise self-efficacy. Many older women believe that they are unable to perform an activity before a first attempt is made, due to a lack of experience or knowledge regarding exercise, particularly if they have been socially discouraged from participating in exercise in their younger years.[41] The lack of sporting opportunities as girls coupled with a strong social commitment to their families may result in older women lacking the confidence to pursue an exercise regimen at this time in their life.[41] These women have now found themselves in a new cultural period whereby they are being told that exercise is an essential component of good health.[40] Exercise and health professionals should consider the self-efficacy of older sedentary women when prescribing exercise. Identifying older women with lower exercise self-efficacy in the early stages of exercise adoption may benefit from informational and motivational instruction to increase their exercise efficacy beliefs.[42]

In regards to whether age would moderate basic affective responses, this study obtained mixed findings. Both groups of women experienced increases in the Felt-Arousal Scale following exercise compared with before and during exercise. In addition, Feeling Scale responses decreased from baseline during exercise for both groups, however this decrease did not persist for the older women when postexercise measures were taken. The older women experienced decreased fatigue and higher positive engagement before, during, and after exercise and higher tranquility levels during and postexercise. Increased revitalization, tranquility and positive engagement postexercise occurred for both groups. These findings suggest that while both groups perceived they were exerting themselves during the exercise bout, the older women found this exertion as a positive experience once they had completed the activity.[43] This further supports the idea that mastery accomplishment was perceived by the older women for completing a bout of moderate-intensity exercise. Past experiences in an exercise activity can therefore shape an individual's self-efficacy.

The fact that physical exhaustion, positive engagement, and tranquility were a function of age may also suggest that the older women had a more enjoyable exercise experience compared with the younger women. Exercise enjoyment is thought to have an influence on the psychological responses to exercise.[2] However, the current study did not measure exercise enjoyment and therefore can only speculate on this relationship. Further studies on the relationship between exercise enjoyment and the affective responses of women of differing ages are warranted.

A reciprocal relationship between self-efficacy and affective responses was demonstrated in the current study and is consistent with the literature.[1,3,17] Results of the correlation analysis revealed that participants who reported greater feelings of tranquility, less fatigue, and more positive feeling states during exercise felt more efficacious postexercise. In addition, participants with greater postexercise self-efficacy had greater feelings of revitalization, tranquility, and less fatigue postexercise. Bartholomew and Miller found participants who had perceived a strong sense of mastery accomplishment reported greater positive well-being following an acute exercise bout.[17] The

mastery experience mechanism may do well toward increasing future exercise self-efficacy for performing stationary cycling in this group of sedentary women.

A number of limitations in the current study should be addressed. The relatively small sample of participants means that interpretation of the current findings should be taken with caution. However, postexercise effect sizes were generally moderate to large, supporting the significant findings. Secondly, the findings are only relevant to sedentary women and may not be able to be replicated for male sedentary participants. As gender specific differences in psychological responses to exercise may exist, further studies including male sedentary participants or differences with active individuals of either gender is recommended. Thirdly, exercise enjoyment was not measured and therefore the author can only speculate as to whether the older participants found the exercise experience to be an enjoyable one. Lastly, only 1 exercise intensity of 60% VO_{2max} for a duration of 20 minutes was employed in the current study. Exercise bouts of varying intensities and durations may elicit quite different responses from participants.

In conclusion, this study found that older sedentary women did not experience more negative affective states following a bout of exercise compared with younger sedentary women. This would suggest that for this group of women, aging does not have an effect on affective states. The older women in particular experienced more positive affective states following a bout of moderate-intensity exercise. As advancing age is associated with an increased risk of chronic cardiorespiratory conditions it is important that older women maintain an active life.

References

1. McAuley E, Blissmer B, Katula J, Duncan TE. Exercise environment, self-efficacy and affective responses to acute exercise in older adults. *Psychol Health*. 2000;15:341–355. doi:10.1080/08870440008401997

2. Raedeke TD. The relationship between enjoyment and affective responses to exercise. *J Appl Sport Psychol*. 2007;19:105–115. doi:10.1080/10413200601113638

3. Focht BC, Knapp DJ, Gavin TP, Raedeke TD, Hickner RC. Affective and self-efficacy responses to acute aerobic exercise in sedentary older and younger adults. *J Aging Phys Act*. 2007;15:123–138. PubMed

4. Pronk, N.P., Crouse, S.F. & Rohack, J.J. Maximal exercise and acute mood response in women. *Physiol Behav*. 1995;57(1):1–4.10.

5. Young PT. The role of hedonic processes in the organization of behavior. *Psychol Rev*. 1952;59(4):249–262. PubMed doi:10.1037/h0057176

6. Gauvin L, Rejeski WJ. The exercise-induced feeling inventory: development and initial validation. *J Sport Exer Psychol*. 1993;15:403–423.

7. Rich SC, Rogers ME. Stage of exercise change model and attitudes toward exercise in older adults. *Percept Mot Skills*. 2001;93(1):141–144. PubMed doi:10.2466/pms.2001.93.1.141

8. Arent SM, Landers DM, Etnier JL. The effects of exercise on mood in older adults: a meta-analytic review. *J Aging Phys Act*. 2000;8:407–430.

9. Rejeski WJ, Focht BC, Messier SP. Obese, older adults with knee osteoarthritis: weight loss, exercise and quality of life. *Health Psychol.* 2002;21(5):419–426. PubMed doi:10.1037/0278-6133.21.5.419

10. Ekkekakis P, Petruzzello SJ. Acute aerobic exercise and affect. Current status, problems and prospects regarding dose-response. *Sports Med.* 1999;28(5):337–374. PubMed doi:10.2165/00007256-199928050-00005

11. Harris AH, Cronkite R, Moos R. Physical activity, exercise coping and depression in a 10-year cohort study of depressed patients. *J Affect Disord.* 2006;93(1-3):79–85. PubMed doi:10.1016/j.jad.2006.02.013

12. Annesi JJ. Relationship between changes in acute exercise-induced feeling states, self-motivation and adults' adherence to moderate aerobic exercise. *Percept Mot Skills.* 2002;94:425–439. PubMed

13. Bandura A. Self-efficacy: toward a unifying theory of behavioral change. *Psychol Rev.* 1977;84(2):191–215. PubMed doi:10.1037/0033-295X.84.2.191

14. Marcus BH, Selby VC, Niaura RS, Rossi JS. Self-efficacy and the stages of exercise behaviour change. *Res Q Exerc Sport.* 1992;63(1):60–66. PubMed

15. McAuley E, Blissmer B. Self-efficacy determinants and consequences of physical activity. *Exerc Sport Sci Rev.* 2000;28(2):85–88. PubMed

16. Sallis JF, Hovell MF. Determinants of exercise behaviour. *Exerc Sport Sci Rev.* 1990;18:307–330. PubMed doi:10.1249/00003677-199001000-00014

17. Bartholomew JB, Miller BM. Affective responses to an aerobic dance class: the impact of perceived performance. *Res Q Exerc Sport.* 2002;73(3):301–309. PubMed

18. McAuley E, Talbot H-M, Martinez S. Manipulating self-efficacy in the exercise environment in women: influences on affective responses. *Health Psychol.* 1999;18(3):288–294. PubMed doi:10.1037/0278-6133.18.3.288

19. Booth FW, Zwetsloot KA. Basic concepts about genes, inactivity and aging. *Scand J Med Sci Sports.* 2010;20:1–4. PubMed doi:10.1111/j.1600-0838.2009.00972.x

20. Kuk JL, Saunders TJ, Davidson LE, Ross R. Age-related changes in total and regional fat distribution. *Ageing Res Rev.* 2009;8(4):339–348. PubMed doi:10.1016/j.arr.2009.06.001

21. Tanaka H, Seals DR. Invited review: dynamic exercise performance in Masters athletes: insight into the effects of primary human aging on physiological functional capacity. *Physiology of Aging.* 2003;95:2152–2162. PubMed

22. Barnett F. Do physical activity levels influence the cardiovascular-related physiological characteristics of postmenopausal women? *Australas J Ageing.* 2009;28(4):216–218. PubMed doi:10.1111/j.1741-6612.2009.00389.x

23. McAuley E, Jerome GJ, Elavsky S, Marquez DX, Ramsey SN. Predicting long-term maintenance of physical activity in older adults. *Prev Med.* 2003;37:110–118. PubMed doi:10.1016/S0091-7435(03)00089-6

24. Treasure DC, Newbery DM. Relationship between self-efficacy, exercise intensity and feeling states in a sedentary population during and following an acute bout of exercise. *J Sport Exer Psychol.* 1998;20:1–11.

25. Thomas S, Reading J, Shephard R. Revision of the Physical Activity Readiness Questionnaire (PAR-Q). *Can J Sport Sci.* 1992;17(4):338–345. PubMed

26. McAuley E, Jacobson L. Self-efficacy and exercise participation in sedentary adult females. *Am J Health Promot.* 1991;5(3): 185–191. PubMed doi:10.4278/0890-1171-5.3.185

27. McAuley E, Mihalko SL. Measuring exercise-related self-efficacy. In Duda, J.L, ed. *Advances in sport and exercise psychology measurement.* Morgantown, WV: Fitness Information Technology; 1998: 371–390.

28. Tellegen A, Watson D, Clark LA. On the dimensional and hierarchical structure of affect. *Psychol Sci.* 1999;10(4):297–303. doi:10.1111/1467-9280.00157

29. Hardy C, Rejeski WJ. Not what but how you feel: the measurement of exercise-induced affect. *J Sport Exer Psychol.* 1989; 11:304–317.

30. Svebak S, Murgatroyd S. Metamotivational dominance: a multimethod validation of reversal theory constructs. *J Pers Soc Psychol.* 1985;48:107–116. doi:10.1037/0022-3514.48.1.107

31. Dunn EC, McAuley E. Affective responses to exercise bouts of varying intensities. *J Soc Behav Pers.* 2000;15(2):201–214.

32. Bozoian S, Rejeski WJ, McAuley E. Self-efficacy influences feeling states associated with acute exercise. *J Sport Exer Psychol.* 1994;16:326–333.

33. Borg GAV. Perceived exertion as an indicator of somatic stress. *Scand J Rehabil Med.* 1970;2:377–381. PubMed

34. Siconolfi SF, Cullinane EM, Carleton RA, Thompson PD. Assessing VO_{2max} in epidemiologic studies: modification of the Astrand-Ryhming test. *Med Sci Sports Exerc.* 1982;14(5):335–338. PubMed

35. Astrand PO, Ryhming I. A nomogram for calculation of aerobic capacity (physical fitness) from pulse rate during submaximal work. *J Appl Physiol.* 1954;7:218–221. PubMed

36. Cohen J. *Statistical power analysis for the behavioral sciences.* San Diego, CA: Academic Press; 1988.

37. McGowan RW, Talton BJ, Thompson M. Changes in scores on the profile of mood states following a single bout of physical activity: heart rate and changes in affect. *Percept Mot Skills.* 1996;83(3):859–866. PubMed doi:10.2466/pms.1996.83.3.859

38. Tanaka H, Seals DR. Endurance exercise performance in Masters athletes: age-associated changes and underlying mechanisms. *J Physiol.* 2008;586(1):55–63. PubMed doi:10.1113/jphysiol.2007.141879

39. Fillingim RB, Blumenthal JA. Psychological effects of exercise among the elderly. In: Seraganian P, ed. *Exercise psychology: the influence of physical exercise on psychological processes.* New York: Wiley; 1993:237–254.

40. O'Brien Cousins S. 'My heart couldn't take it': older women's beliefs about exercise benefits and risks. *J Gerontol.* 2000;55B(5):283–294.

41. Branigan KP, O'Brien Cousins S. Older women and beliefs about exercise risk: what has motherhood got to do with it? *J Women Aging.* 1995;7(4):47–66. doi:10.1300/J074v07n04_05

42. Barnett F, Spinks W. Exercise self-efficacy of post-menopausal women resident in the tropics. *Maturitas.* 2007;58(1):1–6. PubMed doi:10.1016/j.maturitas.2007.04.003

43. McAuley E, Courneya KS. The subjective exercise experiences scale (SEES): development and preliminary validation. *J Sport Exer Psychol.* 1994;16:163–177.

Critical Thinking

1. Why do you think that the older women experience more positive than negative affective responses after moderate-intensity exercise?

2. What are some of the major biological differences between younger and older women?

3. How do you think these differences affect exercise performance?

Create Central

www.mhhe.com/createcentral

Internet References

National Institutes of Health: Senior Health
http://nihseniorhealth.gov/exerciseforolderadults/healthbenefits/01.html

National Institute on Aging: Exercise and Physical Activity
www.nia.nih.gov/health/publication/exercise-physical-activity

FIONA BARNETT is with the Institute of Sport and Exercise Science, James Cook University, Townsville, Queensland, Australia.

Article

Prepared by: Elaina F. Osterbur, *Saint Louis University*

Physician Health

Cognitive Assessment in the Practice of Medicine: Dealing with the Aging Physician

Tania Haddad

Learning Outcomes

After reading this article, you will be able to:

- Discuss the normal process of cognitive aging.

- Identify the effects of aging on fluid and crystalized intelligence.

- Discuss the various solutions to handling the issue of cognitive decline in older physicians.

Over the past century we have observed an increase in the average life span, now approaching 80 years. As a result of increased longevity and economic realities, we have seen a dramatic shift in the age of retirement with some people working well past their mid-60s and often into their 70s.

A 2011 Jackson and Coker retirement survey reported 52 percent of physicians changed their retirement plans since the recession hit.[1] Many physicians practice well beyond the retirement age found among most working individuals. As a physician, it is an honor and a privilege to work without a defined retirement age. But the burning question is: Should there be?

Age-Related Neurocognitive Changes

A recent editorial in the *New York Times*[2] painfully described the involuntary surrender of the medical licenses of a 78-year-old vascular surgeon and a 77-year-old chairman of internal medicine. Both physicians were unaware of any problems.

The vascular surgeon had been reported to the Medical Board of California four years prior. However, it was not until he was referred for neuropsychological examination that proved to be grossly abnormal—demonstrating visual-spatial abnormalities, difficulty with fine motor movements along with an inability to retain information—that he was asked to surrender his license.

The chairman of the internal medicine program was noted by his peers to have cognitive changes. He had trained most of the physicians at the medical center and they were reluctant to confront him and so he continued working. An intervention was finally held by close colleagues and friends who expressed their deep concern and compassion. The doctor subsequently surrendered his medical license.

Normal aging involves sensory and neurocognitive changes. Common age-related sensory changes include impairment of hearing, visual acuity, depth perception and color discrimination.[3] Changes in neurocognitive function can be seen not only in the way knowledge and memory are processed but also in the way older individuals reason through clinical problems that are presented to them.

There is little doubt that clinical reasoning is also affected by aging. Fluid intelligence is the ability to reason through a problem such as finding your way out of a labyrinth. It is associated with age-related decline.[4] Crystallized intelligence represents knowledge that has accumulated over time. It remains largely unchanged until later in life.[4]

The differential effects of age on fluid and crystallized intelligence are well-demonstrated in a study[5] that evaluated the results of older candidates on the American Board of Internal Medicine recertification exam.

The older candidates had higher scores on stable knowledge and lower scores on questions relating to concepts that were new or that had changed over time. Candidates further out from training showed a decrease in scores when compared to their younger counterparts.

These data suggest that age-related decline in test performance may be secondary to examinations that concentrate on questions concerning current data more than on older concepts, and the inability or unwillingness of the physician to update their knowledge base.

Together the combination of age-related decline in analytic processing and reliance on crystallized intelligence[4] can lead to complacency and dependence on past experience in the handling of new problems.

This may cause overlook or neglect in making the appropriate diagnosis and possibly lead to inferior patient care.[4] As Henry David Thoreau said, "It's not what you look at that matters: it's what you see," the problem is "the eye cannot see what the mind does not know."

Using continuous performance testing (CPT), Tanja Mani, PhD,[6] evaluated the effects of aging on various attention factors (see Table 1 for definitions). A CPT is a sustained attention test often used to demonstrate attention deficits.

Participants ranging in age from 19 to 82 years old were asked to press the space bar after observing a target sequence of the letter "K" followed immediately by "A" under clear and noisy conditions.

Mani found that under both conditions accuracy of the tests decreased with age. False alarms and omission errors increased with age suggesting a decline in selective attention and ability to distinguish relevant from irrelevant information.

This decline in selective attention leads to a weakened inhibitory control that may submit one to greater vulnerability to distraction.[7] These results are consistent with those of others[8] but are in opposition to some studies[9, 10] that found that sustained attention was equivalent between different ages.

Determining Competency

The effects of aging are unavoidable. Loss of memory, changes in knowledge base, and the ability to respond appropriately to information presented are all part of the normal aging process.

The practice of anesthesiology is often compared to aviation, however the requirements to maintain currency and proficiency in commercial aviation are far more stringent. In addition to a mandatory retirement age of 65, enacted in 2007 by the Federal Aviation Administration, commercial airline pilots over the age

of 40 must obtain a medical evaluation every six months to act as pilot in command.

These requirements are irrespective of experience (hours of flight time) or rating.[11] The aviation medical evaluation is rigorous and involves neurological and psychological evaluation along with urinalysis and electrocardiogram (yearly after age 40).

These evaluations as well as various medical conditions can mandate early retirement. As with pilots, we as physicians have a social contract of accountability with the public. We take an oath at graduation to do no harm. Yet how do we, the medical community, ensure this?

Increased public concern about the quality and continued competency of physicians has been a major driving force for the change from voluntary recertification to providing time-limited certificates among medical boards.[12] A 2003 Gallup poll found that half of the public surveyed would find another doctor if they were aware their physician's board certification had expired.[13]

The majority of literature that supports recertification extrapolates outcomes data from studies comparing performance between physicians with primary certification and their non-certified counterparts. Because mandated recertification is fairly new, little if any evidence has demonstrated improvement in clinical outcomes from the process.

Only one study[14] evaluated the association between performance on the American Board of Internal Medicine Maintenance of Certification Exam and basic quality of care performance measures. Although this study found a positive correlation between examination score and most of the care measures, more research is required to firmly establish a relationship between the quality of care provided, clinical performance, and patient outcome as measured by cognitive examination.

In addition to a recertification examination, an ongoing accumulation of continued medical education (CME) credits is required. For decades, CME credits have been the accepted currency for physician education after training. It has been the belief that CME brings physicians up to date in their knowledge base, which subsequently leads to improvements in practice and patient outcomes.

However, despite its wide use and acceptance, little evidence exists to show that physicians who participate in CME retain or even use the acquired knowledge appropriately to improve patient care.[15–20] As one researcher noted,[21] "Without enabling or practice-reinforcing strategies, CME participation has little effect on changing physician behavior."

So how do we evaluate the aging physician to determine continued competency? Multiple studies have shown that physicians' self-assess poorly. In a survey of more than 500 retired orthopedic surgeons in which they were asked as to why they retired, the response "I no longer felt competent" was not listed by anyone.[22]

Another survey of surgeons reported that only they were the best judge of their own abilities to continue working.[3] One review[23] observed weak or no association between physicians' self-assessments and external assessments. Of particular import, however, is the finding of an inverse relationship between poor external assessment and the physician's self-assessment.

Table 1 Performance Test Factors Definitions

Sustained attention	Ability to maintain attention, to be alert and ready to act over a period of time.
Selective attention	Ability to distinguish between relevant and irrelevant information and to respond to relevant information while inhibiting response to irrelevant material.
False alarms	Responding to non targets or false recognitions.
Omission errors	Failing to respond to the target.

Does length of time in practice create competency or does accumulation of knowledge and experience help compensate for age-related decline in performance?[24]

The idea that practice makes perfect or that experience will win the day are common themes within medicine. However, the literature is replete with data demonstrating a negative correlation between performance and age that contradicts these well-known sayings.[25−30, 31−34]

One review[25] found that physicians who have been in practice for more years possess less factual knowledge, are less likely to adhere to appropriate standards of care and may have poorer outcomes.

Another researcher[26] demonstrated a 0.5 percent increase in acute myocardial infarction patient mortality for every year since the physician had graduated from medical school. A survey[27] of physicians to assess adherence to current cancer screening guidelines demonstrated that physicians with more than 20 years of practice were less likely to adhere to guidelines.

Another study[28] demonstrated that younger physicians tended to use newer strategies for the management of cardiovascular disease with better outcomes than their older counterparts.

One study[29] demonstrated increased litigation and severity of injury in anesthesiologists over age 65 compared to their younger counterparts. Finally, another researcher[30] analyzed publicly available data from the Oklahoma Board of Medical Licensure and Supervision to determine characteristics of disciplined physicians. They found that the rate of disciplinary action increased over time with each successive 10-year interval since licensure for males.

Although the cause of the increased disciplinary action is not clear, quality of care issues, incompetence, malpractice and negligence complaints were high on the list. Another study[34] found similar results with review of physicians disciplined by the California Medical Board.

Identifying and Managing Declining Competence

There are many variables that contribute to a physician's level of competence. When clinical competency is questioned, treatable and reversible causes should be sought. Although age is just one factor, the literature is replete with data associating increased age with declining performance.

Due to the wealth of information in support of this idea, some institutions have adopted automatic assessments of aging physicians. At the Driscoll Children's Hospital in Corpus Christi, TX,[2] neurocognitive examinations that assess skills specific to a physician's specialty—in conjunction with cognitive tests developed to assess the need for further neuropsychological evaluation[35, 36]—are used to evaluate physicians age 70 or older when up for reappointment.

This policy hopes to provide a more compassionate route to identify physicians with cognitive deficits before something bad happens and another license is involuntarily revoked.[2]

The Lucile Packard Children's Hospital in Palo Alto, CA, and the University of Virginia Medical Center in Charlottesville,

VA,[37] also begin screening doctors at age 70 for signs of cognitive decline.

In Canada, The College of Physicians and Surgeons of Ontario's Peer Assessment Committee found a correlation between older age, male gender, non-certified status, and rural practice as predictors of poor performance.[31] Additional research[32] demonstrated in both longitudinal and cross-sectional studies that advanced age correlated with a decline in performance. As a result of this association, physicians in Ontario are automatically selected for peer review assessment beginning at age 70.

Although there is strong evidence demonstrating a negative correlation between performance and increasing age, data of the characteristics of the participants of the Physician Assessment and Clinical Education (PACE) program between 2002 and 2005 report a mean age of 54.4 years.[38] In a 2012 interview, William Norcross, MD, reported the average age of doctors attending PACE to be about 62.[39]

In the United States, the PACE program receives its referrals from state medical boards, hospital medical staff committees, medical groups, health insurance companies and self-referral.

In Canada, the College of Physicians and Surgeons of Ontario (CPSO) licensing authority conduct comprehensive assessment of physicians when issues of competency are questioned. The Physician Review Program (PREP) consists of detailed assessment activities. Upon completion, each individual is assigned a rating of competency from I (no deficit) to VI (unsafe to practice even with supervision).

A study[39] evaluated the results of extensive remedial continuing medical education (supported by the CPSO) of five physicians whose competency had been questioned. The physicians underwent a three-year program. Upon conclusion of the remedial training only one physician's performance had improved, one physician's performance did not change and three physicians showed a decline in performance.

The physicians that showed a decline in performance had difficulty identifying areas of weakness during the training program in addition to demonstrating little ability to critically self-evaluate. The authors questioned possible early age-related cognitive decline or other conditions leading to neuropsychological deterioration.

In another study,[40] a combination of PREP scores and a battery of neuropsychological tests were administered to each physician. These scores combined predict the possibility that the individual's performance would be impaired by cognitive deficits. These scores were corrected for age with respect to age-appropriate normative data.

In this study, seven out of 27 physicians (ranging in age from 35 to 76) sent for competency evaluations were found to have moderate to severe cognitive problems. Physicians who demonstrated significant neuropsychological impairment also tended to perform poorly at PREP, and very few physicians who performed poorly at PREP had insignificant cognitive impairment.

From the graphic depiction of PREP results (Figure 1) 41 younger individuals received competency ratings from 1 to 4, while competency ratings for older individuals ranged from 3 to 6.

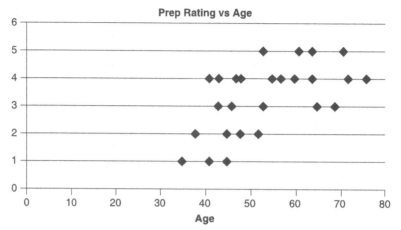

Prep Rating vs Age

Fig. 1. PREP rating categories: 1 = no deficit; 2 = minor deficit; 3 = moderate deficit; 4 = major deficit; 5 = unsafe to practice without supervision; 6 = unsafe to practice even with supervision.

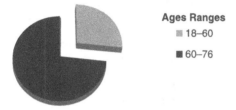

Global Congnitive Score 3, 4
(Percent of total)

Ages Ranges
■ 18–60
■ 60–76

Fig. 2. Neuropsychological categories: 0 = no difficulty; 1 = minimal difficulty; 2 = mild difficulty; 3 = moderate difficulty; 4 = major difficulty. Moderate (3) and severe (4) neuropsychological difficulties (the graphic depiction of the global cognitive scores) represents global cognitive scores for physicians age 18–60 and 60–76. Individuals older than 60 demonstrated more significant cognitive impairment, that perhaps suggests a lower likelihood of ability to remediate.

Competence cannot be passively maintained. Efforts to maintain up-to-date knowledge and skill sets are independent of age and must be our goal for all physicians.

The establishment of focused professional performance evaluation (FPPE) and the recently mandated Ongoing Professional Performance Evaluations (OPPE) require routine monitoring of competency, at least every six months, of all staff members regardless of age.

OPPE has taken many years to define. The challenge now, as noted by Jennifer Hunt, MD,[41] director of quality and safety at Massachusetts General Hospital, will be implementing a process to care for physicians who meet the "designated threshold for errors" allotted by the OPPE standards.

Currently many institutions describe no formal process available. Once OPPE standards become consistently performed and a process to care for individuals who fall below the standard effectively created, then and only then will we be able to maintain our oath to the public and justify the privilege that we have been bestowed.

Summary

Regardless of age, we are all aging physicians. Aging allows for professional maturity, experience and wisdom. Yet it may also present the danger that a physician does not keep pace with new knowledge and current practice standards.[42]

Aging is a fact of life, and unfortunately, we are unable to turn back the sands of time. Although the literature is replete with data demonstrating decreased performance, less adherence to guidelines, and increased disciplinary action with increased age, data from remedial training centers document a wide range of ages referred for evaluation. Thus age alone is not a predictor of neurocognitive decline.

Neurocognitive testing (NCT) is not without value. However, the manner in which it is being used by some institutions is somewhat controversial. At this time use of NCT can be routinely found in aviation, the military (NCAT—Neurocognitive Assessment Tool), sports medicine post-concussion evaluation, and some private commercial enterprises.

Neurocognitive testing is a sensitive and specific test for evaluating individuals who have already been "selected" by either disciplinary action or demonstration of questionable competency.

As noted by the American Academy of Neurology, Canadian Task Force on Preventive Health Care, and the U.S. Preventive Services Task Force, strong evidence supporting routine screening for mild cognitive impairment is lacking (PPV 45–55 percent)[43] while evidence of the harmful effects of false positive NCTs are well demonstrated.[44] False positive errors have been associated with suicide in patients diagnosed with early Alzheimer's dementia.[43]

As a society, we have an obligation to provide the best and safest care possible to the public, to do no harm, while preserving dignity and providing compassion to our colleagues.

It is stressful and painful to call into question the competency of a colleague. The possible loss of livelihood and self-worth to the individual can be devastating. The institution of the Ongoing Professional Performance Evaluations (OPPE) with routine balanced and impartial monitoring of all physicians regardless of age will hopefully allow for questions of competency to be cared for by an established system compassionately, comfortably, and with less stigma to the individual.

So to answer the question presented at the start of this review, should there be a mandatory retirement age in medicine? The answer must be no.

References

1. Jackson & Coker. Jackson & Coker retirement survey. August 2, 2011. (www.Jacksoncoker.com/documents/jcteriement_survey.pdf.)

2. Tarkan L. As doctors age, worries about their ability grow. *The New York Times.* Jan 24, 2011.

3. Greenfield LJ, Proctor MC. When should a surgeon retire? *Advances in surgery* 32:385–93, 1999.

4. Eva K. The aging physician: changes in cognitive processing and their impact on medical practice. *Acad Med* 77:10suppl: S1–S6, Oct. 2002.

5. Day SC, Norcini JJ, Webster GD, Viner ED, Chirico AM. The effect of changes in medical knowledge on examination performance at the time of recertification. *Proc Annu Conf Res Med Edu.* 27:139–44, 1988.

6. Mani TM, Bedwell JS, Miller LS. Age-related decrements in performance on a brief continuous performance test. *Archives of Clinical Neuropsychology.* 20(5):575–86, July, 2005.

7. McDowd JM, Oseas-Kreger DM, Filion DL. Inhibitory processes in cognition and aging. In: *New perspectives on interference and inhibition in cognition.* (Dempster F, Brainerd C, eds) New York: Academic Press, 1995, pp. 363–400.

8. Deaton JE, Parasuraman R. Sensory and cognitive vigilance: effects of age on performance and subjective workload. *Human Performance* 6(1):71–97, 1993.

9. Berardi A, Parasuraman R, Haxby JV. Overall vigilance and sustained attention decrements in healthy aging. *Experimental Aging Research.* 27(1):19–39, Jan-Mar, 2001.

10. Parasuraman R, Nestor P, Greenwood P. Sustained-attention capacity in young and older adults. *Psychology and Aging.* 4(3):339–45, Sept. 1989.

11. Federal Aviation Administration. Code of Federal Regulations: Part 67.

12. Freed GL, Dunham KM, Clark SJ, Davis MM. Perspectives and preferences among the general public regarding physician selection and board certification. *J Pediatr* 156;841–45, May 2010.

13. The Gallup Organization for the The American Board of Internal Medicine. Awareness of and attitudes toward board-certification of physicians. Princeton, NJ: The Gallop Organization, 2003 August.

14. Holmboe ES, Wang Y, Meehan TP, HO S, Starkey KS, Lipner RS. Association between maintenance of certification examination scores and quality of care for medicare beneficiaries. *Arch Intern Med.* 168(13)-:1396–1403, July 14, 2008.

15. Davis DA, Taylor-Vaisey A. Translating guidelines into practice. A systematic review of theoretic concepts, practical experience, and research evidence in the adoption of clinical practice guidelines. *CMAJ* 157:408–416, Aug. 15, 1997.

16. Schrock JW, Cydulka RK. Lifelong learning. *Emerg Med Clin N AM* 24:785–95, Aug. 2006.

17. Davis DA, Thomson Obrien MA, Freemantle N, Wolf FM, Mazmanian PE, Taylor-Vaisey A. Impact of formal continuing medical education. *JAMA* 282:867–74, Sept. 1, 1999.

18. Mazmanian PE, Davis DA. Continuing medical education and the physician as a learner. *JAMA* 288(9):1057–60, Sept. 4, 2001.

19. Grimshaw JM, Shirran L, Thomas R et al. Changing provider behavior: an overview of systematic reviews of interventions. *Med Care* 39(8Suppl):116–45, Aug. 2001.

20. Haddad T. Simulation and the MOCA (part 2). *Anesthesiology News* 38:5, May 2012.

21. Davis D. Does CME work? An analysis of the effect of educational activities on physician performance or healthcare outcome. *Int J Psychiatry Med.* 28(1)21–39, 1998.

22. Green SA. Clinical competence and the aging surgeon. Patient safety, ethical considerations must be respected. American Academy of Orthopedic Surgeons. 8(9):1–6, Sept. 2008.

23. Davis DA, Mazmanian PE, Fordis M, Harrison RV, Thorpe KE, Perrier L. Accuracy of physician self-assessment compared with observed measures of competence. *JAMA.* 296(9):1094–1102, Sept. 6, 2006.

24. Korinek LL, Thompson L, McRae C, Korinek E. Do physicians referred for competency evaluations have underlying cognitive problems? *Academic Medicine* 84(8):1015–21, Aug. 2008.

25. Choudhry NK, Fletcher RH, Soumerai SB. Systematic review: the relationship between clinical experience and quality of healthcare. *Ann Intern Med* 142(4):260–79, Feb. 2005.

26. Norcini JJ, Kimball HR, Lipner R. Certification and specialization: do they matter in the outcome of anterior myocardial infarction? *Acad Med.* 75(12):1193–8, Dec 2000.

27. Czaja R, McFall SL, Warnecke RB, Ford L, Kaluzny AD Preferences of community physicians for cancer screening guidelines. *Ann Intern Med* 120(7):602–8, Apr. 1, 1994.

28. Tocci G, Ferruci A, Guida P, Avogaro A, Corsini A, Cortese C, Giorda CB, Manzato E, Medea G, Mureddu GF, Riccardi G, Titta G, Ventriglia G, Zito G, Volpe M. Impact of physicians' age on the clinical management of global cardiovascular risk: analysis of the results of the evaluation of Final Feasible Effect of Control Training and Ultra Sensitization Educational Programme. *Int J Clin Pract.* 65(6):649–57, June 2011.

29. Tessler MJ, Shrier I, Steele RJ. Association between anesthesiologist age and litigation. *Anesth* 116(3):574–9, Mar. 2012.

30. Khaliq A A, Dimassi H, Huang CY, Narine L, Smego RA. Disciplinary action against physicians: who is likely to get disciplined? *American Journal of Medicine.* 118(7):773–7, July 2005.

31. Norton PG, Dunn EV, Soberman L. What factors affect quality of care? Using Peer Assessment Program in Ontario family practices. *Can Fam Physician* 1997;43:1793–44, Oct. 1997.

32. Norton PG. Faulkner D. A longitudinal study of performance of physicians' office practices: data from Peer Assessment Program in Ontario, Canada. *Jt Comm J Qual Improv* 25(5):252–8, May 1999.

33. Norman GR, Davis DA, Lamb S, Hanna E, Caulford P, Kalgas T. Competency assessment of primary care physicians as part of a peer review program. *JAMA* 270(9):1046–51, Sept. 1, 1993.

34. Kohatsu ND, Gould D, Ross LK, Fox PJ. Characteristics associated with physician discipline. A case control study. *Arch Intern Med* 164(6):653–8, Mar. 22, 2004.

35. Elwood RW. Microcog: assessment of cognitive functioning. *Neuropsychol Rev.* 11(12):89–100, June 2001.

36. Powell DH. *Profiles in cognitive aging.* Cambridge, Mass: Harvard University Press. 1994.

37. Heisel W. Q&A with Dr. William Norcross: Stopping Aging Doctors before they harm. USC Annenberg, Reporting on health, California endowment health journalism fellowship. April 30, 2012.

38. Norcross WA, Henzel TR, Freeman K, Milner-Mares J, Hawkins RE. Toward meeting the challenge of physician competence assessment: the University of California, San Diego Physician Assessment and clinical Education (PACE) Program. *Acad Med* 2009;84:1008–14.

39. Hanna E, Premi J, Turnbull J. Results of remedial continuing medical education in dyscompetent physicians. *Acad Med.* 75(2):174–6, Feb 2000.

40. Turnbull j, Carbotte R, Hanna E, et al. Cognitive difficulty in physicians. *Acad Med.* 75(2):177–81, Feb 2000.

41. Hunt J. OPPE & FPPE joint commission standards. PDF 2010 from [adasp.madoryconsulting.com/meetings/Old/2010/OPPE%20&%20 FPPE%20Joint%20Commission%20Standards%20-%20Hunt.pdf]

42. Weinberger SE, Duffy FD. Practice makes perfect . . . or does it? *Annals of Internal Medicine.* 142(4):302(3), Feb. 15, 2005.

43. Schoenberg MR. Computerized Neuropsychological assessment: the Good the Bad and the Ugly. www.thecjc.org/pdf/gco8/gco8-2.pdf.

Critical Thinking

1. Discuss the pros and cons of a policy that requires cognitive assessment as a requirement for job continuation.

2. Who are the stakeholders affected by policies that restrict employment?

Create Central

www.mhhe.com/createcentral

Internet References

The Joint Commission—Ongoing Professional Performance Evaluations (OPPE)

www.jointcommission.org/mobile/standards_information/jcfaqdetails.aspx?StandardsFAQId=213&StandardsFAQChapterId=74

Institute for Memory Impairments and Neurological Disorders

http://www.alz.uci.edu

TANIA HADDAD, DMD, MD, is an anesthesiologist and partner at Valley Anesthesiology Consultants in Arizona.

Article

Prepared by: Elaina F. Osterbur, *Saint Louis University*

Treatment of Alzheimer's Disease

Yaso Shan

Learning Outcomes

After reading this article, you will be able to:

- Identify the definition and prevalence, pathology, and multiple classification systems of Alzheimer's disease.

- Discuss the theories of development of Alzheimer's disease.

- Discuss current treatment methods and the social/emotional dilemmas in the face of Alzheimer's disease.

Introduction

More than a century ago Alois Alzheimer characterised a disease in a patient who had died from an unusual mental illness (Alzheimer 1907). It is surprising how little is still known and understood about the aetiology, pathogenesis, treatment, management and prevention of AD (Goedert 2009). Diagnosis is difficult, particularly in the early stages, with confirmed diagnosis only possible once dementia has manifested to the point where the distinction between mild cognitive impairment (MCI), arguably a normal part of the ageing process, and AD is not so subtle, precluding any confusion or overlap in symptoms.

So, why has there been such little progress in advancing our understanding of this devastating and incurable disease? The answers may lie in the complexity of human beings and assumptions about normal ageing compared with what constitutes AD and the differences between the two. Experiments on mice have demonstrated significant success in possible drug treatment strategies based on current understanding of pathophysiological mechanisms, yet have failed in clinical trials. Bapineuzumab, for example, demonstrated clear benefits in mice but failed to improve cognition and daily function compared with placebo in patients (Castillo 2012).

Definition and Prevalence

AD is the most common form of dementia. It is a degenerative, incurable and terminal disease. It is the most common form of senile dementia and, along with cerebrovascular disorders, the leading cause of dementia in our population (Alzheimer's Society 2012). On a biological level, AD is described as a clinicopathological state literally meaning the 'loss of the ability to think' (Gandy 2005). Clinically, patients exhibit progressive cognitive failure including loss of the ability to form and retrieve new memories, changes in personality and a loss of the ability to navigate even the most familiar environments. Ultimately, all cortical function is lost and death occurs as a complication of the terminally bed-bound state, for example, with pneumonia or sepsis (Lublin and Gandy 2010). There is also a decline in reasoning, which involves establishing connections, forming judgements and making decisions. However, there is disagreement about the extent of some of these symptoms prior to diagnosis and about the basic nature of the disease itself even among AD specialists. That controversy is no better illustrated than in contemplation of how the disease is initiated at the molecular level (Gandy 2005).

Ageing populations have increased the prevalence of AD. The disease constitutes 62 per cent of all cases of dementia and there were 800,000 people in the UK with a form of dementia in 2012 (more than 17,000 of whom were under 65) (Alzheimer's Society 2012); the number of cases is expected to rise to more than 1.7 million by 2051.

Pathology

AD is defined by a characteristic loss of hippocampal and cerebrocortical neurons (Lublin and Gandy 2010). These regions control memory, thought, language, attention, perception and consciousness. The structural changes in this neurodegenerative process involve the accumulation of a protein called amyloid (which deposits outside the neurones) and neurofibrillary tangles (NFTs), which accumulate inside the neurones. The cerebral amyloid in AD is deposited as military structures known as plaques, which primarily consist of the amyloid-beta (Aβ) peptide (Lublin and Gandy 2010).

Aβ peptide was identified in 1984 as the major constituent that characterises AD (Lublin and Gandy 2010). These amyloid plaques and NFTs have long been regarded as the 'signature' pathological lesions of AD (Armstrong 2011). The discovery of Aβ (Glenner and Wong 1984) as the most important molecular constituent of these plaques resulted in the formulation of the 'Amyloid Cascade Hypothesis' or ACH (Hardy and Higgins 1992), the most important model of the molecular pathology of AD developed over the last 20 years. Essentially, the ACH proposes that the deposition of Aβ is the initial pathological event in the disease leading to the formation of NFTs, cell death and, ultimately, dementia (Armstrong 2009).

ACH has a number of limitations that arise from a lack of understanding of the association between plaques and NFTs (if one exists at all). Of the two original cases described by Alzheimer, both had numerous plaques but only one of them had significant numbers of NFTs (Graeber *et al* 1997), thus creating a controversy that persists to this day as to the relative significance of the two lesions. Armstrong (2011) challenges the ACH with questions on the relationship between the pathogenesis of amyloid plaques and NFTs, and the relationship and significance of these lesions to disease pathogenesis, and suggests limitations to the hypothesis:

- Amyloid plaques and NFTs may be reactive products resulting from neurodegeneration in AD rather than being its cause.
- There is no generally accepted mechanism to explain how the deposition of Aβ leads to the formation of NFTs.

Classification

AD does not develop in a characteristic pattern for all those affected, notably in its onset. Therefore, the disease is classified according to the following (Armstrong 2011):

- Early onset (<65 years)
- Late onset/sporadic AD (SAD)
- Familial AD (FAD)

Early onset AD (<65 years) is usually caused by autosomal dominant mutations in the genes for amyloid precursor protein (APP), presenilin 1 (PS1 or PSE1) and presenilin 2 (PS2 or PSE2). This form of AD accounts for approximately 2–5 per cent of all AD cases (Blennow *et al* 2006). First degree relatives of patients with AD are at higher lifetime risk of developing the disease than the rest of the population (Green *et al* 2002). The risk may be partly due to the presence of the allele Apoε4 (apolipoprotein ε4), which is the only proven genetic factor of risk so far identified in the development of both the early- and late-onset forms of AD (Corder *et al* 1994). The factor increases susceptibility to AD but it is neither necessary nor sufficient for the development of the disease.

Late onset AD or sporadic AD (SAD) is the most common form of AD, accounting for more than 90 per cent of cases and usually occurs after 65 years of age. SAD affects almost 50 per cent of people over the age of 85 and may or may not be hereditary (Alzheimer's Disease Health Center 2012).

Familial AD (FAD) is a rare form of AD that is known to be entirely inherited. In affected families, members of at least two generations have had AD, with a much earlier onset (often in the 40s) (Alzheimer's Disease Health Center 2012). Some sources categorise this along with early-onset AD (Alzheimer's Society 2013). The total known number of cases of FAD worldwide is about 200 people with mutations in three genes shown to be causative of FAD (alzheimersillness.com 2013). The three genes involved account for 30–50 per cent of all autosomal dominant early-onset cases, or around 10 per cent of familial early onset cases (Binetti 2009). The genetic link in some late onset cases of AD (in people aged 65 and over) is more complex than the link for younger people. The presence of a positive family history in the late onset cases is considered as a risk factor, but a clear autosomal dominant pattern of inheritance is rare (Binetti 2009). Recent experiments in mice have added weight to the idea that AD is driven by an infection-like spread of protein aggregates in the brain (Schnabel 2012).

Current Evidence and Theories

Those working on AD research study not only the oligomer theory (Table 1) but also other aspects that may influence the disease profile:

- Oxidative stress.
- Mitochondrial dysfunction.
- Prion/transmission.
- Genetics.
- Inflammation and immune mechanisms.
- Amyloid proteins (Aβ, tau, oligomers).
- Cerebrovascular events and other risk factors.

Oxidative Stress

Free radicals formation can occur as part of normal metabolism. Sometimes, the immune system purposefully creates them to neutralise pathogens (Knight 2000). Normally, the body can handle free radicals, but if antioxidants are unavailable, or if the free radical production becomes excessive, damage can occur (Christen 2000). Of particular importance to AD is that free radical damage accumulates with age. The oxidative stress (OS) hypothesis proposes that the ageing process in the brain is associated with a progressive imbalance between the anti-oxidant defences and the pro-oxidative species. This imbalance can occur as a result of either an increase in free radical production or a decrease in antioxidant defence (Gella and Bolea 2011).

Mitochondrial Dysfunction

Mitochondria are regulators of both energy metabolism and cell death pathways. Extensive literature exists supporting a role for mitochondrial dysfunction and oxidative damage in the pathogenesis of AD (Moreira *et al* 2010).

Prion/Transmission

There is the possibility that some of the SAD cases may arise from an infectious process which occurs with other neurological diseases caused by prions such as CJD. Recent studies (Morales *et al* 2012) on intracellular and extracellular protein aggregation suggest that those aggregates are capable of crossing cellular membranes and can directly contribute to the pathogenesis including AD. Once initiated, neuropathological changes might spread in a 'prion-like manner' and disease progression is associated with intracellular transfer of pathogenic protein (Brundin *et al* 2010).

Table 1 History of Theories about Alzheimer's Disease (1970s to Present)

Date/Theory	Comment
1970s–1980s: Alzheimer's disease is a suspected prion disease	Researchers noted similarities between AD and transmissible spongiform encephalopathies such as scrapie and Creutzfeldt–Jakob disease.
1980s–1990s: Plaques cause AD	Alzheimer's plaque proteins were successfully isolated in 1984 and referred to as amyloid beta (Aβ). It was shown to be quite different to scrapie amyloids. Aβ was determined as a fragment of a larger neuronal membrane protein called amyloid precursor protein (APP) coded by a gene on chromosome 21.
Early 1990s-early 2000s: Confusion and debate	Many of the transgenic mice that over-expressed APP developed the typical brain plaques associated with AD but they did not develop the other major AD amyloid (NFTs), which are made of tau protein, found inside the neurones. These mice also failed to show the profound neuronal losses and memory failures seen in human AD. The NFTs correlated better with dementia.
Late 1990s-present: The oligomeric prion hypothesis	Early experiments showed that Aβ, besides forming plaques can also cluster into soluble 'oligomers' made of comparatively few copies of Aβ. Oligomers were thought to exist only fleetingly as intermediate aggregates on the way to form complex plaques.
	Circumstantial evidence suggests that build-up of Aβ aggregation occurs over decades; it is this which represents the last, lethal stage of disease.

(Adapted from Schnabel 2012)

Genetics

Most AD lacks a predictable, autosomal dominant mode of inheritance (Gandy 2005). While APP and the presenilins (PS1 and PS2) constitute the only known AD genes, at least one important generic risk factor is known for about 25 per cent of the population with AD, and that is the Apoε4 genotype (Mayeux *et al* 1993). However, efforts to link Apoε4 with Aβ accumulation have produced mixed results (Gandy 2005).

Inflammation and Immune Mechanisms

Evidence for the involvement of inflammatory processes in the pathogenesis of AD has been documented for some time (Zotova *et al* 2010). However, it is only recently that inflammation itself has been hypothesised in AD pathology. Much of the data relates to outcomes of two major inflammation-relevant treatment strategies in AD: the use of anti-inflammatory drugs and immunisation against Aβ (Zotova *et al* 2010). For any inflammatory response, there has to be a challenge; the immune system's inflammatory response is after all the body's defence mechanism to a challenge, insult or injury. The type of inflammation in the AD brain is not well defined; it could be a consequence of the disease with the production of Aβ as a direct immune response to a challenge (unknown at present), pointing to an inability of microglia (the brain's immune cells) to clear away ever-growing neuronal debris due to extensive neurodegeneration and synaptic loss. Mixed and often contradictory findings with respect to inflammation in AD indicate the complexity and multifunctional role of the immune system (Zotova *et al* 2010). Inflammation in the CNS (as in the periphery) is a mixture of both destructive and rebuilding processes. It is this balance between the two processes that determines the overall integrity of the tissue or the whole organism (Rogers *et al* 2002). Therefore inflammation should not be viewed as wholly detrimental or wholly beneficial in AD.

Amyloid Proteins (Aβ, Tau, Oligomers)

The build-up of amyloid plaques has characterised AD and has received the bulk of the attention in this pathology. However, there is a gulf in opinion as to whether these plaques are toxic, protective or inert. Of great interest more recently is the significance of the free-floating oligomers (intermediary amyloid proteins), which is gaining prominence as the real culprit in the neurotoxicity that is characteristic of AD (Gandy *et al* 2010).

Cerebrovascular Events

It has been suggested that patients with a clinical history of stroke have an increased risk of developing AD particularly in the presence of vascular risk factors (Honig *et al* 2003). Furthermore, 'silent' cerebral or brain infarcts or silent brain ischemia (SBI) (identified by neuroimaging techniques), even in patients with no history of transient ischaemic attacks (TIAs) or stroke, can contribute to the loss of memory and cognitive function in the elderly. It was found that SBI more than doubles the risk of dementia including AD (Vermeer *et al* 2003, 2007) and AD patients with SBI have lower global cognitive function scores than patients with pure AD (Song *et al* 2007).

Treatment

There are no drug treatments available that can cure AD. At best, medicines abate or improve symptoms, temporarily slow

Table 2 Risk Factors Associated with Alzheimer's Disease

Risk factor hypothesis	Comment
Smoking	Increased risk of Alzheimer's disease (AD) (meta-analysis).
Alcohol	Increased risk of AD.
Overweight and obesity	The higher the BMI, the higher the risk of AD.
BP and management of hypertension	Increased BP, increased risk (observational studies). Antihypertensive drugs offer a protective effect.
Hypercholesterlaemia and statin therapy	Increased risk in middle-aged people 20 years later. Statins reduce risk.
Nutritional factors	Increased antioxidant intake, reduced risk.Increased saturated fat diet, reduced risk.Increased omega 3 EFAs, reduced risk.
Diabetes Mellitus	Diabetes increased risk of AD.Also increased risk of vascular dementia.
CVS and cerebrovascular diseases	Increased risk in stroke patients.Increased incidence of AD in CVD patients.
Psychosocial factors	
Education and socioeconomic status	Low status increased risk.
Social network and social engagement	Poor network and engagement leads to reduced cognitive function & dementia.Social isolation leads to an increased risk.
Physical activity	Physical activity delays onset of dementia and AD (reduced risk).
Mental activity	Protective effect against dementia and AD (reduced risk).

(Adapted from Povova *et al* 2012)

down progression and manage the various symptoms associated with the disease and this may be unique to each patient. Early detection is always advised to delay progression as treatments work best in the early stages of the disease (Hartz *et al* 2010). Acetylcholine (ACh) is a key neurotransmitter in the brain signalling short-term memory and learning. It is broken down by the enzyme acetylcholinesterase, which is in excess in the AD brain. Glutamate is the most common neurotransmitter in the brain and is involved in learning and memory. Dying brain cells in AD release excess amounts of glutamate that causes harm to the brain by over-stimulating healthy brain cells.

The choice of drug for any given patient is mostly determined by the stage of the disease with donepezil, rivastigmine and galantamine prescribed for mild to moderate AD and memantine for moderate to severe AD, who are intolerant to or have a contraindication to cholinesterase inhibitors (National Institute for Health and Care Excellence (NICE) Guidelines March 2011).

New Approaches

The following list summarises the various treatment strategies currently being considered in light of recent advancements in AD research (Lane *et al* 2012):

- Anti-plaque strategies with monoclonal Ab (anti-Aβ42 Ab: oligomeric Aβ42 (for example, Bapineuzumab®, Solanezumab®, Crenezumab®).
- Attack or disrupt the prion-like transmissibility of protein aggregates.
- Target inflammatory pathways/mechanisms on the basis that inflammation is deleterious not beneficial as a result

of an initial trigger or immune challenge (if so, identify that challenge).

- Treatments that mimic the APP gene variant that confers protection against AD.
- Monoclonal Ab or gene therapy/strategy to target the Apoε4 variant.
- Disrupt or inhibit the enzymatic cleavage of APP into amyloid. For example, to inhibit the secretases, BACE1, PS1 or PS2 (such as Semagacestat® a γ−secretase inhibitor).
- Correct or target mitochondrial dysfunction.
- Antioxidant therapy to tackle oxidative stress.

Preventative Strategies

Little is known on whether AD can be prevented. Technological progress is being made on early detection that can make it possible for those with a family history of AD to be vigilant about symptoms and take advantage of assessments early on (McGuire *et al* 2006). This is really based on the premise that AD is a response to injury (Mcguire *et al* 2006); some go on to be healthy as clearing away of plaques is at a sufficient rate to prevent deleterious build-up and some go on to develop dementia and AD.

Predicting Risk

The biggest risk factor is age. However, although risk increases with age, the mechanisms need clarifying so that measures can be taken to give those at risk a chance to plan for that eventuality. Genetic counselling is available for those at risk; given that

Table 3 Current Drug Treatments for Alzheimer's Disease

	Proprietary name (trade name)	Pharmacological mode of action
Cholinesterase inhibitors		Inhibits the enzyme acetylcholinesterase from breaking down the neurotransmitter acetylcholine (ACh). ACh is essential for vital communication between the nerve cells in the brain; the loss of communication is directly linked to the severity of the symptoms associated with AD.
• Donepezil hydrochloride	Aricept®	
• Rivastigmine	Exelon®	
• Galantamine	Reminyl®	
NMDA receptor antagonists		Memantine blocks glutamate, another neurotransmitter which is in excess in AD pathology. However, unlike ACh, excess glutamate further damages brain cells. Therefore, memantine protects brain cells by blocking these effects of excess glutamate.
Memantine	Exiba®	

(Adapted from NICE 2011, Alzheimer's Society 2012)

there is little certainty of how genes link with disease onset, this may be counterproductive by creating a sense of worry unnecessarily.

Dilemmas

The task of professionals who come into contact with patients (psychiatrists, clinical psychologists, community nurses, mental health nurses, GPs, home helps/healthcare assistants, social services, solicitors, police and other authorities) is not an easy one. This condition has a profound and devastating impact on patients and their families.

There is the danger of relying on a lay person's prototype of mental decline where a family member, or carer, has ulterior motives (such as financial gain). Conversely, there may be those in the family who are eager to label a relative showing worrying signs of dementia as being perfectly normal, delaying any prompt treatment. Professionals should remember the vulnerability of patients facing a possible diagnosis of AD and the fear and anxiety that it invokes, not only in those affected but also family members who may worry about being at risk. Given the difficulties in making a diagnosis (especially in the early stages), there are a number of uncertainties and obstacles that make treatment and management of AD particularly difficult. Some of these dilemmas are:

- What is the best point at which power of attorney should be implemented?
- If there is a family history of AD and how worthwhile is genetic counselling? Knowledge can be devastating so can steps be taken to mitigate the risk. Is there sufficient progress in treatment strategies for people diagnosed as being 'at risk'?
- What recourse is there for family members who disagree about the mental capacity of a patient when AD specialists and professionals cannot agree on diagnosis or whether the patient retains the ability to make decisions independent of family influence?
- How much emphasis is given to changes in personality and behaviour, including reasoning abilities, as a diagnostic tool given that most of the cognitive assessments focus on memory and recall?
- Should society be more sympathetic to those who leave or divorce their partner/spouse who has AD because

they are no longer the person/personality they once were or should they stay and honour the 'in sickness and in health' commitment of all relationships?
- How can society, and health and social care in particular, be better integrated to support the needs of people with AD so that they are not to be regarded as a burden?
- What is the right time to advise admitting someone to a care home even if they exhibit moments of extreme lucidity and clarity?
- What support services are available to the carers of AD patients who seek specialist help, counselling or even psychological intervention in a climate of cuts, efficiency savings and a recession?

Conclusion

AD presents a unique problem to an ageing society, not only in terms of cost of care but also in progressing towards effective treatments that can halt the advancement of the disease or reverse its damage to provide a notable quality of life for as long as possible. Questions on best care options will continue to dominate until sufficient progress can be made on the very nature of AD, its pathogenesis and treatments, or even a cure, which seem a long way off at present.

References

Alzheimer A (1907) On a peculiar disease of the cerebral cortex. *Allgemeine Zeitschrift fur Psychiatrie und Psychish-Gerichtlich Medicin.* 64, 146–148.

Alzheimer's Disease Health Center (2012) *Types of Alzheimer's Disease.* www.webmd.com/alzheimers/guide/alzheimers-types (Last accessed: June 4 2013.)

alzheimersillness.com (2013) *2007–2009 Familial Alzheimers Disease - Alzheimers 'What Is Familial Alzheimer's Disease - Early Onset Alzheimers?'* tinyurl.com/mtb8tuv (Last accessed: 4 June 2013.)

Alzheimer's Society (2012) Factsheets.tinyurl.com/kvwmqsy (Last accessed: June 11 2013.)

Alzheimer's Society (UK) (2013) *Genetics of Dementia* www.alzheimers.org.uk/factsheet/405 (Last accessed: June 5 2013.)

Armstrong RA (2009) Alzheimer's Disease and the Eye. *Journal of Optometry.* 2, 3, 103–111.

Armstrong RA (2011) The pathogenesis of Alzheimer's disease: a reevaluation of the 'Amyloid Cascade Hypothesis'. *International Journal of Alzheimer's Disease.* February 7, 630865. doi: 10.4061/2011/630865

Binetti G (2009) *Familial Alzheimer's Disease.* Alzheimer Europe. tinyurl.com/lr5ojvy (Last accessed: June 3 2012.)

Blennow K, de Leon MJ, Zetterberg H (2006) Alzheimer's disease. *Lancet.* 368, 387–403.

Brundin P, Melki R, Kopito R (2010) Prion-like transmission of protein aggregates in neurodegenerative diseases. *Nature Reviews Molecular Cell Biology.* 11, 4, 301–307.

Castillo M (2012) *Anticipated Alzheimer's Drug Bapineuzumab Shows No Patient Benefits in Trial.* CBS News. tinyurl.com/ko49mxh (Last accessed: December 11 2012.)

Christen Y (2000) Oxidative stress and Alzheimer's disease. *American Journal of Clinical Nutrition.* 71(suppl), 621S–629S.

Corder EH, Saunders NJ, Risch WJ *et al* (1994) Protective effects of polipoprotein E type 2 allele for late onset Alzheimer disease. *Nature Genetics.* 7, 180–184.

Gandy S (2005) The role of cerebral amyloid β accumulation in common forms of Alzheimer disease. *Journal of Clinical Investigation.* 115, 5, 1121–1129.

Gandy S, Simon AJ, Steele JW *et al* (2010) Days-to-criterion as an indicator of toxicity associated with human Alzheimer amyloid-β oligomers. *Annals of Neurology.* 67, 6, 220–230.

Gella A, Bolea I (2011) Oxidative stress in Alzheimer's Disease: pathogenesis, biomarkers and therapy. De La Monte S (Ed) *Alzheimer's Disease Pathogenesis-Core Concepts, Shifting Paradigms and Therapeutic Targets* InTech, tinyurl.com/kkta4sh (Last accessed: June 4 2013.)

Glenner GG, Wong CW (1984) Alzheimer's disease and Down's syndrome: sharing of a unique cerebrovascular amyloid fibril protein. *Biochemical and Biophysical Research Communications.* 22, 3, 1131–1135.

Goedert M (2009) Oskar Fischer and the study of dementia. *Brain.* 132, 4, 1102–1111.

Graeber MB, Kösel S, Egensperger R *et al* (1997) Rediscovery of the case described by Alois Alzheimer in 1911: historical, histological and molecular genetic analysis. *Neurogenetics.* 1, 1, 73–80.

Green RC, Cupples LA, Go R *et al* (2002) Risk of dementia among white and African American relatives of patients with Alzheimer disease. *JAMA.* 287, 329–336.

Hardy JA, Higgins GA (1992) Alzheimer's disease: the amyloid cascade hypothesis. *Science.* 256, 5054, 184–185.

Hartz AMD, Miller DS, Bauer B (2010) Restoring blood-brain barrier P-Glycoprotein reduces brain amyloid in a mouse model of Alzheimer's Disease. *Molecular Pharmacology.* 77, 5, 715–723.

Honig LS, Tang M-X, Albert S *et al* (2003) Stroke and the risk of Alzheimer disease. *Archives of Neurology.* 60, 1707–1712.

Knight JA (2000) Review: free radicals, antioxidants, and the immune system. *Annals of Clinical & Laboratory Science.* 30, 2, 145–158.

Lane RF, Shineman DW, Steele JW *et al* (2012) Beyond amyloid: the future of therapeutics for Alzheimer's disease. *Advances in Pharmacology.* 64, 213–71. doi: 10.1016/B978-0-12-394816-8.00007-6.

Lublin AL, Gandy S (2010) Amyloid-β oligomers: possible roles as key neurotoxins in Alzheimer's disease. *Mount Sinai Journal of Medicine.* 77, 43–49.

Mayeux R, Stern Y, Ottoman R *et al* (1993) The apolipoprotein epsilon 4 allele in patients with Alzheimer's disease. *Annals of Neurology.* 34, 752–754.

McGuire BE, Whyte N, Hardardottir D (2006) Alzheimer's Disease in down syndrome and intellectual disability: a review. *Irish Journal of Psychology.* 27, 3/4, 114–129.

Morales R, Duran-Aniotz C, Castilla J (2012) De novo induction of amyloid-β deposition in vivo. *Molecular Psychiatry* 17, 1347–1353.

Moreira PI, Carvalho C, Zhu X *et al* (2010) Mitochondrial dysfunction is a trigger of Alzheimer's disease pathophysiology. *Biochimica et Biophysica Acta.* 1802, 1, 2–10.

National Institute for Health and Care Excellence (2011) *Alzheimer's Disease—Donepezil, Galantamine, Rivastigmine and Memantine (TA217)* www.nice.org.uk/guidance/TA217 (Last accessed: June 2 2013.)

Povova J, Ambroz P, Bar M *et al* (2012) Epidemiological of and risk factors for Alzheimer's disease: a review. *Biomedical Papers.* 156, 2, 108–114.

Rogers J, Strohmeyer R, Kovelowski CJ *et al* (2002) Microglia and inflammatory mechanisms in the clearance of amyloid beta peptide. *Glia.* 40, 260–269.

Schnabel J (2012) *Alzheimer's Disease: Return of the Prion Hypothesis.* The Dana Foundation http://dana.org/news/features/detail.aspx?id=35584 (Last accessed: June 2 2013.)

Song I-U, Kim J-S, Kim Y-I *et al* (2007) Clinical significance of silent cerebral infarctions in patients with Alzheimer disease. *Cognitive and Behavioral Neurology.* 20, 93–98.

Vermeer SE, Prins ND, den Heijer T *et al* (2003) Silent brain infarcts and the risk of dementia and cognitive decline. *New England Journal of Medicine.* 348, 2115–1222.

Vermeer SE, Longstreth WT, Koudstaal PJ (2007) Silent brain infarcts: a systematic review. *The Lancet Neurology.* 6, 611–619.

Zotova E, Nicholl JAA, Kalaria R *et al* (2010) Inflammation in Alzheimer's disease: relevance to pathogenesis and therapy. *Alzheimers Research & Therapy.* 2, 1.

Critical Thinking

1. Does the technology in the advancement of a cure for Alzheimer's disease seem realistic?
2. Discuss the various moral lessons that can be learned when discussing health-care decision making in the face of severe impairment.

Create Central

www.mhhe.com/createcentral

Internet References

Alzheimer's Association
www.alz.org
Caregiver Action Network
http://caregiveraction.org

YASO SHAN is a medical writer and health consultant at Vinings Natural Health Centre in West Sussex.

Shan, Yaso. From *Primary Health Care*, July 2013, pp. 32–38. Copyright © 2013 by RCN Publishing Company Ltd. Reprinted by permission.

Unit 5

Prepared by: Elaina F. Osterbur, *Saint Louis University*

UNIT

Retirement: American Dream or Dilemma?

Since 1900, the number of people in America who are 65 years or more of age has been increasing steadily, but a decreasing proportion of that age group remains in the workforce. In 1900, nearly two-thirds of those over the age of 65 worked outside the home. By 1947, this number had declined to about 48 percent, and in 1975, about 22 percent of men age 65 and over were still in the workforce. The long-range trend indicates that fewer and fewer people are employed beyond the age of 65. Some choose to retire at age 65 or earlier; for others, retirement is mandatory. A recent change in the law, however, allows individuals to work as long as they want with no mandatory retirement age.

Gordon Strieb and Clement Schneider (*Retirement in American Society*, 1971) observed that for retirement to become an institutionalized social pattern in any society, certain conditions must be present. A large group of people must live long enough to retire; the economy must be productive enough to support people who are not in the workforce; and there must be pensions or insurance programs to support retirees.

Retirement is a rite of passage. People can consider it either as the culmination of the American Dream or as a serious problem. Those who have ample incomes, interesting things to do, and friends to associate with often find the freedom of time and choice that retirement offers very rewarding. For others, however, retirement brings problems and personal losses. Often, these individuals find their incomes decreased; they miss the status, privilege, and power associated with holding a position in the occupational hierarchy. They may feel socially isolated if they do not find new activities to replace their previous work-related ones. Additionally, they might have to cope with the death of a spouse and/or their own failing health.

Older persons approach retirement with considerable concern about financial and personal problems. Will they have enough retirement income to maintain their current lifestyle? Will their income remain adequate as long as they live? Given their current state of health, how much longer can they continue to work? The articles in this unit deal with changing Social Security regulations and changing labor demands that are encouraging older persons to work beyond the age of 65.

Article   Prepared by: Elaina F. Osterbur, *Saint Louis University*

Will Baby Boomers Phase into Retirement?

Julie I. Tacchino

Learning Outcomes

After reading this article, you will be able to:

- Define phased retirement.
- Understand the challenges that phased retirement presents.
- Understand the benefits of phased retirement for employees and employers.

Introduction and Overview

For a long time the approach to retirement was very standard—work to a specified age and then jump off the cliff into retirement. Today there is no one standard retirement approach. Given the different needs of the aging workforce and the companies that employ them, the importance of adaptive and innovative retirement strategies for both employees and employers has become critical. One such strategy is phased retirement. Currently, there is no standard legal or agreed-on definition of phased retirement.[1] Phased retirement can be thought of as a broad variety of employment arrangements allowing retirees to continue working reduced workloads while gradually shifting from full-time work to full-time retirement.

A large majority of baby boomers intend to continue working after they reach traditional retirement age, and a majority of those individuals want to work part-time in different fields from their previous careers.[2] This most likely means that phased retirement will grow in the future. In fact, while only 21% of surveyed companies believe that phased retirement is critical to their company's Human Resources strategy today, over 60% believe it will be critical in five years.[3] Of the retirees working in retirement, Rappaport reported that one study found that 31% were working for the same employer as before retirement, 40% worked for a different company, and 27% became self-employed.[4] Further, 45% of working retirees were doing the same type of work they did prior to retirement, 26% were doing different work but using the same skills they had before retirement, and 33% were doing work that was entirely different from the work

they did before retirement.[5] Given the demands of an aging workforce, employers need to come up with formal solutions to retain their older workers and guide them toward their intended retirement goals.

Phased retirement is a great solution to the worker population issue because it comes in many varieties. Phased retirement can be used in jobs that require the same work, jobs that require different work, or jobs that require skills similar to those developed at the full-time job. Through phased retirement employees can stay with their current companies to transfer knowledge to the younger workforce, they can also utilize their skills and abilities at different companies, start their own businesses, or start on completely new "career paths." Phased retirement offers so many different routes providing a variety of exciting choices for retirement-aged workers.

Phased retirement supports different lifestyles—whether it's a client who wants to travel or one who is sick and can no longer work full time. Phased retirement can be a positive option for clients who do not want to, or cannot yet, fully retire. One paradox of phased retirement is that those employees management most wants to retain are more likely to find it hard to limit themselves to part-time work.[6] This is no surprise given that while the younger workers are expected to have a multitude of jobs during their careers, the aged workforce is more likely to have been with the same company throughout their careers. The historical knowledge and skills that the aging workers have accumulated throughout their careers with a given company are invaluable and companies do not want to part with them.

Additionally, people who choose phased retirement are better educated, more likely to have a positive view of work (for example, believe that work is by itself important apart from a means of acquiring money), have greater household wealth and income, and are often in white-collar positions. In other words, they are the same type of people who are more likely to seek the aid of a financial planner.[7] This is also a good description of the baby boomer. Boomers with such characteristics are significant assets for employers, which is why having a formalized phased retirement program is an important tool for companies.

Characteristics of Phased Retirement

Phased retirement is a great retirement option because it can take employees and employers in so many different directions. With the plethora of phased retirement options available, it can be overwhelming to determine which choices are right for employees to follow and for employers to offer. Phased retirement often has one or more of the following characteristics.

Full-Time to Part-Time Employment

The most common characteristic of phased retirement is going from full-time to part-time employment. This can be done in different ways. The employee or former employee can reduce the number of hours worked. For example, the phased retiree cuts back from eight hours per day to four-to-six hours per day. Or the employee or former employee can reduce the amount of days per week worked. For example, the phased retiree cuts back from five days a week to three days per week. The employee or former employee may even reduce the number of weeks worked. This can be done through a variety of methods. For example, the phased retiree could take extended vacation time or limit the work period to seasonal work. Another example of cutting back on the time worked would be having the employee or former employee limit work to projects engaged in on a full-time basis but for a limited period of time.

Other Characteristics

Other characteristics of phased retirement may include the employee or former employee engaging in a job-sharing program, or entering into a contract that provides flexibility in setting hours, or negotiating reduced job duties. Another common characteristic would be doing some sort of consulting work for an ex-employer, another employer, or multiple employers as an independent contractor. For example, a phased retiree who was formerly a tax accountant could work part-time during tax season. With today's technology, engaging in telecommuting or working remotely is a useful tool for phased retirement programs. As phased retirement grows in popularity, the characteristics and options will most likely expand.

Different Approaches to Phased Retirement

With the various characteristics of phased retirement plans, a good way to group phased retirement options is by win-win, where not just the employee but also the employer "wins out" or is favored by the phased retirement option, and employee-favored, where the employee is favored in the phased retirement decision and the employer is most likely not impacted.

Win-Win Phased Retirement Options

Formal and Informal Phased Retirement

One type of phased retirement is the formal phased retirement. Formal phased retirement occurs when formal workplace policies exist that allow an employee to continue working with his or her current employer at a reduced schedule. At the same time, the employee may or may not be receiving retirement benefits. If they exist, formal phased retirement policies often are contained in the personnel policies of the employer. They tend to be most commonly available from large employers.[8] Sponsors of formal phased retirement programs have noted that they do not expect retirees to stay active for very long. One manager said, "Although there are some exceptions, most people work about three years in our program."[9] A formal phased retirement program can be a useful tool for companies. Having a formal program shows the company has an innovative and adaptive style, creates a culture that values employees, and places value on age at a time when many companies devalue age by encouraging early retirement. Companies are used to staying innovative and creative to attract new employees, but it is now crucial they stay innovative to retain all employees, especially those employees nearing retirement age. With the increasing need for phased retirement options, formal phased retirement will most likely grow among companies.

Informal phased retirement is a type of phased retirement in which informal workplace arrangements and practices exist that allow an employee to continue working with his or her current employer at a reduced schedule. At the same time, the employee may or may not be receiving retirement benefits. Informal phased retirement is more common than formal phased retirement. It is often done on a case-by-case basis. Traditionally, employers have been more inclined to accommodate informal phased retirement requests from high-performing workers who require little supervision.[10]

Both formal and informal phased retirements create win-win situations for employers and employees. Employers keep their hard-working "golden" employees longer, possibly allowing them to impart their wisdom to the younger workforce; and employees are able to enjoy their work, while easing into their new lives as retired persons. However, a formal plan is recommended over an informal plan. Standard policies and procedures let employees know their options, and keep employers prepared, structured, and honest when setting up phased retirement plans.

Retire and Rehire

Once an employee has retired, the former employer may rehire him or her for part-time work or a consulting job. In order for the employer's retirement system to be unaffected, there must be a bona fide termination of employment. However, there is no specific legal definition of bona fide termination of employment.[11] This is a definite win-win scenario. Employees who are hired back as consultants for their companies are often paid large amounts for short periods of work, and when an employer needs a consultant, who better to hire than a former employee who already possesses knowledge pertaining to the company and does not require formal training?

Phasing

Phasing a little, or working close to a full-time schedule by only making a modest change in work schedule and conditions, is another win-win phased retirement scenario. When phasing a little, clients typically keep their benefits but they are unlikely to be drawing retirement benefits from the employer. Clients who are phasing a little are often thought of as phasing preretirement.[12] Another strategy is phasing a lot, or work that is dramatically different from a full-time schedule. When phasing a lot, employees will probably lose their employer-provided benefit eligibility. Clients who are phasing a lot are often thought of as phasing postretirement.[13] All of these phasing options are extremely beneficial to the employee, providing flexibility and the ability to retire at his or her own pace. At the same time, employers are able to retain skilled employees who contribute experienced knowledge to the organization. Employers should be prepared to allow flexibility when employees are phasing a little or a lot. Allowing employees to set their own reduced schedules for their convenience (e.g., taking Fridays off), will be more attractive to employees when deciding which phased retirement option is best for them.

Employee-Favored Retirement Options

To reiterate, employers don't necessarily lose in these scenarios, they are just not directly involved with their former employees. In these situations, from the original employer's perspective the employee has completely retired. These scenarios require significant effort on the part of employees, but are a great way to phase into retirement.

Bridge Jobs

Bridge jobs are jobs selected by the employee without the support of a formal employer program. These jobs occur immediately or shortly after the employee has left his or her long-time employer and the employee may or may not yet have started receiving retirement benefits from the prior employer. Bridge jobs spanning a period from the end of work with a full-time employer to full-time retirement out of the labor force are becoming more common.[14] This scenario "bridges" the gap between full-time employment and full-time retirement, allowing employees to hold off on collecting retirement benefits. This is a great retirement savings strategy for two reasons. First, the longer the employee's retirement fund remains untouched, the better. Second, bridge jobs will more than likely pay less than what the employee was paid in his or her previous job. This drop in income, which occurs in many phased retirement plans, is positive because it allows the employee to adapt to a reduced income instead of going from the full-time salary that he or she is used to, to a significantly lower retirement income. Phased retirement is typically a white-collar phenomenon, as evidenced by better education and greater household wealth.[15] Although it is easy to argue that finding a job with a different employer when nearing retirement age is next to impossible, employers in industries similar to that of the retiree's former employer may well value the wisdom and knowledge that comes with the retirement age, making bridge jobs a viable option for retirement-aged individuals. Although it may not be common now, recruiting retirement-aged employees from similar industries will most likely grow

as a competitive strategy for companies as phased retirement grows in popularity.

Wisdom Careers

Another phased retirement program that utilizes one's skills encompasses wisdom careers, which are follow-up careers that capitalize on the retired employee's wisdom, skills, and abilities. Wisdom careers are great options for clients who have been in the same profession or industry for the majority of their careers. The retiree can become a self-employed consultant who uses his or her past experiences to help other companies. Knowledge transfer is invaluable for many industries and career paths. Utilizing the business and/or field wisdom of retired persons is important for employers looking to grow and develop in their industries.

Encore Careers

An encore career is one in which a client retires and starts a new career in a different industry. According to AARP, "Encore careers are increasingly common among Americans 50+. An estimated nine million boomers have found their second acts, and more than 30 million others say they would like to make a career change."[16] Occasionally clients may retire at an early age to "double dip" and get a second pension. They may also retire to start an entrepreneurial venture. No matter what the case, an encore career is an important form of phased retirement to consider. Again, this shows the importance of destandardization of retirement. Retirement age has always been seen as the time to stop working. This adaptive approach makes retirement age a time to start a new career path, showing a complete, 180-degree change in perception.

These are just some phased retirement options that employees can consider and employers can take advantage of or capitalize on. The changing face of retirement requires employers to be innovative and think ahead to create phased retirement programs that entice employees to stay with the company so both the employee and employer can win. While most employers focus on being competitive to recruit those younger in their careers, the need for competitive recruiting and retaining of older workers is becoming essential.

Why Employees Choose Phased Retirement

There are several reasons employees may opt for phased retirement. One reason phased retirement is a growing trend is that continued work is more feasible. Some of today's physically easier, technology-aided jobs make phased retirement more attainable. Advancements in technology have lessened the importance of age as a factor of work and allow retirement-aged employees to continue working and retire at their own leisure. Not only is phased retirement more feasible, it is also more necessary. Pensions are becoming less and less common and employees are in control of their own retirement incomes. There are no guarantees. The reality is that employees need to work longer to ensure they can sustain their retirement incomes, and phased retirement increases retirement income. It allows clients to continue to contribute to their retirement plans; when a client is not satisfied with his or her retirement income, he or she can supplement it with additional income from a phased retirement option. The client may opt for part-time work to correct the situation. With increasing options for sustaining retirement income, what better way to take action and control over one's own retirement bank than to have a phased retirement income?

Phased retirement is also a growing choice among retirees because of the cohort effect. Today's retirees have greater longevity, higher levels of education, and greater occupational profiles, the combination of which provides a basis for staying employed longer.[17] Education and career status are valued in America. People work their entire lives to reach their career goals and often find it is incredibly difficult to leave their careers behind. As we continue to recognize the importance of sustaining a career that was years in the making, more and more employees are feeling comfortable with the decision to work longer periods and extend the "normal" career span.

Additionally, phased retirement allows employees to "try out" leisure activities that could eventually be part of full-time retirement. Retirement is a major life change and phased retirement allows employees to ease into an unfamiliar retirement in their own time and at their own leisure. The ability to negotiate the transition a step at a time allows for better emotional preparation.[18] If we fail to recognize the emotions that come with retirement, then we fail to do our jobs as financial planners. Retirement is not a black and white subject where the only goal is to have enough money to live out one's final years; there is so much more to it. People put their lives into building their careers; phased retirement not only permits acknowledgement of that effort but also allows our clients to adapt to the emotional significance of both having a career and retiring from it.

Phased retirement is a great option also because part-time work allows employees to adjust for age-related changes in stamina or ability. A desire to continue working may not equate to a wish to work full time.[19] Phased retirement allows employees to continue active involvement in the workforce at a pace with which they can be more comfortable.[20] With modern medicine, everything possible is done to keep people alive; why wouldn't the same mentality apply to people's careers? Just because agility declines between the beginning of one's career and what is currently known as the retirement age, does not mean that one has to stop working. Additionally, employees may have more to give. When traditional retirement age arrives, some clients still have plenty of energy and desire to contribute.[21]

In fact, probably the most important, yet most overlooked, reason phased retirement is increasing in popularity is that people want to work. Retirement may be great for some individuals, but how many of us really want to go from working eight hours each day to spending eight hours each day watching TV? Work keeps life interesting and fresh. Employees nearing retirement age won't necessarily want to throw away their careers and embark full time on their hobbies, making phased retirement a great option for the aging workforce.

Employees may be bored in their current careers and they may want to try new work activities. Semiretirement may be a good opportunity to double back and travel down the road not taken. It may allow clients to follow their hearts and passions, and not their wallets, or it may tap into a client's entrepreneurial spirit.[22] Again, it is crucial to adjust our perceptions and recognize that retirement age does not have to mean the end of a career; it might mean the beginning of one. With age and experience come opportunities and options. Phased retirement may be an opportunity to jettison the boring and burdensome projects at work and to choose only those projects that stimulate the client.

Phased retirement also allows for a better work-life balance. Many professional and white-collar jobs have become very demanding, often requiring 50- to 60-hour work weeks. Phased retirement may allow for the intervention of sanity into the client's world by enabling him or her to have some flexibility with how time is spent.[23] Along with achieving a better work-life balance, a person may want to spend some more time with his or her spouse. Phased retirement may be a great option for a client with that desire.[24] Many people have accepted that when in the prime of their careers, work-life balance is at times unachievable. Instead of viewing retirement as a hobby-life balance, why not look at it as a work-life balance in which the life side of the balance finally outweighs the work?

Phasing into retirement can also allow employees to retain benefits. With the rising costs of health care, phased retirement might be necessary to keep employer-provided health insurance, a potentially significant benefit. As people age they are more likely to need better health care. Under the right set of circumstances, phased retirement may allow the client to continue to have employer-sponsored health care; however, this is not always the case. Having a formalized phased retirement plan that allows benefits will certainly put companies at a competitive advantage when recruiting experienced, retirement-aged personnel.

Why Employers Should Encourage Phased Retirement

As discussed earlier, several phased retirement strategies are win-win, where both the employee and employer come out with a winning hand, so to speak. First, these strategies enable employers to retain and recruit older workers who have unique skills and talents.[25] In one survey, 72% of companies said that phased retirement is important for retaining the experience, knowledge, and skills of older workers.[26] This is especially useful for employers whose employees have been with the company for most of their careers. When employees spend their careers in one company, their skills grow and adapt to the company's needs. In addition, older workers who have been with the same company throughout their careers often retain useful, historical knowledge of the company that others may not have. Further, experienced employees often understand the corporate culture and environment. This knowledge is a valuable resource for any company, making phased retirement programs an important offering for employers.

Phased retirement can create effective knowledge-sharing relationships between older mentors and younger protégés.[27] Given all the experience, knowledge, and skills boomers have attained and retained, mentor relationships can help ease the blow that will be sustained when boomers retire. Knowledge transfer is a powerful tool that can help companies retain relevant historical information and useful skills and abilities that are significant to the role the retiree may have. This retention can only occur if the older workforce is able to take the time to share its knowledge with younger protégés. Whenever possible, management should make sure that returning retirees know that an important part of their role is to transfer their critical knowledge to the next generation of employees.[28] It will certainly be an adjustment for current employees who are headed for retirement and retirees who are returning to the workplace to be charged with sharing this knowledge with the younger workforce. Employees are often territorial about their work and having older employees share knowledge with younger employees is rarely welcomed with open arms. It is important to be open and honest with employees about the goal of knowledge sharing. This is often a delicate situation and being open and honest will make them feel important and useful rather than threatened by the idea of sharing their skills and abilities with their potential successors.

Another reason employers should encourage phased retirement is that it accommodates special projects or time-shortened scenarios because retirees comprise a good resource for these contingencies. Again, retirees or employees nearing retirement have accumulated or developed a skill set that makes them effective in their positions. They are already trained so when an employer is in a time-sensitive situation, it is a clear win-win to offer retirees a phased retirement option. Retirees can continue working while employers have the needed human capital on their teams without having to train a new or existing employee. In addition, phased retirement preserves human capital and lowers training costs.[29]

This innovative approach to retirement gives employers a competitive edge in attracting and retaining desirable employees. Having a formalized phased retirement program shows that the company is pioneering a revolutionary change in a transforming workplace. If a company is adapting to one change, it is most likely aware of other needed changes and is willing to make the changes. Employees do not want to work for a company that is antiquated in its policies and procedures. Companies that do not adapt will fail in today's work environment. Additionally, phased retirement programs show employers value their employees because they are looking to retain them past retirement age. Seeing and responding to employee and societal needs by having a formalized phased retirement program gives companies a competitive advantage.

Lastly, another relevant reason employers should encourage phased retirement is that it addresses the potential labor shortage that will occur when boomers retire.[30] "While the percentage of adults ages 65 and older will increase from 17% today to 27% in 30 years—an increase from 37 million to 77 million people—there will not be enough members of the baby bust generation to fill their shoes."[31] This void in human capital that

employers will inevitably experience shows the true value of phased retirement. Having a formal phased retirement policy in place now will help employers avoid the labor shortage as their boomer workforce heads for retirement.

Challenges of Phased Retirement

Although phased retirement programs are a great solution for retirement income gaps for employees and knowledge gaps for employers, there are several challenges associated with phased retirement. As discussed earlier, there is no legal definition of bona fide termination of employment, something that is necessary to terminate and rehire employees without affecting their retirement plans. The lack of legal guidance can pose a barrier for employers who would like to use a retire and rehire program as a phased retirement option.

The type of retirement plan your client has may pose challenges to phasing into retirement—especially if he or she wants to phase before full retirement age. Because defined-benefit plans do not typically allow distributions until age 62, phasing into retirement beforehand could subject the plan to tax consequences.[32] According to Moran, ". . . the IRS has consistently emphasized that a plan cannot allow participants to 'retire' or 'terminate employment,' receive a pension, and then immediately return to work. . .".[33] This creates barriers for clients who would like to phase into retirement before the "normal" or acceptable age of 62, and for companies providing defined-benefit plans, that would like to implement a formalized phased retirement plan.

In addition to legal challenges, there are emotional barriers to phased retirement for your client. While it is a benefit that your client does not have to jump off the cliff to full-time retirement, but instead can climb down at his or her own leisure, it is not easy to release the control to coworkers. This can be especially true of the mentor and protégé relationships. While training and transferring work to the protégé, it is more than likely that the protégé will want to make his or her mark on the work and change it up. It can be quite difficult to watch someone else take something you've been doing one way and flip it upside down. It is important for both employers who support mentor-protégé relationships and employees who take advantage of them to be aware of this emotional barrier.

Although there are challenges to phased retirement, the barriers do not outweigh the positive impact phased retirement can have on employers and employees.

The Future of Retirement

A standard approach to retirement is a thing of the past. It's time to look to the future. It is our responsibility to think ahead and prepare innovative ideas about and creative approaches to the changing face of retirement. Employers need to accommodate employee needs by staying current on retirement trends. Phased retirement plans can be a winning situation for both the employee and employer, allowing employees to ease into one of the biggest changes in life, while allowing employers to retain vital skills and knowledge important for their companies. When companies foresee and adapt to the ever-evolving retirement needs of their employees, talented employees are retained and employers keep a competitive edge, creating a win-win situation.

References

1. Anna Rappaport, "Phased retirement—An important part of the evolving retirement scene." *Benefits Quarterly* 25, no. 2 (2009): 38–50.
2. The New Retirement Survey, Merrill Lynch, 2005.
3. Stephen Miller, "Retiring boomers spark phased retirement interest." *HR Magazine* 53, no. 9 (2008): 32.
4. Rappaport 2009, 41.
5. *Ibid,* 42.
6. David Delong, MetLife Mature Market Institute. "Searching for the Silver Bullet: Leading Edge Solutions for Leveraging an Aging Workforce." November 2007. https://www.metlife.com/assets/cao/mmi/publications/studies/mmi-searching-silver-bullet.pdf.
7. Yung-Ping Chen and John C. Scott, "Phased retirement: Who opts for it and toward what end." *AARP Public Policy Institute.* (2005). http://assets.aarp.org.rgcenter.econ/inb113_retire.pdf.
8. Robert Hutchens, "Phased retirement: Problems and prospects." *Retirement Income Reporter* 14, no. 6 (2008): 6–12.
9. DeLong, 2007.
10. Hutchens, 2008, 9.
11. Rappaport, 2009, 39.
12. *Ibid,* 40–42.
13. *Ibid.*
14. Chen and Scott, 2005, 5.
15. Hutchens, 2008, 7.
16. "Encore career strategies: Finding a career change that suits you for the second half of life." AARP, *Inside E Street,* Feb. 13, 2012. http://aarp.org/work/job-hunting/info-2-2012/encore-career-strategies-inside-estreet.html.
17. Neal E. Cutler, "Working *in* retirement: The longevity perplexities continue." *Journal of Financial Service Professionals* 65, no. 4 (2011): 19–22.
18. Hutchens, 2008, 6.
19. Chen and Scott, 1.
20. Hutchens, 2008, 6.
21. Edelstein, "Choosing a second career over traditional retirement." *RetirementAdvice.com* February 18, 2011. http://retirementadvice.com/choosing-a-second-career-over-retirement/.
22. *Ibid.*
23. Rappaport 2009, 44.
24. *Ibid.*
25. DeLong, 2007.
26. Miller, 2008, 32.
27. DeLong, 2007.
28. *Ibid.,* 24.
29. Tomeka M. Hill, "Why doesn't every employer have a phased retirement program?" *Benefits Quarterly* 26, no. 4 (2010): 29–39.
30. F. Pierce Noble and Erica Harper, "Strategy and policy for phased retirement." *Benefits Quarterly* 26, no. 3 (2010): 11–14.
31. "Time to Develop a Phased Retirement Program?" *Design Firm Management & Administration Report 5,* no. 12 (2005): 2–3. *ProQuest.*Web. Oct. 8, 2012. http://0-search.proquest.com.libcat.widener.edu/docview/223213655/13CDEF825BC5A9483F3/1?accountid=29103.
32. Anne E. Moran, "Phased retirement: Challenges for employers." *Employee Relations Law Journal* 38, no. 2 (2012): 68–74.
33. *Ibid.*

Critical Thinking

1. What is phased retirement?
2. What kind of challenges does phased retirement present?
3. What are the benefits of phased retirement for employees and employers?

Create Central

www.mhhe.com/createcentral

Internet References

AARP
www.aarp.org
Health and Retirement Study (HRS)
www.umich.edu/~hrswww

JULIE I. TACCHINO, MSTFP, graduated in December 2012 from Widener University's Master of Taxation and Financial Planning program. She currently works as a Human Resources Analyst.

Tacchino, Julie I. From *Journal of Financial Service Professionals,* May 2013, pp. 41–48. Copyright © 2013 by Society of Financial Service Professionals. Used with permission.

Article   Prepared by: Elaina F. Osterbur, *Saint Louis University*

Live for Today, Save for Tomorrow

What if working longer meant more fun, not less—and a bigger nest egg, too? You can make it happen if you start planning now.

CARLA A. FRIED

Learning Outcomes

After reading this article, you will be able to:

- Discuss the advantages to older workers of working beyond the anticipated retirement age.

- Explain how working beyond retirement age causes preretirement savings to grow.

- Explain why waiting until your late 70s or early 80s is the best time to begin buying or cashing in on a monthly annuity.

As a senior financial planner, Christine Fahlund is not in the habit of telling people to stop saving for retirement. You wouldn't expect her employer, T. Rowe Price, to be wild about the idea, either. They are in the business of gathering investors' money into mutual funds and 401(k) plans. (Disclosure: Among those plans is the one for employees of AARP.) But in a new strategy that the company has been promoting this year, not only do Fahlund and T. Rowe Price suggest that you stop saving for retirement once you hit age 60; they encourage you to take the money you were previously putting into your 401(k) or other retirement account and—brace yourself—spend it. On fun stuff. "Your 60s should be a time when you start to enjoy yourself more," Fahlund says. "Take more trips. Spend time with the grandkids. Buy the boat or put in the pool you've been dreaming of."

And here's the kicker: If you follow their advice, you could end up with a higher income in retirement than you might have otherwise.

Is this a joke? Did Fahlund and company just snooze through the Great Recession? It's not, and they didn't. What T. Rowe Price calls "practice retirement" could, in fact, be a realistic option for you. But there's a big catch. Two catches, in fact. You have to have significant savings by the time you hit 60. And you have to commit to working well past your early 60s, because you're going to live off that income while your savings and your Social Security benefits sit untouched, gaining in value.

You may already be postponing your retirement: More than 60 percent of workers say they expect to retire at age 65 or later, according to the most recent survey by the Employee Benefit Research Institute, up from 45 percent in 1991. But few view the prospect with enthusiasm. Working longer is Plan B, a sign that something went wrong in your retirement schedule.

"Practice retirement" operates from a different set of assumptions. Steven Sass, director of the Financial Security Project at the Center for Retirement Research at Boston College, says most people think the point of working longer is to

Table 1   How Much You Need to Save

Your Retirement Will be More Comfortable if You Work Well into Your 60s		
If You Plan to Retire at Age 62		
And your total household income is	$50,000	$75,000	$100,000
You'll need this much in savings by age 60	$600,000	$975,000	$1.4 million
If You Plan to Retire at Age 65		
And your total household income is	$50,000	$75,000	$100,000
You'll need this much in savings by age 60	$450,000	$825,000	$1.1 million
If You Plan to Retire at Age 70		
And your total household income is	$50,000	$75,000	$100,000
You'll need this much in savings by age 60	$250,000	$525,000	$700,000

Notes: T. Rowe Price assumes you will want to replace 75 percent of your income and that you will not make any withdrawals from your retirement account, or initiate your Social Security payout, until you retire. The calculation also assumes a portfolio will earn 7 percent before retirement and 6 percent after.
Source: T. Rowe Price.

sacrifice and save. That's not it. "The payoff of working longer," says Sass, who coauthored *Working Longer: The Solution to the Retirement Income Challenge,* "is that you can preserve your retirement savings and delay taking Social Security." Medical researchers have long known that staying on the job pays benefits to the mind and body. By protecting your nest egg, enhancing your benefits, and limiting the number of years your stash needs to support you, working longer has a similar effect on your financial health.

And that creates some opportunities, including the one at the heart of Fahlund's suggestion: Put yourself in a position where you can afford to stop saving, or at least slow down, when you reach 60. Then: Live a little. "Get back to looking forward to your 60s as a time to be enjoyed," she says. "You are delaying retirement, but you don't have to delay enjoyment."

Still sound too good to be true? Here are some answers to your probable concerns:

You'd Need to Save a Fortune to Take "Practice Retirement" at Age 60

Obviously, you can't stop saving at age 60 if you never really started. You need a healthy sum of money in the bank. But the required amount may be less than you're probably thinking.

The table estimates how much you need to squirrel away by age 60 to be able to turn off the savings spigot at that point. What you'll need depends on your current income, as well as the date when you expect to start tapping your savings and collecting Social Security. Bottom line: The longer you keep your hands off the retirement cookie jar, the less you'll need to have saved up by age 60. *Dramatically* less.

For example, a couple with $75,000 in joint household income who want to retire at 62 and have 75 percent of their preretirement income would need $975,000 in savings by age 60. But if they're willing to keep working until age 67, T. Rowe Price estimates they'd need $675,000. Those five extra years on the job cut the amount needed at age 60 by almost one-third. And if the couple don't touch their savings until 70, they need to set aside an even lower amount—$525,000. Hello, mission possible.

One assumption is critical: This model assumes your portfolio will earn 7 percent before you retire and 6 percent in retirement. That might seem too optimistic. To build in a margin of safety, you could assume a 5 percent preretirement return and 4 percent afterward. (By comparison, AARP's financial-planning tool assumes a 6 percent return preretirement, 3.6 percent afterward.) If the more cautious assumption proves accurate, you'd need to work one more year than you anticipated. But even that scenario is probably more affordable than you guessed. That's because the key ingredient in the recipe isn't the rate of return. It's your intention to keep working. "The investment earnings on your contributions at this later stage are less important," says Sass. "The value is that you have a job that supports you and helps you preserve your retirement security by not beginning to draw down your savings. We're talking about a few extra years of working to secure your finances for decades."

Come On—Decades? Working a Few Years More Can't Possibly Make That Much Difference

Most retirement experts say that it does. The Retirement Policy Center at the Urban Institute, for example, estimates that for every year you work past age 62, you increase your eventual retirement income by an average of 9 percent. At that rate, working eight years longer would double your retirement income. Here's why:

- Working longer means your retirement savings need not stretch over so many years. You've probably already heard this longevity riff: A 65-year-old man today has an average life expectancy of 17 years; a woman, 20 years. So you figure, "Okay, if I make it to 65, I will die at 82 or 85."

  But that's not necessarily correct. Your life expectancy isn't a calculation of when you will die; it's the age at which 50 percent of your age group will still be alive. So if you're 65 today, you've got even odds of making it into your mid-80s and beyond. It's even trickier if you're married. There's a better than 60 percent chance that one spouse of a 65-year-old couple today will still be alive at age 90. In other words, if you don't delay retirement—the average American man leaves the workforce at age 64; the average woman, at 62—the chances are good that your nest egg will have to stretch for 30 years.

  That can spread your savings thin. You can see the effect by plugging numbers into AARP's retirement calculator (aarp.org/retirementcalculator). Based on AARP's assumptions, a 60-year-old woman making $75,000 a year who retires at age 62 with a nest egg of $250,000 can sustain an annual income of about $31,000 through age 91. That same nest egg could support a healthier income of nearly $41,000 if she didn't touch her savings and delayed retiring until age 70.

- You give your savings more time to grow. If you work until age 70, your nest egg will be bigger than at 62 because it has eight more years to incubate. As long as you have a respectable amount saved by 60, letting that money grow undisturbed matters more to your financial security than does your adding new cash each year. If you have $250,000 in your 401(k) at age 60, the 7 percent annual rate of return assumed by T. Rowe Price would add $17,500 to your account in the first year alone. That's probably more than you'd contribute to a 401(k) or IRA. Over 10 years that 7 percent rate would lift your savings from $250,000 up to $500,000 by the time you retire, even if you never saved another penny.

- You can delay claiming your Social Security. Individuals can begin receiving benefits as early as age 62. But as the table shows, you'll lock in a higher payout if you hold off. "People's jaws drop when I tell them how much bigger their benefit will be if they wait," says Sass.

What It Takes to Keep Working

Even before the Great Recession triggered massive layoffs, older workers often faced unique job disruption. About one-third of workers ages 51 through 55 in 1992 were involuntarily bounced from their jobs by the time they reached their mid to late 60s, according to a 2009 Urban Institute study. One-fourth lost their jobs because of a layoff or business closing; another 12 percent were forced to stop working because of illness.

But the upside to working through your 60s is so strong that it's worth fighting back to stay on the job, if you can. These principles should help.

Move the Goalposts

If you're still harboring thoughts that retiring at 62 is "right," you risk mentally retiring at 60 or so. That makes you easier pickings if the boss decides to cut overhead. Plan to work until at least your late 60s and you will stay more engaged in your work.

Quitting Is Not an Option

Don't think you can give full retirement a whirl at age 62 and then just go back to work if your new life doesn't shake out as expected. "Retirement is a bit of a black hole," says *Working Longer* coauthor Sass. "It's habit-forming."

Be a Problem Solver

"Look around and see what holes your employer needs to fill, then offer to step in," says Sass. "The more flexible you are, the more valuable you are."

If You Have to Switch Jobs, Plan on Making Less

Some good news: If you've been at your job for a long time, you're in a better position than colleagues with less tenure. "Older workers are better protected from losing a job, but once they lose that job, they have a much harder time [than younger workers] finding a new job," says Richard Johnson, an Urban Institute retirement-policy expert. And the next job will likely be at a lower salary, so don't hold out for a fatter paycheck. Remember, though, that the main goal is to earn enough to cover your living costs.

Take Care of Yourself

A healthier you increases the odds you'll be able to keep working. It also makes it likelier you'll enjoy your 60s—and beyond.

Michael Wilson, a financial planner in Orland, Indiana, notes that the financial crisis makes it crucial to consider delaying. "If your 401(k) tanked, you will be leaning on Social Security even more."

- Finally, you reduce your out-of-pocket health care costs. Not many employers still offer retirement health coverage, so if you retire before 65 you may face stiff private insurance costs until Medicare kicks in. "The longer you can hold on to employer health benefits, the more you'll help preserve your retirement savings," says Richard Johnson of the Urban Institute's Retirement Policy Center.

It's Crazy Not to Save during Your 60s. What if the Market Collapses? What if You Get Sick? What if You Lose Your Job?

Working longer gives you the chance for some immediate gratification in your 60s, but it's not a free ticket to fiscal irresponsibility. Don't stop contributing to your 401(k) if your employer provides a match, for example; instead, dial back your contributions but keep saving enough to qualify for the maximum match. Otherwise you're essentially passing up free money. Don't drag debt into retirement. If you carry credit card balances, pay them off before you get into practice retirement's live-it-up mode. (Then keep them paid off.) Fahlund also recommends making big-ticket purchases while you have the income to cover them. And stay alert to market headwinds. If T. Rowe Price's 7 percent preretirement and 6 percent postretirement return assumptions look dicey after a few years, you may have to adjust by diverting more of your income into savings again, or trimming your expenses, or even delaying retirement by a year or more.

Can you really count on keeping your current job all the way to 70? Even if your employer is willing, your health may have other ideas. If you think that you're hale enough to go the distance, and secure in your position, practice retirement could be a possibility. "You have to take a look at your current job circumstances and ask yourself what is the likelihood you will be with that employer at age 67," Sass says. "If you do change jobs, you will probably lose money."

But don't forget that you can safely earn less than you once did. Since you are no longer diverting 10 or 15 percent of your salary into savings, you can bring home 10 or 15 percent less and still maintain the same quality of life. The aim is simply to resist tapping your savings and Social Security benefits until you are deep in your 60s.

Which brings us to the true benefit of working to a later age: options. One option is to have fun and spend more in a practice retirement. Another is to earn less money and take your foot off the career gas—or do work that's more meaningful to you. As long as you're still earning your living, the choice is yours. And with a Plan B like that, who really misses Plan A?

Social Security: Patience Pays

Your Social Security benefits revolve around your Normal Retirement Age (NRA)—the age at which you are entitled to 100 percent of your benefit. If you were born in 1960 or later, your NRA is 67. If you were born from 1943 to 1954, your NRA is 66, and if you were born from 1955 to 1959 your NRA is somewhere between 66 and 67. If you wait until your NRA or later to claim your benefit, you'll receive much higher monthly payments.

	How much bigger your benefit will be if you defer claiming your benefit until your NRA	Additional annual benefit increase between your NRA and 70	How much bigger your benefit will be if you wait until 70 to start receiving Social Security, compared with taking payouts at 62
If your NRA is 66 . . .	25%	8%	76%
If your NRA is 67 . . .	30%	8%	77%

A new AARP online calculator will give you a personalized snapshot of how waiting can balloon your Social Security benefit. Go to **aarp.org/socialsecuritybenefits.**

Critical Thinking

1. What critical factors should a person consider before deciding to work beyond their anticipated retirement age?

2. If the individual works into their late 60s or early 70s, are they likely to be more or less engaged in their work?

3. In terms of a worker's knowledge and skill in their present job or their flexibility in assuming a new job, what is the biggest advantage in terms of the worker's ability to continue being employed in their later years?

Create Central

www.mhhe.com/createcentral

Internet References

AARP
    www.aarp.org
Health and Retirement Study (HRS)
    www.umich.edu/~hrswww

Article   Prepared by: Elaina F. Osterbur, *Saint Louis University*

Do-It-Yourself Financial Freedom

JANE BRYANT QUINN

Learning Outcomes

After reading this article, you will be able to:

- Discuss the advantages and disadvantages of beginning to withdraw from the Social Security program at age 62.
- Describe the conditions that would qualify a person who never worked to receive Social Security payments.

Safety nets fray when times get hard. Retirements that once looked secure are hanging by a thread. The message for those in their 50s is clear: Mend the nets while there's still time. Those in their 60s and 70s have fewer options. Still, there are ways of making sure your money lasts for life. **Here's how to do it in 12 easy steps:**

1 Get Rid of Debt

Nothing is more destructive of retirement than carrying debt when your paycheck stops. If you're in your early 50s, start debt reduction now. Try to prepay your mortgage, too, so you'll own your home free and clear. If you're retiring now and prepaying would use up too much cash, consider the other extreme: Reduce your payments by taking a new, 30-year mortgage. It's counterintuitive, but it works. Or use your equity to buy a smaller place that will leave you with no house payment or a much smaller one.

Don't fall prey to the slimy promises of commercial debt consolidators. Here are two legitimate and low-cost places to go for help with debt reduction: The National Foundation for Credit Counseling (www.nfcc.org, 1-800-388-2227) and the Association of Independent Consumer Credit Counseling Agencies (www.aiccca.org, 1-800-703-8787).

In the worst case, consider bankruptcy. Never tap retirement accounts to cover unpayable debts. IRAs and 401(k)s are protected in bankruptcy. You'll need those funds for a fresh start.

2 Build a Better Budget

When you're thinking about retirement, nothing is more important than knowing how far your income will stretch. What will your expenses be? How much income will you have, including

prudent withdrawals from your savings? Get your spending under control sooner rather than later. The longer you kid yourself, the greater your chance of running out of money.

3 Increase Your Savings

Save, save, save—even if it means changing your lifestyle or not helping your grandchildren with tuition. The kids have a lifetime to repay their student loans, but you're running out of time. If you arrive at retirement with too little money, you're cooked.

4 Wise up on Investments

Among older people, there's a stampede to safety. Money poured out of stock-owning mutual funds after the panic of 2008–09, and into funds invested in bonds. Many older investors still don't want to take a risk in stocks.

But inflation and taxes will cut the real returns on your bonds and bond funds down to practically nothing. In your 50s and 60s—with 30 or 40 years of retirement ahead—you need to keep some money invested in stocks for long-term growth.

I don't mean individual stocks. For safety reasons, get rid of them—every single share. You have no idea what is going on inside companies, including the one you work for. Even blue chips can be laid low—look what happened to the country's leading banks. Are you holding on to individual stocks to avoid paying tax on capital gains? That tax is probably lower today than it ever will be. Bite the bullet, sell now and diversify.

As a first step, divide your nest egg into three parts:

- Money you'll need within four or five years. Keep it in a bank or a money market fund—any account that is readily accessible when the need arises.
- Money you won't have to touch for 15 years or more. Keep it in well-diversified stock index funds, which track the market as a whole rather than trying to pick individual companies. Low-cost stock index funds are offered by Vanguard and Fidelity Investments. T. Rowe Price has index funds, too, but they cost a little more.
- In-between money. Keep it in bond mutual funds. When interest rates rise (as most people expect to happen in coming years), the value of bond fund shares will fall. But managers will be snapping up those new,

higher-interest bonds, so the income from your fund will rise. When rates fall again, in the next recession, the value of your shares will go back up. If you reinvested your dividends, you'll have more shares working for you, too.

5 Keep Your Job, if Possible

Or get one, if you've already retired. Every extra year of work improves your Social Security benefit, increases your savings (assuming you save) and reduces the number of years that your nest egg has to last. It might bring you health insurance, too. Public schools, hospitals and government agencies offer benefits. Some private companies—including Costco, Home Depot and Wal-Mart—give benefits even to part-timers (usually with a waiting period).

6 Do Whatever you Can to Keep Health Insurance

If your company offers retiree coverage, don't even think of moving to another city or state until you find out if you can take your coverage with you. Most plans won't follow you or will charge you more at a new location.

If you need individual coverage, check with local health insurance agents who can round up plans suitable for you (you can find an agent through the National Association of Health Underwriters). For the lowest premium, pick a policy with a high deductible. You may pay more out of pocket if you become sick, but you're protected from catastrophic, bankruptcy-inducing costs. Once you have signed up, you're in the insurer's PPO network, which gives you discounts of up to 50 percent or so, even on bills you pay yourself.

Health care reform would be helpful for those not yet in Medicare. Any new law is likely to bar rejection for preexisting conditions (at my age, life is a preexisting condition) and provide faster access to generic drugs and subsidies to help cover costs. Those on Medicare will likely see the "doughnut hole"—which requires them to pay some Medicare Part D costs—close over the next few years.

7 Be Smart about Social Security

Draw from your 401(k) or IRA first, and claim Social Security benefits later. If you can wait until 70, your check will be about 76 percent higher than if you had started at 62, and will improve the protection for your spouse as well.

8 Be Smart about Retirement Funds, Too

If you're with a large employer, consider leaving your 401(k) money in your company plan, provided that it offers flexible withdrawal options. Your money will be managed at a much lower cost than you'll find elsewhere, and the funds have been chosen carefully for people in your situation. If you have a traditional pension and take it as a lump sum, don't hand it to a broker or planner who wants to sell you products. Choose index funds yourself or work with a fee-only financial planner (see below).

9 Put off Reverse Mortgages

When you turn 62, salespeople come out in force, urging you to strip the equity out of your home to support your spending now. Don't do it. The fees and effective interest rates are high, and the proceeds are low. Save the reverse mortgage option for your late 70s or early 80s, when other money might be running low. AARP has tons of good information at www.aarp.org/money/personal/reverse_mortgages/.

10 Annuities

When you're retired, there's nothing like receiving a regular check. One way to get it is with an immediate annuity. You take a sum of money and use it to buy an income for life. Your state of health doesn't matter. The fixed payments are based entirely on your age and the type of benefit you want (for cost comparisons, see www.immediateannuities.com). But fixed payments will be whittled away by inflation, so don't buy an annuity too early. Buy in your late 70s or early 80s, when they won't have to last as long.

Stay away from the fancy, tax-deferred annuities that make big promises about future income benefits. They're too complicated to dissect here, so I'll say only that the cost is much higher than you think and the odds are good that they won't perform as you expect. My personal rule is, "if it's complicated, forget it." Deferred annuities with income benefits fit that bill.

11 Work with a Financial Planner

Planners are very helpful in working with budgets and projecting how much you can afford to spend when you retire. But work with fee-only planners, who don't sell products and who charge only for their advice. Planners who take commissions on products could steer you wrong (for example, by selling you those awful, complex annuities). Three places to find a fee-only planner near you: GarrettPlanningNetwork.com, the Alliance of Cambridge Advisors (CambridgeAdvisors.com), and the National Association of Personal Financial Advisors (www.napfa.org).

12 Move in with Your Kids

The last resort, if all else fails. That should be motivation enough to get moving on your own plan for financial success.

Critical Thinking

1. Why is it unwise to take a reverse mortgage on your house at 62?

2. When retired, what is the advantage of keeping a large share of your money invested in stocks rather than in bonds?

3. Why is it wise, if you retire from a large employer who has your retirement money in a 401K plan, to leave it in the plan rather than drawing it out and reinvesting?

Create Central

www.mhhe.com/createcentral

Internet References

AARP
   www.aarp.org
Health and Retirement Study (HRS)
   www.umich.edu/~hrswww

JANE BRYANT QUINN is a financial columnist and the author of *Making the Most of Your Money Now.*

Article   Prepared by: Elaina F. Osterbur, *Saint Louis University*

Top 25 Social Security Questions

Confused about when to claim or whether you're eligible for benefits? We have answers.

STAN HINDEN

Learning Outcomes

After reading this article, you will be able to:

- Describe the variables that best explain why men and women receive the same retirement benefits.

- Cite the reasons why immigrants most often don't receive retirement programs and benefits from their employers.

Here are the most frequently asked questions about Social Security that AARP has received from you.

1. **I am about to turn 62 and plan to file for Social Security. How do I get started?**
   You should apply three months before you want to start collecting. Sign up online or call 1-800-772-1213. Here are some documents you may have to produce: your Social Security card or a record of the number; your birth certificate; proof of U.S. citizenship or lawful alien status; military discharge papers if you served before 1968; and last year's W-2 tax form or tax return if you're self-employed.

2. **How is my Social Security benefit calculated?**
   Benefits are based on the amount of money you earned during your lifetime—with an emphasis on the 35 years in which you earned the most. Plus, lower-paid workers get a bigger percentage of their preretirement income than higher-paid workers. In 2010, the average monthly benefit for retirees is $1,172.

3. **If I remarry, can I still collect Social Security benefits based on my deceased first husband's record?**
   You can—subject to several rules. In general, you cannot receive survivor benefits if you remarry before age 60 unless that marriage ends, too, whether by annulment, divorce or death of your new husband. If you remarry after age 60 (50 if disabled), you can still collect benefits on your former spouse's record. After you reach 62, you may get retirement benefits on the record of your new spouse if they are higher.

4. **Why won't retirees get a cost-of-living adjustment for 2011? Many of us count on this for food, medicine and other bills.**
   COLAs are based on the consumer price index, which tracks inflation. Because inflation has been flat, according to the CPI, there will be no benefit increase—for the second year in a row. AARP is calling on Congress to provide beneficiaries with financial relief.

5. **I am 56 and receive Social Security disability benefits. At what point will I switch to regular Social Security? Will the monthly amount change?**
   When you reach full retirement age, your disability benefits will automatically convert to retirement benefits. The amount will remain the same.

6. **My friend died at 66. She worked full time and had not applied for benefits. What happens to the money she contributed to Social Security? Can her children claim benefits?**
   The money people contribute goes into a fund from which benefits are paid to eligible workers and their families. These include a widower, a surviving divorced husband, dependent parents, disabled children, and children if they have not aged out.

7. **My husband and I are getting a divorce. He wants the settlement agreement to say I will not get his Social Security benefits. Can he do that?**
   No, he has no control over your future benefits. You can qualify for a divorced spouse's benefits if you were married at least 10 years, are now unmarried, are 62 or older, and if any benefit from your own work record would be less than the divorced spouse's benefit.

8. **Cleaning out my mother's home after her death, we found Social Security checks from the 1980s. Can we cash them?**
   No. The checks are negotiable for only 12 months after issue.

9. **My man and I have lived together for over seven years. If he dies, can I collect his Social Security benefits?**

   If your state recognizes your common-law marriage, then you'll likely be eligible for survivor benefits. But you'll have to provide evidence that includes sworn statements, mortgage or rent receipts, or insurance policies.

10. **Do my Social Security contributions go into a personal retirement account for me and earn interest?**

    Although many people think so, the answer is no. Social Security operates under a pay-as-you-go system, which means that today's workers pay for current retirees and other beneficiaries. Workers pay 6.2 percent of their wages up to a cap of $106,800; employers pay the same. The money that younger people contribute will pay for our benefits when we retire.

11. **How much money does the U.S. government owe to the Social Security trust fund, and will it be repaid?**

    To prepare for the boomers' retirement, Social Security has collected more in taxes than it pays in benefits. Surplus funds go into the trust fund and are invested in U.S.-guaranteed Treasury bonds. In 2009, the trust fund held $2.5 trillion in bonds and earned 4.9 percent in interest. These bonds are just as real as U.S. Treasury bonds held by mutual funds or foreign banks. Ultimately, it's up to the American people to ensure the government keeps its promise to retirees, just as it would to other investors.

12. **I have a pension from the Army. Will that affect my Social Security benefits?**

    It will not. You can get both your Social Security benefits and your military pension. If you served in the military before 1957, you did not pay Social Security taxes, but you will receive special credit for some of that service. Special credits also are available to people who served from 1957 to 1967 and from 1968 to 2001.

13. **I didn't work enough to qualify for Social Security. My husband gets it, but he is ill and may not live much longer. Will I be able to collect benefits?**

    Yes, but your benefit will depend on your age and situation: If you are at full retirement age or older, you'll get 100 percent of your deceased husband's benefit. A widow or widower between 60 and full retirement age receives a reduced benefit.

14. **Is it true that some people are collecting Social Security benefits who never paid into the system?**

    Social Security is an earned benefit. In order to collect a retirement benefit, a worker must pay into the system for at least 10 years. In some cases, nonworking family members, such as a spouse, may be eligible for benefits based on the worker's record. Tough rules in place assure that only legal residents can collect Social Security benefits.

15. **I filed for Chapter 13 bankruptcy after being laid off. Do Social Security benefits count as income in bankruptcy, or are they protected?**

    Your benefits are protected. Social Security is excluded from the calculation of disposable income when setting up a debtor repayment plan.

16. **My husband died recently. Can I choose between my own benefit and that as a widow? Can I collect both?**

    Eligibility for a widow's benefit begins at age 60, or 50 if you are disabled. If you are full retirement age, your survivor benefit will be 100 percent of his benefit; if you take it early, the amount will be reduced. You can switch to your own benefit as early as 62. In any event, you can only get one benefit, whichever is higher.

17. **I began drawing Social Security at age 62 in 2006, but I'm still working. Since I'm still paying Social Security taxes, will my benefits increase?**

    If your latest work years are among your highest-earning years, the SSA refigures your benefit and pays you any increase due. This is automatic, with new benefits starting in December of the following year.

18. **My wife is 62 and collects Social Security based on her own work record. Can she receive spousal benefits based on my record when I retire in a few years?**

    If she is eligible for both benefits, yours and hers, Social Security will pay her own benefits first. If she is due additional benefits, she will get a combination of benefits equaling the higher spouse's benefit.

19. **Why would changes in Social Security be considered as a way to help balance the federal budget?**

    Some policymakers say all spending, including Social Security, should be cut. Social Security has not contributed to the deficit. In fact, the trust fund is projected to reach $4.3 trillion by 2023. AARP believes that Social Security benefits should not be targeted to reduce the deficit.

20. **If I retire to a foreign country, can I have my Social Security benefits sent there?**

    If you are a U.S. citizen, you may receive your benefits in most foreign countries, usually by check or direct deposit. If you are not a U.S. citizen, the answer is more complicated, with certain rules applying to certain countries. For specifics, see the Social Security publication "Your Payments While You Are Outside the United States."

21. **I started collecting Social Security at 62. I heard that if I changed my mind, I could pay back the amount I'd collected and get a higher payment. Is that possible?**

    Yes, but the sum you'd be paying back may be quite large, perhaps prohibitive. You must repay all benefits that you and your family received, plus any money withheld from your checks for Medicare Parts B, C and D; also, any tax withheld. For specifics, you'll need to contact Social Security.

22. **Can I collect Social Security and unemployment compensation at the same time?**

    Yes. Unemployment benefits aren't counted as wages under Social Security's annual earnings test, so you'd still receive your benefit. However, the amount of your unemployment benefit could be cut if you receive a pension or other retirement income, including Social Security and railroad retirement benefits. Contact your state unemployment office for information on whether your state applies a reduction.

23. **I am 63 and collecting Social Security. If I work, will my benefit be cut?**

It depends on your income. Between age 62 and the start of the year when you reach full retirement age, $1 in benefits is withheld for every $2 you earn above a limit, which is $14,160 in 2010. In the year you reach full retirement age, $1 is withheld for every $3 above another limit, $37,680 in 2010. In your birthday month, the limits go away—and your benefit will be recalculated upward to compensate for the money that was withheld.

24. **I'm 50. Will Social Security be there when I retire?**

The Social Security trust fund, where accumulated assets are held, currently contains about $2.5 trillion. According to the system's board of trustees, that money and continuing tax contributions will allow payment of all benefits at current rates until 2037. After that, there still will be enough tax revenue coming in to pay about 78 percent of benefits. Congress is being urged to make financial fixes to Social Security to ensure it will be there for you.

25. **I know I can start collecting Social Security at age 62. But should I?**

That depends. If you're healthy and can afford it, you should consider waiting until you reach your full retirement age of 66, or even 70. Here's why. By law, the age when workers can qualify for full benefits is gradually increasing, from 65 to 67. (It will be 67 for anyone born after 1960.) If you claim benefits before reaching full retirement age, they'll be reduced. That's because the goal set by Congress is to pay the same lifetime benefits to an individual regardless of when they're initially claimed. So let's say you claim benefits at age 62 and get $1,000 a month. If you can wait until you're 66, you'll get at least 33 percent more ($1,333). And if you can wait until you're 70, you'll get at least 75 percent more ($1,750). Social Security determines the amount of your benefits based, in part, on your highest 35 years of earnings. So you may get a larger monthly benefit if your extra years of work are your top earning years.

Critical Thinking

1. Should the surplus of funds in the social security account be used by the federal government to reduce the deficit and balance the budget?

2. Can a person receive a social security and an unemployment check at the same time?

3. Is it possible for a wife to receive her husband's social security benefits after his death?

Create Central

www.mhhe.com/createcentral

Internet References

AARP
www.aarp.org
Health and Retirement Study (HRS)
www.umich.edu/~hrswww

STAN HINDEN is a retired *Washington Post* financial writer and author of *How to Retire Happy: The 12 Most Important Decisions You Must Make Before You Retire.*

Unit 6

UNIT

Prepared by: Elaina F. Osterbur, *Saint Louis University*

The Experience of Dying

Modern science has allowed individuals to have some control over the conception of their children and has provided people the ability to prolong life. However, life and death still defy scientific explanation or reason. The world can be divided into at least two categories: sacred and secular. The sacred (that which is usually embodied in the religion of a culture) is used to explain all the forces of nature and the environment that can neither be understood nor controlled. On the other hand, the secular (defined as "of or relating to the world") is used to explain all the aspects of the world that can be understood or controlled. Through scientific invention, more and more of the natural world can be controlled. It still seems highly doubtful, however, that science will ever be able to provide an acceptable explanation of the meaning of death. In this domain, religion may always prevail. Death is universally feared. Sometimes, it is more bearable for those who believe in a life after death. Religion offers a solution to this dilemma. In the words of anthropologist Bronislaw Malinowski (1884–1942):

Religion steps in, selecting the positive creed, the comforting view, the culturally valuable belief in immortality, in the spirit of the body, and in the continuance of life after death. (Bronislaw Malinowski, *Magic, Science and Religion and Other Essays,* Glencoe, IL: Free Press, 1948)

The fear of death leads people to develop defense mechanisms to insulate themselves psychologically from the reality of their own death. The individual knows that someday he or she must die, but this event is nearly always thought to be likely to occur in the far distant future. The individual does not think of himself or herself as dying tomorrow or the next day but years from now. In this way, people are able to control their anxiety about death.

Losing a close friend or relative brings people dangerously close to the reality of death. Individuals come face to face with the fact that there is always an end to life. Latent fears surface. During times of mourning, people grieve not only for the dead but also for themselves and for the finiteness of life.

The readings in this unit address bereavement, grief, and adjustments to the stages of dying.

A Longitudinal Analysis of Social Engagement in Late-Life Widowhood by Linda M. Isherwood, Debra S. King, and Mary A. Luszcz

129

Article

Prepared by: Elaina F. Osterbur, *Saint Louis University*

A Longitudinal Analysis of Social Engagement in Late-Life Widowhood

LINDA M. ISHERWOOD, DEBRA S. KING, AND MARY A. LUSZCZ

Learning Outcomes

After reading this article, you will be able to:

- Describe the role that social activities and contact with children has on the adjustment to late-life widowhood.

- Identify the group of individuals who were found to have low levels of social engagement in widowhood.

Widowhood is one of the major transitions faced in older age (McCallum, 1986) and is considered part of the normative aging process (Baltes & Baltes, 1990). Widowhood engenders a far greater impact on an individual than purely an emotional loss; the transition to widowhood also involves the adjustment to a new role as a single person and the subsequent changes in life that this entails (Carr & Utz, 2002). Social engagement—having close relationships and participating in social activities—strongly influences the ability of the widowed spouse to successfully adapt to widowhood (Bennett, Gibbons, & Mackenzie-Smith, 2010). Therefore, it is important to understand how relationships and social activities change as a consequence of widowhood, and the potential role that social engagement has in protecting widowed people from the strain of bereavement and promoting healthy aging.

Active social engagement has been shown to play an important role during later life and in models of healthy aging. Continuing active engagement in life, along with the avoidance of disease and disability, and the maintenance of cognitive and physical functioning, has been proposed as a vital component of healthy aging (Rowe & Kahn, 1998). With ageing, undesirable changes (or losses) relating to physical, psychological, and social domains become more prevalent (Baltes & Baltes, 1990). The more resources an individual has, including ongoing social resources such as strong social networks and opportunities for social activity, the better their ability to cope with the losses associated with older age (Baltes & Lang, 1997).

By definition, those who have been widowed have lost a key figure in their network of social partners, with potentially an associated reduction in social engagement. The central purpose of this article is to examine the changes in social engagement which occur over time among widowed older adults. Social contact during the earlier stages of bereavement tends to be focused on adult children (Guiaux, van Tilburg, & van Groenou, 2007) and is an important source of emotional support (Ha, 2010). Friends play a more important role in terms of contact and support later in widowhood (Guiaux et al., 2007; Ha, 2008) and this contact is often centered around social activities (Chambers, 2005). Our study examines two key aspects of social engagement: the extent of contact with children and participation in social activities during late-life widowhood.

It is particularly important to understand the social engagement experiences of older widowed men and women for their experiences are likely to be different from that of those widowed at younger ages. Unlike their younger counterparts, the older widowed person is more likely to also be coping with other concurrent stressors such as health concerns, reduced mobility, financial pressures, relocation, cognitive decline, and loss of friends or family members (Carr, 2006). The life-span developmental perspective—which provided the theoretical grounding for this study—emphasizes that transitions during the life course are shaped by contextual factors (Baltes, 1987). Therefore, concomitant changes relating to aging may also have implications for social engagement, and hence the experience of social engagement during late-life widowhood must be viewed against this background.

Relationships with family, friends, and the wider social network take on increased significance following the death of a spouse (Feldman, Byles, & Beaumont, 2000). Social contact with network members during widowhood is an important factor in the facilitation or impediment of successful adjustment to spousal bereavement (van Baarsen, van Duijm, Smit, Snijders, & Knipscheer, 2002). Frequency of contact with others has been associated with well-being in widowhood (Bisconti, Bergeman, & Boker, 2006; Lund, Caserta, & Dimond, 1993) and a lack of social contact identified as a major risk factor for post-bereavement loneliness (Pinquart, 2003).

Two previous studies have examined longitudinal change in contact with the social network during widowhood. These studies produced equivocal results possibly due to methodological differences in their design. Guiaux and colleagues (2007) explored changes in contact and support with the social network before and after widowhood over a 10-year period with outcome data collected every 3 years. Immediately following their loss, widowed individuals reported higher levels of contact with their social network than their still-married peers, with contact peaking at 2.5 years after widowhood. In a study of 108 bereaved spouses interviewed six times in the first 2 years of widowhood, Lund and colleagues (1990) found that contact with family and close friends reached its highest point at 2 months post-bereavement; contact with the primary social network then fell after this point (particularly for older widowed males).

Social activities may also play an important role in the process of adaptation to widowhood. Social activities are those activities which are performed with others and, more than any other activity domain, have been associated with physical and emotional well-being (Adams, Leibbrandt, & Moon, 2011). Kleiber and colleagues (2002) propose that social activities have four different functions during negative life events: activities may act as a buffer; generate hope for the future; provide continuity; and play a central role in personal transformations. Participation in social activities during widowhood has been associated with lower levels of loneliness (Pinquart, 2003), guilt and sadness (Sharp & Mannell, 1996), enhanced morale and reduced stress (Patterson & Carpenter, 1994), and better physical and mental health (Janke, Nimrod, & Kleiber, 2008a). Older widowed individuals may be at risk of lower levels of social participation as significant declines in activity levels have been associated with aging (Bennett, 2005), in particular due to reduced financial status, shrinking of social networks owing to deaths of friends, deterioration in physical health (Bennett, 1997), and poorer perceived health status (Patterson, 1996).

There have been no consistent findings regarding the impact of widowhood on levels of social activity. Previous studies examining participation in social activities have differed considerably in their design, in particular in the timing of measurements, the use of a married control group, and whether pre-loss measures were collected. These studies also measured social activity in very different ways, which could account for the disparate findings. In a comparison of married and widowed older adults and their participation in 20 different activities (solitary as well as social), Bennett (2005) found that widowhood (and especially recent bereavement) led to a decrease in overall levels of activity. Likewise, a study exploring patterns of leisure activity in a sample of recently widowed older adults (Janke, Nimrod, & Kleiber, 2008b) found that the majority of participants reduced their involvement in activities following widowhood.

Meanwhile, other studies have reported increased participation in social activities during widowhood. A study by Utz and colleagues (2002) comparing levels of formal and informal social participation of recently widowed and married participants found that frequency of informal activities increased after widowhood; widowed and married participants reported similar levels of formal activities. Donnelly and Hinterlong (2010), however, in a quasi-replication of the study by Utz et al., found that widowed individuals tended to increase participation in both informal and formal activities. A study examining leisure activity

in a female sample aged 50 years or older (Janke et al., 2008a) found that while widowed women increased their involvement in all activities (except gardening) over time, married participants decreased their participation in most leisure activities.

The main purpose of this study was to explore the changes and continuities which occur in social engagement during late-life widowhood. Previous widowhood research has recommended the use of prospective longitudinal data, married control groups, and collecting data prior to widowhood to ensure that pre-loss characteristics and resources can be controlled (Carr & Utz, 2002). This study follows these recommendations. Previous longitudinal studies have reported differing findings with regard to trajectories of change in social engagement in late-life widowhood. To date, there has been no consensus regarding the relationship between widowhood and the frequency of contact and social activities in later life. Contact in widowhood (particularly during the early stages) tends to be focused on adult children (Guiaux et al., 2007). To our knowledge, there have been no previous studies examining trajectories of change in contact with children during widowhood.

The majority of longitudinal studies of bereavement have focused on the earlier stages of the widowhood transition and used data drawn over two or three occasions. Very little is known of the longer-term outcomes of widowhood with regard to changes in social contact and activities. This study provides an opportunity for an extended longitudinal investigation of social engagement in late-life widowhood as data are available from five occasions over a 16-year period, enabling an examination of social engagement in early and later widowhood.

The particular aspects of social engagement focused on in this study were personal and phone contact with children and participation in social activities. Two primary research questions were developed:

1. Do widowed and married participants exhibit different levels of contact with children and participation in social activities over time?
2. What are the predictors of contact with children and participation in social activities during late-life widowhood?

Method
Participants

Participants were drawn from the Australian Longitudinal Study of Ageing (ALSA). Commenced in 1992, the ALSA aims to enhance understanding of biological social, and psychological factors associated with age-related changes in the health and well-being of older people (aged 65 years and over). To date, the ALSA has collected 11 waves of data: six major waves comprised of in-depth face-to-face interviews, clinical assessments, and self-completed questionnaires; and five waves utilizing shorter telephone interviews. Data on personal and phone contact with children and participation in social activities collected over the first five major waves (T1 = 1992 − 1993, T3 = 1994 − 1995, T6 = 2000 − 2001, T7 = 2002 − 2003, T9 = 2007 − 2008) of the ALSA were used for the longitudinal analyses.

ALSA participants who, at baseline, were married and had at least one living child were included in the sample for this study ($N = 1,266$). The widowed sub-sample was comprised of 344 participants who experienced spousal loss after baseline. The married participant group ($N = 922$) were continuously married throughout their participation in the ALSA. On average, 2.27 observations were available for each married participant. Widowed participants had an average of 3.69 observations each, representing 9.38 years in study.

Measures
Dependent Variables

Personal contact with children—The frequency of personal contact with children was determined by the question "Think of your children and/or children-in-law who do not live with you. In the past 12 months, how often did you have personal contact with at least one of them?" Frequencies were coded never (0), less than once a month (1), almost once a month (2), two or three times a month (3), once a week (4), and more than once a week (5).

Phone contact with children—The frequency of phone contact with children was ascertained by the question "Again, think of your children and/or children-in-law who do not live with you. In the past 12 months, how often did you have phone contact with at least one of them?" Frequencies were again coded never (0), less than once a month (1), almost once a month (2), two or three times a month (3), once a week (4), and more than once a week (5).

Social Activities—Questions regarding participation in social activities in the ALSA were derived from the Adelaide Activity Profile (AAP). The AAP is an instrument for the measurement of lifestyle activities of older people relating to domestic chores, household maintenance, service to others, and social activities (Clark & Bond, 1995). Participants were asked about their frequency of participation in eight social activities over the previous 3 months: voluntary or paid employment; inviting people to the home; telephone calls to friends or family; social activities at a center or club; attendance at religious services or meetings; outdoor social activities; recreational or sporting activities; going for a drive or outing. The scores from the individual questions were summed to create a total social activities score (0 to 24).

Predictor variables and covariates—A number of variables identified in previous widowhood studies were used as either predictors or control variables at different stages in the analyses. These variables included socio-demographic (sex, age, marital status, household income, education), physical health (number of chronic conditions, self-rated health), psychological health (cognitive impairment, depression), and social network variables (number of children, child in close proximity). Sex, age, and education (time-invariant predictors) were based on self-reported data at baseline. All other covariates (time-varying predictors) used in this study were measured at each of the five major waves. The coding for these variables is outlined in Table 1.

Statistical Analysis

Multi-level modeling (MLM) was used to investigate longitudinal change in contact with children and in social activities.

MLM has several advantages over repeated measures statistical models: both within-individual change and between-individual differences can be modeled; the number of observations can vary across participants thus allowing for missing data; occasions of measurement do not need to be fixed but can vary in their timing; and both time-varying (measures collected repeatedly over time) and time-invariant (attributes which are stable and measured only once) predictors can be included in the model (Singer & Willett, 2003). MLM enables both fixed and random effects to be modeled. Fixed effects describe the average patterns of change within a population, while random effects enable within- and between-person variance to be accounted for in the model.

Hox (2010) recommends that if categorical data has at least five categories and the distributions are symmetric, then the potential bias introduced to the model is small and multi-level modeling can be used. The outcome variables for contact with children were therefore treated as linear dependent variables in the multilevel analysis. All the MLM analyses were conducted using SPSS Version 17.0 Linear Mixed Models program.

Comparison of Widowed and Married Participants

In order to ascertain whether widowed and married participants exhibited different levels of contact with children and participation in social activities over time, a series of multi-level models were developed. A forward modeling approach was used with predictors added to the model in subsequent steps. Predictors were retained in the model if overall model fit was improved. In order to ascertain the model of best fit for each of the outcome variables, the deviance statistic (-2LL) of the current model was compared to that of the previous model.

An unconditional growth model (Singer & Willett, 2003) was initially developed containing the random and fixed effects of "time in study." Hence, both the average rate of change over time in social engagement and the between-person variability in this change could be modeled. "Time in study," which was 0 for each participant at baseline, enabled exploration of changes in social engagement with each additional year in study. The fixed effects of "widowed status" at each wave were then added into the model enabling comparisons in levels of social engagement of widowed and married participants over time. Dummy variables for marital status (Married = 0, Widowed = 1) were created for each occasion of measurement. A fixed quadratic function of time in study explored whether change was better represented using a more complex polynomial function of time rather than a linear model (Singer & Willett, 2003). A final model controlled for socio-demographic, health, and network variables in order to ascertain whether marital status was a significant predictor of social engagement.

Predictors of Change for Widowed Participants

The predictors of change in contact with children and participation in social activities during late-life widowhood were then explored. The analysis again began with an unconditional

Table 1 Descriptive Statistics for Participants at Baseline

Variable	Classification	Widowed (n = 344)		Married (n = 922)	
		n	(%)	n	(%)
Sex	Male	113	32.8	571	61.9
	Female	231	67.2	351	38.1
Age	65-74	5	48.1	372	40.3
	75-84	222	42.0	444	48.2
	85 +	95	9.9	106	11.5
	Mean (SD)	76.25	(5.79)	76.96	(5.84)
Household income	≤ $12,000	61	17.7	144	15.6
	$12,000-$30,000	234	68.0	623	67.6
	> $30,000	30	8.7	91	9.9
	Missing	19	5.5	64	6.9
Education	≤ 14 years	176	51.2	522	56.6
(age left school)	> 14 years	164	47.7	394	42.7
	Missing	4	1.2	6	0.6
Chronic conditions	0-1	251	73.0	633	68.5
	2-3	85	24.7	278	30.1
	4 +	8	2.3	13	1.4
	Mean (SD)	1.03	(0.97)	1.14	(0.99)
Self-rated health	Excellent/very good	153	44.5	315	34.2
	Good	107	31.1	277	30.0
	Fair/poor	84	24.4	325	35.2
	Missing	0	0.0	5	0.5
CES-D	No depression (<16/40)	307	89.2	789	85.6
	Depression (≥ 16/60)	36	10.5	119	12.9
	Missing	1	0.3	14	1.5
	Mean	7.42	(7.14)	7.58	(7.15)
MMSE	No cognitive impairment (>23/30)	294	85.5	708	76.8
	Cognitive impairment (≤ 23/30)	47	13.7	197	21.3
	Missing	3	0.9	17	1.8
	Mean	27.04	(3.19)	26.06	(4.32)
Number of children	1	56	16.3	132	14.3
	2	112	32.6	329	35.7
	3	93	27.0	238	25.8
	4 +	83	24.1	223	24.1
	Mean (SD)	2.74	(1.32)	2.79	(1.46)
Child in close proximity	0 children	27	7.8	83	9.0
	≥ 1 child	317	92.2	839	91.0
	Missing	0	0.00	1	0.1

growth model containing the fixed and random effects of "time in study." However, in this analysis, "time in study" was centered on widowhood (where time = 0 was the date of widowhood for each participant) enabling changes in the social engagement variables for each additional year in study before and after widowhood to be identified. Predictors (fixed effects only) were then added to the model in order to ascertain whether they had a significant relationship with levels of social engagement during widowhood. The predictors were added individually beginning with the time-variant predictors (Hox, 2010). Finally, fixed quadratic functions of time in study were added to the model. Using the date of widowhood as a breakpoint, "quadratic time before widowhood" and "quadratic time after widowhood" were calculated at each wave (Guiaux et al., 2007).

Results

Descriptive statistics for the widowed and married participants at baseline are presented in Table 1. The distribution of men and women according to marital status varied. Females comprised the majority (67.2%) of the widowed sub-sample while males formed the majority (61.9%) of the married participants, $\chi^2(1, 1266) = 84.14, p < .001, phi = .26$. Although small, significant differences were found between the married and subsequently widowed participants at baseline. Widowed participants were significantly younger, $t = 2.73 (618.28), p = .006$, reported better self-rated health, $(\chi^2 (5, 1262) = 26.58, p < .001, phi = .15$, and exhibited higher cognitive performance, $t = -4.34 (809.24), p = <.001$.

The results from the multi-level models of best fit for each of the social engagement variables are reported in Table 2.

Personal Contact with Children
Comparison of Widowed and Married Participants

Preliminary models suggested that widowed participants had higher levels of personal contact with their children than their married counterparts. However, once the final quadratic model of best fit controlled for psychological and physical health, social network variables, and socio-demographic factors, the difference between widowed and married participants, $\gamma = 0.117, p = .099$, was no longer significant, indicating that marital status is not predictive of personal contact with children in later life. For the average participant, personal contact with children decreased significantly over time, $\gamma = -0.044, p = .002$, reaching a low point at 11.0 years in study after which contact began to increase.

Predictors of Change for Widowed Participants

The model of best fit introduced health, social network, and socio-demographic predictors into the linear multi-level model. Controlling for all the predictors in this model, the average participant had 4.145 units ($p < .001$) of personal contact with their children at the time of widowhood (where a score of 4 indicates weekly contact and 5 is more than once a week). This frequent level of personal contact did not change significantly over time, $\gamma = -0.002, p = .783$, suggesting that fact-to-face contact with children does not vary with the length of widowhood.

Close proximity to children, $\gamma = -1.869, p < .001$, was the only predictor significantly related to personal contact with children. Hence widowed participants with at least one child living within an hour's travel had considerably higher levels of personal contact with their children.

Phone Contact with Children
Comparison of Widowed and Married Participants

After controlling for health, socio-demographic, and network variables, the quadratic model of best fit showed a small but significant difference between widowed and married participants in level of phone contact, $\gamma = 0.154, p = .024$, indicating that widowhood is associated with more phone contact with children than remaining married. The trajectories of change in phone contact for married and widowed participants are shown in Figure 1. Phone contact with children significantly decreased over time ($\gamma = -0.068, p < .001$), reaching a low-point for the average participant at 8.5 years in study, after which contact started to increase again.

Predictors of Change for Widowed Participants

Controlling for the predictors in the linear model of best fit, the average participant had 4.336 units ($p < .001$) of phone contact with their children at the time of widowhood. Change in phone contact over time was not significant, $\gamma = -0.009, p = .125$, suggesting that the frequency of phone contact does not change during the different phases of widowhood.

Income, $\gamma = 0.100, p = .047$, and sex, $\gamma = -0.438, p = < .001$, were found to be significant predictors of phone contact with children during widowhood. Having a higher income or being female were both predictive of higher levels of phone contact with children.

Social Activities
Comparison of Widowed and Married Participants

The model of best fit suggested that the average married participant had a social activities score of 6.517 ($p < .001$) at baseline, reducing by 0.059 ($p = .001$) with each passing year. Widowed participants on average scored 1.376 ($p < .001$) higher on the social activities scale compared to married participants, suggesting that widowhood is associated with more participation in social activities in older age.

Predictors of Change for Widowed Participants

Controlling for the predictors in the quadratic model of best fit, the average participant had a social activities score of 7.357 ($p < .001$) at the time of widowhood. With each additional year after widowhood, social activities increased by 0.197 ($p < .001$). The quadratic parameters for time before and after widowhood were both significant, $\gamma = 0.020, p = .001; \gamma = -0.017, p = .009$, indicating that the increase in social activities tapered off with time after widowhood. Figure 2 illustrates the average trajectory in social activities score during the transition to widowhood. Before widowhood, social activities were lowest at 4.9 years prior to bereavement. Activities then increased until 5.8 years after widowhood when participation began to decrease again.

Table 2   Social Engagement—Multi-Level Models of Best Fit

Parameters	Comparison between widowed and married participants		
	Personal contact[a]	Phone contact[a]	Social activities[b]
Fixed effects			
Intercept	3.913***	4.213***	6.517***
Time in study	−0.044**	−0.068***	−0.059**
Widowed status	0.117	0.154*	1.376***
Quadratic time in study	0.002*	0.004***	—
Random effects			
Variance residual	0.611***	0.663***	5.177***
Variance intercept	0.747***	0.731***	6.953***
Variance slope	0.004***	0.001	0.027***
Covariance	−0.026***	−0.014*	−0.148**
Model fit			
-2LL	7335.420	7342.084	12700.735
df	18	18	17
Parameters	Predictors of change for widowed participants		
	Personal contact[c]	Phone contact[c]	Social activities[d]
Level-1 fixed effects			
—Intercept	4.145***	4.336***	7.357***
Time in study	−0.002	−0.009	0.197***
Cognitive impairment	0.067	−0.150	−0.969*
Depression	−0.078	0.026	−0.856*
Self-rated health	—	—	−0.464**
Chronic conditions	—	—	—
Close proximity to children	−1.869***	—	—
Number of children	—	—	—
Income	−0.031	0.100*	0.025
Quadratic time before widowhood	—	—	0.020**
Quadratic time after widowhood	—	—	−0.017**
Level-2 fixed effects			
Sex	—	−0.438***	−0.529
Age	—	—	−0.115***
Education	−0.093	0.047	0.955**
Random effects			
Variance residual	0.643***	0.599***	5.751***
Variance intercept	0.555***	0.618***	5.954***
Variance slope	0.004**	0.001	0.021*
Covariance	−0.007	−0.003	−0.052
Model fit			
-2LL	2723.162	2616.007	4718.699
df	11	11	15

Note: df indicates the number of parameters used in the model.

[a] Model included the fixed and random effects of time in study, the fixed effects of widowed status and quadratic time in study, and also controlled for socio-demographic, health, and network variables.

[b] Model included the fixed and random effects of time in study, the fixed effects of widowed status and also controlled for socio-demographic, health, and network variables.

[c] Model included the fixed and random effects of time in study and the fixed effects of socio-demographic, health, and network predictors.

[d] Model included the fixed and random effects of time in study, the fixed effects of quadratic time before and after widowhood, and the fixed effects of socio-demographic, health, and network predictors.

*$p < .05$, **$p < .01$, ***$p < .001$.

A Longitudinal Analysis of Social Engagement in Late-Life Widowhood by Linda M. Isherwood, Debra S. King, and Mary A. Luszcz

135

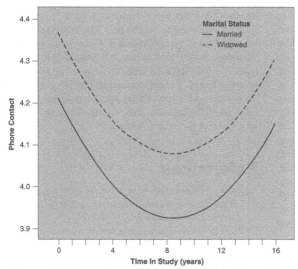

Figure 1   Average change in phone contact with children for married and widowed participants.

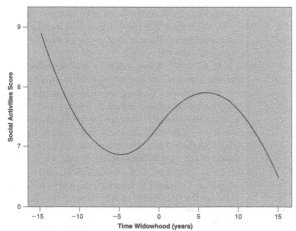

Figure 2   Average change in social activities score during widowhood.

Cognitive impairment, $\gamma = -0.969$, $p = .013$, depression, $\gamma = -0.856$, $p = .010$, self-rated health, $\gamma = -0.464$, $p = .002$, age, $\gamma = -0.115$, $p < .001$, and education, $\gamma = 0.955$, $p = .004$, were all found to be significant predictors of participation in social activities during widowhood. Thus, having an absence of cognitive impairment and depressive symptomatology, better self-rated health, being younger, and having a higher level of education were associated with greater levels of social activity during widowhood.

Discussion

This study explored the levels and predictors of social engagement during late-life widowhood. As the results indicate, levels of social engagement remain high during older age and the

transition to widowhood served to enhance phone contact with children and participation in social activities.

Contact with Children

Comparisons between widowed and married participants indicated that frequency of phone contact with children was greater for the widowed participants. Both married and widowed participants were found to have similarly high levels of face-to-face contact with their children. These results concur with the findings or Guiaux and colleagues (2007) that widowed individuals have higher levels of overall contact with their children compared to married older adults. However, Guiaux et al. used a measure of total contact with children in their study and did not differentiate between personal and phone contact. The current study, while showing that contact with children may increase overall with widowhood, also suggests that there are differences in the trajectories of personal and phone contact in later life. Hence, it is important to distinguish the nature of the contact.

Around the time of widowhood, participants reported on average high levels of both personal and phone contact with their children. Neither type of contact was shown to change significantly over time, indicating that the length of widowhood does not have an impact on the intensity of contact with children. The consistency of contact with children during widowhood found in this study differs from the findings or previous studies which have shown increased levels of contact with the social network during widowhood (Lund et al., 1990; Guiaux et al., 2007). However, it is difficult to fully compare the results of the current study with these previous studies given the methodological differences between them. Socio-emotional selectivity theory proposes that older adults place an increasing focus on close relationships (Carstensen, 1992). Our findings of sustained high levels of contact with children throughout widowhood confirm the importance of the parent-child relationship during this transition.

Nonetheless, these average effects varied as a function of other individual difference factors which were shown to influence the amount or type of contact. Living in close proximity to at least one child was found to significantly predict the level of personal contact with children, while having a higher income and being female were significant predictors of higher levels of phone contact. Previous research with an older cohort has suggested that wives tend to act as "kin-keeper" during a marriage facilitating social interactions for the couple and that widowed men may consequently be at more risk of social isolation (Chipperfield & Havens, 2001). Our findings concur that males, as well those from lower socio-economic groups, and individuals who do not have a child living nearby may experience lower levels of social contact during widowhood.

Social Activities

Longitudinal comparisons of married and widowed individuals revealed that becoming widowed leads to a significant increase in the extent of participation in social activities. This confirms the results of previous studies (Donnelly & Hinterlong, 2010; Janke et al., 2008a; Utz et al., 2002) which also found that widowed individuals had higher levels of participation in social activities. However, these studies only examined social activities during earlier stages of widowhood (18 months and up to 3 years and 5 years post-bereavement respectively); moreover, the study by Janke and colleagues (2008a) used an exclusively female sample. The current study, by examining the experiences of older widowed males and females up to 15 years post-widowhood, enables a longer-term view of social activity following spousal bereavement.

Participation in social activities during widowhood was shown to increase initially with each year after bereavement, reaching a peak at 5.8 years after which time participation began to fall. Age, poorer self-rated health, cognitive impairment, depression, and lower levels of education were all found to be detrimental to participation rates in social activities. Hence, as Bennett (2005) suggests, the very old (who are more likely to be suffering from cognitive decline and physical and mental health problems) may be less able to participate in social activities with others during widowhood.

The results should be interpreted in the context of several limitations. Timing between data collection was not uniform and varied between 2 to 6 years. The larger time intervals may have masked shorter-term fluctuations in social engagement, particularly during the initial stages of widowhood. This study focused on contact with children following spousal bereavement; contact with members of the wider social network was unable to be ascertained as the relevant data was not collected at all time points of the ALSA. An overall measure of social activity was used in the study. We were therefore unable to differentiate whether change occurred in the frequency of particular social activities over time, that is, between levels of participation in formal and informal activities.

These limitations are counterbalanced by the strengths of the study. The data on social engagement was drawn from a population-based study over a 16-year period which, to our knowledge, provides the longest exploration of social engagement in widowhood. Our findings thus enhance understanding of the longer-term impact of widowhood on levels of social engagement. Trajectories of change in contact with children during the transition to widowhood were examined for the first time, differentiating between personal and phone contact. By only including participants who were married at baseline, the study was able to control for pre-loss characteristics. A large sample of older adults was used with a wide age range (65-94 years at baseline) and length of widowhood (up to 15 years).

The results of this study showed that the transition to widowhood is characterized by enhanced levels of social engagement. Frequency of phone contact with children and participation in social activities were shown to be higher for the widowed participants in this study; and social participation increased during the first 6 years of widowhood. High levels of social engagement during widowhood may not only assist individuals in successfully overcoming the challenges of spousal bereavement but may also enhance healthy aging.

However, opportunities for social engagement in widowhood were not found to be uniform. In particular, the very-old, males,

and those in lower socio-economic groups, in poorer health, or without a child living nearby may have restricted opportunities for social contact and activities in widowhood and thus be more vulnerable to social isolation. It is important that practitioners identify those bereaved individuals who may be more at risk of lower levels of social engagement. Promoting opportunities for contact and social activity could have a positive impact on older adults' adjustment to widowhood and provide enhanced opportunities for healthy aging.

References

Adams, K. B., Leibbrandt, S., & Moon, H. (2011). A critical review of the literature on social and leisure activity and wellbeing in later life. *Ageing & Society, 31,* 683–712.

Baltes, P. B. (1987). Theoretical proposition of life-span developmental psychology: On the dynamics between growth and decline. *Developmental Psychology, 23,* 611–626.

Baltes, P. B., & Baltes, M. M. (1990). Psychological perspectives on successful aging: The model of selective optimization with compensation. In P. B. Baltes & M. M. Baltes (Eds.), *Successful aging: Perspectives from the behavioral sciences* (pp. 1–34). Cambridge: The Press Syndicate of Cambridge University.

Baltes, M. M., & Lang, F. R. (1997). Everyday functioning and successful aging: The impact of resources. *Psychology and Aging, 12,* 433–443.

Bennett, K. M. (1997). A longitudinal study of wellbeing in widowed women. *International Journal of Geriatric Psychiatry, 12,* 61–66.

Bennett, K. M. (2005). Psychological wellbeing in later life: The longitudinal effects of marriage, widowhood and marital status change. *International Journal of Geriatric Psychiatry, 20,* 280–284.

Bennett, K. M., Gibbons, K., & Mackenzie-Smith, S. (2010). Loss and restoration in later life: An examination of dual process model of coping with bereavement. *Omega, 61,* 315–332.

Bisconti, T. L., Bergeman, C. S., & Boker, S. M. (2006). Social support as a predictor of variability: An examination of the adjustment trajectories of recent widows. *Psychology and Aging, 21,* 590–599.

Carr, D. (2006). Methodological issues in studying late life bereavement. In D. Carr, R. M. Nesse, & C. B. Wortman (Eds.), *Spousal bereavement in late life* (pp. 19–48). New York: Springer.

Carr, D., & Utz, R. (2002). Late-life widowhood in the United States: New directions in research and theory. *Ageing International, 27,* 65–88.

Carstensen, L. (1992). Social and emotional patterns in adulthood: Support for socioemotional selectivity theory. *Psychology and Aging, 7,* 331–338.

Chambers, P. (2005). *Older widows and the lifecourse: Multiple narratives of hidden lives.* Aldershot: Ashgate Publishing Ltd.

Chipperfield, J. G., & Havens, B. (2001). Gender differences in the relationship between marital status transitions and life satisfaction in later life. *Journal of Gerontology: Psychological Sciences, 56B,* 176–186.

Clark, M. S., & Bond, M. J. (1995). The Adelaide Activities Profile: A measure of the lifestyle activities of elderly people. *Aging: Clinical & Experimental Research, 7,* 174–184.

Donnelly, E. A., & Hinterlong, J. E. (2010). Changes in social participation and volunteer activity among recently widowed older adults. *The Gerontologist, 50,* 158–169.

Feldman, S., Byles, J. E., & Beaumont, R. (2000). 'Is anybody listening?' The experiences of widowhood for older Australian women. *Journal of Women & Aging, 12,* 155–176.

Guiaux, M., van Tilburg, T., & van Groenou, M. B. (2007). Changes in contact and support exchange in personal networks after widowhood. *Personal Relationships, 14,* 457–473.

Ha, J. (2008). Changes in support from confidants, children, and friends following widowhood. *Journal of Marriage and Family, 70,* 306–318.

Ha, J. (2010). The effects of positive and negative support from children on widowed older adults' psychological adjustment: A longitudinal analysis. *The Gerontologist, 50,* 471–481.

Hox J J. (2010). *Multilevel analysis: Techniques and application.* New York: Routledge.

Janke, M. C, Nimrod, G., & Kleiber, D. A. (2008a). Leisure activity and depressive symptoms of widowed and married women in later life. *Journal of Leisure Research, 40(2),* 250–266.

Janke, M. C, Nimrod, G., & Kleiber, D. A. (2008b). Reduction in leisure activity and well-being during the transition to widowhood. *Journal of Women and Aging, 20,* 83–98.

Kleiber, D. A., Hutchinson, S. L., & Williams, R. (2002). Leisure as a resource in transcending negative life events: Self-protection, self-restoration, and personal transformation. *Leisure Sciences: An Interdisciplinary Journal, 24,* 219–235.

Lund, D., Caserta, M., & Dimond, M. (1993). The course of spousal bereavement in later life. In M. Stroebe, W. Stroebe, & R. Hansson (Eds.), *Handbook of bereavement: Theory, research and intervention.* Cambridge: Cambridge University Press.

Lund, D. A., Caserta, M. S., van Pelt, J., & Gass, K. A. (1990). Stability of social support networks after late-life spousal bereavement. *Death Studies, 14,* 53–73.

McCallum, J. (1986). Retirement and widowhood transitions. In H. Kendig (Ed.), *Ageing and families: A support networks perspective.* Sydney: Allen & Unwin.

Patterson, I. (1996). Participation in leisure activities by older adults after a stressful life event: The loss of a spouse. *International Journal of Aging & Human Development, 42,* 123–142.

Patterson, I., & Carpenter, G. (1994). Participation in leisure activities after the death of a spouse. *Leisure Sciences, 16,* 105–117.

Pinquart, M, (2003). Loneliness in married, widowed, divorced, and never-married older adults. *Journal of Social and Personal Relationships, 20,* 31–53.

Rowe, J. W., & Kahn, R. L. (1998). *Successful aging.* New York: Pantheon Books.

Sharp, A., & Mannell, R. C. (1996). Participation in leisure as a coping strategy among bereaved women. In D. Dawson (Ed.), *Proceedings of the Eighth Canadian Congress on Leisure Research.* Ottawa, ON: University of Ottawa.

Singer, J. D., & Willett, J. B. (2003). *Applied longitudinal data analysis: Modeling change and event occurrence.* Oxford: Oxford University Press.

Utz, R. L., Carr, D., Nesse, R., & Wortman, C. B. (2002). The effect of widowhood on older adults' social participation: An evaluation of activity, disengagement, and continuity theories. *The Gerontologist, 42,* 522–533.

van Baarsen, B., van Duijn, M. A. J., Smit, J. H., Snijders, T. A. M., & Knipscheer, K. P. M. (2002). Patterns of adjustment to partner loss in old age: The widowhood adaptation longitudinal study. *Omega, 44,* 5–36.

Critical Thinking

1. How did the transition to widowhood affect the levels of social engagement of these individuals?

2. How did the social activities of widowed persons compare to those of married persons?

3. What is a major problem the older persons may experience if their level of social engagement declines during widowhood?

Create Central

www.mhhe.com/createcentral

Internet References

Agency for Health Care Policy and Research
www.ahcpr.gov

Growth House, Inc.
www.growthhouse.org

Hospice Foundation of America
www.HospiceFoundation.org

Article   Prepared by: Elaina F. Osterbur, *Saint Louis University*

End-of-Life Concerns and Care Preferences: Congruence among Terminally Ill Elders and Their Family Caregivers

DANIEL S. GARDNER AND BETTY J. KRAMER

Learning Outcomes

After reading this article, you will be able to:

- Identify the group of individuals who were found to have low levels of social engagement in widowhood.

- Describe the main function of denial in the grieving process.

- Explain why confusion is normal for those whose social world has been destroyed.

- List the areas of congruence regarding the end-of-life preferences between terminally ill people and their family caregivers.

Introduction

In the past several decades, it has become clear that there are substantial disparities between the way older Americans wish to die and the way their last days are realized. This discrepancy is due, in part, to well-documented gaps in the quality of care that people receive at the end of life (Field & Cassel, 1997; SUPPORT, 1995). Although most people prefer to die in their own homes (Higginson & Sen-Gupta, 2000; Tang & McCorkle, 2003; Thomas, Morris, & Clark, 2004), a majority of deaths occur in hospitals or nursing homes (Gallo, Baker, & Bradley, 2001; Pritchard, Fisher, Teno, Sharp, Reding, Knaus, et al., 1998). And despite considerable advances in medical and supportive approaches to pain management, a significant number of older adults with advanced and terminal illness experience serious pain and discomfort (SUPPORT, 1995; Teno, Clarridge, Casey, Welch, Wetle, Shield, et al., 2004). In an effort to better understand the needs and enhance the care of dying individuals and their families, end-of-life researchers have explored these and other disparities between end-of-life preferences and outcomes.

Barriers to quality end-of-life care include the unpredictable nature of terminal illness, communication difficulties in familial and social relationships, and the complex care needs of dying patients and their families (Kramer & Auer, 2005). Quality care is also hindered by systemic-level factors, including the emphasis on curative and life-sustaining intervention over quality of life and supportive care, health care financing and service delivery structures that move patients between multiple care settings with minimal coordination and poor continuity of care, a lack of providers trained in the fundamentals of palliative care (e.g., biopsycho-social-spiritual aspects of grief and loss, effective clinical communication, attention to family systems), and the absence of evidence-based practice knowledge in this area (Emanuel, von Gunten, & Ferris, 2000; Field & Cassel, 1997; Morrison, 2005). Further, end-of-life care models that represent the standard of care—hospice and palliative care—are under-utilized and often inaccessible to the poor, racial and ethnic minorities, and elders with uncertain disease pathways.

Less is known about the subjective end-of-life experiences, concerns, and preferences of older patients and their family members (Cohen & Leis, 2002; Singer, Martin & Kellner, 1999; Vig, Davenport, & Pearlman, 2002). Recently there have been calls for research to better understand factors that affect patients' and families' perceptions of quality of life and quality of care at the end of life (Field & Cassel, 1997; Kramer, Christ, Bern-Klug, & Francoeur, 2005; NIH, 2004; SUPPORT, 1995). This study explores the challenges, concerns, and preferences of low-income elders receiving palliative care, and focuses on congruence and incongruence between the elders and their primary family caregivers.

Quality of Life and Care at the End of Life

The Institute of Medicine defined a "good death" as one with minimal suffering, which satisfies the wishes of dying patients and their families, while adhering to current medical, cultural and ethical standards (Field & Cassel, 1997). Researchers often operationalize a good death as the degree to which an individual's dying experiences correspond with their preferences for quality of life and quality of care at the end of life (Engelberg, Patrick, & Curtis, 2005). A growing literature has sought to shed light on the aspects of care that are most important to terminally ill elders and their family members (Heyland, Dodek, Rocker, Groll, Gafhi, Pichora et al., 2006; Laakkonen, Pitkala, & Strandberg, 2004).

When faced with advanced life-threatening illness, most people wish to be free of pain and symptoms (Heyland et al., 2006; Vig & Pearlman, 2004), to be treated with dignity and respect (Chochinov, Hack, Hassard, Kristjianson, McClement, & Harlos, 2002; Steinhauser, Christakis, Clipp, McNeilly, McIntyre, & Tulsky, 2000), and to maintain a sense of autonomy and control over their last days (Singer et al., 1999; McSkirmning, Hodges, Super, Driever, Schoessler, Franey, et al., 1999; Vig & Pearlman, 2004). Nearly all prefer to be informed of their prognoses and have time to put their affairs in order (Heyland et al., 2006; McCormick & Conley, 1995; Terry, Olson, Wilss, & Boulton-Lewis, 2006). Dying elders hope to avoid becoming burdens to their families (McPherson, Wilson, & Murray, 2007; Vig & Pearlman, 2004) and typically eschew the use of artificial means to prolong life (Heyland et al., 2006; Singer et al., 1999; see Steinhauser et al., 2000 for divergent findings). There is, however, a great deal of heterogeneity in what constitutes a "good death." Ultimately, end-of-life preferences are individual, dynamic and multidimensional, and vary across contexts such as age, gender, disease course, care setting, financial resources, and social and familial relationships (Thomas et al., 2004).

Congruence in Patient and Family Perspectives

During the course of advanced and terminal illness, elders increasingly rely on family members to identify and communicate their emotional and physical needs and concerns (McPherson, Wilson, Lobchuk, & Brajtman, 2008; Waldrop, Kramer, Skretny, Milch, & Finn, 2005). Much of the research on patients' end-of-life care preferences is also based on the report of family surrogates or healthcare proxies (Teno et al., 2004). However, the accuracy of family members' assessments of dying patients' concerns and preferences is uncertain. Studies have documented significant incongruence between patients and family members on their evaluations of quality of life (Farber, Egnew, Herman-Bertch, Taylor, & Guldin, 2003; McPherson & Addington-Hall, 2003), frequency and severity of pain and other physical and psychological symptoms (McPherson et al., 2008; Mularski, Curtis, Osborne, Engelberg, & Ganzini, 2004; Sneeuw, Sprangers, & Aaronson, 2002), and end-of-life preferences (Engelberg et al., 2005; Moorman & Carr, 2008; Shalowitz, Garrett-Myer, & Wendler, 2006; Steinhauser et al., 2000). Farber and colleagues (2003) describe these differences as reflecting the often highly divergent "cultural perspectives" of patients and their formal and informal caregivers around death and dying.

Although findings have been inconsistent, congruence in the end-of-life preferences and perceptions of elders and their

family caregivers has been found to range from moderate to poor. There is some evidence of greater agreement around objective and measurable factors such as patient functioning and mobility, and less regarding subjective factors such as pain and depression (Desbiens & Mueller-Rizner, 2000; Engelberg et al., 2005; McPherson & Addington-Hall, 2003; Tang & McCorkle, 2003). Congruence may be more likely when surrogate decision-makers are younger and female (McPherson & Addington-Hall, 2003; Zettel-Watson, Ditto, Danks, & Smucker, 2008), family income is higher (Desbiens & Mueller-Rizner, 2000), the illness is of longer duration, or the patient is closer to death (Sneeuw et al., 2002). Notably, there is evidence that families who have had explicit discussions about dying and the patient's wishes are more likely to agree with each other about end-of-life care preferences (Engelberg et al., 2005; Sulmasy, Terry, Weisman, Miller, Stallings, Vettese et al., 1998).

Despite gaps in our understanding of the correspondence between individual and family experiences of dying and preferences for end-of-life, very few studies have focused on congruence among paired patient-family caregiver dyads (Engelberg et al., 2005). And there remains a critical lack of knowledge about the shared and distinct challenges, concerns, and preferences of older adults and their family caregivers at the end of life (Vig et al., 2002). Empirical inquiry in this area may help to enhance familial understanding of older patients' concerns and the accuracy of surrogate decision-making, and to ultimately improve the quality of life at the end of life. The study described here uses qualitative methods to delve more deeply into the subjective experiences of terminally ill elders and their family caregivers, describe their end-of-life preferences and identify areas of congruence and incongruence.

Methods
Study Design

These data were collected as part of a larger longitudinal research study exploring the process and experience of end-of-life care provided to frail elders with advanced chronic disease enrolled in an innovative, fully "integrated" managed care program (Kramer & Auer, 2005). The design was an embedded case study (Scholz & Tietje, 2002), involving in-depth data collection with multiple sources of data. Case study research design makes it possible to examine processes, perceptions and outcomes regarding naturalistic phenomena of which the researcher seeks multiple perspectives (Yin, 2003). The results reported here address the congruent and incongruent end-of-life perceptions, challenges, concerns, and care preferences of elders and their primary family caregivers.

Research Site and Sample

Elder Care of Dane County, a not-for-profit organization, has provided community-based health and social services for older adults since 1976. The Elder Care Partnership (ECP) program, the largest program offered by this organization, provides comprehensive, fully integrated health, psychosocial, and long-term care to low-income frail elders. The program integrates practices that are consistent with clinical practice guidelines for quality palliative care (National Consensus Project, 2004). Detailed descriptions of the study and site can be found elsewhere (Kramer & Auer, 2005).

Study participants were purposively selected by interdisciplinary team members from the pool of elders (aged 65 years or older) enrolled in ECP. Enrollees had annual incomes below $10,000, seven to eight chronic medical conditions, and functional limitations in three or more Activities of Daily Living. Team members were asked to identify elders who were likely to die within 6 months, spoke English, were cognitively able to understand and respond to interview questions, and had a family member involved in their care. Once the elder completed consent procedures and agreed to participate, team members invited the identified primary family caregiver to participate in an interview with the Principal Investigator (PI; second author).

Data Collection

In-depth, semi-structured, face-to-face interviews, which ranged from 1 to 2 hours long, were conducted by the project PI, a university professor and Project on Death in America Social Work Leader. Elders and their identified family caregivers were interviewed separately at a time and place selected by the participant, most often in the participant's home. The interviews were not standardized in order to facilitate greater exploration of issues deemed most important to respondents (Padgett, 2008). Instead, each interview was structured around open-ended questions reflecting the study aims, including questions designed to explore the perceived challenges and concerns of the participants, their end-of-life preferences, and the extent to which they had discussed these issues with family members:

- What has been most difficult or challenging to you and your family members at this time?
- What are your [your family member's] concerns or worries?
- What is most important to you about the care you [your family member] receive[s] in your [their] last days?
- If you could plan it perfectly, what kind of death would you hope for [for the patient]? What would make a "good" death?

Additional questions and probes were used to explore participant preferences about the location of death, the desire for family members to be present, and the importance of family communication and saying "goodbye" during the elder's last days. In addition, the interviewer asked about the extent to which they had talked about the elders' end-of-life preferences, and their comfort or difficulty in doing so.

Data Analysis

All of the interviews were recorded on audiotape and transcribed verbatim, with participant consent. The researchers employed qualitative methods that entailed detailed readings and re-readings of each transcript, team coding, and thematic and conceptual analysis. Data analysis followed a form of *template analysis* (Crabtree & Miller, 1999) that begins with an a priori set of coding categories (i.e., a "template") based on the researchers' domains of interest (end-of-life challenges and worries or fears, care concerns, preferences, and family communication). Two researchers independently read the transcripts, identified segments that were relevant to the research domains, and used the preliminary coding template to search for and identify patterns and themes in the data. These themes were then tested within and across cases, and refined in order to generate broader and more integrated conceptual domains. Upon reaching theoretical saturation, a thematic conceptual matrix (Patton, 2002) was developed to examine the congruent (i.e., like) and incongruent (distinct) themes relevant to the domains of elder and family caregiver end-of-life challenges, concerns, and care preferences.

While no tests were conducted of inter-rater reliability, the research team employed several strategies to ensure analytic rigor. The protocol included: extended engagement, or the use of long interviews with extensive probing and clarification; independent team coding and peer debriefing; deviant case analysis in the development and testing of a final thematic schema; and careful auditing that involved documentation (including verbatim transcripts, field notes, and analytic memos) of the data collection and analytic process (Padgett, 2008).

Findings
Study Participants

Ten elders (five women and five men) and ten family caregivers (six women and four men) completed face-to-face interviews (see Table 1). The mean age of the elders was 85 years old (range: 64-101), and family members were a mean 53 years old (range: 47-67). Family caregivers included four daughters, three sons, one daughter-in-law, one grandson, and one wife. Nine of the dyads were non-Hispanic white, and one was African American. Elders were enrolled in the program an average of 2.6 years (range: 1.5-4), and all had multiple chronic health conditions. The most debilitating diagnoses included serious heart disease ($n = 5$), lung disease ($n = 3$), and cancer ($n = 2$). Five of the elders lived alone and five lived with their family caregivers (four with an adult child and one with a spouse).

Domains of Care

Four domains of end-of-life care framed the results of our analysis: a) the *challenges* or day-to-day difficulties related to the patient's terminal illness; b) participants' *worries* or fears about the patient's death and dying; c) *care concerns* regarding the patient's end-of-life care by formal and informal caregivers; and d) participants' hopes and preferences for a *good death*. These domains reflect a range of end-of-life concerns and preferences that were expressed and elaborated on by study participants, some of which are shared or congruent, and others which are distinct to either elders or their family members (see Table 2).

Challenges

Elders and their family caregivers identified four primary illness-related challenges they struggled with on a daily basis.

Table 1 Elder and Family Caregiver Dyads

Elder	Family Caregiver
97-year-old African-American female with heart disease	47-year-old African-American grandson; single, live-in caregiver
86-year-old white female with lung disease	50-year-old white daughter; lives separately
89-year-old white male with heart disease	56-year-old white son; married, lives separately
82-year-old white female with lung cancer	52-year-old white daughter; single, lives separately
101-year-old white female with heart disease	67-year-old white son; single, live-in caregiver
84-year-old white male with heart disease	47-year-old white daughter; divorced, lives separately (in same town)
80-year-old white male with heart disease and accident-related injuries	48-year-old white daughter-in-law (married to step-son); lives separately
86-year-old white male with prostate cancer	56-year-old daughter; single, live-in caregiver
82-year-old white female with lung disease and accident-related injuries	48-year-old white son; married, lives with elder
64-year-old white male with lung disease	55-year-old white wife; live-in

Table 2 Congruence & Incongruence among Elders & Family Caregivers

Domain	Themes	Incongruent Elder	Family	Congruent Both
Challenges	Experiencing decline			X
	Accepting dependence	X		
	Providing adequate care		X	
	Living with uncertainty			X
Worries	Pain & suffering			X
	Meeting elders' care needs		X	
	Becoming a burden	X		
	Anticipating the impact on survivors			X
Concerns about EOL Care	Receiving competent, consistent & responsive care			X
	Managing pain			X
	Being treated with dignity and respect			X
	Living while dying			X
A "Good Death"	Dying at home			X
	Dying quickly, without suffering			X
	Avoiding life support			X
	Being prepared	X		
	Addressing spiritual needs		X	

Experiencing Physical and Functional Decline

Elders spoke articulately about their efforts to participate in normal daily activities in the face of decreased energy and declining physical and functional capacities, as is illustrated here:

I like to walk. I can't get out and walk. I have to have a walker so sometimes the kids take me in a wheelchair and we can walk around the campgrounds, or we'll go down by the lake. I'd like to be able to walk, too. But I can't do it. I can't go up and down the stairs so I have to stay here and let somebody else go down and do my laundry. I haven't been down the stairs in the basement for two years. (83 year-old female elder)

I can't do the things I want to do, like mow the lawn or walk down the block. It's hard to breathe . . . Yeah, feels like you're ready to die—takes your breath right away from you. (64-year-old male elder)

Family caregivers also struggled with the changes in their loved ones' functioning, often within the context of lifelong relationships:

It's just that I can't be with him like I'd like to be . . . we've been married almost 37 years so it's a long time, and, just to see him going downhill like he is. (55-year-old wife)

Accepting Increasing Dependence

Closely associated with physical and functional decline, many elders struggled to contend with the diminished autonomy and increasing dependence on others:

> I miss driving . . . I have to depend on other people and I was always so independent. It bothers me when I have to ask people to haul me around and pick me up, but they don't care, they don't say anything, but I—that's one thing that bugs me but I can't change it so I'll just go on the way it is. (80-year-old male elder)

Some family caregivers were aware that decreased autonomy could be challenging for the elders, but rather than viewing dependence as a challenge they emphasized the benefits of relying on others:

> He was able to take his own baths and do everything and then wham-o, here he is. He's in bed all the time and somebody has to help him bathe or whatever . . . although I tell him it's *teamwork,* that we're doing this as a team. (56-year-old daughter)

Providing Adequate Care

Family caregivers spoke at length about caring for the elders, often emphasizing the challenges and responsibilities inherent in the role of family caregiver.

> Basically, I'm her number one health advocate. I've had to deal with these situations where people didn't want [her] to go to the hospital and I knew she had to, or just on and on with different things that have happened. So, I just kind of focus on her. (48-year-old son)

The challenge of providing care was often experienced as stressful by family members, given the elder's changing medical needs and the complex nature of family history and relationships:

> Part of my life is on hold right now because I'm staying here to take care of her. . . . I'm married and I have a wife and we want to enjoy our life together, so as painful as it is to see your parent leave your life, it's also going to be a big transition when I finally get on with my life . . . it's really a dichotomy because you feel selfish when you think about yourself and your own situation and what your preferences are and what you'd do if you were just living in your own house with your own family versus taking care of a parent. So, it's pretty hard. (48-year-old son)

Living with Uncertainty

Both elders and family caregivers talked about the difficulties they had in coping with their uncertain futures. Although all participants were aware that the elders had limited prognoses, many struggled with not knowing how and when their terminal decline would occur:

> About death? I've had pains and stuff, you know, and I had to go to the hospital and all that. I don't know if I'm gonna come home again or not. You don't know that—if you're that bad—and these blood clots can move. They can hit you just like that and you're gone. (64-year-old male elder)
>
> For me, it's never knowing when he's going into an attack, and if I'm at work . . . I told them at work—I said there'll be days when I can't come in because he isn't good, or I'll have to leave because something's gone wrong. (55-year-old wife)

Worries or Fears about Dying

Elders and family caregivers were encouraged to talk about their concerns, worries, and fears related to dying. In response to direct questions, most of the elders initially denied any fears of death or dying. As the interviews progressed, however, elders and family caregivers raised a variety of concerns about the future. Four areas of concern or worry were expressed by a majority of the participants.

Pain and Suffering

The principal concern shared by elders and family caregivers was that the elder would experience unmanageable pain or physical discomfort as they were dying.

> I'm concerned about pain and cancer, I never had anyone in my family that's had cancer, my ideas of it are strictly from novels or movies, so they give you enough pain medication to control the pain then you're going to be nauseated and sleepy and even [lose] your mind, hallucinating even, so that's not something I look forward to. (82-year-old female elder)
>
> I guess I'm . . . afraid of the pain, if she might have a lot of pain. I don't know, it really is kind of terrifying. I don't know what it's going to be like when the, if the cancer really hits. The best thing would be if she would die from some secondary, related, symptomatic illness like pneumonia or something. (52-year-old daughter)

Meeting Elders' Increasing Needs

Family caregivers were particularly worried about their capacity to respond to the intensifying needs of the elders, and that they might lack the necessary supports and resources to continue providing care at home. Several participants feared having to place elders in long-term care institutions in the future:

> I suppose my biggest concern . . . is that he will regress and have a physical deterioration that will make it virtually impossible for him to be able to continue in that apartment, making a full time placement in a nursing home type facility necessary. That's going to be hard in a lot of ways. There's the physical move and taking care of all the stuff that will need to be moved over there, and then there's just the emotional aspect for [Elder] in terms of being in a place where he just damn well doesn't want to be. (48-year-old daughter-in-law)

A related concern was that the elder might not be aware of—or might hide—signs of his or her decline.

> I think probably one of my biggest concerns with my mother is whether or not she'll be totally honest and recognize when something is really wrong. And so that,

that's got me some concern to the point when she did fall the last time and she was in the nursing home . . . she had fallen a couple of times earlier in the week and hadn't told anybody that she had been dizzy and that she had fallen and if she, if she had told anybody either her home nurse or us, that that was going on, then we would have intervened, so it raised questions about whether or not she could be on her own or not. (50-year-old daughter)

Family caregivers often feared a sudden decline in the elder's health, and, in particular, "something happening with no one around." Several family members expressed anxiety and guilt about going to work or returning to their own homes, and leaving the elder in the care of others.

Well, I worry every single day about her falling down and stuff like that, and what's going to be the next trigger that sends her back to the hospital for the next surgery that she can barely tolerate or not at all—that whole thing. (48-year-old son)

Becoming a Burden

A major concern of most of the elders was the fear of experiencing a long trajectory of decline, and becoming a burden on their families:

Well, I'd like to go fast. I don't want to suffer a lot and make everybody else suffer a lot. That would be important. My husband had Alzheimer's and that was just pathetic, watching him for ten years go downhill . . . most families now-a-days are half crazy with trying to make a living . . . they have to spend so much time with the woman working and the man working, and then to add the care of an elderly patient is just too much for them, it overburdens them so that they, the parent or the aunt or grandmother, whoever it is, begins to feel well I don't want to bother my children with this, I'll just let it go which is what I do to some extent. (82-year-old female elder)

Family caregivers did not share the concern that their elders were becoming burdens; most did not question their responsibility to provide care and support for the elders.

Anticipating Survivors' Wellbeing

Many elders worried about the needs and wellbeing of their families after their impending death. They were primarily concerned about family members' grief and ability to cope with the loss:

Just to keep my daughter as calm as possible—that's the main thing. I don't want to upset her any more than I have to. What can you do? Your parents die, that's going to happen, so . . . there is nothing to be done about it but I want to, want her to be as calm as possible. (82-year old female elder)

One elder was also specifically anxious about the spiritual wellbeing of her children and grandchildren after she died:

Well, to know that they're taken care of—their health and they're able to—their religion—stay with that. And then

I hear about some of them giving up religion and they're all becoming atheists—it makes me feel kind of blue. I don't like to hear that. (101-year-old female elder)

Some elder participants worried more about practical concerns (e.g., medical bills, taxes, or loss of income) that would affect their loved ones. Many expressed regrets that they would not be around to look out for family members after death.

Well, the thing I'd be concerned about is my wife and the kids, and the house and stuff, you know? All the bills should be paid, or whatever. Well, she'd be living here by herself, you know? And if she was taken care of, or whatever she has to do—I don't think she'd ever get remarried again, but I imagine it'd be tough for her to keep on rolling, keeping the house maybe. The taxes ain't cheap. (64-year-old male elder)

I just hope that the kids will get along fine, and the grandkids, that's it. And hope the world straightens out a little bit better. All this terrorism and stuff, I don't like that but that's way beyond my help. (80-year-old male elder)

Family caregivers echoed these concerns with their own worries about life after the elder's death. Some concerns were about their anticipation of grief and loss, but several caregivers worried about pragmatic matters such as arranging funeral plans and paying bills.

[My fears are] stupid. [Laughs], My worries are about her funeral, okay? That it will come at a really bad time, like when I'm in the middle of three hundred and forty report cards and my house is a mess, you know, and that kind of stuff that, that I won't know what to do. That there will be a division, and fighting like over the paintings and things like that [Laughs]. I want her to write people's names on the backs of the paintings so I won't have to deal with it. (50-year-old daughter)

Concerns about End-of-Life Care

In addition to their worries about dying, elders and family caregivers articulated their concerns and care preferences regarding the care the elders would receive from healthcare team members in their last days. Specifically, they reported four major preferences.

Receiving Competent, Consistent and Responsive Care

Elders and family caregivers felt that quality care required the involvement of skilled healthcare professionals who were competent, "consistent and responsive" to the elders' needs. For elders, it was of critical importance to feel they could depend on reliable caregivers that met their basic needs:

Well [hospice] volunteers means that no one person would come every week, instead you would probably get a stream of people coming in, none of whom you knew and I don't like that idea at all . . . . Just that whoever takes care of me shows me respect . . . taking good care of me. You know, keeping me clean and fed and whatever. If I can't eat—well that's another thing but . . . I just think to take good care of me, see that my needs were taken care of. (82-year-old female elder)

For family members, these concerns seemed to be associated with their anxieties about meeting the elders' escalating needs as death approached (see above). Their descriptions of adequate care often emphasized the medical and concrete aspects of care (e.g., keeping the elder safe and clean, and ensuring their adherence to medication regimens):

> I think hygiene is way up on the scale as far as her, granny's is. Her body is so fragile and her skin is so, you know, tender, so I mean for them making sure she's gets the proper hygiene. And medical, um, well granny won't take a lot of medical, but I mean, but they're there for any medical needs. But, I think, just trying to make her comfortable as possible. (48-year-old grandson)

Managing Pain

Elders and family caregivers were concerned that the elders receive good pain control and prompt alleviation of physical discomfort at the end of their lives. For several participants, this was a primary reason for choosing hospice or palliative care services:

> Well that, the hospitals, they never used to give you enough painkiller to make enough difference because they said you were going to become addicted. Well what difference does it make at that point? And so I would want someone managing that and I . . . I think I would want to go to hospice and let them handle it. (86-year-old female elder)
>
> I happen to be a big proponent of hospice-type transitions from life to death. And, I'm a big believer in you make the person comfortable. At that point, I don't care if he gets hooked on a particular drug. It's irrelevant. But if he could have his needs tended to, the pain alleviated, and the transition as smooth as possible, I'd rather see that—except to go quickly. (48-year-old daughter-in-law)

Being Treated with Dignity and Respect

Elders and family caregivers also agreed that respectful treatment was of paramount concern in end-of-life care. For elders, this meant appreciating their need for autonomy and control, and being cared for in a courteous, compassionate manner. Family members also articulated the importance of having providers who treated the elders with dignity and valued each patient as a unique, "whole person":

> Just that, that whole, you know, just having respect and beauty and concern around. . . . But a nursing home staff in all fairness is totally overloaded, I mean so it's not like totally all their fault. It's our system's fault, it's like, we don't value that so much. (50-year-old daughter)
>
> To try to meet the person on their own level. In my mother's case, in other words, to try and find out what is important to that person and take an interest in those things with them. Share with them those things. If someone thinks clipping coupons is important, than the social worker who's coming says look at all these coupons

I found, we can go get such and such at so and so or if the person is a musician and the social worker would come and say well I have a new recording of so and so's orchestra doing such and such. (52-year-old daughter)

Living While Dying

Many of the elders thought it was important to continue living as they had their entire lives. "Focusing on living" instead of dying included eating the foods they loved, participating in activities they enjoyed (e.g., walking, sewing, card-playing, and socializing) with friends and family.

> Just comradeship. . . . [Having] people that are around that I will talk with, or will talk with me, and you would miss them if you don't see them at least once a week, or more than that. (84-year-old male elder)

This concern was associated with the desire to be treated with dignity and respect, and to die at home in the context of intimate surroundings, people, and routines! Elders emphasized the critical importance of having a measure of control over their lives and choice in their care during the dying process.

> Well, if I could eat—to get some decent food—and they wouldn't cut me off my martinis or beer. That's about all. (80-year-old male elder)

Although not often a primary concern, most family caregivers expressed an understanding of how important it was for the elder to continue "living while dying," and sought to provide them with opportunities to enjoy their cherished activities.

> Well, I think she wants to maintain a sense of normalcy, that things are still the way they used to be as much as possible. So even if life is slipping away, she still can enjoy it. She can still feel at home. So little things, like being able to watch her favorite television shows. . . . Being able to get out—she likes to get out and drive around. You know, just anything that would make her feel normal. So eating the types of things that she's enjoyed in the past, being able to go to a movie with us, go for a drive with the relatives. All the types of things like that. (48-year-old son)

A "Good Death"

In response to a being asked to describe a good death, participants expressed their fundamental end-of-life preferences for the elders' final days.

Dying at Home

Almost all participants expressed a preference for the elder to die at home. Dying at home was viewed as a more "natural death," where elders could more easily be surrounded by friends and family, and their final wishes could best be met. Several family caregivers worried that the patient's needs might outstrip the supports and resources necessary to keep the elder at home until death, but preferred that the death take place at home if at all possible.

Dying Quickly, without Suffering

For elders and family members, the ideal death was seen as one where the elder dies swiftly, "peacefully, and without pain." One patient summed this perspective up memorably:

> Just let me die. Quickly. Fast. And painlessly.... Stand out there and have lightning strike me, or anything that would do me in like that! (84-year-old male elder)

Many imagined a "natural" death, spending their last moments comfortably ensconced in a favorite chair or sitting in a garden surrounded by natural beauty. Some hoped they would simply be able to "go to sleep and not wake up":

> Good death would be able to roll out in a wheelchair onto a garden patio and be surrounded by beautiful flowers, you know, I mean that would be all right. Just that . . . having respect and beauty and concern around you. (50-year-old daughter)
>
> He would sit down in his chair and he wouldn't wake up. That would be ideal. (48-year-old daughter-in-law)

Avoiding High-Tech Life Support

For most elders, the desire to die naturally meant not having to accept unwanted intervention, and not taking advantage of feeding or breathing "tubes," or other medical technologies meant to prolong their lives.

> Well, I don't want this—I don't want to be resuscitated. If I'm going I want to go, and that's supposed to prevent them from putting me on any machines. I don't want to wake up a lunatic or something, you know, be alive—breathing but not knowing what's going on. I don't want that.... I want to go—no life saving treatments for me. It might be a terrible thing to say.... It's my life. (80-year-old male elder)

For the most part, family caregivers reported that they respected these concerns and believed it important to follow their elders' preferences, even if they did not share them:

> Um yes, we, we talked, we talked about it and she just basically wants to be at home, not hooked up to any machines um, you know, just to die naturally, you know, just go. She don't want to go to a revival or resuscitory thing, you know, she dies, she just wants to die, you know. (47-year-old grandson)

Being Prepared

The elders expressed a preference to be made aware of their impending death so that they could "get things in order." Many worked to develop a sense of completion in their lives, had arranged their financial and other affairs, and felt to some extent prepared to die. Those who did not feel a sense of completion or closure reported that having time for preparation was quite important to them.

> Well, I wouldn't want to go in my sleep. I'd want to prepare better. I'd want some doctor to say "[Name], you only have two days, three days, six days," whatever and then I can prepare myself better—get things straightened out with the kids, get my will set, and just have a priest with me and that's all. I don't want to die in my sleep. (80-year-old male elder)

Family caregivers were not aware of and did not share the elders' desire to be prepared for death, although some shared regrets that they had not talked enough or spent enough time with elders when they were still "able to do things."

Addressing Spiritual Needs

Many family members hoped their loved ones would achieve "peace of mind" at the end of their lives, and felt this was an important component of a good death. This sense of peace was most often expressed in spiritual or religious terms; several family members hoped that elders would achieve "spiritual closure" through faith and prayer, and wanted them to have access to clergy to talk with about their spiritual concerns.

> I guess it's um, being taken care of spiritually . . . contacting the people at the church. And have somebody come talk to him, and um, give him a peace of mind. (56-year-old son)

Although we asked questions about faith, spirituality, and religion, there was a great deal of variability in the extent to which faith was important to the elders. Most denied that having their spiritual or faith needs addressed were essential to a "good death" in the way they were to family caregivers.

Communication about End-of-Life Care Preferences

As part of our analysis, the researchers examined the ways in which families talked about death and dying, and how family communication influenced the congruence between participants in expressed challenges, concerns, and preferences. When asked about the extent to which they had discussed dying or their care preferences with family members, the majority of elders and family members—six of the ten dyads—indicated they had not done so. Three elders believed the lack of communication was due to their own lack of desire to talk about dying or end-of-life care with family members. Two others reported that it was difficult to talk about these subjects with family, either due to their own or their family members' discomfort.

> It doesn't make me feel uncomfortable but I can't think of anything that I could, that I can add to it that I haven't already thought about.... No, I think I'd like to talk to them about that. They don't seem to want to talk about it—'cause it's an unpleasant thing and they don't always go for it—kind of push it back. But I want to talk a little more about this. (82-year-old male elder)

Four families indicated that they had talked about dying and discussed the elders' care preferences. Even though she had talked with her husband, one caregiver indicated that she found these conversations about dying and his care preferences extremely uncomfortable.

In order to examine the relationship, if any, between participants' communication patterns and congruence in end-of-life care preferences, we compared the responses of families who reported communication constraints with those who reported open communication. As illustrated in Table 3, the level of congruence was much higher among families reporting open communication regarding dying and end-of-life care. None of the four families with open communication and half of the six families with communication constraints shared end-of-life concerns or preferences that were not congruent. Examples of the latter include: the 84-year-old male elder who stated a preference to be alone at the time of death, and his 47-year-old daughter who reported he wished to be surrounded by family; the 101-year-old female elder who expressed a strong desire to be kept informed of her evolving health status whose 67-year-old son preferred her not to be informed of these changes; and the 64-year-old male elder who expressed a strong desire to die at home without the use of life-sustaining machines, contrasting his 55-year-old wife's preference for him to die at the hospital, with full access to medical and technological resources.

Discussion

The findings of this study were generally consistent with the empirical literature on congruence between patients and surrogate decision-makers, which suggests that agreement about dying and end-of-life care ranges from poor to moderate (Engelberg et al., 2005; Moorman & Carr, 2008; Mularski et al., 2004). Elder participants acknowledged their need for support and care as their illnesses progressed, but—in contrast to family caregivers—most strongly valued their independence, and wanted to maintain control over their lives and continue to participate in activities they enjoyed. This parallels the finding that family members often underestimate the patient's need for autonomy and control over their own care (Farber et al., 2003; McSkimming et al., 1999; Singer, et al., 1999; Vig & Pearlman, 2004). Elders were greatly concerned about becoming a burden on their families, echoing another well-documented finding, particularly with older patients (McPherson et al., 2007; Vig & Pearlman, 2004).

The lack of apparent spiritual or religious needs on the part of the elders may be due, in part, to the lack of minority elder participants; a wealth of prior research suggests spirituality is of primary importance to African Americans and Latinos at the end of life (Born, Greiner, Sylvia, & Ahluwalia, 2004; Waters, 2001). One African-American elder shared that she spent all of her waking hours in prayer, but she too denied a desire to talk with others about her faith. This may reflect a perception that spiritual needs are felt to be intrinsic, and not as something that requires intervention from others.

Family caregivers felt most challenged by the responsibilities of managing and providing adequate care, and were concerned about their capacity to meet their loved ones' physical and spiritual needs as the illness progressed. The preeminence of these concerns is consistent with the literature (Terry et al., 2006) and reflects the high level of cognitive, emotional, and physical investment made by family caregivers at the end of life (Waldrop et al., 2005). Although other researchers have found strong congruence around the importance of preparation and a sense of completion in determining a good death (Engelberg et al., 2005; Steinhauser et al., 2000), in this study only elder participants identified this as a significant preference. Unlike the elders, family caregivers were concerned about elders' spiritual wellbeing, and felt that achieving "peace of mind" was essential to experiencing a good death.

Despite these differences, elders and family caregivers reported many congruent concerns and preferences. Consistent with the literature on quality of life at the end of life, most elders and family caregivers preferred that the elder die at home (Tang & McCorkle, 2003; Steinhauser et al., 2000), and for death to come swiftly, without pain or suffering (Heyland et al., 2006; Vig & Pearlman, 2004). Experiencing loss related to the elders' physical, functional, and cognitive decline, and managing advanced illness in the face of an uncertain and unpredictable future were among the most difficult challenges reported by the elders and their caregivers. Accepting the inherent uncertainty and ambiguity of the dying process may indeed be one of the more significant challenges for terminally ill patients and their families (Bern-Klug, 2004; Gardner, 2008; McKechnie, Macleod & Keeling, 2007). Elders and family caregivers also shared concerns about the wellbeing of survivors following the patient's eventual death.

There was particularly consistent agreement regarding end-of-life care preferences, specifically around the importance of reliable, high-quality care, and the avoidance of life-sustaining treatment. Another shared concern was that elders be treated with dignity and respect by formal caregivers, and would be allowed to continue living until death, a finding echoed in the literature (Chochinov et al., 2002). A finding not compatible with prior literature was the shared preference of elders and family caregivers to avoid using life-sustaining treatment. Many studies suggest that family members are less likely than older patients to prefer life-support, and that surrogates often underestimate elders' preference for aggressive measures at the end of life (Hamel, Lynn, Teno, Covinsky, Wu, Galanos et al., 2000; Pruchno, Lemay, Field, & Levinsky, 2005). The present finding may be another artifact of a sample that includes few minority elders, who are more likely than white patients to

Table 3 Communication Patterns and Congruence in End-of-Life Care Preferences

Communication Pattern	Congruence	Incongruence
Communication Constraints	3	3
Open Communication	4	0

prefer life-sustaining medical treatment (Phipps, True, Harris, Chong, Tester, Chavin et al., 2003; Steinhauser et al., 2000). Nonetheless, the findings suggest the need for further exploration of patients and family preferences for life-sustaining treatment.

Replicating findings from prior research (Parker, Clayton, Hancock, Walder, Butow, Carrick et al., 2007; Teno, Lynn, Wenger, Phillips, Murphy, Connors et al., 1997), a minority of families had communicated with each other about end-of-life concerns and preferences. Despite the advantages of open family communication (Metzger & Gray, 2008), the literature on advance care planning and family communication suggests that less than 20% actually talk about dying and their preferences for care (Bradley & Rizzo, 1999; Rosnick & Reynolds, 2003; Teno et al., 1997). Lack of communication can contribute to family conflict between the elder and family surrogates, difficulties in decision-making and advance care planning, and ultimately to poorer quality end-of-life care (Kramer, Boelk, & Auer, 2006). This corroborates our finding that a lack of communication was associated with greater incongruence, and suggests the importance of future research on the impact of family conflict on end-of-life experiences and outcomes.

Conclusions & Implications

While many of these findings were consistent with the literature on congruence in patient and caregiver perceptions, the current study is unusual in that it compared the subjective experiences of older chronically and terminally ill patients with those of their matched family caregivers. This study confirms that end-of-life concerns and care preferences found with broader populations also apply to frail elders and their caregivers. The findings further suggest that there may be more family congruence around preferences for end-of-life care than around challenges, concerns, and wishes related to dying. Open family communication was associated with greater congruence in patient and family preferences, which supports prior findings that open communication is associated with better adjustment in family caregivers after the death of their loved ones (Kramer, 1997; Metzger & Gray, 2008). These results have important implications for intervention and research, as they highlight potential sources of unmet needs and conflict among dying elders and their family members.

Although there were more areas of congruence than incongruence among family members, the findings of this study suggest that healthcare professionals providing end-of-life care would be prudent to view family reports as imperfect proxies for elder's concerns, challenges, and preferences. Principle domains of incongruence included the elders' difficulties in accepting dependence, their fears of becoming a burden, and desire to be prepared for death. Unlike the elders, family caregivers were primarily concerned with providing adequate care to meet the elders' physical and spiritual care needs. The study highlights the need for more focused and comprehensive assessment of terminally ill elders and their family caregivers, and for sensitivity to potential differences in preferences and concerns.

It is perhaps not surprising that elders and family caregivers viewed the end-of-life experience somewhat differently, given their different ages, roles, and perspectives. Incongruence presents difficulties only when patients and caregivers with different views are unable to communicate openly and resolve differences with each other (de Haes & Teunissen, 2005). Family conflict and communication constraints can present significant barriers to the provision of quality care, the completion of advance directives, and the attainment of a "good death" (Covinsky, Fuller, Yaffe, Johnston, Hamel, Lynn et al., 2000; Kramer et al., 2006). Terminally ill elders and their families may therefore derive particular benefit from interventions that address congruent and incongruent experiences, and teach communication and family problem-solving skills around the end-of-life and end-of-life care. Working to enhance families' efforts to talk about and resolve differences, and to make informed decisions about care is fundamental to facilitating advance care planning, and reducing inappropriate procedures and hospitalizations.

There were some limitations to this study, which involved a small, non-representative sample of primarily white, low-income elders, recruited purposively from a unique comprehensive health and long-term care program in the Midwest. Casual generalizations should not, therefore, be made to other populations of terminally ill elders and family caregivers. The sample lacked heterogeneity in terms of race/ethnicity, and cultural factors have been shown to be important variables in end-of-life preferences (Phipps et al., 2003). There was also a good deal of variability in medical diagnosis, elders' living situations, and family caregivers' relationships to the elder, all of which may have influenced the findings.

Despite these limitations, this qualitative study identifies subjective concerns and care preferences of terminally ill elders and their family caregivers at the end of life. The findings highlight the need for more focused and comprehensive assessment of terminally ill elders and their family caregivers, and attention to potential differences in patient and family preferences and concerns. Further research into this population's unique needs and perceptions, including the dynamics of family communication and decision making at the end of life, is necessary to further healthcare efforts to better meet elders' psychosocial needs, enhance their wellbeing, and facilitate a "good death." Understanding elders' experiences and preferences, identifying areas of congruence and incongruence, and improving communication in families are essential to providing quality end-of-life care to all dying patients and their families.

References

Bern-Klug, M. (2004). The Ambiguous Dying Syndrome. *Health and Social Work, 29*(1), 55–65.

Born, W., Greiner, K., Sylvia, E., & Ahluwalia, J. (2004). Knowledge, attitudes, and beliefs about end-of-life care among inner-city African Americans and Latinos. *Journal of Palliative Medicine, 7*(2), 247–256.

Bradley, E., & Rizzo, J. (1999). Public information and private search: Evaluating the Patient Self-Determination Act. *Journal of Health Politics, Policy and Law, 24*(2), 239–273.

Chochinov, H., Hack, T., Hassard, L., Kristjianson, S., McClement, S., & Harlos, M. (2002). Dignity in the terminally ill: A cross-sectional, cohort study. *The Lancet, 360*(9350), 2026–2030.

Cohen, S. R., & Leis, A. (2002). What determines the quality of life of terminally ill cancer patients from their own perspective? *Journal of Palliative Care, 18*(1), 48–58.

Covinsky, K., Fuller, J., Yaffe, K., Johnston, C., Hamel, M., Lynn, J., et al. (2000). Communication and decision-making in seriously ill patients: Findings of the SUPPORT project. *Journal of the American Geriatrics Society, 48*(5), S187–S193.

Crabtree, B., & Miller, W. (1999). Using codes and code manuals: A template organizing style of interpretation. In B. F. Crabtree & W.L. Miller (Eds.), *Doing qualitative research* (2nd ed., pp. 163–178). Thousand Oaks, CA: Sage.

de Haes, H., & Teunissen, S. (2005). Communication in palliative care: A review of recent literature. *Current Opinion in Oncology, 17*(4), 345–350.

Desbiens, N., & Mueller-Rizner, N. (2000). How well do surrogates assess the pain of seriously ill patients? *Critical Care Medicine, 28,* 1347–1352.

Emanuel, L., von Gunten, C., & Ferris, F. (2000). Gaps in end-of-life care. *Archives of Family Medicine, 9,* 1176–1180.

Engelberg, R., Patrick, D., & Curtis, J. (2005). Correspondence between patients' preferences and surrogates' understandings for dying and death. *Journal of Pain and Symptom Management, 30*(6), 498–509.

Farber, S., Egnew, T., Herman-Bertch, J., Taylor, T., & Guldin, G. (2003). Issues in end-of-life care: Patient, caregiver, and clinician perceptions. *Journal of Palliative Medicine, 6*(1), 19–31.

Field, M. J., & Cassel, C. K. (Eds.). (1997). *Approaching death: Improving care at the end of Life.* Institute of Medicine. Washington, DC: National Academy Press.

Gallo, W., Baker, M., & Bradley, E. (2001). Factors associated with home versus institutional death among cancer patients in Connecticut. *Journal of the American Geriatrics Society, 49,* 771–777.

Gardner, D. (2008). Cancer in a dyadic context: Older couples' negotiation of ambiguity and meaning in end-of-life. *Journal of Social Work in End-of-life and Palliative Care, 4*(2), 1–25.

Hamel, M., Lynn, J., Teno, J., Covinsky, K., Wu, A., Galanos, A., et al. (2000). Age-related differences in care preferences, treatment decisions, and clinical outcomes of seriously ill, hospitalized adults: Lessons from SUPPORT. *Journal of the American Geriatrics Society, 48*(5/Supplement), S176–S182.

Heyland, D., Dodek, P., Rocker, G., Groll, D., Garni, A., Pichora, D., et al. (2006). What matters most in end-of-life care: perceptions of seriously ill patients and their family members. *Canadian Medical Association Journal, 174*(5), 627–633.

Higginson, I., & Sen-Gupta, G. (2000). Place of care in advanced cancer: a qualitative systematic literature review of patient preferences. *Journal of Palliative Medicine, 3*(3), 287–300.

Kramer, B. J., & Auer, C. (2005). Challenges to providing end-of-life care to low-income elders with advanced chronic disease: Lessons learned from a model program. *The Gerontologist, 45,* 651–660.

Kramer, B. J., Boelk, A., & Auer, C. (2006). Family conflict at the end of life: Lessons learned in a model program for vulnerable older adults. *Journal of Palliative Care 9*(3), 791–801.

Kramer, B. J., Christ, G., Bern-Klug, M., & Francoeur, R. (2005). A national agenda for social work research in palliative and end-of-life care. *Journal of Palliative Medicine 8,* 418–431.

Kramer, D. (1997). How women relate to terminally ill husbands and their subsequent adjustment to bereavement. *Omega: Journal of Death and Dying, 34*(2), 93–106.

Laakkonen, M., Pitkala, K., & Strandberg, T. (2004). Terminally ill elderly patients' experiences, attitudes, and needs: A qualitative study. *Omega: Journal of Death and Dying, 49*(2), 117–129.

McCormick, T., & Conley, B. (1995). Patients' perspectives on dying and on the care of dying patients. *Western Journal of Medicine, 163*(3), 236–243.

McKechnie, R., Macleod, R., & Keeling, S. (2007). Facing uncertainty: The lived experience of palliative care. *Palliative and Supportive Care, 5,* 367–376.

McPherson, C., & Addington-Hall, J. (2003). Judging the quality of care at the end of life: Can proxies provide reliable information? *Social Science and Medicine, 56,* 95–109.

McPherson, C., Wilson, K., & Murray, M. (2007). Feeling like a burden: Exploring the perspectives of patients at the end of life. *Social Science & Medicine, 64*(2), 417–427.

McPherson, C., Wilson, K., Lobchuk, M., & Brajtman, S. (2008). Family caregivers' assessment of symptoms in patients with advanced cancer: Concordance with patients and factors affecting accuracy. *Journal of Pain Symptom Management, 35*(1), 70–82.

McSkimming, S., Hodges, M., Super, A., Driever, M., Schoessler, M., Franey, S. G., et al. (1999). The experience of life-threatening illness: Patients' and their loved ones' perspectives. *Journal of Palliative Medicine, 2*(2), 173–184.

Metzger, P., & Gray, M. (2008). End-of-life communication and adjustment: Pre-loss communication as a predictor of bereavement-related outcomes. *Death Studies, 32*(4), 301–325.

Moorman, S., & Carr, D. (2008). Spouses' effectiveness as end-of-life surrogates: Accuracy, uncertainty, and errors of overtreatment or undertreatment. *Gerontologist, 48*(6), 811–819.

Morrison, S. (2005). Health care system factors affecting end-of-life care. *Journal of Palliative Medicine, 8*(Supplement 1), S79–S87.

Mularski, R., Curtis, R., Osborne, M., Engelberg, R., & Ganzini, L. (2004). Agreement among family members and their assessment of the quality of dying and death. *Journal of Pain and Symptom Management, 28*(4), 306–315.

National Consensus Project (2004). *Clinical practice guidelines for quality palliative care.* Brooklyn, NY.

National Institutes of Health (NIH). (2004). *State-of-the-science conference on improving end-of-life care: Conference statement.* Bethesda, MD: National Institutes of Health.

Padgett, D. K. (2008). *Qualitative methods in social work research: Challenges and rewards* (2nd ed.). Thousands Oaks, CA: Sage Publications, Inc.

Parker, S., Clayton, J., Hancock, K., Walder, S., Butow, P., & Carrick, S. et al. (2007). A systematic review of prognostic/end-of-life communication with adults in the advanced stages of a life-limiting illness: Patient/care-giver preferences for the content, style, and timing of information. *Journal of Pain and Symptom Management, 34*(1), 81–93.

Patton, M. (2002). *Qualitative research and evaluation methods* (3rd ed.). Thousands Oaks, CA: Sage Publications, Inc.

Phipps, E., True, G., Harris, D., Chong, U., Tester, W., Chavin, S., et al. (2003). Approaching the end of life: Attitudes, preferences, and behaviors of African-American and white patients and their family caregivers. *Journal of Clinical Oncology, 21*(3), 549–554.

Pritchard, R., Fisher, E., Teno, J., Sharp, S. Reding, D., Knaus, W., et al. (1998). Influence of patient preferences and local health system characteristics on the place of death. (SUPPORT Investigators: Study to Understand Prognoses and Preferences for Risks and Outcomes of Treatment). *Journal of the American Geriatrics Society, 46*(10), 1242–1250.

Pruchno, R., Lemay, E., Field, L., & Levinsky, N. (2005). Spouse as health care proxy for dialysis patients: Whose preferences matter? *Gerontologist, 45*(6), 812–819.

Rosnick, C., & Reynolds, S. (2003). Thinking ahead: Factors associated with executing advance directives. *Journal of Aging & Health, 15*(2), 409–429.

Scholz, R. and Tietje, R. (2002). *Embedded case study methods: Integrating quantitative and qualitative knowledge.* Thousand Oaks, CA: Sage Publications.

Shalowitz, D., Garrett-Meyer, E., & Wendler, D. (2006). The accuracy of surrogate decision makers: A systematic review. *Archives of Internal Medicine, 166*, 493–497.

Singer P., Martin D., & Kellner M. (1999). Quality end-of-life care: patients' perspectives. *Journal of the American Medical Association, 281*, 163–168.

Sneeuw, K., Sprangers, M., & Aaronson, N. (2002). The role of health care providers and significant others in evaluating the quality of life of patients with chronic disease. *Journal of Clinical Epidemiology, 55*(11), 1130–1143.

Steinhauser A., Christakis N., Clipp E., McNeilly M., McIntyre L., & Tulsky J. (2000). Factors considered important at the end of life by patients, family, physicians, and other care providers. *Journal of the American Medical Association, 284*(19), 2476–2482.

Sulmasy, D., Terry, P., Weisman, C., Miller, D., Stallings, R., Vettese, M., et al. (1998). The accuracy of substituted judgments in patients with terminal disease. *Annals of Internal Medicine, 128*(8), 621–629.

SUPPORT Principal Investigators (1995). A controlled trial to improve care for seriously ill hospitalized patients: The study to understand prognosis and preferences for outcomes and risks for treatments (SUPPORT). *Journal of the American Medical Association, 274*(20), 1591–1598.

Tang, S., & McCorkle, R. (2003). Determinants of congruence between the preferred and actual place of death for terminally ill cancer patients. *Journal of Palliative Care 19*(4), 230–237.

Teno, J., Clarridge, B., Casey, V., Welch, L., Wetle, T., Shield, R., et al. (2004). Family perspectives on end-of-life care at the last place of care. *Journal of the American Medical Association, 291*(1), 88–93.

Teno, J., Lynn, J., Wenger, N., Phillips, R., Murphy, D., Connors, A., et al. (1997). Advance directives for seriously ill hospitalized patients: Effectiveness with the patient self-determination act and the SUPPORT intervention. SUPPORT Investigators. *Journal of the American Geriatric Society, 45*(4), 500–507.

Terry, W., Olson, L., Wilss, L., & Boulton-Lewis, G. (2006). Experience of dying: Concerns of dying patients and of carers. *Internal Medicine Journal, 36*(6), 338–346.

Thomas, C., Morris, S., & Clark, D. (2004). Place of death: Preferences among cancer patients and their carers. *Social Science & Medicine, 58*, 2431–2444.

Vig, E., Davenport, N., & Pearlman, R. (2002). Good deaths, bad deaths, and preferences for the end of life: A qualitative study of geriatric outpatients. *Journal of the American Geriatric Society, 50*(9), 1541–1548.

Waldrop, D., Kramer, B.J., Skretny, J., Milch, R., & Finn, W. (2005). Final transitions: Family caregiving at the end of life. *Journal of Palliative Medicine, 8*(3), 623–638.

Waters, C. (2001). Understanding and supporting African Americans' perspectives of end-of-life care planning and decision making. *Qualitative Health Research, 11*, 385–398.

Vig, E., & Pearlman, R. (2004). Good and bad dying from the perspective of terminally ill men. *Archives of Internal Medicine, 164*(9), 977–981.

Yin, R. (2003). *Case study research: Design and methods* (3rd ed.). Thousand Oaks, CA: Sage Publications.

Zettel-Watson, L., Ditto, P., Danks, J., & Smucker, W. (2008). Actual and perceived gender differences in the accuracy of surrogate decisions about life-sustaining medical treatment among older spouses. *Death Studies, 32*(3), 273–290.

Critical Thinking

1. What are the barriers to quality end-of-life care?

2. What were the major worries and fears about dying expressed by the elders and their family caregivers?

3. What were the end-of-life preferences for the elders in their final days?

Create Central

www.mhhe.com/createcentral

Internet References

Agency for Health Care Policy and Research
www.ahcpr.gov

Growth House, Inc.
www.growthhouse.org

Hospice Foundation of America
www.HospiceFoundation.org

Acknowledgements—The authors' extend their appreciation to Elder Care Partnerships staff and administration, and to End-of-Life committee members who provided ongoing support and consultation. Special thanks to the elders and their family members who offered their valuable insights.

Article Prepared by: Elaina F. Osterbur, *Saint Louis University*

The Myriad Strategies for Seeking Control in the Dying Process

TRACY A. SCHROEPFER, HYUNJIN NOH, AND MELINDA KAVANAUGH

Learning Outcomes

After reading this article, you will be able to:

- List the six thematic areas that people who are terminally ill spoke of concerning the parts of their lives over which they felt they had control.

- Indicate the two areas of life that severely ill people could not control.

R esearch on end-of-life care has produced evidence that achieving a sense of control is viewed by terminally ill individuals (Singer, Martin, & Kelner, 1999; Volker, Kahn, & Penticuff, 2004b; Wilson et al., 2007) and those who care for them (Teno, Casey, Welch, & Edgman-Levitan, 2001) as playing an important role in the quality of their dying process. Terminally ill individuals have been found to consider the ability to exercise control as a desirable psychosocial outcome (Singer et al.) and a psychological comfort (Ganzini, Johnston, McFarland, Tolle, & Lee, 1998). Furthermore, the inability to achieve a sense of control has been associated with moderate to extreme suffering for some terminally ill individuals (Wilson et al., 2007) and a desire to hasten death for others (Back, Wallace, Starks, & Pearlman, 1996; Chin, Hedberg, Higginson, & Fleming, 1999; Coyle & Sculco, 2004; Oregon Department of Human Services [ODHS], 2000). Although sense of control evidently plays a key role in the psychological wellbeing of terminally ill individuals, less clear are the aspects of the dying process over which terminally ill individuals want to exercise control and the strategies they use for doing so.

In this article, we seek to advance our understanding of the role control plays in the dying process of terminally ill elders by investigating the aspects of the dying process over which terminally ill elders seek to exercise control, the strategies they use to do so, and whether they desire to exercise more control. By gaining a deeper understanding of the role control plays in the dying process of elders, health care and service providers and informal caregivers can work toward ensuring that elders exercise control in their dying process, thereby working toward the goal of improving the quality of end-of-life care.

Current Knowledge of Control's Role in the Dying Process

The literature on the role of control in the dying process is continually expanding. Some information is available regarding the aspects of the dying process over which individuals, not necessarily elders, desire to exercise control, as well as the way in which they want to do so.

Aspects to Control

The factors motivating the consideration of a hastened death have been studied both retrospectively and prospectively. In retrospective studies, health care professionals or survivors of the deceased are asked to write case studies or respond to surveys concerning the factors cited by now deceased patients, who had considered or requested a hastened death. In prospective studies, individuals with a terminal illness (an illness likely to result in death), or who have been defined as terminally ill (less than 6 months to live), are directly asked about their consideration to hasten death and their reasons for doing so. Both retrospective and prospective studies provide insight into aspects of the dying process over which terminally ill individuals would like to exercise control.

Retrospective studies have found that loss of control over bodily functions (Back et al., 1996; Chin et al., 1999; ODHS, 2007) and physical symptoms (Volker, 2001) have served as factors motivating the consideration of a hastened death. A desire for control over the manner of death was found in both retrospective (Back et al.; Ganzini et al., 2002; ODHS, 2000; Volker) and prospective studies. In prospective studies, respondents who feared dying might become intolerable felt that having control over the manner of their death provided them with a sense of control (Ganzini et al., 1998; Schroepfer, 2006), as it did for those who feared a loss of control more generally (Chapple, Ziebland, McPherson, & Herxheimer, 2006). Respondents also noted that exercising control over the manner of death served to enhance their feelings of control over the disease itself (Albert et al., 2005), provided psychological comfort (Ganzini et al., 1998), and afforded a way to exercise control in an "untenable situation" (Coyle & Sculco, 2004, p. 703).

Other studies have sought to gain understanding about the aspects of dying over which terminally ill elders seek control by posing the question directly to bereaved caregivers, terminally ill individuals, and individuals living with a terminal illness. In one retrospective study, bereaved family members included in their definition of quality end-of-life care the ability for their deceased loved ones to have exercised control over their own health care decisions and daily routine (Teno et al., 2001). In another retrospective study (Volker, Kahn, & Penticuff, 2004a), advance practice nurses reported that patients sought control over decisions related to dying, transitioning to dying, and end-of-life care, as well as over their comfort and dignity. In prospective studies, terminally ill individuals reported seeking to exercise control in end-of-life decisions (Singer et al., 1999; Volker et al., 2004b), over their dignity and physical comfort, the place of their death, and in preparing family for their pending death (Volker et al., 2004b). Although not all of the respondents in the aforementioned studies were elders, the information provides insight into aspects of the dying process over which terminally ill elders may desire to exercise control. To determine the control strategies used for doing so, an understanding must first be gained regarding the conceptualization of control.

Perceived Control Theories and Evidence

Numerous studies have been conducted on sense of control or, as it is often referred to in the literature, perceived control, which has to do with the *expectation* or *perception* of "engaging in actions" either to attain desirable outcomes or to evade those seen as undesirable (Rodin, 1986, p. 141). Perceived control is often presented as a "one-process construct," but Rothbaum, Weisz, and Snyder (1982) have advanced the argument that it may actually be a "two-process construct" consisting of primary and secondary control (p. 8). These researchers define primary control as the perception that the individual has the ability to *directly* influence a desired outcome or avoid an undesirable one. Such beliefs develop when individuals endeavor to change *directly* the external environment to fit their own needs and are successful. Secondary control, in contrast, is the perception that the individual has the ability to influence more *indirectly* a desired outcome (Rothbaum et al.). This perception is formed when individuals endeavor to *fit* into their external environment and are able to do so. Thus, primary control attempts are focused on the external world and secondary control attempts on the individual's internal self.

The life-span model of successful aging proposed by Schulz and Heckhausen (1996), which incorporates their life-span theory of control (Heckhausen & Schulz, 1995), builds on the notion of a two-process construct and argues that humans seek to exert control over the environment throughout their life span to attain goals. They propose three control strategies for doing so: selective primary control, compensatory primary control, and compensatory secondary control. Selective primary control involves individuals' "investment of resources" such as their time, abilities, or efforts to attain a particular goal (Schulz & Heckhausen, 1996, p. 710). When individuals' own resources are no longer sufficient to attain a particular goal, then compensatory primary control strategies become necessary, which require the assistance of others. Finally, compensatory secondary control involves the use of cognitive strategies on the part of individuals, which can include comparing their situation to someone whose situation is worse, disengaging from prior goals, augmenting the value of a new goal, or diminishing the value of an old goal (Heckhausen & Schulz). The use of compensatory secondary control strategies can work to maintain or lessen the losses that an individual is experiencing in his or her life.

Control Strategies Used

We are unaware of any research that has focused on control strategies used by elders in their dying process; however, evidence is available regarding the use of primary and secondary control strategies by elders with acute and chronic health conditions. In general, elders with chronic conditions have been found to use primary and secondary control strategies (Wrosch & Schulz, 2008). Due to age-related declines in late life, however, the tendency has been for elders to move toward using more compensatory secondary control strategies (Heckhausen, 1997). For elders experiencing a high number of health problems, Wrosch, Heckhausen, and Lachman (2000) found that the secondary control strategies of positive reappraisal and lowered aspirations were more strongly associated with their subjective well-being compared with elders who persisted in using primary control strategies.

Whether the findings regarding the control strategies used by elders with acute and chronic conditions hold true for terminally ill elders remains unclear at this time, as do the aspects over which terminally ill elders desire to exercise control. This study seeks to provide such insight by interviewing terminally ill elders about the aspects of their dying process over which they exercise control, the ways in which they exercise such control, and whether they would want more control.

Design and Methods
Participants

A purposive sample of 102 respondents was obtained at hospices throughout southern Wisconsin. Eligible respondents had to be at least 50 years of age, been told by a physician that they had 6 months or less to live, and deemed mentally competent by their nurse or social worker. Although age 50 would not normally be considered the lower age limit for elders, prior research experience with hospice populations (Schroepfer, 2006, 2007, 2008) has shown that to have enough male respondents, the age of inclusion needs to be lowered.

Procedure

A single-session face-to-face interview was conducted with each of 102 elders utilizing a mixed-method survey instrument. Interviews were audiotaped so that the qualitative portion could be captured verbatim, and the quantitative portion checked against what the interviewer recorded in the survey booklet. Interviews ranged in length from 23 to 178 min, with a mean of 63 min. Of the 102 respondents who completed the interview process, 18 respondents were dropped from the analysis because they declined to answer the control questions of interest. We have no way of knowing whether declining to answer these questions was systematically related to the level of control they exercised in their dying process. We do know, however, that a comparison between these 18 respondents and the 84 who completed the control questions revealed no differences in regard to age, gender, marital status, education, primary hospice diagnosis, or quality of life. Therefore, the final sample size used for analysis was 84.

Data Collection

Respondents were asked a series of questions regarding the control they were experiencing in their lives to determine the type of control strategies they were using. To learn about the aspects of the dying process over which they exercised control, respondents were asked if there were parts of their life over which they *felt* they had control. If respondents answered yes, they were asked to specify the parts. To determine the type of control strategy they used, they were next asked a series of questions regarding each part of their life over which they felt they had control. First, respondents were asked if *they* did things to directly control or be in charge of that part of their life. If they said yes, they were asked to talk about what they did and how satisfied they were with it. Next, respondents were asked if there were other people whom they believed helped them control that part of their life. If yes, they were asked to talk about how these individuals helped them exert control. Finally, all respondents were asked if there were other parts of their life over which they would like to exercise control. If they said yes, they were asked to specify the parts and what they felt prevented them from having control. If they said no, they were asked why they did not want more control.

Quantitative data were gathered on respondents' demographic information to explore whether the control strategies utilized by respondents differed based on their age, education, gender, marital status, or primary hospice diagnosis. Age was coded as a continuous variable, as was education, which was based on the number of years of schooling that respondents had completed. The respondents' gender was coded as a dummy variable (0 = female and 1 = male), as was their marital status (0 = not married and 1 = married/partner). Respondents' primary hospice diagnosis was grouped into four categories: cancer and, respiratory, heart, and muscular diseases.

To determine whether the use of control strategies was associated with respondents' quality of life, quantitative data were gathered via a quality-of-life measure. Based on a previous study (Schroepfer, 2006) that sought to determine the factors that led terminally ill elders to consider or not consider a hastened death, nine factors were reported by elders as important to experiencing a quality dying process. These factors included having a reason for living, being able to maintain dignity, not feeling like a burden, living a life full of meaning and full of enjoyment, and feeling a sense of purpose, independent, useful, and hopeful. A thorough review of related literature produced several surveys containing one or more of the items but none that encompassed all nine items or that were designed for elders.

To address this problem, we used items from three survey instruments. The first is the Functional Assessment of Chronic Illness Therapy (FACIT)—spiritual well-being, a 12-item scale that has been designed to measure the spiritual domain of quality of life. Three items were borrowed from the eight-item subscale: a reason for living, a sense of purpose, and life has meaning. Tested in cancer populations (Peterman, Fitchett, Brady, Hernandez, & Cella, 2002), this survey has been found to have internal consistency, high test–retest correlations, concurrent validity, discriminant validity, and a positive association with measures of quality of life. Four items were borrowed from the FACIT—palliative care: burden, dependence, usefulness, and hope. This scale is newer and currently undergoing psychometric testing. The third survey, the Structured Interview for Symptoms and Concerns (SISC), is a 13-item instrument designed specifically for patients receiving palliative care for advanced cancer. This instrument has been found to have high interrater reliability, good test–retest correlations, and concurrent validity. The two items taken from this survey measuring dignity and enjoyment of life were reworded, as was the response set. The reason for rewording the items is that they are worded as questions in the SISC, a format that does not fit with the statement format of the other items. Rewording of the response set occurred because it appears complicated and could prove burdensome to terminally ill elders. These items were measured on a 5-point ordinal scale ranging from 0 = *not at all* to 4 = *very much*. All nine items were summed, resulting in a possible score range of 0–36 wherein a higher score represented a higher quality of life.

Quantitative Analytic Approach

Bivariate analyses were conducted to determine if the control strategies used by respondents differed based on age, education, gender, marital status, and primary hospice diagnosis, as well as respondents' quality-of-life scores. One-way analysis of variance (ANOVA) statistics were run to test the association between the control strategies used by respondents and their age, education, and quality-of-life scores. Cross-tabulations using the Pearson chi-square association test were conducted to test differences based on gender, marital status, and primary hospice diagnosis.

Qualitative Analytic Approaches

Using Schulz and Heckhausen's (1996) theoretical framework, we conducted a directed content analysis (Hsieh & Shannon, 2005) of the information concerning what respondents or others did to control the various parts of their dying process over which they felt they exercised control. Directed content analysis uses theory to predetermine the categories that will be used in exploring the qualitative data. For this study, the first author read each interview transcript multiple times and grouped responses into the following control strategy categories: selective primary control, compensatory primary control, and compensatory secondary control. Responses coded into selective primary control were those in which respondents described externally investing their efforts alone into attaining a particular goal. Respondents' descriptions of exercising control externally with assistance from others were coded into compensatory primary control. Finally, responses that described the use of cognitive strategies to exercise control internally were coded into one of three types of compensatory secondary control strategies: adjustment of goals by lowering aspirations, self-protective positive reappraisal (Wrosch et al., 2000), and self-protective social comparisons (Chipperfield & Perry, 2006). As a reliability check, two members of the research team independently coded the responses based on the strategies identified. Initially, the team members were 76 % in agreement and, after a discussion of the differing categorizations, arrived at a consensus on the remaining 24 %.

Once the directed content analysis of the control strategies had been concluded, the two team members independently coded (a) the aspects of the dying process over which elders reported exercising control and (b) the aspects over which they desired to exercise control. This analysis did not employ a theoretical framework and so the team members utilized conventional content analysis (Hsieh & Shannon, 2005). Using an inductive method, themes were identified from repeated readings of the transcripts (Patton, 1990) and preliminary codes generated to represent the themes. Separately, the team members repeatedly read through and categorized the responses to the question regarding the parts of life over which respondents felt they had control. This same approach was used with responses to the questions regarding whether respondents felt there were other parts of their life they would like to control. If respondents answered yes, then team members categorized the parts that respondents wanted to control and what they felt prevented them from exercising that control. If respondents answered no, then responses regarding why they did not want more control were categorized. As with the directed content analysis, a reliability check was conducted between the two members of the research team, with an 82 % initial agreement and full consensus reached upon discussion.

Results

The demographic characteristics of the 84 respondents were varied. Respondents ranged in age from 51 to 96 years, with a mean age of 76 years. The vast majority of respondents ($n = 82$; 98 %) were White and 2 (2 %) Black. Regarding gender and marital status, a little over half were female (55 %; $n = 46$) and 42 % ($n = 35$) married/partnered, 33 % ($n = 28$) widowed, and 25 % ($n = 21$) single/separated/divorced. Respondents were fairly well educated, with a range of 7–25 years of school completed and a mean of 13 years. The vast majority of respondents had some form of cancer (88 %; $n = 74$), and others were diagnosed with respiratory (5 %; $n = 4$), heart (4 %; $n = 3$), neurological (2 %; $n = 2$), and renal (1 %; $n = 1$) diseases.

Control Strategies Exercised

All 84 respondents described the way in which they exercised control (see Table 1). Of these respondents, 83 reported using

Table 1 Qualitative Themes Regarding Control Exercised in the Dying Process ($N = 84$)

Theme	n (%)
Control strategies exercised	
Selective primary control	1 (1)
Compensatory primary control	19 (23)
Selective and compensatory primary control	42 (50)
Compensatory primary and secondary control	8 (9)
Selective primary control, and compensatory	14 (17)
Primary and secondary control	
Aspects of life over which control was exercised	
Decision making	50 (59)
Independence	18 (21)
Mental attitude	18 (21)
Instrumental activities of daily living	18 (21)
Activities of daily living	14 (17)
Personal relationships	9 (11)
Desire for more control	
Yes ($n = 43$; 51 %)	
Independence	14 (33)
Body functioning	13 (30)
Illness	10 (23)
Generativity	6 (14)
No ($n = 41$; 49 %)	
Satisfied with current level of control	31 (76)
Physical condition prevents exercising more control	7 (17)
God's in control	1 (2)
No explanation provided by respondent	2 (5)

a primary control strategy in combination with another primary or compensatory secondary control strategy; only one reported exercising a single primary control strategy. This 84-year-old never-married woman described using selective primary control. Although she had cancer, her focus was not on the illness itself but on the goal of strengthening her legs so she could be more mobile. When asked if other people helped her exercise control, she said no. Thus, although it was likely that others were assisting because her mobility was limited, she did not feel their doing so helped in her exercise of control.

Nineteen (23 %) of the 84 respondents reported they could no longer completely rely on their own resources to attain their goals and so asked for assistance (compensatory primary control). Respondents viewed asking others for assistance in a positive light noting that the assistance enabled them to maintain some control:

> I feel like I'm probably . . . see, I'm not a quitter and I may have to ask for help but I do . . . and that way I can stay on a schedule and maintain a life that I feel that I'm still contributing something to my family. (62-year-old married woman)

Awareness of the need for assistance to exercise control did not necessarily mean that respondents would not like to exercise control on their own (selective primary control). For example, a 62-year-old married woman was used to having full control of her own home and stated, "Oh yeah, I would definitely like to go back to the way it was before all of this happened and be able to maintain my complete house and not have to ask for help in anything."

Forty-two (50 %) of the 84 respondents used a combination of selective and compensatory primary control. These respondents were able to use their own personal skills and resources to attain some goals but required assistance to attain others. For example, one 70-year-old divorced man exercised selective primary control in regard to attaining his goal of setting a daily schedule for eating, bedtime, and leisure activities; however, to attain his goal of bathing himself, he required assistance (compensatory primary control).

Compensatory secondary control was used in combination with compensatory primary control by 8 (9 %) respondents and in combination with selective and compensatory primary control by 14 (17 %) respondents. For respondents who exercised compensatory secondary control, at least one of the following three strategies was used: lowering aspirations, positive reappraisal, and social comparison. The eight respondents, who used a combination of compensatory primary and secondary control, used one of each type of control strategies. The 14 respondents who used a combination of selective primary control, and compensatory primary and secondary control, each reported one selective and one compensatory primary control strategy and one or two secondary control strategies. For those using compensatory secondary control, lowering aspirations was the most common strategy used: 16 (73 %) of the 22 respondents spoke about adjusting their goals (lowering their aspirations) concerning exercising control. For example, an 88-year-old divorced woman sought to reframe her own inability to write checks any longer such that it was something her daughter needed to experience: "I think she [daughter] just offered [to write her checks] and I said sure . . . I said that's fine. I felt it would be a good experience for her."

Quantitative analyses were conducted to determine whether respondents' demographic characteristics differed by these control strategy groups (CPC; SPC and CPC; CPC and CSC; and SPC, CPC, and CSC; Table 2). By necessity, the sole respondent who reported using only selective primary control was dropped from these analyses given the absence of variation. One-way ANOVA and chi-square tests revealed no significant differences in respondents' age, gender, marital status, education, or primary hospice diagnosis by the control strategy grouping reported (see Table 2).

Table 2 Demographics and Quality of Life of Elders Adopting Control Strategies ($N = 84$)

Demographic	SPC (1 %; $n = 1$)	CPC (23 %; $n = 19$)	SPC & CPC (50 %; $n = 42$)	CPC & CSC (9 %; $n = 8$)	SPC, CPC, & CSC (17 %; $n = 14$)
Age (in years), M	80.0	77.5	76.1	74.8	72.8
Education (in years), M	15.0	12.8	13.2	12.8	15.1
Gender, %					
Female ($n = 46$)	100.0	63.2	54.8	37.5	50.0
Male ($n = 38$)	0.0	36.8	45.2	62.5	50.0
Marital status, %					
Not married ($n = 49$)	100.0	57.9	64.3	50.0	42.9
Married ($n = 35$)	0.0	42.1	35.7	50.0	57.1
Primary diagnosis, %					
Cancer ($n = 74$)	100.0	84.2	95.2	75.0	78.6
Respiratory ($n = 4$)	0.0	5.3	2.4	12.5	7.1
Heart disease ($n = 3$)	0.0	5.3	0.0	12.5	7.1
Neurological ($n = 2$)	0.0	5.3	0.0	0.0	7.1
Renal failure ($n = 1$)	0.0	0.0	2.4	0.0	0.0
Quality of life, M		18.5 [a]	23.2 [b]	24.1 [a,b]	24.7 [b,*]

Notes: The levels of significance for continuous variables are based on one-way analysis of variance tests. Means in the same row that have different superscripts differ at $p \le .05$. SPC = selective primary control; CPC = compensatory primary control; CSC = compensatory secondary control.

*$p < .05$.

A one-way ANOVA test was also conducted on the control strategy groups and respondents' quality-of-life score (see Table 2). The overall mean for quality of life was 22.6, with a range of 6–35: higher scores represent higher quality of life. Based on the finding of a significant F ratio, $F(3, 79) = 5.15$; $p < .01$, Tukey's honestly significant difference post hoc test was run to determine, through pairwise multiple comparisons, the control strategies that did and did not differ in regard to quality of life. The post hoc tests results revealed that respondents who used a combination of selective and compensatory primary control ($p < .05$) or a combination of selective primary control, compensatory primary control, and compensatory secondary control ($p < .05$) reported a significantly higher quality of life than respondents who used only compensatory primary control. No significant difference was found between respondents who used compensatory primary and compensatory secondary control and those who used only compensatory primary control. Although this group does not significantly differ, the result is likely due to the small sample size ($n = 8$). Thus, the overall finding from these tests suggests that exercising more than one control strategy was associated with higher quality of life than exercising only one control strategy.

Aspects of Life over Which Control Was Exercised

Respondents were asked to name and discuss the parts of their lives over which they exercised control, and they named anywhere from one ($n = 27$; 32 %), to two ($n = 34$; 40 %), to three ($n = 14$; 17 %) to four parts ($n = 9$; 11 %). Content analysis of these discussions revealed six thematic areas regarding the parts of their lives over which respondents felt they exercised control: decision making, independence, mental attitude, instrumental activities of daily living (IADLs), activities of daily living (ADLs), and personal relationships.

Decision Making

Exercising control through decision making was reported by 50 (59 %) of the 84 respondents, one of whom exercised control by herself and the others who did so with assistance. These respondents talked about making decisions or participating in the decision-making process with others regarding where to live, their finances, plans for death, how people provided their care, treatments they chose to receive, and their daily schedule and activities. Respondents noted that making a decision and having it supported by others provided them with a sense of control. A 72-year-old married woman stated, "I could tell her [daughter] this is what I want to do and we do it together. I feel like I'm a little bit more in control." Several respondents noted that it was not the size of the decision or what was being decided; rather, it was having a decision to make that made them feel more in control. An 86-year-old widower made this point when he said, "It's really small things like the choice of where you want to eat. It's nice if somebody gives you a choice."

Independence

Eighteen (21 %) of the 84 respondents reported that being independent was a part of their life over which they exercised control. Independence was expressed by respondents as the ability to "go where I want and do what I want," "live my own life," and "don't have to ask for help from others." These 18 respondents spoke in adamant tones when talking about having control over their independence, as illustrated by a 73-year-old married man's, "I can do what I damn well please!" and a 79-year-old widow's, "I don't *have* to ask for help from others." Control over independence was clearly very important.

Mental Attitude

Exercising control internally over their own mental attitude was discussed by 18 (21 %) of the 84 respondents. Using this compensatory secondary control strategy, a 77-year-old married man noted, "Well, I have control over my feelings; I have control over my mind." . . . An 81-year-old married man reported, "Well, I can control my mental attitude toward the disease, knowing that its terminal and I can't do much about that." . . . This ability to exercise control internally was viewed in a positive light, as expressed by one 72-year-old divorced woman who said, "Well, my viewpoint . . . is you cannot always control certain things you find yourself in but you (can) always choose your attitude."

Instrumental Activities of Daily Living

The ability to exercise control over one's IADLs was reported by 18 (21 %) respondents. Respondents spoke about being able to control their finances, order groceries over the telephone, and perform basic household chores. For example, a 67-year-old divorced woman reported exercising control over household chores: "Yesterday, my grandsons were here and they came to do the lawn and stuff like that, so I can still direct them and take care of the outdoors without being outdoors."

Activities of Daily Living

Fourteen (17 %) respondents reported exercising control over ADLs. The importance of doing so is evident in the following statement by a 73-year-old married man:

> . . . I uh, you know, I wash myself up every morning and uh, brush my teeth and all of those little tasks—don't need any help other than my wife will—we usually do it in this room and she'll bring in the equipment, you know. But if I had to, I could go into that bathroom next door and take care of it. It's just a little simpler this way so, but I could do it, and I know I could.

Although still needing assistance with her bath, a 76-year-old divorced woman made a point to let the interviewer know that she still exercises some control over her bath: "Yeah, they [hospice certified nursing assistant] insist I should be helped with a bath, but I can still lift myself up out of the tub." Concerning ADLs, the 14 respondents were all quick to point out that they exercised control, even if they were receiving assistance.

Personal Relationships

Nine (11 %) of 84 respondents talked about having control over how they relate with their family and friends. They talked about the value those relationships held for them and how they felt they had control over making sure they were positive relationships. An 81-year-old married man talked about how concerned he was by the impact his illness had on his loved ones and how he wanted to make certain the impact was positive.

> I try to influence my family's feelings toward my situation. I get the impression that . . . I'm concerned that they are also concerned about my situation—that it's affecting them now. They're calling every day, they try to come every day. So I'm sure it's had a direct effect on their lives.

In addition to making sure their impact on loved ones was positive, respondents also talked about ensuring that those relationships were as normal as possible. One 86-year-old widower talked about how he made sure that he and his girlfriend "date just like anybody else."

Desire for More Control

Although all 84 respondents reported experiencing a sense of control in their dying process, the question remained whether they felt it was enough. All 84 respondents were asked whether there were other parts of their life that they would like to control and 43 (51 %) answered yes. When asked to identify those parts, four thematic areas surfaced: independence, body functioning, illness, and generativity. Having identified the part of their life they wanted to control, they were then asked to talk about what prevented them from doing so.

Fourteen (33 %) respondents noted that they would like to exercise more control over their ability to be independent such as being able to stay in their house alone sometimes or being able to get in their car and drive wherever they wanted by themselves. It is interesting to note that when describing how they would exercise control in regard to their independence, all 14 respondents discussed the importance of being alone sometimes, a desire that may have resulted from the constant presence of caregivers. One 76-year-old divorced woman stated, "I would like to be independent again. . . . do what I want and go where I want . . . navigate by myself." When asked what prevented them from exercising such control, all 14 noted that it was their illness, which left them fatigued, nauseous, dizzy, or in pain.

Exercising control over their own bodies was the desire of 13 (30 %) of the 43 respondents. The functions that respondents wanted more control over were incontinence, sexual performance, muscle and leg movement, appetite, physical strength, and memory. Lacking control over functions that people normally can control was very upsetting, as evidenced by one 90-year-old married man who was struggling with incontinence: "Well, accidents happen without any warning a lot of times." Again, when asked what prevented their exercising control, all 13 people stated that it was their illness.

The third most common theme to emerge was the desire to control their illness: 10 (23 %) respondents spoke about wanting to control the impact their illness had on their ability to function physically in their daily lives. They also spoke of wanting to control their illness such that it would not be terminal. A 76-year-old divorced woman who was terminally ill with lung cancer said wistfully, "Just maybe—the only thing,

oh, that's more or less a desire . . . that they x-ray me once, and see that the spots are gone . . . controlling these spots on my lungs." Although the desire was strong to exercise such control and fight their illness, respondents stated that what prevented them from doing so was that it was "not realistic."

The fourth theme that arose was the desire expressed by six respondents (14 %) to exercise control now and after their death on behalf of the next generation, a stage of development referred to by Erik Erikson as generativity (Erikson, Erikson, & Kivnick, 1986). Erikson's seventh stage of his developmental theory, generativity versus stagnation, proposes that as part of their own development, adults assist the younger generation in leading meaningful lives. Although Erikson proposes this as a midlife stage of development, terminally ill elders who reported seeking to be instrumental in their children and grandchildren's future lives ranged in age from 62 to 84 years. For example, a 62-year-old divorced woman longed to assist financially loved ones in difficult circumstances. A 73-year-old married man talked about his need for ensuring his grandchildren's future education, and an 81-year-old married man who had lung cancer wanted to talk with young people about the dangers of smoking. Perhaps knowing that time was limited, these respondents felt the need to make a lasting impact on the next generation. When asked what prevented them from doing so, they talked about their children's resentment and need for independence. One 71-year-old widow stated:

> He's a 21-year-old man . . . I guess I would like him to have ways of being helped physically, medically, healthcare-wise. I can't do any of that. . . . [I]f I were healthy, I couldn't do those things. People have to do for themselves what they have to do. I'd like to make his life easier because there are things that I've seen because I'm older.

For the 41 (49 %) respondents who answered no to the question regarding whether there were other parts of their life that they would like to control, all but 2 (5 %) provided an explanation. The vast majority (76 %; $n = 31$) reported they were satisfied with their current level of control. Some of these individuals reported their satisfaction was due to their still exercising the same amount of control as before their illness: "I'm still kind of fully in charge of what I've done before." Others spoke of feeling happy or peaceful with life in its current state: "I'm satisfied—life is where it should be." The other eight respondents provided different explanations. Seven (17 %) respondents stated that their physical condition left them unable to control other parts of their lives. An 84-year-old widow noted, "I'm not capable of doing the thing I would want to control." The eighth respondent, a 55-year-old divorced woman, remarked she did not want control because "God's in control."

Discussion

The results from this study offer an understanding of the role control plays in the dying process of terminally ill elders and the potential association it has with quality of life in the dying process. The 84 elders interviewed provided information about the strategies they used to exercise control in their dying process, the aspects over which they exercised control, and whether they desired to exercise more control.

Control Strategies

Either on their own (selective primary control) or with the assistance of another (compensatory primary control), all 84 elders were exercising a form of primary control to attain a particular goal. The fact that these elders sought to exercise primary control, although they were very ill and their time was limited, is evidence of its importance.

Another important finding concerned the mix of control strategies that terminally ill elders used to exercise control. Although about a fifth of respondents exercised only one primary control strategy, the majority used two to four primary and secondary control strategies. Respondents had goals they wanted to attain and appeared to choose a control strategy that fit with the abilities they possessed related to that goal. It is also significant that although the exercise of primary control is visible to others, the exercise of secondary control may not be; yet, changing the internal self to fit with the external world did provide these respondents with a sense of control. For example, one 63-year-old married woman, who was chair bound during the day, spent her days alone. A hospice worker came by each day and the woman always asked the worker to turn on the radio before she left. She loved to listen to the radio and felt that by asking the worker, she had control over being able to do so. One day, however, she forgot to have the worker turn on the radio. Unable to do so herself (selective primary control) or ask others to do it for her (compensatory secondary control), she turned to a compensatory secondary control strategy: "I didn't have any of them to turn on my radio. My God, I thought, well all right, no sound but I could (still) hear the birds." The use of multiple strategies is not only evidence of these elders' desire to exercise control but their adaptability in doing so.

Findings from the study also reveal that the use of multiple strategies appears to be associated with quality of life in the dying process. Although the sole use of selective primary control could not be tested due to only one elder reporting its use, comparisons were made between the use of only compensatory primary control and the use of other combinations of control strategies. The one-way ANOVA test revealed that exercising more than one control strategy (compensatory primary control) was associated with a higher reported quality of life in the dying process, which has important implications for practitioners.

Aspects Controlled

The aspects respondents reported exercising control over provided insight into the world of terminally ill elders, which, due to being home or facility bound for the most part, was a smaller world than when they were healthy. As their world grew smaller, the areas in which they could exercise control became more limited. The six thematic areas that respondents spoke of concerning the exercise of control were decision making, independence, mental attitude, IADLs, ADLs, and personal relationships. Being able to make decisions that influenced their

world and future death, to come and go and be alone, to choose their attitude, to perform IADLs or ADLs, and to ensure their relationships were positive, were the key aspects of the dying process over which respondents sought to exercise control. Realizing at some level that their world and often their ability to exercise control were constrained in ways they had not been before, respondents appeared to adapt by focusing on areas inside their world, being flexible in how they exercised control, as well as how much control they exercised.

More Control?

Study results revealed that over half of the respondents wanted to exercise more control in their dying process. Just as independence was an aspect of the dying process that many respondents reported exercising control over, 14 respondents who were not currently exercising such control desired to do so. The severity of their illness prevented exercising this control, just as it did in two other areas: their illness and bodily functions. Although they desired control in these areas, terminally ill elders were realistic regarding their inability to do so.

Perhaps the most surprising finding was that respondents wanted to exercise more control over the future success of their children and grandchildren. Erickson proposed generativity as a stage of development that takes place at midlife. Although these elders were not in midlife, perhaps in the final stage of life, the need to ensure the success of the next generation presented itself yet again. An alternative explanation may simply be that in providing for the next generation, these elders were able to leave behind a legacy of love.

Study Limitations and Future Implications

Although this qualitative study employed a large sample size, and new understandings were gained on the role of control in the dying process of terminally ill elders, limitations were present. First, 98 % of the sample were Caucasian elders. Future research should be conducted with other racial/ethnic elders to determine the extent to which culture influences the role of control in an elder's dying process. The role of the individual and the exercise of control tend to be Western values and so not all groups may view control in the same manner as the current study participants. Second, the lives of terminally ill elders are not stagnant; rather, they can shift very quickly due to advancing illness. The 84 respondents who volunteered to participate in the study may have done so because they were less ill than others who were not recruited. They may still have been at a point in their illness where they could exercise primary control more readily and rely less on secondary control strategies. The current study was cross-sectional in nature and so the results are based on one time point in the respondents' dying process. A longitudinal study following elders throughout their dying process would provide greater insight into whether they continue to be adaptive in the use of control strategies and what they seek to control changes. Third, the respondents participating in the current study were all receiving hospice care either at home or in a hospice inpatient facility. Future studies should look at elders who are dying in other environments and not receiving hospice care, such as a hospital or nursing home. It is not clear from the current study whether the environment itself and the type of end-of-life care being provided influenced respondents' control strategies or the aspects of the dying process over which they desired control. Fourth, the respondents in this sample were terminally ill (less than 6 months to live), but it is feasible that elders with terminal or chronic conditions may experience similar physical limitations that impact their exercise of control. Certainly, the findings for this study's terminally ill respondents bear similarities to the research findings discussed in the literature review on elders with chronic conditions in that they, too, have been shown to use a mix of primary and secondary control strategies (Wrosch & Schulz, 2008) and to use compensatory secondary control strategies, including positive reappraisal and lowering aspirations (Heckhausen, 1997). Future research should look more closely at the exercise of control for elders with acute, chronic, and terminal conditions to determine the similarities and differences in regard to how control is exercised and its relationship to quality of life. Fifth, in order for terminally ill elders to exercise control in their dying process, particularly when the control strategy is compensatory and necessitates the assistance of others, family members must be supportive of their doing so. A recent study (Schroepfer, 2008) found that the relational content of social relationships defined as the "functional nature or quality of social relationships" (House, Umberson, & Landis, 1988, p. 302) was related to the consideration of a hastened death. Quantitatively, poor or conflictual support was found to be a highly significant predictor of the consideration to hasten death, and, qualitatively, if an elder felt his or her own suffering or the suffering his or her care placed on loved ones was burdensome, he or she was likely to consider a hastened death. The current study did not include measures of the relational content of those who indirectly or directly supported the elders in their exercise of control in the dying process, or the impact of relational content on their quality of life. Future studies on exercising control in the dying process should quantitatively include relational content measures and qualitatively include questions on not only how others assist an elder in the exercise of control but also the elder's experience with their doing so. Sixth, the finding regarding the association of control strategies with quality of life was limited to a bivariate analysis. Future research on this finding should employ the use of multivariate analyses to control for relevant control and predictor variables.

Practice Implications

The knowledge gained from these interviews has important implications for practitioners and family members providing care to elders during their dying process. Being cognizant of the life an elder had prior to his or her dying process and how that life has changed since the illness is important knowledge for family members to remember and practitioners to garner. As the health that once allowed an elder to be very much a part of the world outside his or her home or facility declines, so does the size of his or her world. Understanding this, family members and practitioner can seek to support the elder's exercise of control within that smaller world, as well as the strategies he or she chooses to use. If family members and the practitioner are assisting the elder with a task, then supporting the elder's need to exercise control as much as possible is key for the elder in exercising compensatory primary control. If an elder is physically limited to such a point that exercising primary control alone or with the assistance of another is not practical, then it is important that family members and the practitioner be aware that the elder may seek to exercise control internally over his or her mental attitude. Based on the expression of an elder's attitude, it may appear that he or she is giving up; however, it may actually be that he or she is taking a realistic approach to the situation and using the compensatory secondary control strategy of lowering his or her aspirations. Based on the elder's situation, the family and the practitioner must then determine whether the elder is lowering his or her aspirations unnecessarily or simply being realistic. Family members or the practitioner can then work with the elder to either reframe his or her situation in a way that allows for raising aspirations or, in the case of a realistic viewpoint, support the elder's use of the control strategy. Because the exercise of more than one control strategy appears to be associated with a reportedly higher quality of life in an elder's dying process, then family members and practitioners can work to ensure that elders have the opportunity to do so whenever possible.

Decision-making, independence, mental attitude, IADLs, ADLs, and relationships were aspects of the dying process over which the respondents sought to exercise control. Providing the support and the opportunities for such control to be possible is an important role for family and the practitioner. For example, elders who talk about the importance of their always having been independent may necessitate their family members and practitioners locating such opportunities. The elders in the current study tended to equate independence with time alone; thus, family members and the practitioner can work to ensure that the elder has a period of privacy each day. Another example is the role decision making plays in the dying process. The study's respondents were not focused on the size of a decision or the need to make one alone: They primarily wanted to be a part of the process and have the support of others in doing so. These interventions and others based on familial knowledge and a thorough assessment of an elder's pre- and post-terminal illness life will assist family members and practitioners in ensuring that elders' control preferences are supported in their final stage of life.

Funding

Support for this study was provided by the John A. Hartford Foundation Faculty Scholars Program in Geriatric Social Work.

References

Albert, S. M., Rabkin, J. G., Del Bene, M. L., Tider, T., O' Sullivan, I., Rowland, L. P., et al. (2005). Wish to die in end-stage ALS. *Neurology, 65,* 68–74.

Back, A., Wallace, J., Starks, H., & Pearlman, R. (1996). Physician-assisted suicide and euthanasia in Washington state: Patient requests and physician responses. *Journal of the American Medical Association, 275,* 919–925.

Chapple, A., Ziebland, S., McPherson, A., & Herxheimer, A. (2006). What people close to death say about euthanasia and assisted suicide: A qualitative study. *Journal of Medical Ethics, 32,* 706–710.

Chin, A., Hedberg, K., Higginson, G., & Fleming, D. (1999). Legalized physician-assisted suicide in Oregon—The first year's experience. *New England Journal of Medicine, 340,* 577–583.

Chipperfield, J. G., & Perry, R. P. (2006). Primary- and secondary-control strategies in later life: Predicting hospital outcomes in men and women. *Health Psychology, 25,* 226–236.

Coyle, N., & Sculco, L. (2004). Expressed desire for hastened death in seven patients living with advanced cancer: A phenomenologic inquire. *Oncology Nursing Forum, 31,* 699–706.

Erikson, E. H., Erikson, J. M., & Kivnick, H. Q. (1986). *Vital involvement in old age.* New York: W. W. Norton.

Ganzini, L., Harvath, T., Jackson, A., Goy, E., Miller, L., & Delorit, M. (2002). Experiences of Oregon nurses and social workers with hospice patients who requested assistance with suicide. *New England Journal of Medicine, 347,* 582–588.

Ganzini, L., Johnston, W. S., McFarland, B. H., Tolle, S. W., & Lee, M. A. (1998). Attitudes of patients with amyotrophic lateral sclerosis and their care givers toward assisted suicide. *New England Journal of Medicine, 339,* 967–973.

Heckhausen, J. (1997). Developmental regulation across adulthood: Primary and secondary control of age-related challenges. *Developmental Psychology, 33,* 176–187.

Heckhausen, J., & Schulz, R. (1995). A life-span theory of control. *Psychological Review, 102,* 284–304.

House, J. S., Umberson, D., & Landis, K. R. (1988). Structures and processes of social support. *Annual Review of Sociology, 14,* 293–318.

Hsieh, H., & Shannon, S. E. (2005). Three approaches to qualitative content analysis. *Qualitative Health Research, 15,* 1277–1288.

Oregon Department of Human Services. (2000). *Oregon's Death with Dignity Act: The second year's experience.* Portland: Oregon Health Division.

Oregon Department of Human Services. (2007). *Ninth annual report on Oregon's Death with Dignity Act.* Portland: Oregon Health Division.

Patton, M. (1990). *Qualitative evaluation and research methods* (2nd ed.). Newbury Park, CA: Sage.

Peterman, R. H., Fitchett, G., Brady, M., Hernandez, L., & Cella, D. (2002). Measuring spiritual well-being in people with cancer: The Functional Assessment of Chronic Illness Therapy–Spiritual Well-Being Scale (FACIT–Sp). *Annals of Behavioral Medicine, 24,* 49–58.

Rodin, J. (1986). Health, control and aging. In M. M. Baltes & P. B. Baltes (Eds.), *The psychology of control and aging* (pp. 139–165). Hillsdale, NJ: Lawrence Erlbaum.

Rothbaum, F., Weisz, J. R., & Snyder, S. S. (1982). Changing the world and changing the self: A two-process model of perceived control. *Journal of Personality and Social Psychology, 42,* 5–37.

Schroepfer, T. A. (2006). Mind frames towards dying and factors motivating their adoption by terminally ill elders. *Journal of Gerontology: Social Sciences, 61,* S129–S139.

Schroepfer, T. A. (2007). Critical events in the dying process: The potential for physical and psychosocial suffering. *Journal of Palliative Medicine, 10,* 136–147.

Schroepfer, T. A. (2008). Social relationships and their role in the consideration to hasten death. *The Gerontologist, 48,* 612–621.

Schulz, R., & Heckhausen, J. (1996). A life span model of successful aging. *American Psychologist, 31,* 702–714.

Singer, P. A., Martin, D. K., & Kelner, M. (1999). Quality end-of-life care: Patients' perspectives. *Journal of the American Medical Association, 281,* 163–168.

Teno, J. M., Casey, V. A., Welch, L. C., & Edgman-Levitan, S. (2001). Patient-focused, family-centered end-of-life medical care: Views of the guidelines and bereaved family members. *Journal of Pain and Symptom Management, 22,* 738–751.

Volker, D. (2001). Oncology nurses' experiences with requests for assisted dying from terminally ill patients with cancer. *Oncology Nursing Forum, 28,* 39–49.

Volker, D. L., Kahn, D., & Penticuff, J. H. (2004a). Patient control and end-of-life care. Part I: The advanced practice nurse perspective. *Oncology Nursing Forum, 31,* 945–953.

Volker, D. L., Kahn, D., & Penticuff, J. H. (2004b). Patient control and end-of-life care. Part II: The patient perspective. *Oncology Nursing Forum, 31,* 954–960.

Wilson, K. G., Chochinov, H. M., McPherson, C. J., LeMay, K., Allard, P., Chary, S., et al. (2007). Suffering with advanced cancer. *Journal of Clinical Oncology, 25,* 1691–1697.

Wrosch, D., Heckhausen, J., & Lachman, M. W. (2000). Primary and secondary control strategies for managing health and financial stress across adulthood. *Psychology and Aging, 15,* 387–399.

Wrosch, C., & Schulz, R. (2008). Health-engagement control strategies and 2-year changes in older adults' physical health. *Psychological Science, 19,* 537–541.

Critical Thinking

1. What were given as examples of the person's control over the "instrumental activities of daily living"?

2. What were given as examples of the person's control over the "activities of daily living"?

3. What were given as examples of the elderly person's control over decision making?

Create Central

www.mhhe.com/createcentral

Internet References

Agency for Health Care Policy and Research
www.ahcpr.gov

Growth House, Inc.
www.growthhouse.org

Hospice Foundation of America
www.HospiceFoundation.org

Article   Prepared by: Elaina F. Osterbur, *Saint Louis University*

Six Steps to Help Seniors Make the CPR/DNR Decision

There's a lot of misinformation and misunderstandings when it comes to cardiopulmonary resuscitation (CPR) or a do not resuscitate (DNR) order. Here's an insider's view and six steps you can follow to help seniors have meaningful conversations to make this critical decision and feel confident it is right.

VIKI KIND

Learning Outcomes

After reading this article, you will be able to:

- Identify the traditional form of CPR and why this concept has changed over time.
- Discuss the six steps in the decision-making process.
- Identify health goals that may influence a CPR/DNR process.

A common and extremely important decision seniors face when writing their advance health-care directives or experiencing a medical crisis is whether to choose cardiopulmonary resuscitation (CPR) or to request a do not resuscitate order (DNR). There is a lot of misinformation and misunderstandings when it comes to the CPR decision. As a Certified Senior Advisor (CSA)®, you are in a position to provide relevant and accurate information to help seniors and their families make a decision that reflects the senior's values and health goals.

How CPR Has Changed

CPR used to be very simple to understand. *Cardio* stands for heart; *pulmonary* stands for lungs; and *resuscitation* means to revive from death. In the past, when a patient died, someone would push on the person's chest to try to restart the heart while giving mouth-to-mouth resuscitation to help the person breathe. But over time, CPR has become more complex as health-care professionals discover different and advanced ways to try to bring a person back to life. What seemed like an easy question,

"Does the person want CPR?" has turned into a decidedly complicated decision.

Do You Want to Be a DNR?

There are three ways to say "do not resuscitate"—DNR, DNAR, and AND; the differences are very important. The second choice, "do not *attempt* resuscitation" (DNAR), more appropriately explains that just because you attempt CPR doesn't mean it will work.

The third and newest term, "allow natural death" (AND), is a more gentle way of saying "do not resuscitate." Instead of telling you what won't be done for the senior, the doctor is offering the senior a peaceful, natural death without resuscitation efforts. Along with introducing the concept of allowing a natural death, this language creates an opportunity to discuss what the senior might envision at the end of life, as well as the benefits of hospice and palliative care.

Steps to Having the CPR/DNR Conversation

As a clinical bioethicist, my approach to the CPR/DNR conversation is threefold:

- Educate the person about CPR.
- Help the person put the medical decision into the context of his or her life.
- Have the person make the decision.

If the senior or the senior's decision maker would like your assistance, the following steps will help you guide and support the person in making a choice that represents the senior's values and health goals.

Step 1: Inform
Ask the Senior, "What Do You Know about Cardiopulmonary Resuscitation (CPR)?"

Most seniors will say, "They push on your chest, blow in your mouth, and/or shock you with paddles." You need to explain that CPR also includes *medications* to help restart your heart and *intubation,* which means they put a tube down your throat. Also, you will be put on a *breathing machine* (sometimes called a ventilator or a respirator). I have been shocked to see how many seniors are outraged when I tell them what really happens during CPR, because they never would have chosen to be put on a ventilator. They are also angry that they didn't have all the facts.

Another option that may be offered is the misleading choice of being a "chemical code only," which means medicine will be given but no chest compressions. As nurses and doctors will tell you, if the doctor gives the medicine but doesn't do the chest compressions to move the blood around, the medicine will not circulate in the body. Without circulation, the medicine cannot do its job. That said, if family members can't accept that the senior is going to die, this choice is occasionally offered, even though it very probably won't work. Some seniors, families, and physicians also find comfort in this choice because "something is being done." But as a bioethicist, I don't think people should be offered options that have no benefit. If a person wants CPR, then he or she should choose everything CPR offers to have a chance at being brought back to life.

Step 2: Explain
Help Seniors Understand the Chance of CPR Working for Them.

If you ask health-care professionals, "How many of you would like to die by CPR?" no one ever raises a hand. What they know is that the chance of CPR working is minimal—sometimes even 0 percent. On television shows such as *ER,* CPR brings the patient back to life about 75 percent of the time (Diem, Lantos, & Tulsky, 1996), but in real life it only works, at best, 17 percent of the time on healthy patients (Peberdy et al., 2003). In many situations, the chance of success is zero.

In the article "CPR Survival Rates for Older People Unchanged," by Serena Gordon (2009), William Ehlenbach, M.D., the lead author of a study on CPR in the elderly, explains that "CPR has the highest likelihood of success when the heart is the reason, as in an ongoing heart attack or a heart rhythm disturbance. If you're doing well otherwise, CPR will often be successful. But, if you're in the ICU [intensive care unit] with a serious infection and multiple organ failure, it's unlikely that CPR will save you."

Step 3: Discuss
"You May Come Back to Life in a Worse Condition Than You Were Before, Both Mentally and Physically."

Most people don't understand what can happen if CPR brings someone back to life. When the health-care team is pushing on the person's chest, there is a chance of broken ribs or a collapsed lung. The longer the patient isn't able to breathe, the greater the chance is for brain damage. There may also be damage to the windpipe if the person is placed on a ventilator.

Another way that television shows mislead you is by letting you think a person will be healthy enough to go home about 67 percent of the time (Diem, Lantos, & Tulsky, 1996). In reality, if CPR is able to bring the patient back to life, the chance of this person going home with good brain function is about 7 percent (Kaldjian et al., 2009). Some patients may survive CPR but are never able to leave the hospital. Others may remain hooked up to ventilators for the rest of their lives. The success rate will depend on the health of the patient, the patient's age, how quickly the CPR was begun, and other medical factors.

Step 4: Reflect
"The Type of Death You May Be Choosing with CPR May Not Be the Kind of Death You Want."

With CPR, the senior might not have the opportunity for a peaceful and profound death experience. When you picture the last minutes of a person's life, do you see strangers straddling the patient on a bed, pushing on the patient's chest, while the family waits outside in the waiting room? Or do you see a time with family and friends gathered around the bedside, with words of love being expressed, music being played, or prayers being said?

The CPR decision is about more than medicine. It frames the dying experience for the patient and their loved ones. I would encourage people to balance the chance of CPR working and bringing the person back in a good condition with the desire for a dignified death. This is why many health-care professionals wouldn't want to die by CPR; there is nothing peaceful or dignified about this type of death.

Step 5: Clarify
"I Want to Make Sure You Understand There May Be a Time in Your Life When You Would Want CPR and a Time When CPR Would No Longer Be an Option You Would Choose."

This is where to stop and re-emphasize the difference between choosing CPR when you are healthy and choosing CPR at the end of your life. The senior's medical instructions should clarify in what health condition the senior would choose a DNR.

5 CPR Decision-Making Tips for Seniors

1. Make sure you understand what really happens during CPR.
2. CPR doesn't work like you see on television.
3. CPR will not change the underlying cause of your condition, and it might make you worse.
4. Think about the kind of death you are choosing.
5. The decision about CPR is only one part of a good end-of-life plan.

The senior might say, "While I am still healthy and able to interact with the people I care about, I would want to receive CPR. When I near the end of my life, or when I can no longer enjoy spending time with my loved ones, I would not want to receive CPR." This decision is more than a "medical choice"; it is really a quality-of-life choice. Thus, the senior will need to define what makes his or her life worth living.

Step 6: Process
Moving the Medical Decision into the Context of the Senior's Life.

At this point in the conversation, the goal is to help the senior process what he or she has just learned. Let the senior lead the conversation and explore what CPR represents to him or her. Leave some silence for the senior to consider the significance of these issues. If the senior is hesitant, you can try asking one of these questions: "For many people, CPR just prolongs the dying process. What do you think about this?" or "Is there value in fighting until your last breath, even if this might increase your suffering?"

But don't rush the senior because you are uncomfortable in the silence. He or she may need some time to think about what you have shared. You might also encourage the senior to take his or her time with the decision by saying, "You don't need to make a decision about this today."

What Else May Affect the Decision?
Decision Maker's Emotions

As a bioethicist, I get called in to resolve conflicts when a loved one is demanding CPR for the patient and the doctor is frustrated because he or she knows CPR won't work since the person is terminal. When a family member says to me, "I won't sign the DNR," I ask the person, "Why don't you want to sign it?" Then I listen. The demand for CPR may be desperation, grief, guilt, familial obligations, religious beliefs, a fear of death, misunderstanding what CPR can do, or a reaction to a past negative experience with the health-care system.

The other day, a family was refusing to sign the DNR and the health-care team thought that they were refusing because

they were very religious. It turns out that the family was not making the decision based on their religious values. They were refusing to sign the DNR because a family member had once come back to life when everyone had said there was no hope. Given their experience, they believed not only that miracles can happen, but that they do happen. Once the health-care team understood the family's perspective, it made sense to them why the family was so insistent on "doing everything."

Professional's Beliefs

As professionals, we may get caught up in thinking we always know what is best for the clients we are serving. We approach these situations with our own perspective about what would be the "right decision." But these types of choices are not about us and our agendas—they are about the senior.

It is important to educate the senior about CPR but then you have to let the individual make his or her own decision. These end-of-life conversations are a process, not a one-time event. Don't push the person to sign the DNR. Pushing the senior will erode the trust he or she has in you and will create a confrontational relationship.

When the Person Wants CPR and the Doctor's Choice

If the person chooses CPR, I would encourage the senior to find out if the hospital has a family presence policy that allows loved ones to witness any attempts at resuscitation. Being able to be in the room has been shown to help the family feel comforted by knowing that all efforts were made to help their loved one. The family will also have the opportunity to say good-bye during the CPR attempt, instead of being told after the fact that the senior has died. Of course, the hospital has the right to refuse to have the family in the room if the family is disruptive.

There are times when a patient can want CPR but the doctor can refuse. This is when CPR no longer has a chance of working and is therefore no longer a valid medical option. A patient cannot make the doctor give an ineffective or non-beneficial treatment, and sometimes CPR falls into that category because it simply won't work.

Another issue is when certain doctors won't agree to a DNR because of moral opposition. While doctors are allowed to live by their morals and to refuse to participate in acts that go against their values, they are still obligated to let patients know about valid medical options and then let the patient or the decision maker decide. If the doctor is unwilling to do this, then he or she should help the patient find a physician who will discuss and honor the DNR decision.

Lastly, make sure that the DNR request in an advance directive is transferred into the hospital chart. If the DNR is not on the chart, it doesn't exist. Encourage the senior or the decision maker to review the advance health-care directive with the health-care team in the emergency room and again when moved to an inpatient room.

Our role as CSAs in the CPR/DNR conversation is to educate, to understand the senior's perspective, and to support the person who has this difficult choice to make. Encourage the seniors and the families you work with to ask for a meaningful conversation with their health-care providers. The ultimate goal is to ensure that the senior's health goals are listened to and respected.

References & Related Reading

Diem, S. J., J. D. Lantos, and J. A. Tulsky. 1996. "Cardiopulmonary Resuscitation on Television: Miracles and Misinformation." *New England Journal of Medicine* 334: 1578–82.

Ehlenbach, W. J., A. E. Barnato, J. R. Curtis, W. Kreuter, T. D. Koepsell, R. A. Deyo, and R. D. Stapleton. 2009. "Epidemiologic Study of In-Hospital Cardiopulmonary Resuscitation in the Elderly." *New England Journal of Medicine* 361: 22–31.

Gordon, S. 2009, July 1. "CPR Survival Rates for Older People Unchanged." *HealthDay: News for Healthier Living.*

Kaldjian, L. C., Z. D. Erekson, T. H. Haberle, A. E. Curtis, L. A. Shinkunas, K. T. Cannon, and V. L. Forman-Hoffman. 2009. "Code Status Discussions and Goals of Care among Hospitalised Adults." *Journal of Medical Ethics* 35(6): 338–42.

Peberdy, M. A., W. Kaye, J. P. Ornato, G. L. Larkin, V. Nadkarni, M. E. Mancini, R. A. Berg, G. Nichol, and T. Lane-Truitt. 2003. "Cardiopulmonary Resuscitation of Adults in the Hospital: A Report of 14, 720 Cardiac Arrests from the National Registry of Cardiopulmonary Resuscitation." *Resuscitation* 58(3): 297–308.

Critical Thinking

1. How do states differ in their requirements for advance directives?
2. What is the role of the family in the CPR/DNR decision-making process?

Create Central

www.mhhe.com/createcentral

Internet References

Caring Connections
   www.caringinfo.org/i4a/pages/index.cfm?pageid=32891
MedlinePlus
   www.nlm.nih.gov/medlineplus/advancedirectives.html

VIKI KIND is a clinical bioethicist, professional speaker, hospice volunteer, and author of the award-winning book *The Caregiver's Path to Compassionate Decision Making: Making Choices for Those Who Can't.*

Article   Prepared by: Elaina F. Osterbur, *Saint Louis University*

"Affordable" Death in the United States: An Action Plan Based on Lessons Learned from the *Nursing Economic$* Special Issue

Christine T. Kovner, Edward Lusk, and Nellie M. Selander

Learning Outcomes

After reading this article, you will be able to:

- Identify the end-of-life reforms and why they are necessary.

- Discuss the advantages and disadvantages of palliative care and hospice care.

- Discuss the proposed action plan and the impact it could potentially achieve in end-of-life care.

The preceding six articles presented in this special issue of *Nursing Economic$* illustrate with uncommon clarity the nature and scope of the end-of-life cost problems facing the U.S. health care system. They tactfully navigate the sensitive and often contentious subject of death, while acknowledging that it must be addressed by patients, by their families, and ultimately by all Americans, if we are to efficiently and expertly dodge the catastrophic effects of the "perfect cost storm" that several of the authors reference. The storm—rising health care costs, particularly at the end-of-life, and the aging baby-boomer generation—is just beginning to lap at our shores; predictably soon it will be a tsunami. Taking the necessary actions to deal with the nexus of the Cost and the Dignity of Death issues will require making difficult decisions about the extent and types of care delivered, as well as the mode of health care delivery offered in the United States. The authors of the articles that you have just read provide convincing evidence for why and how these decisions should now be made. To give a sense of the most salient points that each of the preceding authors make, we will next summarize them. Following our summaries, we will offer an eight-point action plan that policymakers and lobbyists would do well to consider to avoid the impending tsunami that inaction will surely invite.

Lessons Learned from Papers Addressing the Question, How Can We Afford to Die?

In "End of Life Care in the United States: Current Reality and Future Promise—A Policy Review," Lisa A. Giovanni, BSN, RN, details the end-of-life reforms, or lack thereof, in the 2010 Patient Protection and Affordable Care Act and the inherent potential of the 1991 Patient Self-Determination Act, specifically as it pertains to advance directives and their ability to curtail end-of-life health care costs. Stressing "that the unique needs of the terminally ill remain poorly addressed," she explains the benefits of hospice and palliative care and advance directives, and suggests their integration, bringing forward their individual benefits but also anticipating the synergy created by folding these initiatives together. Giovanni also raises an alert that must be considered—that of disparity in access and funding for these cost-controlling measures.

Marlene McHugh, DNP, DCC, FNP-BC; Joan Arnold, PhD, RN; and Penelope R. Buschman, MS, RN, PMHCNS-BC, FAAN, in their article, "Nurses Leading the Response to the Crisis of Palliative Care for Vulnerable Populations," posit that nurses are innately qualified to provide palliative care. They poetically suggest that the qualities and duties of palliative care compose the essence of nursing and that all nurses can be palliative care generalists, whereas nurses with more specialized, advance knowledge in the field can lead the implementation and expansion of palliative care. Beyond simply encouraging the expansion of palliative care, McHugh and co-authors argue palliative care must be expanded to vulnerable populations, as these populations are especially in need of palliative care and should have easy access to it. The authors go on to detail recent innovations in encouraging and expanding palliative care in the United States and recommend all nurses should be aware of these initiatives. Ultimately, the authors want patients, not settings, to dictate the quality and type of care received at end-of-life. They conclude with a hopeful vision of the future: "all nursing care is palliative care" and adopting this viewpoint "can transform health with nurses taking the lead."

In "Death Is Not an Option How You Die Is: Reflections from a Career in Oncology Nursing," Brenda M. Nevidjon, MSN, RN, FAAN, and Deborah Mayer, PhD, RN, AOCN, FAAN, describe the fears associated with dying that they have witnessed in decades of practice in oncology nursing and which they also support with evidence. Nevidjon and Mayer also address the costs associated with dying and ask the profound question, "Life at what cost?" By denying that death is an inevitable reality, we make it impossible to discuss our end-of-life care rationally. Nevidjon and Mayer provide resources and cite examples of successes in beginning this conversation, but assert that providers have not gone far enough. Ultimately, they suggest that to answer this question, providers must begin the end-of life conversation in their own homes.

Deborah Witt Sherman, PhD, CRNP, ANP-BC, ACHPN, FAAN, and Jooyoung Cheon, MS, RN, in "Palliative Care: The Paradigm of Care Responsive to the Demands for Health Care Reform in America," go beyond asserting that something must be done to curtail costs and improve the quality of end-of-life care and identify a remedy: palliative care. Sherman and Cheon offer convincing evidence that palliative care is poised to become a "universally available approach" to health care, which addresses both the quality of life needs of patients and families as well as the costs of delivering end-of-life treatment and services. Although they address the differences between hospice and palliative care, they focus quite intently on palliative care because of its broader potential (it can be coupled with curative treatments and it can be used to ease the suffering associated with long-term, not just end-of-life, diseases) and because of its proven cost-saving and quality-improving characteristics. The logical extension of their idea is that costs at the end of life, which seems to be the most contentious aspect of "controlling" health care costs in general, can be routinely subsumed in the palliative care domain and so controlled. In addition to documenting the positive aspects of palliative care, Sherman and Cheon offer convincing evidence that advance practice nurses, as a result of their educational training, proficiency in practice, and professional commitment, are and should continue to be the integral players in the rapid and continued expansion of palliative care nationally and internationally.

Virginia P. Tilden, DNSc, RN, FAAN; Sarah A. Thompson, PhD, RN, FAAN; Byron Gajewski, PhD; and Marjorie Bott, PhD, RN, provide a well-documented rendering of the escalating cost problem created by high nursing home employee turnover rates in their article, "End-of-Life Care in Nursing Homes: The High Cost of Staff Turnover." The consequence of this high turnover is further compounded by a new trend the authors cite: "By 2020, 40% of those over 65 are projected to die in nursing homes." Tilden and colleagues study of 85 Midwestern nursing homes also found that high turnover rates were significantly related to lower quality of dying for patients and their families. Similar to the end-of-life health care conundrum at large, the problem with high nursing home employee turnover is both economic and personal. They argue performance-linked reimbursement policy is the "hammer" that will, over time, put the health care delivery system back on track. To this extent, they see the active employment of incentive systems and punitive reimbursement policy as measures to reduce costs by minimizing staff turnover. This intelligent design uses both carrot and stick incentives at a time when they are needed.

Dorothy J. Wholihan, DNP, ANP-BC, GNP-BC, ACHPN, and James C. Pace, DSN, MDiv, ANPBC, FAANP, offer an exciting plan to engage Americans in conversation regarding their end-of-life care—something every human will have to confront eventually. Their article, "Community Discussions: A Proposal for Cutting the Costs of End-of-Life," proposes initiating discussions of end-of-life care earlier in life—before people are terminally ill. Although this is not a new concept, they suggest these discussions should take place in the community, not in the ICU. By opening up the topic of end-of-life care to the community, the issues and apprehensions surrounding creating and implementing advance directives are lessened. As evidence for this, the authors cite numerous studies showing early adoption and sensitive cultural creation of advance directives makes these documents more effective. Ultimately, the potency of the authors' argument is that if scripted properly, based on individual, family, and community beliefs and norms, advance directives can contribute to a dignified end-of-life strategy consistent with the community discourse an individual is engaged in over his or her lifetime. This may finally allow the health care delivery system to move away from providing heroic and ineffective end-of-life treatments and toward a more palliative approach.

These six works competently address the myriad issues warranting consideration in the development of an action plan, which addresses the question, "How can we afford to die?" These articles have many common arguments and fit together nicely; that is to say, our proposed action plan basically wrote itself.

The Action Plan

Following are the eight central points of our action plan derived from a synthesis of the research summarized in this special issue. We fully recognize the complicated systemic-dynamic change necessary to achieve our action plan will require pilot testing, redesign refinements, further pilot testing, a full-scale launch, and then periodic monitoring and evaluation. We propose this action plan because, at some point, systemic change will happen; we want these change efforts to be pro-active—driven by design rather than re-active—not spawned by panic. After outlining our proposed action plan, we will discuss its desirability, feasibility, and sustainability.

1. All individuals over 18 years old should have advance directives long before they find themselves at the "seventh age:" the end of life. Nurses, physicians, and other health care providers should be required to follow these advance directives. Many of the authors

who have contributed to this special issue suggest and demonstrate advance directives have significant cost-cutting potential, but recognize that even when patients do complete them, they are not always honored. The contributing authors posit ways to increase completion and use of advance directives. These suggestions, which we believe to be the essentials in scripting effective advance directives, are: (a) reimbursement policies should compensate health care providers for helping their patients to complete advance directives, (b) advance directives should be discussed and created in the context of an individual's community, and (c) cost sensitivity should be discussed transparently as part of the intended effect of the advance directives.

2. Hospice and palliative care (as defined in the "Introduction" to this special issue) must be available for all patients treated at hospitals or using services that are supported in part by any municipal/local, state, or federal-derived revenue. Derived revenue is any tax revenue that accrues by way of the taxing/redistribution authority following the accounting principles as laid out in Statement No. 34 of the Governmental Accounting Standards Board.

3. The decision to provide a patient with hospice and/or palliative care will be determined by the patient, his or her family, case manager, and nurses and physicians of the organization where the patient is receiving care. All the while, the patient's advance directive must be kept in mind and adhered to in accordance with the patient's wishes. This is, of course, where the cost sensitivity of the advance directive will play a major role in dealing with the nexus of the Cost and Dignity of Death issues.

4. Traditional reimbursement sources will bear the cost of providing individuals with hospice and palliative care; specifically, private insurance with no/low deductibles or co-pays and a combination of municipal, state, and federal sources. Reimbursement agreements should be as simple as possible, following the usual concept of equitable redistributions. This may sound daunting; however, simple rules such as "telescoping" where one first exhausts private insurance, then municipal, then state, and finally federal may make the funding and reimbursement processes simpler and more equitable. We also propose that an individual's personal wealth should not be exhausted before municipal, state, or federal sources are used.

5. To increase the availability of hospice and palliative care facilities, for which there will be a sharp increase in demand due to the aging baby-boomer generation as well as the fact the central feature of our action plan requires the expansion of such facilities, legislators and other elected officials should consider incentivizing or subsidizing new construction or conversions of hospice and palliative care facilities using tax abatements, payments in lieu of taxes, or issuing bonds on behalf of private firms in order to lower the cost of development. This may be particularly viable in cities experiencing high vacancy and foreclosure rates where the cost of purchasing land is already low. One such city is Cleveland, which is home to the world-renown Cleveland Clinic.

6. Social networking should be used by health care organizations and local, state, and federal governments to promote choosing hospice or palliative care over heroic, and often futile, end-of life treatments. Successfully increasing the use of hospice and palliative care is contingent upon convincing individuals and their caregivers to choose these less-expensive and quality-of-life improving options, as well as detailing them in their advance directives. As Wholihan and Pace recommend, a way to encourage individuals to include hospice care in their advance directives is through extensive and intensive community dialogue and communication. Additionally, fully using social networking in this regard may also be beneficial. This is the powerful communication tool, made famous by Mark Zuckerberg's *Facebook,* and should not to be dismissed as a fad. Although we were unable to find scholarly sources connecting social networking and improved health outcomes or increased engagement in health care decision making, some studies indicate social networking may increase civic and social engagement (Pasek, More, & Romer, 2009; Valenzuela, Park, & Kee, 2009). Make no mistake: everything is contingent upon developing sensible advance directives.

7. A greater number of nurse faculty at U.S. colleges and universities will be required to meet the increased demand by nurses who need advance training and education in hospice and palliative care. Nurses can, and traditionally, have played a major role in hospice or palliative care; expanding hospice or palliative care will necessitate an increase of the numbers of specialized nurses (American Association of Colleges of Nursing, 2005).

8. We recommend that Tilden and colleagues' list of punitive reimbursement policies (penalties for hospital re-admission, value-based and pay-for-performance plans, and other payment reforms that emphasize quality and penalize systems that deliver poor care), as well as possible incentives, be linked to documented patient outcomes and be audited by the Government Accounting Office (GAO). We recommend the GAO audit the expansion of hospice and palliative care because of the unbiased, analytical role it has played in objectively evaluating U.S. legislation and governmental actions. GAO-audited and approved services would be reimbursed. Un-audited or unnecessary/non-recommended treatments would not be reimbursed under this proposed system, *unless the treatment was in accordance with a patient's advance directive.* This "unless-caveat" regarding the advance directives needs to be considered carefully; if many patients have advance directives that make positive, cost-conscious systemic change impossible, most of the other efforts discussed as part of our action plan will go for naught.

Other Important Contextual Issues

- The GAO audit will include an assessment of the benefits of a specific treatment or service relative to its cost for a particular patient population under examination. The audit will focus on a series of questions. For example, "How was the treatment or service delivered given the alternatives?" or "What were the benefits of the treatment relative to its cost?" The answers to such questions will be considered relative to reasoned *a priori* expectations for the group within which the particular patient falls. That is to say: Context matters in assessing the effects of medical treatment plans.

- As an additional control as well as enrichment of the development of the patient treatment plan, nurses should be integrated into the treatment team decision making group on hospice and palliative care units. Nurses, as a result of their training and experience, can make significant contributions in developing hospice and palliative treatment plans. Specifically, we suggest hospice and palliative care treatment plans are signed by both a trained hospice or palliative care nurse and the patient's physician. This additional documenting voice is just a simple way of recording the opinion of another health care professional as part of the treatment plan. Over time, such dual recording will likely improve the quality of care.

- It is clear that increasing hospice and palliative care use and advance directives will require the creation of many systemic support initiatives; as a result, we recommend that our action plan be the purview of an independent decision making group that is out of the influential reach of partisan lobbying. Simply put: Lobbying is counterproductive to effective cost and quality control; the case in point is that in most countries that have more socialized health care delivery systems lobbying is illegal. We imagine this group would maintain its independence and operate within the governmental context, following the models of the Federal Reserve Board and the Public Company Accounting Oversight Board.

Features of the Eight-Point Action Plan

Let us now consider the features of this action plan. Following we discuss the desirability, feasibility, and sustainability of the action plan presented here.

Desirability. We believe expanding and incentivizing hospice and palliative care and respecting advance directives, which are central aspects of the eight-point action plan, is desirable because of their inherent effectiveness and efficiency. Specifically, effectiveness is addressed because patients' advance directives will dictate the progression of their care, thus potentially avoiding heroic, ineffective, and unwarranted end-of-life treatments. Additionally, the action plan will be efficient by curtailing costs by adhering to the GAO-audited reimbursement procedures as set forth in action plan item eight.

Feasibility. The expansion of hospice and palliative care would not be feasible, from a cost or dignity perspective, if the execution of the eight-point action plan worked against the legal, religious, moral, or financial fabric of American social and cultural norms and expectations. Engaging communities in discussions of health, recommending cost-sensitive advance directives, using discharge planning in hospitals, suggesting hospice or palliative care at the end-of-life alternatives, and financing health care through insurance and audited redistributive measures have all long been used by those trying to curtail health care costs in the United States. Expanding and incentivizing hospice and palliative care is only a modest re-organization of these aspects of the U.S. health care delivery system, the action plan of which will realign these systemic features to conserve resources and preserve individual end-of-life dignity.

Sustainability. Sustainability is the most difficult-to-predict aspect of the eight-point action plan. Expanding and incentivizing the use of hospice and palliative care with an eye to conservation of scarce resources will, by definition, move the U.S. health care delivery system in the sustainability direction. Simply put: Economies affected by cost-sensitive incentives will translate into more resources being available to cover needed services. However, the Patient Protection and Affordable Care Act of 2010 (the first health legislation in decades seeking to directly help millions of uninsured Americans) will undoubtedly put greater financial pressure on the current reimbursement system, as many more millions of citizens obtain access to health care. This increased pressure may compromise the gains made in affecting economies through the eight-point action plan. Here is where experimentation, monitoring, and redesign will be needed to maintain the hospice and palliative care initiatives as features of the U.S. health care delivery system. This of course may call into question the distribution of resources of all of the federal programs from the Department of Defense to the Department of Health and Human Services as in the Zero-Based Budget context.

Concluding Comments

A recent poll from the California Health Foundation notes there is a great disparity between what people say they want (to die a natural death at home) and what actually occurs. Eighty-two percent of respondents reported "that it was important to have end-of-life wishes in writing," and yet less than 25% had done so (Wood, 2012). Ultimately, this special issue begs the question: Given our political and economic realities of 2012, can we realistically imagine positive, cost-reducing changes in the way we deliver health care in the United States? To realize the expansion of our hospice and palliative care action plan, many details must be worked out. For example, how will the incentives listed by Tilden and co-authors be employed given the GAO audit? And how will the appointment process to the independent decision making group be organized and monitored? Of course this is normal; one should not read this special issue of *Nursing Economic$* and think, "Well, I see problems here and there," and then stop thinking. One should see this special issue as a catalyst for developing ways to deal with the difficulties of negotiating end-of-life care. In this regard we appreciate the "spirit" of Peter Neumann's (2012) editorial where he introduces the central issue that defined this special issue of *Nursing Economic$*. Neumann begins with the following "directive" taken from the American College of Physician [ACP] Ethics Manual:

> Physicians have a responsibility to practice effective and efficient health care and to use health care resources responsibly. Parsimonious care that utilizes the most efficient means to effectively diagnose a condition and treat a patient respects the need to use resources wisely and to help ensure that resources are equitably available (p. 585).

With this as the logical backdrop, Neumann systematically considers the difficulties in "doing what is needed" and keeping everyone satisfied and also controlling the resources needed to affect the needed delivery. He offers the following as guidance to begin the discussion needed to avoid the impending storm:

> The challenge is how to have a more honest conversation. A candid discussion could set expectations, inform policy debates, and help the country prioritize uses for resources within and outside the health care sector. There seems to be little evidence, however, that such a conversation will take place, at least in the public sphere. There is no political advantage in talking realistically about our problems. The election-year rhetoric will continue to emphasize prevention, quality, and health information technology. On the campaign trail, the speechifying will be about fraud and abuse, the evils of rationing, and the need to improve our way to sustainability. That is why the new ACP guidelines are so valuable. Their focus on responsibility, their direct acknowledgment of the need to consider constraints, their recognition that less care may be better care, and their call for individual physicians to use resources wisely are rare and welcome. The ACP should be applauded for its engagement of costs. Is "parsimonious" the right word? Perhaps there are better ones, but "frugal," "prudent," "thrifty," "cost-conscious," and others would also raise objections. Whatever we call this necessary quality, the conversation could use a dose of reality. Calling it parsimonious is a reasonable start (p. 586).

To close this important *Nursing Economic$* special issue, let us have the courage to be proactive, evaluate the impact of our actions, make modifications, and continue to learn and evolve the health care delivery system to produce a responsive and responsible way to address the problems that we have gotten ourselves into. As Pogo so wisely quipped: "We have met the enemy and he is us." Let's prove him wrong.

References

American Association of Colleges of Nursing. (2005). Faculty shortages in baccalaureate and graduate nursing programs: Scope of the problem and strategies for expanding the supply. Retrieved from http://www.aacn.nche.edu/publications/whitepapers/faculty-shortages

Neumann, P.J. (2012). What we talk about when we talk about health care costs. *New England Journal of Medicine, 366*(7), 585–586.

Pasek, J., More, E., & Romer, D. (2009). Realizing the social Internet? Online social networking meets offline civic engagement. *Journal of Information Technology & Politics 6*(3–4), 197–215.

Valenzuela, S., Park, N., & Kee, K.F. (2009). Is the social capital in a social network site?: Facebook use and college students' life satisfaction, trust, and participation. *Journal of Computer-Mediated Communication 14*(4), 875–901.

Wood, D. (2012). Nurses critical to fulfilling patients' end-of-life wishes. *Nurse Zone: Nursing News*. Retrieved from http://www.nursezone.com/Nursing-News-Events/morenews/Nurses-Critical-to-FulfillingPatients%E2%80%99-End-of-life-Wishes_39216.aspx

Additional Readings

Activities of Daily Living Evaluation. (2002). *Encyclopedia of nursing & allied health*. Retrieved from http://www.enotes.com/topic/Activities_of_daily_living

CBS. (2009). Why the Federal Reserve needs to be independent. *Money Watch*. Retrieved http://www.cbsnews.com/8301-505123_162-39740151/why-the-federal-reserve-needs-to-be-independent

CBS. (2011). There goes the neighborhood. *60 Minutes*. Retrieved from http://www.cbsnews.com/8301-18560_162-57344513/there-goes-the-neighborhood

Hulse, C., & Cooper, H. (2011, July 31). Obama and leaders reach debt deal. *New York Times*. Retrieved from http://www.nytimes.com/2011/08/0 1/us/politics/01FISCAL.html

Kelley, M.A., Angus, D., Chalfin, D.B., Crandall, E.D., Ingbar, D., Johanson, W., . . . Vender, J.S. (2004). The critical care crisis in the United States. *CHEST 125*(4), 1514–1517.

Krause, J.H. (2010). Following the money in health care fraud: Reflections on a modern-day yellow brick road. *American Journal of Law and Medicine 36*(2–3), 343–369.

Morris, L. (2009). Combating fraud in health care: An essential component of any cost containment strategy. *Health Affairs 28*(5), 1351–1356.

Newport, F. (2011). Congress ends 2011 with record-low 11% approval. *Gallup*. Retrieved from http://www.gallup.com/poll/151628/Congress-Ends-2011-Record-LowApproval.aspx

Poulsen, G. (2011). *Improving quality, lowering costs: The role of health care delivery system reform*. Testimony before the Senate Health, Education, Labor and Pensions Committee. Retrieved from http://help.senate.gov/imo/media/doc/Poulsen.pdf

Robert, H.M. (1915). *Robert's Rules of Order: Revised for deliberative assemblies*. Retrieved from http://www.bartleby.com/176

Social Security Advisory Board. (2009). *The unsustainable cost of health care*. Retrieved from http://www.ssab.gov/documents/TheUnsustainableCostofHealthCare_508.pd

Critical Thinking

1. The article suggests that there is an "impending tsunami that inaction will surely invite." What is this tsunami?

2. What is meant by community discussions regarding advance directives?

3. How will the cost of health care be affected by these proposed changes in its delivery?

Create Central

www.mhhe.com/createcentral

Internet References

American Association of Colleges of Nursing
www.aacn.nche.edu

AARP
www.aarp.org

CHRISTINE T. KOVNER, PhD, RN, FAAN, is a Professor, College of Nursing, and Nurse Attending, NYU Langone Medical Center, New York University, New York, NY. EDWARD LUSK, PhD, MBA, MA, CPA, is a Professor of Accounting, State University of New York—Plattsburgh, Plattsburgh, NY, and Emeritus, the Department of Statistics, the Wharton School of the University of Pennsylvania, Philadelphia, PA. NELLIE M. SELANDER, MUP, is a Research Assistant, College of Nursing, New York University, New York, NY.

Kovner et al., Christine T. From *Nursing Economic$*, May/June 2012, pp. 179–184. Copyright © 2012 by Jannetti Publications, Inc., East Holly Avenue/Box 56, Pitman, NJ 08071-0056; (856) 256-2300, FAX (856) 589-7463; for a sample copy of the journal, please contact the publisher. Used with permission. www.nursingeconomics.net

Article   Prepared by: Elaina F. Osterbur, *Saint Louis University*

Palliative Care: A Paradigm of Care Responsive to the Demands for Health Care Reform in America

DEBORAH WITT SHERMAN AND JOOYOUNG CHEON

Learning Outcomes

After reading this article, you will be able to:

- Discuss the cost savings of palliative care and its impact on quality of life.

- Discuss the health-care demands for palliative and hospice care in the United States.

- Discuss the provisions in the Affordable Care Act and how the act affects end-of-life-care decisions.

In March 2010, the affordable Care Act was passed by Congress and signed into law by President Obama. This act expands access to health care to over 30 million Americans (Pelosi, 2010). The Act increases insurance coverage for pre-existing conditions, and increases projected national medical spending with the expansion of Medicaid to include more low-income Americans (Foster, 2009; Keehan et al., 2011), while projecting a reduction in spending on Medicare of $400 billion over a 10-year period (Pelosi, 2010). The Affordable Care Act of 2010 requires the Centers for Medicare and Medicaid Services to implement a 3-year demonstration project which allows patients to receive aggressive treatment as well as palliative/hospice care concurrently (Office of the Legislative Counsel, 2010). This will require a rethinking of hospice eligibility criteria to be less stringent than having a current prognosis of 6 months or less to live for patients with advanced illness (Casarett, 2011). This moves in the right direction as the addition of palliative-hospice care to aggressive treatment reduces health care utilization and costs (Brumley et al., 2007; Temel et al., 2010).

The project also evaluates the cost saving of palliative home health care programs and will evaluate patients' quality of life. The expectation is that the results of this 3-year project will indicate that palliative care, in addition to life-sustaining treatment, will improve patients' survival when compared to usual care (Temel et al., 2010). Palliative care has great relevance to efforts to reform the health care system, insuring quality, consistency, and effectiveness of health care delivery (Meier & Beresford, 2009).

Palliative Care as a Paradigm of Care

Palliative care is a paradigm of care, which expands the traditional disease-model of treatment to anticipate, prevent, and alleviate the suffering associated with serious, progressive, chronic, life-threatening illness at any point during the illness trajectory (National Consensus Project [NCP] for Quality Palliative Care, 2009). It is now recognized as a specialty in medicine, nursing, and social work with an inherent interdisciplinary nature (Grant, Elk, Ferrell, Morrison, & von Gunten, 2009). Palliative care addresses the physical, emotional, social, and spiritual needs of patients and their families with the goal of improving their quality of life. This occurs through the aggressive treatment of pain and other symptoms, as well as optimizing function and assisting patients and families with health care decision making (NCP, 2009). Through conversations with patients and families regarding advanced care planning, palliative care focuses on matching treatments with the patient's and family's values and preferences (Meier & Beresford, 2009). It improves communication across all care settings and results in continuous and well-coordinated care during illness transitions.

The experience of serious life-threatening illness is overwhelming for patients. Studies indicate that 53% of patients averaged across all disease stages report pain, with one-third rating pain as moderate to severe (Giese-Davis et al., 2011; Morrison, Flanagan, Fishberg, Cintron, & Siu, 2009; Morrison et al., 2003; Satin, Linden, & Phillips, 2009). Often concurrent with pain are associated symptoms of depression, delirium, or functional decline. Patients with cancer also report nonpain symptoms such as dyspnea, anxiety, and insomnia (Mitchell et al., 2011; Spiegel, 2011; van den Beuken-van Everdingen et al., 2009). These symptoms are exacerbated by the uncertainty associated with severe illness and often have an impact on spiritual and social well-being which impairs quality of life (Meier & Brawley, 2011). The ultimate outcome is impaired quality of life with spiritual and social ramifications. Palliative care focuses on addressing all aspects of suffering, which not only improves quality of life, but survival. With consideration regarding the goals of care, palliative care considers the risk and benefit ratio of tests, procedures, and treatments, which may adversely affect quality of life, create additional suffering, providing limited benefit while driving up the costs of health care (Meier & Brawley, 2011).

The impact of illness is felt not only by the patient but also by family caregivers. Wright and colleagues (2008) documented the association between patients' end-of-life care and quality of life of caregivers. The burdens of family caregiving include time and logistics, physical tasks, financial costs, emotional burdens, and other health risks (Rabow, Hauser, & Adams, 2004). The physical stress of caregiving can lead to significant physiological changes and medical illness with a greater risk of mortality. In turn, health risks and serious illness require increasing utilization of health care resources and escalated health care costs as caregivers suffer from heart disease, hypertension, and impaired immune function, placing them at greater risk for cancers, HIV/AIDS, and other infections (Family Caregiver Alliance, 2006). Emotionally, caregivers suffer from symptoms of anger, depression, and anxiety and often become demoralized and exhausted (Zarit, 2006). As a vulnerable population, many caregivers of advanced cancer patients either meet DSM-IV criteria for, or are being treated for, psychiatric problems (Vanderweker, Laff, Kadan-Lottick, McColl, & Prigerson, 2005), and demonstrate impaired cognitive functioning (McGuire et al., 2000). Caregiving demands result in lost wages or leaving the workforce entirely, both of which have severe economic implications, and personal, social, and institutional consequences. As leisure, religious, and social activities are abandoned, there is heightened marital and family stress, with long-term consequences for the health and the stability of the family (Dumont, Dumont, & Mongeau, 2008). Given that palliative care offers patient and family-centered care, it promotes a sense of safety in the health care system for both patients and their family caregivers (NCP, 2009).

The Similarities and Differences of Palliative and Hospice Care

In response to the central question of "How we can afford to die?" we contend that palliative and hospice care offer holistic and comprehensive care that is individualized to the needs of patients and families, and consistent with their goals of care. Palliative care thereby limits unwanted, inappropriate, and ineffective interventions which drive up the cost of health care significantly. Palliative care can be provided at the same time as life-prolonging treatments. In contrast, hospice care, as a form of palliative care, is the care of patients and families during the last few weeks or months of life. Both palliative and hospice care are based on the principles of patient/family-centered care and holistic care including comprehensive assessment and treatment which is offered by an interdisciplinary team of health professionals. The difference between palliative care and hospice care is essentially the timing; palliative care is offered from the time of diagnosis with life-threatening illness through the death of the patient and into the bereavement period for families, while hospice care is offered at the end of life (Jennings, Ryndes, D'Onofrio, & Baily, 2003).

The clinical models of palliative care include palliative consultation services, inpatient palliative care units, and community home-based programs in nursing homes and assisted living facilities as well as care in ambulatory outpatient clinics. Similarly, hospice care can be offered in hospice units of hospitals or nursing homes as well as in residential hospices and home hospices.

The Increasing Demand for Palliative Care

Palliative care is poised to become a universally available approach to meet the needs of the sickest and most vulnerable populations and is an important factor in improving health care in America (Meier, 2010). With the increase in life expectancy for patients with cancer, HIV/AIDS, or end-stage organ diseases, as well as the expected growth of the aging population, palliative care is in demand. Seminal data from the 1994 SUPPORT studies indicate more than 50% of caregivers of Americans hospitalized with a serious illness report less than optimal care and more than 30% of families report significant economic burden (Covinsky et al., 1994). Teno and colleagues (2004) report that 1 in 4 patients report inadequate treatment of pain and dyspnea; 1 in 3 families report inadequate emotional support; and 1 in 3 patients report they receive no education related to the treatment of their symptoms following a hospital stay nor are arrangements made for follow-up care after hospital discharge. Given these significant gaps in care, hospitals are recognizing the value of palliative care in providing relief of pain and other symptoms, continuity of the care, as well as educational and emotional support for patients and families experiencing serious illness (Teno et al., 2004). As such, palliative care is important in health care reform where the emphasis is quality health outcomes while considering the value and cost of care.

Cost Savings and Health-Related Outcomes of Palliative Care

The Federal Government estimates the U.S. population ages 85 and over will grow from 5.3 million in 2006 to nearly 21 million by 2050 (Federal Interagency Forum on Aging Related Statistics, 2008). In the United States, capita spending on health care outranks anywhere else in the world with a reported $2.4 trillion spent on health care in 2008 (Medicare Payment Advisory Commission, 2009). Furthermore, 68% of all Medicare spending will be to address the needs of Medicare patients with greater than four chronic conditions. "Five percent of Medicare enrollees with the most serious illness account for over 43% of Medicare expenditures with the top 25% of enrollees accounting for 85% of the costs" (Congressional Budget Office, 2005).

Additionally, there is a rapid growth in the eligible nursing home population which represents 6%–7% of the Medicaid population, but over half of the Medicaid expenditures (Huskamp, Stevenson, Chernew, & Newhouse, 2010; Kaiser Family Foundation, 2011; Meier, Lim, & Carlson, 2010; Mitchell et al., 2009). Hospitals are responding to the economic crisis and escalating cost of health care by cutting administration costs, reducing staffs, reducing services, divesting assets, and considering merger and other economic restraints which have significant implications related to quality of care (American Hospital Association, 2008).

Increased cost of health care does not equate with a higher quality of care. Although it is estimated the U.S. Gross National Product (GNP) will increase from 16% to 20% by 2015 for medical spending, data indicate higher medical spending does not lead to better patient's outcomes. In fact, regions of highest utilization, such as having the greatest number of specialist visits, hospital days, and ICU use, have the highest mortality rates (Fisher, Wennberg, Stukel, & Gottlieb, 2004; Fisher et al., 2003; Mitka, 2006).

Morrison and colleagues (2008) examined the cost and ICU outcomes associated with palliative care consultation in eight U.S. hospitals. For individuals with live discharges, it was reported that palliative care, when compared to usual care, reduced the total costs of admission by $2,642, lowered the cost per day by $279, as well as lowered the direct costs per admission by $1,696. Palliative care also significantly lowered the costs of direct costs per admission, laboratory costs, and ICU costs. For individuals who had a hospital death, palliative care significantly lowered the total cost of admission by $6,896, lowered the total costs per day by $549, and lowered the direct costs per admission by $4,908. For this population, significant reductions also occurred for direct costs per day, laboratory costs, and ICU costs.

Morrison and colleagues (2008) indicated that for a 400-bed hospital, the annual cost savings by palliative care is more than $1.3 million per year. Penrod and colleagues (2010) further reported patients receiving palliative care were 44% less likely to be admitted to an ICU when compared to usual care patients. Evidence clearly indicates palliative care reduces the overuse of unnecessary, marginally effective, or ineffective treatments and leads to less hospital re-admissions as a result of greater continuity of care and the development of safe transition plans upon initial discharge (Morrison et al., 2008; Penrod et al., 2010; Penrod et al., 2006; Smith et al., 2003).

Brumley and colleagues (2007) also reported the palliative care shifts care out of hospital to the home. Specifically, palliative care significantly increases home health visits while lowering physician office visits, emergency visits, hospital days, and skilled nursing facilities days. According to a report published by the Institute of Medicine, savings greater than $6 billion per year would occur if palliative care teams were fully integrated into the nation's hospitals (Morrison et al., 2011).

In addition to cost savings, data indicate palliative care is beneficial in achieving positive health-related outcomes for patients, families, and health professionals. More specifically, palliative care outcomes include:

- Improvement of quality care while lowering length of stay and cost.
- Emotional, spiritual, and social support of patients and families.
- Improvement of quality of life for patients and families.
- Improvement in patient/family satisfaction.
- Handling of time-intensive family/patient/team meetings.
- Better coordination of care.
- Specialty-level assistance to the attending physician.
- Support for attending physicians and discharge planning staff.
- Improvement in nurse and physician satisfaction (NCP, 2009).

Given that health care spending continues to increase in most countries as a percentage of the GNP, Higginson and Foley (2009) affirm there is intensive pressure to reduce health care costs, which are particularly high in the last year of life. They conclude palliative care not only results in cost savings for health care systems, but quantifiable benefits in the reduction of pain and suffering, and improvement in the quality of care and quality of life. In short, the palliative care/hospice partnership creates a common sense allocation of health care resources as patients move across the illness trajectory and approach the end of life. With palliative and hospice care, the wishes and preferences of patients and families are respected, often with a desire to withdraw life-prolonging treatments and insure their comfort and dignity as death approaches.

Palliative Care Responds to the Health Care Demands in America

The 2008 State-by-State Report Card of America's care of serious illness indicates that over the last 10 years, palliative care has been one of the fastest-growing trends in health care (National Palliative Care Research Center, 2011). The report card indicates 85% of large hospitals with 300 or more beds have a palliative care team. However, only 54% of public hospitals, 26% of for-profit hospitals, and 37% of community hospitals offer palliative care services (National Palliative Care Research Center [NPCRC], 2011). Although it is recognized that palliative care is the new paradigm for managing serious illness and 92% of people polled believe palliative services should be available at all hospitals, millions of Americans with serious illness do not have access to palliative care. Despite a 138% increase in the number of palliative care programs, the accessibility and availability of such programs vary greatly by region and by state (NPCRC, 2011).

In 2008, the nation's palliative care report card indicated an overall grade of C. The good news is the overall grade improved to a grade of B in 2011 (NPCRC, 2011), indicating that overall, states now exceed the minimal standards of quality palliative care. In fact, although more than half of the 50 states received a grade of B, seven states now report they have more than 80% of hospitals with palliative care services, thereby receiving a grade of A, indicating excellence in palliative care. Clearly, there is still improvement to be made as 12% of states received a non-passing grade of D or F. In many of these states, there are disparities given geographic availability and the shortage of trained palliative care health professionals. Furthermore, public and community provider hospitals are often the only options for Americans without health care insurance as well as for those living in geographically isolated areas. The result is greater health disparities resulting from less access to palliative care for these underserved populations. The mandates of health care reform will lead institutions to voluntary certification in palliative care as recommended by the Joint Commission on Accreditation of Healthcare Organizations and an expectation for hospitals to achieve Magnet® status.

Global Demands for Palliative Care

Palliative care is a global imperative as 56 million people die each year in resource-rich as well as resource-poor countries with associated physical and emotional suffering (Seymour et al., 2009). "At the end of the first decade of the 21st Century, the provision of palliative care is beginning to feature in the political and policy agendas of many different countries as they seek to respond to the challenges of epidemiological and socio-demographic change, particularly given aging populations" (Seymour, 2011, p. 18).

With the belief that palliative care should be regarded as a human right, Wright, Wood, Lynch, and Clark (2008) have mapped the levels of palliative care development globally. Although palliative care is now regarded as a human right, the distribution of services is generally unavailable in many countries in the world. The typology of worldwide palliative care was constructed by identifying countries with: (a) no identified hospice/palliative care activities; (b) the capacity for developing palliative care, however no palliative services available; (c) the provision of localized palliative care; (d) and countries where palliative care is being integrated with mainstream health care services. The results of this mapping determined palliative care services can be found in 115 out of 234 countries. More specifically, the results indicated there was no identified activities in 78 (33%) countries, 41 (18%) countries had capacity building, and 80 (34%) countries had localized provision of palliative care, while 35 (15%) countries approached integration.

With over half of the world's countries still without palliative care, the challenges that remain include the awareness of palliative care to improve quality of life for patients and families, increased access to opioid medications, education, and government support for palliative care. Centeno and colleagues (2007) suggested the importance of implementing different models of palliative care service delivery. They proposed not only hospice consultation support teams, but day centers which

are common in the United Kingdom, as well as mobile teams. In an aging society with stretched budgets, the future will bring new challenges to sustain, expand, and optimize the 8,000 dedicated palliative care services that currently exist in the world (Gomes, Harding, Foley, & Higginson, 2009).

International Recommendations for the Advancement of Palliative Care

As a global leader in hospice and palliative care, funding and financing issues in the Australian hospice and palliative care sector is informative (Gordon, Eagar, Currow, & Green, 2009). In Australia, responsibilities for managing the health care system are shared by both levels of government—the states and territories. The delivery of palliative care services therefore is the responsibility of both states and territories. The funding of palliative care varies according to the type of care offered by specialist providers, generalist providers, and support services in nongovernment, private, and public sectors. In Australia, there is no national model for funding inpatient or community services, as these services are a states/territories responsibility. Given that palliative care is evolving at a rapid rate in Australia, it is recommended that flexible evidenced-based models of care delivery emerge along with equally flexible funding and financing models with consideration of the case mix of patient and type of providers (Gordon et al., 2009).

In directing the future of the palliative care field, Gomes and colleagues (2009) and Lynch and co-authors (2009) reported on the outcomes of an international meeting of clinicians, health economists, researchers, policymakers, and advocates. Based on this meeting, seven recommendations related to palliative care were identified: (a) the need for shared definitions of palliative care, (b) identification of the strengths and weakness of different payment systems, (c) determination of country-specific and international research priorities, (d) consideration of appropriate economic evaluation methods, (e) evaluation of the cost of palliative care, (f) the need for palliative care education and training programs for interdisciplinary health care professionals, and (g) the development of national standards to regulate and determine palliative care planning and development. Countries such as the United Kingdom, Canada, Australia, and the United States are at the forefront in providing quality palliative and hospice care and national as well as international leaders in the specialty are addressing these recommendations.

Advance Practice Nurses Play a Pivotal Role in Palliative Care

With the rapid growing increase in both the number and quality of palliative care programs in the United States and worldwide, the contribution of advance practice nurses in advancing the specialty is striking. "Advance practice nurses often embody in a single person palliative care's focus on the whole person and the medical practitioner's ability to diagnose conditions, prescribe medications and order treatment interventions while recouping salary costs through billing for consultations" (Meier & Beresford, 2006, p. 624). The importance of whole-person care is emphasized by Meier and Brawley (2011), who state that "New delivery and payment models that promote quality of care, instead of the current fee-for-service model that promotes quantity of care, may change incentives that encourage procedures and interventions over whole-person care" (p. 2751).

In many hospitals, it is the advance practice nurse who spearheads the development, implementation, and evaluation of palliative care services. Advance practice nurses have pivotal leadership roles as clinical consultants, administrators, educators, health policymakers, and researchers. With advance nursing degrees in adult primary care, geriatrics, psychiatric nursing, pediatrics, or family nursing, palliative care nurses combine their primary specialization with specialist-level knowledge in palliative care gained through concurrent master's degrees or post-master's certification in palliative care. Palliative care competencies and expertise are demonstrated by passing the Advance Practice Palliative Care Certification Examination offered by the National Board for Certification of Hospice and Palliative Nurses. Eligibility to take the examination requires documentation of an advanced practice master's degree in nursing and 500 clinical hours in palliative care within the year prior to taking the examination. Advance practice nurses can bill for their services given they have achieved advance practice nursing licensure and certification and are working within their scope of practice as defined by their certification agency.

As a leader in palliative care, advance practice nurses are often the health professionals who make the case to hospital administration to implement a palliative program. The unique missions, needs, and the constraints of the hospital must be considered when designing a successful palliative care program (Center to Advance Palliative Care, 2011). In developing a business plan, the advanced practice nurse considers interdisciplinary resources, feasibility and accessibility, cost control, revenue generation, integrating and leveraging of existing services, deciding the palliative care program structure and model, where to house the program, as well as how to coordinate patient care across settings. The business plan includes the operational plan for implementation such as space needs, staffing roles and requirements, basic policies and procedures, and projections of patient volume and program capacity. The operational plan explains the program start-up and ongoing costs, as well as the expected sources of revenue or cost avoidance.

In creating the business plan, the advance practice nurse utilizes financial and strategic planning tools. The advanced practice nurse demonstrates how the palliative program will contribute to the hospital's financial viability, with consideration of program volume, length of stay, daily census, hospital billing revenues, estimated cost savings, and potential contributions by philanthropy (Center to Advance Palliative Care, 2011). The executive summary of the plan describes the context for the proposal, the program's key features, the needs or problems identified through institutional and market analysis, and how the palliative program will meet these needs as well as the expected impact and outcomes for quality care. With advanced clinical knowledge and expertise related to health care systems, advance practice nurses are credited for the rapid advancement of the specialty and for their futuristic perspectives on addressing the demands of health care reform while providing quality care.

Health Care for the Seriously Ill and Dying: An Exemplary Action Plan in the State of Maryland

Within the context of cancer care and a focus on quality and affordable health care, the Maryland Cancer Control Plan for Palliative and Hospice Care (Sherman et al., 2011) provides a valuable action plan or "Blueprint for Success in Palliative and Hospice Care." This comes at a time when citizens of Maryland and all of the United States most need a complement to health care, including cancer care. With an aging population in the State of Maryland and nationally, an increase in the number of cancer diagnoses, and an increase in the number of survivors of cancer and other life-threatening illness who still face a number of physical and emotional symptoms, a comprehensive "all hands on deck" approach to health care is critical. Quality and affordable health care during any stage of the illness trajectory, particularly as the disease progresses and death approaches, involves collaborative efforts of patients, families, communities, health care professionals, institutions, health care policymakers, legislators, and payers (see Table 1). By active involvement and joint efforts, these key stakeholders can insure quality of care and quality of life, lower cost, increased access, coordination and continuity, and the reduction of health disparities (Sherman et al., 2011).

Maryland's Action Plan for Palliative and Hospice Care (Sherman et al., 2011, p. 4) highlights the importance of the achievement of the "4 A's"—Awareness, Acknowledgment, Access, and Action—by each of the identified stakeholder groups.

- *Awareness* implies knowledge and appreciation gained through one's perceptions or by means of information about palliative and hospice care.
- *Acknowledgment* is the recognition and acceptance of the value of palliative and hospice care.
- *Access* is the right, privilege, or ability to make use of resources and information related to palliative and hospice care.
- *Action* is the development, implementation, and evaluation of initiatives to promote palliative and hospice care, which will lead to inclusion of palliative and hospice care into the standards of care and setting of future goals.

According to Maryland's Action Plan, each of the identified stakeholder groups develops an awareness of palliative

Table 1 Identification of Key Stakeholder Groups in Palliative and Hospice Care

Patients, Families, and Communities

- *Patients:* Individuals with a diagnosis of cancer at any phase of the illness experience.
- *Family:* Any individual who provides direct or indirect support of a patient experiencing cancer.
- *Community:* A group of interacting people living in a common location and who share common values or interests.

Health Care Professionals and Associated Staff

- *Health Care Professionals:* All members of the palliative care and hospice interdisciplinary team including physicians, nurses, social workers, psychologists, chaplains, pharmacists, physical or occupational therapists, as well as patients' oncologist or primary care physician.
- *Associated Staff:* All individuals involved in the caring process who offer direct or indirect support in the care of oncology patients and their families across all health care settings.

Institutions

All health care delivery systems that provide palliative or hospice care, such as medical centers, hospitals, rehabilitation hospitals, sub-acute and long-term care facilities, assisted-living facilities, hospices (inpatient, home, or residential), or related office/outpatient clinics.

Health Care Policymakers, Legislators, and Payers

State and Congressional legislators, the state executive branch of government, two key federal agencies, the Centers for Medicare and Medicaid and the Centers for Disease Control and Prevention, insurers, philanthropists, as well as the business community, including employers and caregiver advocacy organizations.

Source: Sherman et al. (2011)

care, acknowledges its value, promotes access to quality palliative and hospice care, and takes action to implement a standard of practice in palliative and hospice care. Goals, objectives, and strategies related to palliative and hospice care (see Table 2) have been identified for each of the stakeholder groups in relation to the 4 A's, which serve as cornerstones of the blueprint for success for palliative and hospice care for patients and families experiencing cancer in the state of Maryland.

As described in Maryland's Action Plan, patients, families, and communities must become educated about palliative and hospice care, and advanced care planning. This will lead to conversations with health care providers, hospital administrators, policymakers, and insurers, which might not have occurred otherwise. Their knowledge and resulting expectations related to palliative and hospice care will drive the creation of health care environments where physical symptoms and emotional and spiritual needs are acknowledged and

Table 2 Goals, Objectives, and Strategies

A more detailed version of the Goals/Objectives/Strategies can found on the Palliative and Hospice Care page of the Maryland Cancer Plan web site: www.marylandcancerplan.org.

Goal: Implement a blueprint for success for palliative and hospice care for patients and families experiencing cancer in the state of Maryland.

Objective 1 (Awareness): By 2015, develop an awareness campaign to educate Maryland citizens about palliative and hospice care within 50% of Maryland jurisdictions.

Strategies (by stakeholder group):

1. *Patients/Families/Communities* should seek information on palliative and hospice care and advanced care planning from their health care providers, public library, national and local cancer agencies, and local health department.
2. *Health Care Professionals and Associated Staff* should increase communication related to palliative care issues in patients' conversations, health care publications, and media/marketing.
3. *Institutions* should initiate palliative care activities with the goal of obtaining buy-in from various constituencies.
4. *Health Care Legislators/Policymakers/Payers* should conduct an internal education effort on strategies to reduce barriers that Maryland residents face in regard to quality palliative and hospice care. The education effort should include widespread distribution, discussion, and the development of an action plan based on:
   - The 2009 Workgroup Report on "Hospice Care, Palliative Care and End of Life Counseling," released by the Maryland Attorney General's Counsel for Health Decisions Policy workgroup, and
   - Reports of the Maryland State Advisory Council on Quality of Care at the End of Life.

(continued)

Objective 2 (Acknowledging the Value): By 2015, increase the participation in and support of palliative and hospice care initiatives by stakeholders as outlined in the strategies.

Strategies (by stakeholder group):

1. *Patients/Families/Communities* should participate in campaigns that support/promote palliative and hospice care and advanced care planning.
2. *Health Care Professionals and Associated Staff* should actively participate in palliative education and palliative care initiatives as demonstrated by attendance at national conferences, increase in certification and credentialing rates, and referral to palliative care services and hospice care.
3. *Institutions* should develop a strategic plan that incorporates goals and related tactics to institutionalize palliative care as it relates to ongoing professional education, implementing and maintaining supportive services for patient/families, supporting research and evidence-based practice, and driving health care policy and legislative initiatives that promote palliative care.
4. *Health Care Legislators/Policymakers/Payers* should conduct outreach efforts via email, town halls, and focus groups to educate constituents about the knowledge, financial, and administrative barriers Maryland cancer patients and their families face in regard to palliative and hospice care and get their input on options to reduce them.

Objective 3 (Access): By 2015, increase access to palliative and hospice care services in Maryland.

Strategies (by stakeholder group):

1. *Patients/Families/Communities* should request access to palliative and hospice services.
2. *Health Care Professionals and Associated Staff* should develop and implement educational programs (formal and informal) related to palliative and hospice care.
3. *Institutions* should:
   - Develop a mechanism to track the percentage of palliative care consultations for hospital patients admitted with cancer, and
   - Ensure clinical support through hiring a skilled and credentialed/certified team of interdisciplinary palliative care professionals and associated support staff in order to implement a palliative care consult service or other delivery models (such as an inpatient unit, outpatient clinic, home care program, and/or establishing partnerships with community hospices).
4. *Health Care Legislators/Policymakers/Payers* should explore legislative options for expanding access to and payment for palliative and hospice care, building on best practices.

Objective 4 (Action): By 2015, stakeholders will take ownership of the Blueprint for Success and act on 70% of the strategies recommended for each stakeholder group.

Strategies (by stakeholder group):

1. *Patients/Families/Communities* should advocate for effective and compassionate palliative care across health care settings to insure that the goals of care are achieved.
2. *Health Care Professionals and Associated Staff* should incorporate the National Quality Forum Preferred Practices of Palliative Care as a standard of care within the institution.
3. *Institutions* should initiate quality improvement studies to evaluate the provision of quality palliative care by tracking:
   - Requests for palliative care consults.
   - Patient/family and community outcomes.
   - Health care professional outcomes.
   - Economic outcomes.
4. *Health Care Legislators/Policymakers/Payers* should support pilot programs that test:
   - The feasibility and impact of training lay workers to serve as palliative and hospice care counseling coaches and navigators.
   - Reimbursement models for providing end-of-life care counseling.
   - The impact of innovative clinical-financial models of palliative and hospice care for cancer patients and their families designed to reduce knowledge, financial, and administrative barriers to their use.

Source: Sherman et al. (2011)

addressed in a holistic manner throughout the illness trajectory. Increased awareness, improved communication, and the expectation to be involved in decisions regarding health care will ensure a better quality of life regardless of the quantity of life.

Health care professionals and associated personnel are being educated to staff the rapid national increase in palliative care programs. Through medical, nursing, and social work training programs; graduate programs in nursing; the integration of palliative care into nursing and medical school curricula; and interprofessional fellowship programs in palliative care, educational initiatives are well underway across the country. Such education reinforces the importance of interprofessional collaboration and teamwork. By developing palliative care and hospice competencies, health professionals develop the science and art of palliative care, educate and mentor those entering the profession and other colleagues, and inform patients and families about the value of palliative and hospice care, thus increasing referrals and promoting access to quality care (Sherman et al., 2011).

At the institutional level, administrators also are important stakeholders as they recognize national priorities and initiatives related to palliative care and acknowledge its value to quality patient care. It is critical administrators incorporate palliative care goals and tactics into the institution's strategic plan, and budget substantial resources for educational outreach to insure appropriate utilization of palliative care. This conveys the message of the value of palliative and hospice care in terms of cost savings, cost avoidance, quality care, and patient and family satisfaction. Furthermore, administrators utilize philanthropic and other contributions, which can add to a revenue base for hiring a skilled and credentialed team of interdisciplinary professionals. As in the State of Maryland, each state's attorney general's office should expect health care facilities to develop systems to utilize health professionals currently trained in palliative and hospice care. They will staff services and promote the coordination of care across health care settings, while monitoring the frequency and quality of care provided by practitioners (Sherman et al., 2011).

Maryland's Action Plan recognizes health care legislators, policymakers, and payers need to be aware of the barriers to access to quality palliative care and develop a Bill of Rights related to palliative and hospice care. These critical stakeholders can facilitate changes in health policy, quality standards, and reimbursement incentives to provide for ongoing education and training in palliative care and insure excellence in care across the illness trajectory. Change can also be affected as state governments promote the development of Centers of Excellence in palliative care, which in turn support community provider hospitals, as well as 24/7 urgent care centers and clinics which are challenged in providing continuity of care. By developing and instituting initiatives which support quality improvement studies, data can be tracked regarding the number of palliative care consults, patient and family outcomes, health care professional outcomes, and financial and economic outcomes.

In addition, policy solutions can fund career development awards in palliative care and increase the number of dollars spent on educating health professionals, as well as addressing the more complex issues of payment reform and reimbursement for palliative care services. Further consideration should also be given to the legislative agenda to address relevant health care reform initiatives such as the comparative effectiveness of palliative care and hospice with traditional hospital care, bundled payments, and funding of demonstration projects that test the integration of comprehensive palliative care in the care of patients with complex medical needs. Health care policymakers should be encouraged to implement programs that will improve the quality of care while slowing the growth of total health care spending in the nation: it is this platform that defines palliative care and its goals (Sherman et al., 2011).

Conclusion

In thinking about the metaphor of "a perfect storm" with all of the issues of quality care, affordability of care and economic constraints both nationally and internationally, the emergence of palliative care as a specialty in the United States is a means of "tackling a perfect storm" (NPCRC, 2011, p. 11). Over the last 10 years, there has been growing recognition of the importance of concurrent palliative care regardless of prognosis and of whether the goal of care is cure, life prolongation, or solely comfort (Meier & Brawley, 2011). "Palliative care ensures that the person is viewed in his or her entirety, not as a collection of organs and medical problems" (NPCRC, 2011, p. 12). Not only does palliative care reduce costs and improve quality of care, it reduces high levels of suffering and distress among patients with serious illness at any age and at any stage of disease; improves communication; addresses the needs of family caregivers; reduces unwanted, unnecessary, and painful interventions; improves patient, family, and staff's satisfaction; and improves survival (NPCRC, 2011).

Palliative care is an economic imperative in reducing the cost of health care. But, even more importantly, palliative care is a humanistic imperative to insure quality of life is promoted during all phases of the illness experience for both patients and their family caregivers. "The interface of energies and visions between patients, families, communities, healthcare professionals, institutions, healthcare policymakers, legislators, and payers is critical to create much-needed reform as well as the crafting of policies that will promote the well being of patients, families, and communities facing serious, life-threatening illness. It is this interface that provides not only an informed perspective but can achieve a 'meeting of the minds' to insure high-quality care and continuous care" (Sherman et el., 2011, p. 7). Palliative care, as a relatively new paradigm of care, responds to the demand for health care reform in America.

References

American Hospital Association. (2008). *The economic crisis: Impact on hospitals.* Retrieved from http://www.aha.org/content/00-10/08-fullsurveyresults.pdf

Brumley, R., Enguidanos, S., Jamison, P., Seitz, R., Morgenstern, N., Saito, S., . . . Gonzalez, J. (2007). Increased satisfaction with care and lower costs: Results of a randomized trial of in-home palliative care. *Journal of the American Geriatrics Society, 55*(7), 993–1000.

Casarett, D.J. (2011). Rethinking hospice eligibility criteria. *JAMA, 305*(10), 1031–1032.

Centeno, C., Clark, D., Lynch, T., Racafort, J., Praill, D., De Lima, L., . . . EAPC Task Force. (2007). Facts and indicators on palliative care development in 52 countries of the WHO European region: Results of an EAPC task force. *Palliative Medicine, 21*(6), 463–471.

Center to Advance Palliative Care. (2011). *Building a hospital-based palliative care program.* Retrieved from http://www.capc.org/building-a-hospital-based-palliative-care-program

Congressional Budget Office (2005). *High-cost Medicare beneficiaries.* Retrieved from http://www.cbo.gov/ftpdocs/63xx/doc6332/05-03-MediSpending.pdf

Covinsky, K.E., Goldman, L., Cook, E.F., Oye, R., Desbiens, N., Reding, D., . . . Phillips, R.S. (1994). The impact of serious illness on patients' families. SUPPORT investigators' study to understand prognoses and preferences for outcomes and risks of treatment. *JAMA, 272*(23), 1839–1844.

Dumont, I., Dumont, S., & Mongeau, S. (2008). End-of-life care and the grieving process: Family caregivers who have experienced the loss of a terminal-phase cancer patient. *Qualitative Health Research, 18*(8), 1049–1061.

Family Caregiver Alliance (2006). *Caregiving.* Retrieved from http://www.caregiver.org/caregiver

Federal Interagency Forum on Aging Related Statistics (2008). *Older Americans 2008: Key indicators of well-being.* Retrieved from http://www.aoa.gov/agingstatsdotnet/Main_Site/Data/2008_Documents/OA_2008.pdf

Fisher, E.S., Wennberg, D.E., Stukel, T.A., & Gottlieb, D.J. (2004). Variations in the longitudinal efficiency of academic medical centers. *Health Affairs (Project Hope) (Suppl. Variation),* VAR19–32.

Fisher, E.S., Wennberg, D.E., Stukel, T.A., Gottlieb, D.J., Lucas, F.L., & Pinder, E.L. (2003). The implications of regional variations in Medicare spending. Part 2: Health outcomes and satisfaction with care. *Annals of Internal Medicine, 138*(4), 288–298.

Foster, R.S. (2009). *Estimated financial effects of the "Patient Protection and Affordable Care Act of 2009," as Proposed by the Senate Majority Leader on November 18, 2009.* Retrieved from https://www.cms.gov/ActuarialStudies/Downloads/SPPACA_2009-12-10.pdf

Giese-Davis, J., Collie, K., Rancourt, K.M., Neri, E., Kraemer, H.C., & Spiegel, D. (2011). Decrease in depression symptoms is associated with longer survival in patients with metastatic breast cancer: A secondary analysis. *Journal of Clinical Oncology, 29*(4), 413–420.

Gomes, B., Harding, R., Foley, K.M., & Higginson, I.J. (2009). Optimal approaches to the health economics of palliative care: Report of an international think tank. *Journal of Pain and Symptom Management, 38*(1), 4–10.

Gordon, R., Eagar, K., Currow, D., & Green, J. (2009). Current funding and financing issues in the Australian hospice and palliative care sector. *Journal of Pain and Symptom Management, 38*(1), 68–74.

Grant, M., Elk, R., Ferrell, B., Morrison, R.S., & von Gunten, C.F. (2009). Current status of palliative care—clinical implementation, education, and research. *CA, 59*(5), 327–335.

Higginson, I.J., & Foley, K.M. (2009). Palliative care: No longer a luxury but a necessity? *Journal of Pain and Symptom Management, 38*(1), 1–3.

Huskamp, H.A., Stevenson, D.G., Chernew, M.E., & Newhouse, J.P. (2010). A new Medicare end-of-life benefit for nursing home residents. *Health Affairs (Project Hope), 29*(1), 130–135.

Jennings, B., Ryndes, T., D'Onofrio, C., & Baily, M.A. (2003). Access to hospice care: Expanding boundaries, overcoming barriers. *The Hastings Center Report, (Suppl.),* S3–7, S9–13, S15–21.

Kaiser Family Foundation (2011). *Medicaid's long-term care beneficiaries: An analysis of spending patterns across institutional and community-based settings.* Retrieved from http://www.kff.org/medicaid/upload/7576-02.pdf

Keehan, S.P., Sisko, A.M., Truffer, C.J., Poisal, J.A., Cuckler, G.A., Madison, A.J., . . . Smith, S.D. (2011). National health spending projections through 2020: Economic recovery and reform drive faster spending growth. *Health Affairs (Project Hope), 30*(8), 1594–1605.

Lynch, T., Clark, D., Centeno, C., Rocafort, J., Flores, L.A., Greenwood, A., . . . Wright, M. (2009). Barriers to the development of palliative care in the countries of central and eastern Europe and the commonwealth of independent states. *Journal of Pain and Symptom Management, 37*(3), 305–315.

McGuire, D.B., DeLoney, V.G., Yeager, K.A., Owen, D.C., Peterson, D.E., Lin, L., & Webster, J. (2000). Maintaining study validity in a changing clinical environment. *Nursing Research, 49*(4), 231–235.

Medicare Payment Advisory Commission. (2009). *Report to Congress: Medicare payment policy.* Retrieved from http://www.medpac.gov/documents/Mar09_March%20report%20testimony_WM%20FINAL.pdf

Meier, D.E. (2010). The development, status and future of palliative care. In D.E. Meier, S.L. Isaacs, R. Hughes (Eds.), *Palliative care: Transforming the care of serious illness.* San Francisco, CA: Jossey-Bass. Retrieved from http://www.rwjf.org/files/research/4558.pdf.

Meier, D.E., & Beresford, L. (2006). Advanced practice nurses in palliative care: A pivotal role and perspective. *Journal of Palliative Medicine, 9*(3), 624–627.

Meier, D.E., & Beresford, L. (2009). Palliative care seeks its home in national health care reform. *Journal of Palliative Medicine, 12*(7), 593–597.

Meier, D.E., & Brawley, O.W. (2011). Palliative care and the quality of life. *Journal of Clinical Oncology, 29*(20), 2750–2752.

Meier, D.E., Lim, B., & Carlson, M.D. (2010). Raising the standard: Palliative care in nursing homes. *Health Affairs (Project Hope), 29*(1), 136–140.

Mitchell, A.J., Chan, M., Bhatti, H., Halton, M., Grassi, L., Johansen, C., & Meader, N. (2011). Prevalence of depression, anxiety, and adjustment disorder in oncological, haematological, and palliative-care settings: A meta-analysis of 94 interview-based studies. *The Lancet Oncology, 12*(2), 160–174.

Mitchell, S.L., Teno, J.M., Kiely, D.K., Shaffer, M.L., Jones, R.N., Prigerson, H.G., . . . Hamel, M.B. (2009). The clinical course of advanced dementia. *The New England Journal of Medicine, 361*(16), 1529–1538.

Mitka, M. (2006). Less may be more when managing patients with severe chronic illness. *JAMA, 296*(2), 159–160.

Morrison, R.S., Dietrich, J., Ladwig, S., Quill, T., Sacco, J., Tangeman, J., & Meier, D.E. (2011). Palliative care consultation teams cut hospital costs for Medicaid beneficiaries. Health Affairs (Project Hope), 30(3), 454–463.

Morrison, R.S., Flanagan, S., Fischberg, D., Cintron, A., & Siu, A.L. (2009). A novel interdisciplinary analgesic program reduces pain and improves function in older adults after orthopedic surgery. *Journal of the American Geriatrics Society, 57*(1), 1–10.

Morrison, R.S., Magaziner, J., Gilbert, M., Koval, K.J., McLaughlin, M.A., Orosz, G., . . . Siu, A.L. (2003). Relationship between pain and opioid analgesics on the development of delirium following hip fracture. *The Journals of Gerontology. Series A, Biological Sciences and Medical Sciences, 58*(1), 76–81.

Morrison, R.S., Penrod, J.D., Cassel, J.B., Caust-Ellenbogen, M., Litke, A., Spragens, L., . . . Palliative Care Leadership Centers' Outcomes Group. (2008). Cost savings associated with US hospital palliative care consultation programs. *Archives of Internal Medicine, 168*(16), 1783–1790.

National Consensus Project for Quality Palliative Care (NCP). (2009). *Clinical practice guidelines for quality palliative care* (2nd ed.). Pittsburgh, PA: National Consensus Project for Quality Palliative Care. Retrieved from http://www.nationalconsensusproject.org/guideline.pdf

National Palliative Care Research Center (NPCRC). (2011). *America's care of serious illness: A state-by-state report card on access to palliative care in our nation's hospitals.* Retrieved from http://reportcard-live.capc.stackop.com/pdf/state-by-state-report-card.pdf

Office of the Legislative Counsel. (2010). *Compilation of Patient Protection and Affordable Care Act of 2010, S 3140, 111th Congress, 2nd Session.* Retrieved from http://docs.house. gov/energycommerce/ppacacon.pdf

Pelosi, N. (2010). *Letter to the Honorable Nancy Pelosi providing estimates of the spending and revenue effects of the reconciliation proposal.* Washington, DC: Congressional Budget Office. Retrieved from http://www.cbo.gov/ftpdocs/113xx/doc11379/AmendReconProp.pdf

Penrod, J.D., Deb, P., Dellenbaugh, C., Burgess, J.F., Jr, Zhu, C.W., Christiansen, C.L., . . . Morrison, R.S. (2010). Hospital-based palliative care consultation: Effects on hospital cost. *Journal of Palliative Medicine, 13*(8), 973–979.

Penrod, J.D., Deb, P., Luhrs, C., Dellenbaugh, C., Zhu, C.W., Hochman, T., . . . Morrison, R.S. (2006). Cost and utilization outcomes of patients receiving hospital-based palliative care consultation. *Journal of Palliative Medicine, 9*(4), 855–860.

Rabow, M.W., Hauser, J.M., & Adams, J. (2004). Supporting family caregivers at the end of life: "They don't know what they don't know." *JAMA, 291*(4), 483–491.

Satin, J.R., Linden, W., & Phillips, M.J. (2009). Depression as a predictor of disease progression and mortality in cancer patients: A meta-analysis. *Cancer, 115*(22), 5349–5361.

Seymour, J. (2011). Changing times: Preparing to meet palliative needs in the 21st century. *British Journal of Community Nursing, 16*(1), 18.

Seymour, J.E., Kennedy, S., Arthur, A., Pollock, P., Cox, K., Kumar, A., & Stanton, W. (2009). *Public attitudes to death, dying and bereavement: A systematic synthesis.* Retrieved from http://tinyurl.com/35g6lsc

Sherman, D.W., Evans, S., Halstead, L., Kelleher, C., Kenworthy, C., Olson, L., & Piet, L. (2011). In *Maryland comprehensive cancer control plan: Palliative and hospice care* (pp. 1–10). Retrieved from http://fha.mary land.gov/cancer/cancerplan

Smith, T.J., Coyne, P., Cassel, B., Penberthy, L., Hopson, A., & Hager, M.A. (2003). A high-volume specialist palliative care unit and team may reduce in-hospital end-of-life care costs. *Journal of Palliative Medicine, 6*(5), 699–705.

Spiegel, D. (2011). Mind matters in cancer survival. *JAMA, 305*(5), 502–503.

Temel, J.S., Greer, J.A., Muzikansky, A., Gallagher, E.R., Admane, S., Jackson, V.A., . . . Lynch, T.J. (2010). Early palliative care for patients with metastatic non-small-cell lung cancer. *The New England Journal of Medicine, 363*(8), 733–742.

Teno, J.M., Clarridge, B.R., Casey, V., Welch, L.C., Wetle, T., Shield, R., & Mor, V. (2004). Family perspectives on end-of-life care at the last place of care. *JAMA, 291*(1), 88–93.

van den Beuken-van Everdingen, M.H., de Rijke, J.M., Kessels, A.G., Schouten, H.C., van Kleef, M., & Patijn, J. (2009). Quality of life and non-pain symptoms in patients with cancer. *Journal of Pain and Symptom Management, 38*(2), 216–233.

Vanderwerker, L.C., Laff, R.E., Kadan-Lottick, N.S., McColl, S., & Prigerson, H.G. (2005). Psychiatric disorders and mental health service use among caregivers of advanced cancer patients. *Journal of Clinical Oncology, 23*(28), 6899–6907.

Wright, A.A., Zhang, B., Ray, A., Mack, J.W., Trice, E., Balboni, T., . . . Prigerson, H.G. (2008). Associations between end-of-life discussions, patient mental health, medical care near death, and caregiver bereavement adjustment. *JAMA, 300*(14), 1665–1673.

Wright, M., Wood, J., Lynch, T., & Clark, D. (2008). Mapping levels of palliative care development: A global view. *Journal of Pain and Symptom Management, 35*(5), 469–485.

Zarit, S. (2006). Assessment of family caregivers: A research perspective. In *Family Caregiver Alliance (Eds.), Caregiver assessment: Voices and views from the field.* Report from a National Consensus Development Conference (Vol. II) (pp. 12–37). San Francisco, CA: Family Caregiver Alliance.

Critical Thinking

1. In the face of long-term growth of older Americans, how will demand change in a decade, in a quarter-century?

2. Will the acceptance of palliative and hospice care as viable end-of-life treatment measures lead to new technologies?

Create Central

www.mhhe.com/createcentral

Internet References

Family Caregiver Alliance
    www.caregiver.org/jsp/content_node.jsp?nodeid=368
Medicare Payment Policy: March 2013—Medicare Payment Advisory Commission
    www.medpac.gov/documents/Mar13_entirereport.pdf

DEBORAH WITT SHERMAN, PhD, CRNP, ANP-BC, ACHPN, FAAN, is a Professor, University of Maryland, School of Nursing, Baltimore, MD. **JOOYOUNG CHEON, MS, RN,** is a Doctoral Student, University of Maryland, School of Nursing, Baltimore, MD.

Sherman, Deborah Witt and Cheon, Jooyoung. From *Nursing Economic$,* May/June 2012, pp. 153–162, 166. Copyright © 2012 by Jannetti Publications, Inc., East Holly Avenue/Box 56, Pitman, NJ 08071-0056; (856) 256-2300, FAX (856) 589-7463; for a sample copy of the journal, please contact the publisher. Used with permission. www.nursingeconomics.net

Article   Prepared by: Elaina F. Osterbur, *Saint Louis University*

Palliative Care: Impact on Quality and Cost

Jessica D. Squazzo

Learning Outcomes

After reading this article, you will be able to:

- Discuss the definition of palliative care.
- Identify the role of family in the discussion of palliative care.
- Discuss the professional's role in the management of palliative care options for patients and families.

Palliative care is an emerging piece of the healthcare system that many predict will have a profound ability to improve quality of care, communication and coordination for seriously ill patients and their families and, through this process, reduce reliance on emergency departments and hospitals. Different in name and function than hospice and end-of-life care, palliative care is a unique, team-oriented approach to caring for the sickest of patients who are also, without doubt, the costliest.

Though not a new concept, it is perhaps one of the least understood service lines. It is, however, showing signs of growth, with the number of U.S. hospitals offering palliative care rising rapidly, according to the Center to Advance Palliative Care. Data from the Center and the American Hospital Association reveal that the number of programs in U.S. hospitals with 50 or more beds increased from 658 (24.5 percent) to 1,635 (66 percent) from 2000 to 2010—a 145.8 percent increase.

One person on the front lines of the emergence of palliative care programs in the U.S. healthcare system is Diane E. Meier, MD, FACP, director of the New York-based Center to Advance Palliative Care. "My mission is to improve access to palliative care across all settings," Meier told the audience at the ACHE program "Palliative Care: Impact on Quality and Cost." The program, funded in part by the Foundation of ACHE's Fund for Innovation in Healthcare Leadership, was held Sept. 11, 2012, in conjunction with ACHE's Atlanta Cluster Program.

During her keynote address, Meier, who is also vice chair of public policy and professor of geriatrics and palliative medicine and Catherine Gaisman Professor of Medical Ethics at Mount Sinai School of Medicine in New York City, made the case for why palliative care is so important to healthcare today and how organizations can begin to develop such programs.

According to Meier, it isn't difficult to make the business case for establishing palliative care programs, especially at a time when, she said, the largest cause of bankruptcy in the U.S. is healthcare bills, and a very large portion of our population is underinsured.

"It is the costliest, very small proportion of patients that drive the vast majority of spending," she said. "Healthcare spending is highly concentrated on the sickest and most vulnerable 5 percent of patients. Palliative care models have been shown to improve quality of life for these patients and families, to prolong life in a number of studies and, as a result, to enable patients to avoid the preventable crises and emergencies that land them in the hospital. The costliest patients are palliative care patients. That's why palliative care is so critical to improving quality and reducing costs."

Defining Palliative Care

Meier said one key way to help organizations think about palliative care and distinguish it from other service lines is to remember that, "Palliative care is not what we do when there's nothing else to do." Palliative care is delivered *at the same time* as appropriate disease-related therapies, she said. "You don't move to hospice until disease-directed therapies are no longer working or their burdens begin to outweigh their benefits."

Palliative care differs from hospice or end-of-life care because the patients benefiting from palliative care programs aren't necessarily dying. Often they are patients who are very sick but have a good prognosis and are expected to live. Most people with serious and complex chronic illness in the United States are not dying, but living with significant burden of illness for many years. Meier said the fact that there are pediatric palliative care programs operating at some organizations highlights the importance of not linking palliative care to end-of-life care. In Meier's program at Mount Sinai, they are very accustomed to taking care of patients who are likely to be cured, such as bone marrow transplant patients, she said.

Meier shared the Center to Advance Palliative Care's definition of palliative care with the audience. The definition was crafted using language that was most highly rated among the public, according to a public opinion survey conducted by the Center, so as to use language that is meaningful and important to patients and families:

"Palliative care is specialized medical care for people with serious illnesses. This type of care is focused on providing patients with relief from the symptoms, pain and stress of a serious illness—whatever the diagnosis. The goal is to improve quality of life for both the patient and the family. Palliative care is provided by a team of doctors, nurses and other specialists who work with a patient's other doctors to provide an extra layer of support. Palliative care is appropriate at any age and at any stage in a serious illness, and can be provided together with curative treatment."

As described in the above definition, palliative care is delivered by a care "team." The team consists of key players such as physicians, nurses and advance practice nurses, social workers, chaplains or spiritual advisors, pain management specialists and others. The emphasis is on treating the patient's medical condition but also helping him or her through the difficult practical challenges and emotional and spiritual distress that accompany a serious illness.

Patients' family members and other loved ones also play a key part in palliative care. In a successful palliative care program, they are part of the conversation at the moment treatment begins. Palliative care programs also provide the proper counseling and support, including bereavement programs, if necessary, to patients' loved ones.

Meier said the impact of serious illness on patients' family members—including increased mortality and morbidity and post-traumatic stress disorder—cannot be ignored. "The cost to society from this is incalculable . . . [resulting in] people who can't function as mothers, who can't go to work, who can't return to their role in society," she said. "That is a fault in the system we don't think about much."

Palliative care addresses three domains, said Meier. By addressing these domains, quality of care is improved and because patients feel better and remain in control, costs are reduced:

- Physical, emotional and spiritual distress
- Patient-family-professional communication about achievable goals for care and the decision making that follows
- Coordinated, communicated continuity of care and support for practical needs of both patients and families across settings

Evidence showcasing these and other benefits of palliative care programs is mounting, with hundreds of studies showing how palliative care can improve care quality, Meier said. A Harvard Medical School/Massachusetts General Hospital study published by the *New England Journal of Medicine* in 2010 found that in a randomized trial of patients receiving standard cancer care with palliative care co-management from the time of diagnosis versus a control group receiving standard cancer care

only, the group receiving palliative care co-management experienced improved quality of life, reduced major depression, reduced "aggressiveness" in treatment (e.g., less chemotherapy before death, less likely to be hospitalized during the last month of care, etc.), *and improved survival rates* (11.6 months versus 8.9 months). Other studies have pointed to cost savings including reductions in use of costly imaging and pharmaceuticals and reductions in ED visits and time spent in the ICU.

Making Palliative Care Work

Meier provided attendees with an overview of what it takes in a healthcare organization to make palliative care succeed. At the top of the list is medical staff engagement. "If you don't have respectful and strong relationships with front-line medical staff working with the patients and families, it won't work," Meier said. "A social worker alone can't do it. Palliative care teams without a doctor are not going to work well." Meier says having medical staff on the palliative care team provides added credibility to the information presented to patients and their families.

Other strategies for convincing physicians and others in the organization to get on board with palliative care include identifying opinion leaders in the organization and getting their interest and investment to help you sell the idea to others; interviewing others in the organization about what problems/issues they perceive and how they feel they should be addressed (this aids in relationship building); gathering quality data; focusing on quality; and, finally, seeking senior leadership's support for a universal, systemwide palliative care screening checklist. "Palliative care should be part of the admission process," said Meier. "They should be screening for unmanaged illness just as they screen for pressure ulcer or fall risk."

Palliative care is sure to gain more ground in the future, as it is already on the radar of several national healthcare groups such as the National Quality Forum, which has listed it as one of six of its National Priorities for action; The Joint Commission, which in September 2011 released its Palliative Care Advanced Certification Program; MedPAC; and the Institute for Healthcare Improvement.

"Palliative care is key to survival under a capitated, global budget," said Meier. "When fee-for-service goes away and you're not managing the sickest 5 percent in the best way possible, they will bankrupt your budget."

After her keynote address, Meier introduced the program's three panelists, who each discussed their organization's experiences with palliative care.

Advance Care Planning

Bernard "Bud" Hammes, PhD, director, medical humanities, and director, Respecting Choices, at Gunderson Lutheran Health System in La Crosse, Wis., discussed advance care planning (ACP) as a complement to palliative care. He said the health system, which serves approximately 560,000 people in 19 counties in western Wisconsin, has invested heavily in the quality of the planning process—the process of knowing and honoring a patient's informed plans.

Hammes outlined the three key desired outcomes of advance care planning:

- Creating an effective plan, including selecting a well-prepared healthcare agent or proxy when possible and creating specific instructions that reflect informed decisions geared toward a person's state of health
- Having advance care plans available to the treating physician
- Incorporating the plans into medical decisions when and wherever needed

"Planning isn't enough," said Hammes. "We have to make sure these plans are available to the treating physicians, and they incorporate them correctly into decisions."

Hammes discussed the relationship of ACP to advance directives. According to Hammes, the successful implementation of an advance directive is directly tied to the quality of the planning process or advance care planning. "If the process of planning has a poor quality to it, the plan will not work," said Hammes. "Quality of communication with the patient and the family predicts the quality of the outcome."

There are four key elements in designing an effective ACP program, according to Hammes. They are:

1. **Systems design**—build an infrastructure that assists in hardwiring excellence, including effective, standardized documentation, reliable medical records storage and retrieval, and an ACP team and referral mechanism. According to Hammes, advance care planning must be made routine among staff members and a part of the care process. "It has to be hardwired into how we relate to our patients," he said. "No matter where patients are being treated, the written care plan must be available to the treating physicians."
2. **Advance care plan facilitation skills training**—build confidence among staff and create an effective ACP team. Hammes said Gunderson Lutheran Health has experienced success with teams featuring "facilitators" who on behalf of doctors talk with patients about their values and goals in order to develop their care plans. Facilitators help take some of the burden off already-busy physicians.

   Once the team is in place, staff training and use of a standardized curriculum are paramount. This ensures delivery of a consistent, reliable ACP service, according to Hammes.
3. **Community education and engagement**—reach out to communities with consistent messages about advance care planning. Because care in the La Crosse region involves two integrated health systems, all ACP-related materials distributed throughout the community have the names of both systems on them so patients know they can contact both systems related to their advance care plans, according to Hammes. This makes it possible to work effectively with all community groups and institutions.
4. **Continuous quality improvement**—measure and improve. Hammes noted the importance of continuously measuring your organization's ACP program—and constantly looking for ways to improve it.

"We didn't create a successful system because we were smart—we created a successful system because we were persistent," said Hammes. "We redesigned it and redesigned it until it worked."

Making the Case for Palliative Care

Stacie T. Pinderhughes, MD, director of palliative medicine at Banner Good Samaritan Medical Center in Phoenix, told the audience about her experience with setting up a palliative care program at the system, which comprises 23 acute-care hospitals, when she began her job at the organization in 2010. She shared several important lessons learned.

One key lesson was to know your organization s culture before you jump in. For Pinderhughes, she was fortunate to be at a hospital where "the doctors were very receptive and open to the whole concept of palliative care," she said.

That buy-in from physicians is critical to the success of a palliative care program, according to Pinderhughes. But there was some education of physicians that had to be done, especially among the specialty groups such as hospitalists, primary care doctors and the hospital's two large intensivist groups.

She recalled how it was helpful at Good Samaritan to have physicians round with the palliative care team to gain a better understanding of how a palliative care program works and see the variety of services it offers. According to Pinderhughes, it also helped clinicians understand that palliative care is different from hospice care. "We made a deliberate decision at Banner Health System to debrand palliative care from hospice," she said.

During year one of the palliative care program, the team consisted of Pinderhughes, a nurse practitioner and one social worker. Pinderhughes said bringing a social worker on board helped make connections in the community, an important aspect of palliative care.

Another key lesson Pinderhughes and her colleagues learned was the importance of getting C-suite buy-in. Showing senior leaders the cost benefit of a palliative care program is key.

"We found significant cost avoidance among these patients, which got the attention of the C-suite early," recalled Pinderhughes. In the first year of its program, Good Samaritan's palliative care team had seen approximately 500 patients. Since the program's start, Pinderhughes said, the total cost avoidance attributed to Good Samaritan's palliative care program is approximately $1.5 million.

At the end of the program's first year, a Palliative Care System Developmental Initiative was convened and charged with developing a stable platform for the delivery of palliative care across the healthcare continuum. This group called together stakeholders across the system, including providers, risk management staff and administrators. The group began the process of defining palliative care for the system and developed a business plan, a plan for educating others about the program and an IT infrastructure for documentation. The palliative care team also defined the program's mission and vision (and alignment with Banner Health's overall mission and vision) and defined its patient population.

Pinderhughes recalled how crucial it was to have the CFO's support with developing the business plan. Good Samaritan's CFO was involved from the beginning, even accompanying the palliative care team on walk rounds. "Now he is an effective ally in the C-suite," said Pinderhughes.

Pinderhughes said the team created tools to ensure palliative care at Good Samaritan was standardized. The team created an information card, which they distributed to physicians, residents, nurses, social workers and case managers. The organization's EHR now includes a Palliative Care Rounding Tool in which palliative care team members document information. Palliative care information is also captured on the Palliative Medicine H&P (history and physical) Template the team developed.

Banner Health is now looking at developing palliative care programs in several of its hospitals and plans to work with its ACO to develop palliative care further across other settings. "We've laid the infrastructure, now we're moving to the design phase," Pinderhughes said.

Buy-In from the C-Suite

When John M. Haupert, FACHE, became CEO of Grady Health System in Atlanta in 2011, one of his priorities was improving the way the system was managing the significant number of patients in need of hospice and palliative care. At least one-third of those patients were being improperly placed in the ICU.

As a safety net provider for Atlanta and one of the nation's largest public hospitals with 625 acute-care beds, Grady's payor mix is 30-30-20-20 (charity, Medicaid, Medicare, commercial). "To make this work economically takes a lot of work," Haupert told the audience.

The development of Grady's palliative care program is one major solution developed to help more efficiently and economically manage the most vulnerable among Grady's patient population. Haupert and his staff established a vision statement for palliative care at the system, which "has become our calling card for everything we do, every action we take and every action we put our energy behind," he said. The vision is: "The program assists patients and their families by providing relief from the symptoms, pain, and stress of a serious illness with the goal of improving their quality of life. The program affirms life and recognizes death as a normal process; helps people live as actively as possible and, in the event of terminal illness, neither postpones nor hastens death but helps them experience the end of their life with dignity and comfort."

Haupert said the vision is inclusive and looks at the full continuum of palliative and hospice services. "We wanted to avoid a model consisting of just life-prolonging care," Haupert said. An ideal model, he said, is a palliative care team working *with* hospice care staff and supportive services including after-care support.

The palliative care program at Grady is constantly evolving and improving as the organization learns what works best to serve its patient population. The focus is always on doing what's best for patients and their families in difficult times. "We have a lot of work to do to treat people with the dignity they deserve," Haupert said.

Grady's palliative care program has been developed in three levels. The organization is currently working to get from level two to level three, and Haupert says they have identified the following factors that must be in place to make that happen:

- **Enhanced leadership**—including identifying clinical leaders
- **Established operational infrastructure**—including implementation of a palliative care service scorecard and deployment of resources to meet demand for services
- **Enhanced system integration**—including clinical partnerships with other service lines such as oncology and internal medicine

Haupert knows firsthand the importance of having C-suite buy-in for a palliative care initiative. "With my commitment, we will get there and make this happen," he said.

Attendee Tammie Quest, MD, associate professor of emergency medicine and director, Emory Center for Palliative Care, which has a close working relationship with Grady Health, emphasized Haupert's sentiment. It makes a difference in the success of a palliative care program when you work with senior leaders who are "incredibly motivated and enthusiastic," she said.

"When you don't have that from the C-suite, it's really hard to take these programs to the next level."

Critical Thinking

1. What are the considerations that need to be discussed between professionals and patients in order to ensure that patients are making informed decisions?
2. What is the role of advance directives in the palliative care treatment option?

Create Central

www.mhhe.com/createcentral

Internet References

National Hospice and Palliative Care Organization
   www.nhpco.org
Open Society Foundations: Health: Palliative Care
   www.opensocietyfoundations.org/topics/palliative-care

JESSICA D. SQUAZZO is senior writer with *Healthcare Executive*.

Unit 7

UNIT

Prepared by: Elaina F. Osterbur, *Saint Louis University*

Living Environment in Later Life

Old age is often a period of shrinking life space. This concept is crucial to an understanding of the living environments of older Americans. When older people retire, they may find that they travel less frequently and over shorter distances because they no longer work and many neighborhoods have stores, gas stations, and churches in close proximity. As the retirement years roll by, older people may feel less in control of their environment due to a decline in their hearing and vision as well as other health problems. As the aging process continues, elderly people are likely to restrict their mobility to the areas where they feel most secure. This usually means that an increasing amount of time is spent at home. Estimates show that individuals aged 65 and above spend 80 to 90 percent of their lives in their home environments. Of all other age groups, only small children are as neighborhood- and housebound. The house, neighborhood, and community environments are, therefore, more crucial to elderly individuals than to any other adult age group. The interaction with others that they experience within their homes and neighborhoods can either be stimulating or foreboding, pleasant or threatening. Across the country, older Americans live in a variety of circumstances, ranging from desirable to undesirable.

Approximately 70 percent of people who are elderly live in a family setting, usually a husband-wife household; 20 percent live alone or with nonrelatives; and the remaining number live in institutions such as nursing homes. Although only about 5 percent of elderly people live in nursing homes at any one time, 25 percent of people aged 65 and above will spend some time in a nursing home setting. The longer one lives, the more likely he or she is to eventually live in a total-care institution. Because most older Americans would prefer to live independently in their own homes for as long as possible, their relocation—to other houses, apartments, or nursing homes—is often accompanied by a considerable amount of trauma and unrest. The fact that aged individuals tend to be less mobile and more neighborhood-bound than any other age group makes member's living environment crucial to their sense of well-being. Articles in this unit focus on some alternatives available to aged people, from family care to assisted living to nursing homes.

Article

Prepared by: Elaina F. Osterbur, *Saint Louis University*

Design and Technologies for Healthy Aging

CLAUDIA B. RÉBOLA AND JON SANFORD

Learning Outcomes

After reading this article, you will be able to:

- Identify the disparities between the design of technology and the needs of older adults.

- Discuss the Design and Technologies for Healthy Aging (DATHA) coalition.

- Identify DATHA's infuences in the design of environments, products, and technologies to the needs of older adults.

Encouraging healthy aging at home and in the community is not only important to relieve our overtaxed healthcare system, but it is also a vehicle for promoting independence and quality of life among older adults. While remaining in the community provides substantial benefits for older adults and society as a whole, there are a variety of challenging issues for successful aging at home. Unfortunately, many homes and communities are not designed to support the needs of older adults for healthy aging. Similarly, the healthcare information and communication technologies developed to facilitate healthy aging are often unusable or unacceptable to the older adults who must use them.

Together, design and technology can have significant positive impacts on how older adults are able to age successfully. Yet, new design and technologies are not always enthusiastically embraced or widely adopted. A key barrier to the adoption and use of supportive design and technology by older adults has been a disconnect between the needs of the users and the solutions. Without an understanding of the actual problems faced by older adults and the functionality, value, design, cost, privacy, trust, and acceptance of all users, including older adults, their families, and service providers, new designs and technologies will not be successfully implemented. In order to bring about successful solutions, an effective design must solve a relevant problem; fit the artifact, system, or service to the needs of the person through considering appropriate aesthetics and ergonomics, technical processes, requirements for manufacture, marketing opportunities, and economic constraints; and be implemented or marketed.

While giving form to products, spaces, and technologies, the designer's primary activity is to provide a humanizing link between the designs and the people who must use them. However, designers are typically disconnected from the problems and needs of older adults in the community. Therefore, the development of effective, useful, and implementable solutions for healthy aging necessitates that designers join forces with practitioners, providers, and researchers in the aging community to engage in an integrated multidisciplinary approach toward healthy aging.

In order to address the disparity between the design of environments, products, and technologies and the needs of older adults, the Design and Technologies for Healthy Aging (DATHA) coalition was developed at the Georgia Institute of Technology in Atlanta, Georgia. The purpose of the initiative is to bring together service providers, researchers, and industry to address the following three key questions: What are the real problems facing older adults in the community? How can design and technology effectively solve those problems to facilitate healthy aging at home? How can we get new evidence-based design and technological solutions to market?

By bringing together the highly fragmented aging community with expertise in a range of relevant issues, including housing, community planning, health, universal design, technology, psychology of aging, rehabilitation, and research, DATHA provides a forum for integrating the various individual efforts in the Atlanta area focused on design and technology. Most importantly, it brings together academic researchers with the knowledge of solving problems with service providers who understand what the problems are and industry representatives who understand how to get solutions into the hands of the users. As such, DATHA serves as the catalyst for a major shift in the way design and technology for healthy aging is conceptualized and implemented—from research and development that is investigator-initiated and technology-centered to a need-driven, user-centered approach.

The specific aims of the DATHA coalition are to promote academic and industry partnerships to engage in multidisciplinary research, education, and practice of design and technology for healthy aging. From the practice perspective, it promotes multidisciplinary academic–industry communities of practice that support sustainable infrastructures around universal design and technologies to deliver real-life design and technological innovations for healthy aging. From the educational perspective, it aims to advance implementation of user-centered technologies, products, and universal design practices by educating students and professionals across a range of health, social science, and design and technology disciplines about the benefits of healthy aging by design and technology. From the research perspective, it aims to assess, implement, and evaluate design and technologies to meet needs for healthy aging in different types of living options, including aging in place in one's home, continuing care retirement communities, active aging communities, and natural occurring retirement communities.

With these specific aims, DATHA focuses on four major areas of interest: *people, services, policy,* and *environment.* People include interests in the following: health; limitations in activities of daily living; safety issues; community mobility; physical activity; communication and social connectedness; health literacy; medication adherence; recreation and leisure; and demographic trends shaping the market. Services include a focus on health promotion and management, facilitating activities of daily living safety; community mobility; medication adherence; telehealth; and recreation. Policy includes financing/lending opportunities, including low- to moderate-income housing; trends in the seniors' housing industry; health trends and impacts on our communities; planning and zoning to facilitate community development; and public health, fiscal, and regulatory impacts of aging and environment. Finally, environment includes universal design to facilitate aging-in-place; innovative technologies for healthy aging and healthcare delivery; and livable communities.

As a means of creating key partnerships among the various interests in the aging community, DATHA sponsors a monthly forum where practitioners, professionals, and providers are invited to share their work, interests, and issues. Presentations are deliberately short and evocative to provoke discussion, engage in problem-solving, and develop innovative solutions. This special issue is the result of those monthly forums.

The five articles in this issue reflect the breadth of DATHA's interests, covering efforts undertaken in psychology, industrial design, and computing at Georgia Institute of Technology, the Center for Health and Aging at Emory University, the Rehab R&D Center at Atlanta, VA Medical Center, and the Area Agency on Aging at the Atlanta Regional Commission. As a whole, the articles provide an understanding of the range and types of design and technological challenges to enable older adults to age successfully in their home environments. The first four articles focus on communication and design of communication technologies. The first two examine communication of information between healthcare providers and recipients, including the importance of interpersonal relationships for developing communication technologies and the impact design of health technologies on communication of health information. The third article examines the importance and use of the Internet as a source of health information and health literacy, while the fourth focuses on the design of social communication technologies to make the enable older adults maintain social networks. The final article provides a context for the other four by proposing a new way to approach the design of communities to promote physical activity, social interaction, and easy access of health and supportive services that are essential for healthy aging.

In the first article, *Challenges for home health care providers: A needs assessment,* McBride, Beer, Mitzner, and Rogers present the results of a three-phased needs assessment that provides a detailed and systematic investigation into the challenges faced by home healthcare providers. They assert that identifying difficulties with care provision in the home is a critical step that must occur before interventions can be properly designed and implemented. The authors clearly demonstrate the need to understand team dynamics among healthcare providers, patients, and families, and how these dynamics may be different from traditional healthcare settings. This information will allow for a clearer distinction of each individual's role and responsibilities in the healthcare plan and provide the basis for developing improved communication devices for sharing information between healthcare providers and recipients.

In the second article, *Using telehealth technology to support family caregivers: Description of a pilot intervention and preliminary results,* Griffiths, Davis, Wachtel, Lin, Ward, Painter, Forrester, Nagamia, Patton, Connell, Parmelee, and Johnson discuss how instructional technology can aid family caregivers in the technical aspects of their tasks and duties. The authors developed a program to train family caregivers and to enable them provide health information on a daily basis using an off-the-shelf home-messaging unit. Findings indicate that such technologies and programs are not accepted by caregivers, but can promote successful aging in the community by providing a valuable link to healthcare professionals.

In the third article, *Predictors of reported Internet use in older adults with high and low health literacy: The role of socio-demographics and visual and cognitive function,* Echt and Burridge discuss the importance of the Internet access and use by older adults to support the autonomy and independence. This study found that health literacy and visual and cognitive function predict older adults' Internet use differentially as a function of socio-demographic characteristics. They envision that this knowledge can be used to inform the design of more inclusive, user-centered information technology that will overcome barriers to access and usability of the Internet-based health information.

In the fourth article, *Sympathetic devices: Communication technologies for inclusion,* Rébola and Jones investigate the impact of design and technology on preventing social isolation and loneliness among older people. This article presents an iterative process of applied action research studies that resulted in the design of several communication technology devices for older adults. Based on testing with older adults to provide feedback on the aesthetics and design experience, as well as ease-of-use, usefulness, and acceptance of technologies, one device was selected for future development.

In the final article, *Atlanta's lifelong communities initiative,* Rader, Keyes, and Berger discuss the relationship between the community environment, including buildings, infrastructure and services, and the ability of older adults to maintain independence and successfully age in place. They propose a new paradigm of Lifelong communities, which involves the coordination of housing location with community design, the removal of barriers that inhibit aging in place, and the development of new guidelines to promote physical activity, social interaction, and access to health and supportive services.

As reflected in this issue's articles, DATHA has been able to achieve, through its monthly forums, the goal of serving as a catalyst for interdisciplinary communities of practice and academic–industry partnerships to support design and technology for healthy aging. In addition, DATHA has created not only an opportunity for interdisciplinary research and design related to healthy aging but also set a forum for educating and engaging a wide audience from students, faculty, and professionals about the needs for healthy aging. The next steps for DATHA are to develop a mechanism for responding rapidly to needs of older adults, clinicians, and practitioners and for deploying solutions to support healthy aging, especially in Georgia so that older adults can benefit from healthier aging in place by design and technology.

Critical Thinking

1. What types of technology would be of the greatest benefit to the long-term-care needs of older adults?

2. Would the costs of technology be a burden to bear for both society and older adults?

Create Central

www.mhhe.com/createcentral

Internet References

MetLife Mature Market Institute: Aging in Place 2.0
  www.metlife.com/mmi/research/aging-in-place.html#insights
National Aging in Place Council
  www.ageinplace.org

Article   Prepared by: Elaina F. Osterbur, *Saint Louis University*

A Little Help Can Go a Long Way

"Aging in Place" Requires Good Luck, Support Network

David Crary

Learning Outcomes

After reading this article, you will be able to:

- Identify the services that residents in Verona, New Jersey, receive that assist them in remaining in their current home as they age.

- Identify the goal of educational initiatives in Verona for older people who are attempting to age in place.

Retirement communities may have their perks, but Beryl O'Connor says it would be tough to match the birthday surprise she got in her own backyard when she turned 80 this year.

She was tending her garden when two little girls from next door—"my buddies," she calls them—brought her a strawberry shortcake. It underscored why she wants to stay put in the house that she and her husband, who died 18 years ago, purchased in the late 1970s.

"I couldn't just be around old people—that's not my lifestyle," she said. "I'd go out of my mind."

Physically spry and socially active, O'Connor in many respects is the embodiment of "aging in place," growing old in one's own longtime home and remaining engaged in the community rather than moving to a retirement facility.

According to surveys, aging in place is the overwhelming preference of Americans over 50. But doing it successfully requires both good fortune and support services—things that O'Connor's pleasant hometown of Verona has become increasingly capable of providing.

About 10 miles northwest of Newark, Verona has roughly 13,300 residents nestled into less than 3 square miles. There's a transportation network that takes older people on shopping trips and to medical appointments, and the town is benefiting from a $100,000 federal grant to put in place an aging-in-place program called Verona LIVE.

Administered by United Jewish Communities of MetroWest New Jersey, the program strives to educate older people about available services to help them address problems and stay active in the community. Its partners include the health and police departments, the rescue squad, the public and public schools, and religious groups.

Among the support services are a home maintenance program with free safety checks and minor home repairs, access to a social worker and job counselor, a walking club and other social activities. In one program, a group of middle-school girls provided one-on-one computer training to about 20 older adults.

Social worker Connie Pifher, Verona's health coordinator, said a crucial part of the overall initiative is educating older people to plan ahead realistically and constantly reassess their prospects for successfully aging in place.

"There are some people who just can do it, especially if they have family support," said Pifher, "And then you run into people who think they can do it, yet really can't. You need to start educating people before a crisis hits."

There's no question that aging in place has broad appeal. According to an Associated Press-LifeGoesStrong.com poll conducted in October 2011, 52 percent of baby boomers said they were unlikely to move someplace new in retirement. In a 2005 survey by AARP, 89 percent of people age 50 and older said they would prefer to remain in their home indefinitely as they age.

That yearning, coupled with a widespread dread of going to a nursing home, has led to a nationwide surge of programs aimed at helping people stay in their neighborhoods longer.

Critical Thinking

1. What support is probably the most critical for families that want to age in place?

2. What percent of the population over 50 would prefer to age in place in a 2005 poll that was taken?

3. What do older people dread most about their living arrangements?

Create Central

www.mhhe.com/createcentral

Internet References

American Association of Homes and Services for the Aging
www.aahsa.org

Center for Demographic Studies
http://cds.duke.edu

Guide to Retirement Living
www.retirement-living.com

The United States Department of Housing and Urban Development
www.hud.gov

Article   Prepared by: Elaina F. Osterbur, *Saint Louis University*

Happy Together

Villages are helping people age in place.

Sally Abrahms

Learning Outcomes

After reading this article, you will be able to:

- Describe the variety of niche communities that exist for older adults today.
- Identify the fastest-growing niche communities in the country at the present time.

For years, boomers have denied they are going to get old. Now, with knees that need scoping and birthday cakes with way too many candles, the defiant generation is finally thinking about the future—especially where and how to live.

Visits to their parents in sterile, regimented assisted living or nursing homes are leaving boomers dismayed. They want better choices for Mom—and for themselves. While they may be a decade or more away from needing care, they're overhauling or honing traditional models and inventing new ones.

In choosing how they want to age, and where, boomers are helping shape the future of housing. "They have changed expectations every decade they've gone through; I don't think it will stop now," says John McIlwain, senior fellow for housing at the Urban Land Institute. Down the road, he says, "there won't be one single trend. People will be doing a lot of different things." They already are. The common denominator in existing and still-to-be-created models, say experts, is the desire to be part of a community that shares common interests, values or resources. People want to live where neighbors know and care about one another and will help one another as they age. That doesn't mean they'll become primary caretakers; if it gets to that point, outside professionals may need to help.

They also won't necessarily retire from their jobs if they live in a "retirement" community. Today's housing options reflect the attitude of older Americans: Stay active, keep learning, develop relationships and have fun for as long as possible.

Niche Communities

The concept: Live with others who share similar lifestyles, backgrounds or interests. **The numbers:** Around 100 across the country. **The price:** Depends on community type.

Prices can range from $800 a month for a rental at an RV park or $1,700 at an artists' community, up to several hundred thousand dollars to buy a unit at a university community, with monthly addons of $2,000 or more that include some meals, housekeeping, social activities and medical care.

"With 78 million baby boomers, housing options are virtually unlimited," says Andrew Carle, founding director of the Program in Assisted Living/Senior Housing Administration at George Mason University in Virginia. In the next 20 years, he says, name an interest group and there'll be a community for it. "Will there be assisted living for vegetarians or a community for Grateful Dead fans? Residential cruise ships with long-term care? Absolutely."

Today's niche communities are already varied. They're geared to healthy adults but often have an assisted care component. They include places like Rainbow's End RV Park in Livingston, Texas, which offers assisted living, Alzheimer's day care, respite for caregivers and short-term care for the sick or frail. The Charter House in Rochester, Minn., provides a home for former Mayo Clinic staffers, among others. The Burbank Senior Arts Colony in Los Angeles attracts retired or aspiring artists, musicians, actors and writers. Aegis Gardens in Fremont, Calif., caters to older Asians.

The swanky Rainbow Vision in Santa Fe, N.M., is primarily—but not exclusively—for gay, lesbian, bisexual and transgender (GLBT) clients. While it has assisted living, there's also a cabaret, an award-winning restaurant and a top-notch spa. With 3 million GLBT older Americans—a figure projected to nearly double by 2030—and typically no adult children to care for them, such communities are expected to multiply.

Hands down, the fastest-growing niche community sector is university-based retirement communities (UBRCs). So far there are 50 or more on or near such college campuses as Dartmouth, Cornell, Penn State and Denison University. While residents are usually in their 70s, 80s and up—besides independent living, there is assisted living and nursing care—UBRCs will appeal to boomers, the most highly educated demographic, when they grow older, says Carle. Residents can take classes and attend athletic or cultural events at the nearby college campus, professors lecture at the UBRC, and young students can complete internships.

Five years ago, Harvey Culbert, 75, a former medical physicist from Chicago, and his wife moved to Kendal at Oberlin, which is affiliated with the Ohio college. He has audited, for free, a course in neuroscience, sings in a college group, and is taking voice lessons from a retired Kendal music teacher. "I'm always interested in improving what I do," he says.

Cohousing

The concept: A group, usually composed of strangers at the start, creates a communal-type housing arrangement that is intergenerational or all older people, with separate units but some shared common space. The group may buy the property, help design it, make all rules by consensus and manage it independently. Residents eat some dinners together and often form deep relationships. **The numbers:** 112 intergenerational cohousing communities, with another 40 to 50 planned; four elder cohousing projects, with 20 or so in the works. More than half are in California. **The price:** $100,000 to $750,000, monthly fees $100 to $300; 10 percent of projects offer rentals for $600 to $2,000 a month.

Intergenerational cohousing is geared to families with younger children but also draws boomer couples and singles. The youngest elder cohousing residents are in their 60s. Members live in separate, fully equipped attached or clustered units, and share outdoor space and a common house where communal meals take place. The common house also contains a living room and guest (or caretaker's) quarters. What's in the rest of the space depends on the members; it could be a media or crafts room, or a studio for exercise and meditation.

"I think cohousing is a marvelous way to live," says Bernice Turoff, an 85-year-old widow and member of the intergenerational Nevada City Co-housing community in California. "It's a close community where people really care about one another. If you get sick, 14 people say, 'How can I help you?'"

Charles Durrett, her neighbor and an architect who, along with his wife, Kathryn McCamant, brought the concept of cohousing to the United States from Denmark in the 1980s, says older members act as surrogate grandparents. Last year, when one of the older residents was dying, all ages pitched in to help or visit.

Today, older boomers live in both intergenerational and elder cohousing. "I'd be surprised if cohousing doesn't double every couple of years in the next 20 years," says Durrett. Getting popular: cohousing in cities.

Green House

The concept: A new style of nursing home created by gerontologist William Thomas that looks, feels and operates more like a cozy house than an institution. Ten or so residents live together and get ultra-individualized care from nursing staff that knows them well and cooks their meals in an open country-style kitchen. **The numbers:** 87 Green House projects serving 1,000 residents; 120 projects in development. **The price:** The same Medicaid and Medicare coverage offered to traditional nursing homes; the minority paying out of pocket are charged the going rate in the area for a more conventional nursing home.

Residents' private bedrooms and bathrooms surround a living and dining room that looks like it could be in a single-family home; a screened-in porch or a backyard offers outdoor access. As much as possible, residents make their own decisions, such as when they'll wake up.

Proponents point to studies showing a Green House can improve an older person's quality of life, provide at least comparable, if not better, care than a traditional nursing home, and reduce staff turnover. "The good news and the bad news is that you get to spend the rest of your life with 10 people," says Victor Regnier, a professor of architecture and gerontology at the University of Southern California.

Stanley Radzyminski, 90, might not be able to communicate with a few dementia residents in his Green House at Eddy Village Green in Cohoes, N.Y., but says, "I really like it here. I have my own room and privacy, and if I need help, the staff is outstanding. We all want to think we can take care of ourselves, but it's not always possible."

The Village Model

The concept: Live in your own home or apartment and receive discounted, vetted services and social engagement opportunities. **The numbers:** 56, with 17 in the Washington, D.C., area alone, and 120 in development around the country. **The price:** $100- to $1,000-a-year membership fee, with an average of $500 for a single member, $650 or so for a household.

Growing quickly in popularity, this model will become even more popular in the coming years, say housing experts. That's because studies show most older people want to age in place. The first village was established in 2002 at Beacon Hill Village in Boston; in the last four years alone, 90 percent of the villages have formed.

Village members call a central number for help of any kind. That might be transportation to the grocery store or the doctor, or the name of a plumber, acupuncturist, computer tutor, caregiving agency, home modifications specialist, babysitter for visiting grandkids, dog walker or home delivery company. Because the village may have up to 400 members (although new groups may have fewer than 100), vendors find it an attractive market. The group buys theater tickets in bulk, for example, or contracts with a service provider; consolidated services save everyone money.

Villages offer plenty of opportunities to socialize, whether it's taking yoga down the street with neighbors, attending outings to museums or movies, or participating in a book club, walking group or supper gathering.

Rita Kostiuk, national coordinator for the Village to Village Network, which helps communities establish and manage their own villages, has noticed something about the new people calling for information: "The majority are boomers."

On the horizon: Already, demographers are seeing more older Americans moving, or contemplating moving, into cities and suburban town centers. Rather than being saddled with a house requiring nonstop upkeep or feeling isolated in the burbs, they're within walking distance of shops, entertainment and public transportation. So their ability or desire to drive is not a big deal.

Another trend: divorced, widowed or never-married older women living together. Some who don't know one another are keeping such agencies as nonprofit Golden Girls Housing in Minneapolis busy. Golden Girls offers networking events for women who want to live together, lists requests for women looking, and steers them to services that can help. They don't match women, though; women do that themselves. Others opting for this setup are already friends.

David Levy, a gerontologist and lawyer by training, runs seven groups a week for caregivers. Inevitably, the conversation turns from the parents they care for to themselves. "These boomer women may be estranged from, or never had, kids, have diminished funds, and not a significant other on the horizon. They want to know, 'What's going to happen to me? Who will be there for me?'" he says.

It looks like they'll have choices.

Critical Thinking

1. What will the effect of the Green House concept be on nursing homes in the future?

2. What is the advantage that the villages offer to older people in terms of their preferred living choices?

3. What attracts older persons to moving to downtown cities and suburban town centers?

Create Central

www.mhhe.com/createcentral

Internet References

American Association of Homes and Services for the Aging
www.aahsa.org

Center for Demographic Studies
http://cds.duke.edu

Guide to Retirement Living
www.retirement-living.com

The United States Department of Housing and Urban Development
www.hud.gov

SALLY ABRAHMS writes about aging, boomer health, and workplace issues. She lives in Boston.

City Governments and Aging in Place: Community Design, Transportation, and Housing Innovation Adoption by Amanda J. Lehning

195

Article

Prepared by: Elaina F. Osterbur, *Saint Louis University*

City Governments and Aging in Place: Community Design, Transportation, and Housing Innovation Adoption

AMANDA J. LEHNING

Learning Outcomes

After reading this article, you will be able to:

- Cite the most effective strategy to get cities to adopt innovations that benefit older adults.

- Discuss what should be included in the successful advocacy to the local government for changes that would benefit older adults.

The physical environment of many cities in the United States presents barriers to elder health, well-being, and the ability to age in place. These include community design that separates residential and commercial areas (Handy, 2005), the absence of adequate alternative transportation services (Rosenbloom & Herbel, 2009), and limited accessible housing (Maisel, Smith, & Steinfeld, 2008). Recent studies (e.g., AARP Public Policy Institute, 2005) suggest an emerging consensus regarding the innovative policies and programs needed to address these physical barriers, including the following: (a) zoning and infrastructure changes that could allow older adults to remain connected to their community, (b) developing a range of transportation services and mobility options, and (c) creating a wide variety of housing supports and choices. City governments often provide services that may help older adults age in place, including senior centers, recreation programs, and social services. However, there are no previous studies that have explored city government adoption of policies that address the impact of the physical environment on older adults. Informed by an internal determinants and diffusion framework, there are two aims of this mixed-methods study. The first is to examine the characteristics associated with city government adoption of community design, housing, and transportation innovations that affect older adults. The second is to use qualitative interviews to explain the quantitative findings and provide additional findings around the process of adopting these innovations.

A growing interest in adapting the physical environment of communities to better meet the needs of older adults is a reaction to a confluence of factors, including the aging of the U.S. population, a projected increase in disability and chronic disease in future cohorts of older adults, and an inadequate long-term care system. Due to the aging of the Baby Boomer generation and increased longevity, by the middle of the 21st century, a projected 88.5 million Americans will be aged 65 and older (U.S. Census Bureau, 2009). Although the percentage of older adults with a disability decreased in recent years (Crimmins, 2004), the 85 and older population, whose members experience a greater incidence of functional and cognitive impairment, is expected to triple over the next 40 years (U.S. Census Bureau, 2008). In addition, research indicates an increase in chronic illness among Baby Boomers compared with the previous cohort (Martin, Freedman, Schoeni, & Andreski, 2009), suggesting that improvements in morbidity and disability rates will reverse in the near future. The growing number of older adults who require assistance with functioning will rely on a U.S. long-term care system characterized by high costs (Komisar & Thompson, 2007), unmet need (Zarit, Shea, Berg, & Sundstrom, 1998), and poor quality (U.S. Government Accountability Office, 2005). Further, even as 93% of older adults want to remain in their own homes (Feldman, Oberlink, Simantov, & Gursen, 2004) and governments attempt to reduce long-term care costs and increase the supply of community-based services, public reimbursement continues to favor institutional care (Harrington, Ng, Kaye, & Newcomer, 2009).

Physical Environments and Elder Health and Well-being

Community Design

In recent decades, the percentage of older adults living outside of cities has steadily increased, and a majority of elders today are suburbanites (Frey, 1999). Thus, many older adults live in communities characterized by the separation of commercial and residential areas, creating a situation in which access is severely restricted for those who no longer operate their own vehicle. The distances between residential and commercial areas, combined with the absence of sidewalks in many suburban neighborhoods, discourages walking as a mode of transportation or physical activity.

Research suggests that zoning and infrastructure changes can positively affect the health and well-being of community residents. First, mixed-use and walkable neighborhoods can help individuals maintain or increase their life space (Beard, Blaney, Cerda, Frye, Lovasi, Ompad, Rundle, & Vlahov, 2009), thereby improving access to goods and services. Second, residents of neighborhoods with a variety of walking destinations score higher on measures of social capital (Leyden, 2003). Third, mixed-use and walkable neighborhoods are related to increased physical activity (Berke, Koepsell, Moudon, Hoskins, & Larson, 2007) and decreased limitations of instrumental activities of daily living (IADL; Freedman, Grafova, Schoeni, & Rogowski, 2008).

Transportation

The majority of older adults get around their communities in a car, with 75% as the driver and 18% as a passenger (Feldman et al., 2004). Impairments such as reduced cognitive functioning, however, hamper the ability of many older adults to drive safely (Lynott et al., 2009). Older nondrivers make 15% fewer trips for medical appointments and 65% fewer trips for religious, social, or community activities compared with their driving counterparts (U.S. Government Accountability Office, 2004). Policies and programs that help older adults continue to safely operate their own vehicle, such as improving the visibility of street signs and simplifying intersections, could positively affect elder health and well-being. Approximately 33% of older adults do not have public transportation in their communities (Rosenbloom & Herbel, 2009), and many that do experience inadequate service that is viewed as unsafe, unresponsive, and inconvenient (Adler & Rottunda, 2006). Complementary paratransit services mandated by the Americans with Disabilities Act of 1990 address the mobility needs of some elders (Koffman, Raphael, & Weiner, 2004), although eligibility criteria mean that approximately 40% of older adults with a disability do not qualify for these services (Rosenbloom, 2009). A recent study found that the negative impact of driving cessation on elder well-being can be avoided if transportation needs are met through other modes of travel (Cvitkovich & Wister, 2003), suggesting that alternative transportation services, such as senior vans, can benefit elders.

Housing

The cost of maintaining a home presents a significant barrier to aging in place, and in a recent survey more than 50% of older respondents reported spending more than 30% of their income on housing (Feldman et al., 2004). Further, the majority of housing in the United States includes design features that make it inaccessible to individuals with disabilities (Maisel et al., 2008). Federal laws such as the Fair Housing Amendments of 1988 mandate the inclusion of accessible features (i.e., wide entrances and interior doors, accessible light switches) in new multifamily housing (Kochera, 2002), but do not address accessibility in single-family homes or small multifamily buildings (American Planning Association, 2006). In addition, regulatory barriers such as restrictions for converting a garage into a dwelling unit not only keep densities low but also limit the housing options of older adults (Rosenthal, 2009). For example, in many communities zoning ordinances prevent the development of accessory dwelling units (ADUs; Pollack, 1994), an attached or detached permanent structure located on the same lot as a single-family home that includes a private kitchen and bathroom. For older adults who need to downsize because of financial or physical functioning reasons (e.g., difficulty climbing stairs), ADUs serve as an alternative form of housing, whereas for older adults who can remain in their own home but require some financial or personal care support, adding their own ADU creates a rental unit or a living space for a caregiver (Pynoos, Nishita, Cicero, & Caraviello, 2008).

Changing the home environment is associated with improved outcomes for individuals with a disability (Wahl, Fange, Oswald, Gitlin, & Iwarsson, 2009). Incorporating accessibility features is associated with a lower risk of health problems (Liu & Lapane, 2009), slower decline in IADL independence (Gitlin, Corcoran, Winter, Boyce, & Hauck, 2001), and reduced health care expenses (Stearns et al., 2000).

Purpose of the Study

As described earlier, there is growing evidence that community design, transportation, and housing innovations can have a positive impact on elder health, well-being, and the ability to age in place. However, there is little evidence as to why city governments may institute these policies and programs. To begin to address this gap in the literature, this study examined city government adoption of 11 innovations by testing 3 hypotheses informed by an internal determinants and diffusion framework. In addition, this study used qualitative interviews to explain the quantitative findings and provide additional findings around the process of adopting these innovations.

A combined internal determinants and diffusion framework is often used to guide investigations into the process of adopting an innovation, defined as a program or policy that is new to the adopting unit (Berry & Berry, 1999; Walker, 1969). Diffusion models propose that governments adopt innovations because they are influenced by other governments; policymakers often must devise solutions to problems quickly within the context of limited resources and therefore look to others as they determine the appropriate policy response (Colvin, 2006). Internal determinants models propose that factors within a government jurisdiction, such as community characteristics, determine whether the government will adopt innovations (Berry & Berry). The author selected this framework because it has been applied to previous investigations of the adoption of policy agendas rather than only one specific policy (e.g., Walker), has been used in research on local government innovations (e.g., Shipan & Volden, 2005), and allows flexibility in terms of the specific internal characteristics influencing policy adoption.

This study tested three hypotheses informed by previous studies using an internal determinants and diffusion framework.

The first hypothesis, based on the ideas of Berry and Berry (1999), is three diffusion factors will be positively associated with the adoption of these innovations. First, because uncertainty regarding the potential impact of an innovation can be overcome by observing its effects in nearby jurisdictions, governments will adopt innovations that are perceived as being beneficial elsewhere. Second, governments want to gain a competitive advantage to, for example, attract high-income households to increase their tax base, and therefore adopt policies that have popular support in other jurisdictions. Third, governments are more likely to adopt innovations when citizens advocate for these changes.

The second hypothesis is five community characteristics will be positively associated with the adoption of these innovations. In previous studies, larger total population and higher socio-economic status of the population have positively influenced innovation adoption (Shipan & Volden, 2005; Walker, 1969). In the United States, recognition of older adults as a distinct social group that deserves special consideration in matters of public policy dates back to the passage of the Social Security Act of 1935 (Elder & Cobb, 1984). Therefore, the percent of older adults living in the community could be associated with the adoption of these innovations. Further, many of these innovations are designed for those who have a physical disability, suggesting the inclusion of the percent of the adult population with a disability.

The third hypothesis is two government characteristics will be positively associated with innovation adoption. First, higher per capita government spending may be a proxy for fiscal health, and local governments that are in poor fiscal health may be more conservative than innovative, particularly in terms of innovations that require a commitment of financial resources (Wolman, 1986). Second, policy entrepreneurs, or those who work within government to promote and advocate for policy innovations (e.g., elected officials), may be particularly influential in terms of increasing awareness and consideration of innovations (Mintrom, 1997).

Methods

This study used a sequential explanatory mixed-methods design, which involves a larger quantitative study followed by a smaller qualitative study (Creswell & Plano Clark, 2007). As this is the first study to examine the factors that influence the adoption of these specific innovations, the use of both quantitative and qualitative methods provided a more in-depth understanding of this topic. Qualitative interviews also allowed the author to expand beyond the quantitative findings to collect information that would be difficult to capture using a more structured online survey, including the process of innovation adoption.

The University of California Berkeley Committee for the Protection of Human Subjects classified this study as exempt from Institutional Review Board approval.

Quantitative Phase
Sample and Data Collection Procedures

The sample for this study included all 101 cities located in the San Francisco Bay Area. City governments were selected because they have jurisdiction over the use of land, including aspects of community design, housing, and transportation (Feldstein, 2007). Primary data were collected via online surveys developed by the author. Following a small pilot of the survey, the author sent an invitation to participate via electronic mail to the director of city planning in each city. Survey data collection took place between March and August of 2009. A total of 62 of 101 (61.4%) city planners returned completed surveys, and these data were combined with secondary data from the 2000 U.S. Census and the California 2000 *Cities Annual Report*.

Measures

Table 1 describes the measures and distribution of the dependent and independent variables. For the dependent variables, the survey asked respondents if their city had adopted the 11

Table 1 Description of Measures and Sample (*N* = 62)

Variables	Description	Frequency (%)
Dependent variables		
Community design	0: Zero or one innovation adopted	22 (35.5)
• Incentives to encourage mixed-use neighborhoods	1: Both innovations adopted	40 (64.5)
• Changes in infrastructure to improve walkability		
Transportation (range: 0–5)	0	13 (21.0)
• Education programs for older drivers	1	18 (29.0)
• Assessment programs for older drivers	2	25 (40.3)
• Infrastructure changes to improve older driver safety	3	5 (8.1)
• Alternative transportation	4	1 (1.6)
• Slower-moving vehicle ordinance	5	0

(continued)

Table 1 Description of Measures and Sample (*N* = 62)

Variables	Description	Frequency (%)
Housing (range: 0–4)	0	0
• Accessory dwelling unit ordinance	1	15 (24.2)
• Developer incentives to guarantee housing units for seniors	2	19 (30.6)
• Incentives to make housing accessible	3	15 (24.2)
• Home modification assistance	4	13 (21.0)
Total number of innovations (range: 0–11)	0	0
	1	2 (3.2)
	2	4 (6.5)
	3	4 (6.5)
	4	5 (8.0)
	5	17 (27.4)
	6	12 (19.4)
	7	11 (17.7)
	8	5 (8.1)
	9	2 (3.2)
	10	0
	11	0
Independent variables		
Diffusion factors		
Benefits	0: No knowledge of benefits in other jurisdictions	7 (11.3)
	1: Knowledge of benefits in other jurisdictions	55 (88.7)
Advantage	0: Does not believe other cities gained an advantage by adopting innovations	15 (24.2)
	1: Does believe other cities gained an advantage by adopting innovations	47 (75.8)
Public advocacy	0: Has not experienced public advocacy from residents to adopt innovations	18 (29.0)
	1: Has experienced public advocacy from residents to adopt innovations	44 (71.0)
Community characteristics		
Size (range: 2,125–776,733)	0: Population size < 50,000	42 (67.7)
	1: Population size ≥ 50,000	20 (32.3)
Education (range: 48.2%–98.8%)	0: Percent of the population with a high school diploma ≤ 89	31 (50.0)
	1: Percent of the population with a high school diploma >89	31 (50.0)
Income (range: 37,184–200,001)	0: Household median income ≤ 67,352	31 (50.0)
	1: Household median income >67,352	31 (50.0)
65 + (range: 5.1%–45.1%)	0: Percent of the population aged 65 and older ≤ 11.1	31 (50.0)
	1: Percent of the population aged 65 and older >11.1	31 (50.0)
Disability (range: 8.5%–25.5%)	0: Percent of the adult population with a disability ≤ 15.2	31 (50.0)
	1: Percent of the adult population with a disability >15.2	31 (50.0)
Government characteristics		
Spending (range: 294–6,550)	0: City per capita government spending ≤ 1,013	31 (50.0)
	1: City per capita government spending >1,013	31 (50.0)
Policy entrepreneur	0: No individual within government has advocated for innovation adoption	28 (45.2)
	1: An individual within government has advocated for innovation adoption	34 (54.8)

City Governments and Aging in Place: Community Design, Transportation, and Housing Innovation Adoption by Amanda J. Lehning

199

community design, transportation, and housing innovations shown in the table. Due to the distribution of frequencies, the community design outcome was dichotomized to compare cities with both innovations to those with one or none. Transportation, housing, and total number of innovations were measured as count variables.

For the independent variables, the survey asked respondents whether they had knowledge of benefits of these innovations in other jurisdictions, believed other cities gained an advantage by adopting these innovations, experienced public advocacy to adopt these innovations, and if there was an individual within government advocating for adoption. Data on community characteristics were obtained from the 2000 U.S. Census (the most recent year that included all necessary data for cities in the sample), and the California 2000 *Cities Annual Report* provided information on per capita government spending. Population size was coded into categories of less than 50,000 versus 50,000 or more, a demarcation of small and large cities used by federal agencies (e.g., the Office of Management and Budget) and professional organizations (e.g., National League of Cities). Due to problems with functional form, the author transformed continuous variables for community characteristics into dichotomous variables using median splits.

Statistical Analysis

The author calculated four different regression equations to examine the association between internal determinants and diffusion factors and innovation adoption. Tolerance and variance inflation factor results indicated that multicollinearity is not a concern with independent variables. Logistic regression was used to estimate odds ratios for the dichotomous outcome variable of community design innovations. Poisson regression was used to analyze the other three outcome variables (i.e., transportation, housing, and total number of innovations) as these measured counts of the number of innovations adopted. As recommended by Cameron and Trivedi (2009), robust standard errors for the parameter estimates were obtained to adjust for minor underdispersion.

Qualitative Phase
Sample and Data Collection Procedures

After completing the survey, 28 city planners indicated their willingness to participate in a follow-up interview. Ten interview participants were selected using maximum variation sampling, which allows the researcher to explore phenomena using cases that vary by characteristics (Sandelowski, 2000). The author selected interview participants representative of community characteristics (e.g., high and low education, high and low income, high and low percent of the population 65 and older, high and low percent of the population with a disability) and a range in the total number of innovations adopted. The researcher conducted, recorded, and transcribed the interviews in November and December of 2009. Interviewees were asked about the decision process involved in adopting innovations, including how the idea developed and facilitators of and barriers to adoption.

Data Analysis

Following the recommendation of Miles and Huberman (1984), qualitative data analysis consisted of three concurrent activities: data reduction, data display, and conclusion drawing/verification. Analysis of interview data was informed by previous research but was also inductive in nature, with data reduction starting at the basic level of line-by-line coding (Padgett, 1998). Following the first review of all interview transcripts, the researcher developed initial codes, which were refined after multiple iterations through the data. During data display, the researcher created spreadsheets for each code that included direct quotes as well as data from the online surveys (i.e., community characteristics and specific innovations adopted by the local government of the interview participant). This visual display allowed the researcher to further refine codes, establish a set of themes expressed by multiple interview participants, and draw conclusions about the data. The researcher then verified conclusions by a final review of the interview transcripts, a procedure that has been used by other qualitative researchers to determine the validity of qualitative data analysis (Miles & Huberman).

Results
Quantitative

Table 2 presents the results of the regression of internal determinants and diffusion factors on innovation adoption. Model 1 presents the logistic regression for the adoption of community design innovations. Cities that experienced public advocacy or had a higher percent of the population with a disability had an increased odds of adopting both community design innovations. However, these results should be interpreted with caution as wide confidence intervals indicate problems with the precision of the model.

Model 2 presents the regression of the number of transportation innovations, and public advocacy was significantly associated with innovation adoption. As shown in Model 3, cities with a higher percent of the population aged 65 and older adopted fewer housing innovations and those with a higher percent of the population with a disability adopted more housing innovations. In Model 4, which presents the regression of the total number of innovations, the relationship between percent of the population with a disability and innovation adoption was also significant. In addition, higher per capita government spending was negatively associated with innovation adoption, whereas the existence of a policy entrepreneur was positively associated with innovation adoption.

Qualitative

Qualitative interviews uncovered potential explanations for the quantitative findings and also additional findings. Three concepts were identified through analysis of the qualitative interviews: advocacy and public resistance, disability and age, and city and resident economic resources.

Advocacy and Public Resistance

Advocacy by city residents was described as a facilitator of the adoption process. According to one city planner, "Every large

Table 2 Regression Results for the Adoption of Community Design, Transportation, and Housing Innovations (*N* = 62)

Internal determinants and diffusion variable	Model 1ᵃ: community design, OR (95% CI)	Model 2ᵇ: transportation, *B* (95% CI)	Model 3ᵇ: housing, *B* (95% CI)	Model 4ᵇ: total number of innovations, *B* (95% CI)
Diffusion factors				
Benefits	1.46 (0.29–7.40)	.09 (−.29 to .46)	.02 (−.19 to .23)	−.01 (−.34 to .33)
Advantage	2.26 (0.40–12.81)	−.03 (−.43 to .37)	−.07 (−.29 to .16)	.08 (−.16 to .31)
Public advocacy	4.28* (0.88–20.73)	.35** (.02 to .68)	.11 (−.13 to .35)	.17 (−.04 to .38)
Community characteristics				
Size	3.39 (0.55–20.70)	−.03 (−.41 to .34)	.12 (−.07 to .32)	.11 (−.06 to .27)
Education	1.34 (0.23–7.77)	−.02 (−.39 to .35)	−.10 (−.34 to .14)	−.06 (−.22 to .10)
Income	2.00 (0.17–22.81)	−.15 (−.62 to .33)	.17 (−.058 to .39)	.05 (−.10 to .20)
65+	0.70 (0.16–3.08)	.04 (−.33 to .42)	−.26** (−.51 to .02)	−.11 (−.26 to .03)
Disability	8.79* (0.69–112.14)	.19 (−.33 to .72)	.28** (.03 to .54)	.22** (.05 to .40)
Government characteristics				
Spending	0.28 (0.06–1.28)	−.15 (−.49 to .18)	−.08 (−.267 to .11)	−.12* (−.26 to .01)
Policy entrepreneur	0.85 (0.18–3.91)	.21 (−.12 to .53)	.07 (−.16 to .30)	.15* (−.02 to .32)

Note: OR = odds ratio; CI = confidence interval.
ᵃ Logistic regression.
ᵇ Poisson regression.
*$p < .10$. **$p < .05$.

project had its genesis with some sort of citizens' group that came to the city with a concept and got that to move forward." Another said, "We respond to things we're pushed to do." A third city government respondent reported that "Activists come to public meetings and they share info about their needs. It is clear what they want: they call me and they definitely call their council people."

Public resistance, often discussed as concerns about mixed-use neighborhoods and higher-density development, is perceived by city planners as a barrier to adopting these innovations. One city planner referred to "the traditional NIMBY [not in my backyard] people." Another interviewee noted "There are parts of town where people don't want more dense neighborhoods . . . People prefer single-family homeownership." Another planner recalled resistance to an accessible apartment building: "The concerns raised were about how it would affect parking in the neighborhood and wanting to make sure it would be well managed and well designed."

Disability and Age

Several interviewees mentioned advocacy by and on behalf of younger individuals with disabilities. One planner explained, "When we built more accessible housing, it wasn't seniors per se, but a disability group pushed the city. The basic idea was 'why are you spending all this money to keep people in institutions when you could keep people in their homes?'." Another interview participant noted the increased visibility of

individuals with disabilities in this region compared with other parts of the United States: "There are probably not more people here with disabilities, but they are more out in the community." A third interviewee said, "I think, anecdotally, this area is a magnet for people with disabilities because we have such great services."

City and Resident Economic Resources

Interviewees indicated that they viewed some of these innovations as a way to improve the fiscal health of their city. The following quote is from a city with relatively low spending that adopted a high number of innovations: "We see all these policies and provisions coming into place to make downtown more vital, more interesting, and more economically competitive. The thought process is getting more people into downtown." Similarly, another city planner explained that a recent push by a city to create more walkable mixed-use neighborhoods was motivated in part because "people want more lively places, more lively streets, and they want more of a 24-hr presence."

In terms of resident economic resources, some cities do not see any need for public supports for their more economically advantaged aging residents. For example, as one city planner explained: "This is an affluent community, so it doesn't require as much public assistance. I think the seniors do need household assistance and sometimes medical assistance . . . We are going to promote increased density near the commercial district, and also second units so you can have your nurse living nearby, but most of these services are private in this community." According to another, "there is a sense that we have addressed a good chunk of part of the need, and I mean by income levels. I tend to focus on below market housing, but there are other niches outside of my scope. There could be a need for empty nester housing but that is not part of our focus."

Discussion

This mixed-methods study is the first attempt to explore local government adoption of community design, transportation, and housing innovations that could improve elder health, well-being, and the ability to age in place. The quantitative phase tested three hypotheses informed by an internal determinants and diffusion framework using data collected via online surveys with city planners. The qualitative phase used data collected through telephone interviews designed to explain and supplement the quantitative results.

The first hypothesis proposed that three diffusion factors would be positively associated with the adoption of community design, transportation, and housing innovations that could benefit older adults: knowledge of benefits in other jurisdictions, a belief that cities gain an advantage from adopting innovations, and public advocacy. Only public advocacy was significant, and only for community design and transportation innovations. In qualitative interviews, a number of participants reported that resident advocacy influences policy decisions. However, interviews also suggest that public resistance can present a barrier to innovation adoption. Similar to a recent study examining barriers to the adoption of ADU ordinances (Liebig et al., 2006), public resistance came up in discussions about mixed-use and higher-density development, ranging from NIMBY sentiments to residential concerns about parking problems.

The second hypothesis proposed that five community characteristics would be positively associated with innovation adoption: population size, population education, household median income, percentage of the population aged 65 and older, and percent of the adult population with a disability. This hypothesis was partially supported as the percent of the population with a disability was associated with the adoption of community design, housing, and total number of innovations. The percent of the population aged 65 and older was not significant in three of the models and was negatively associated with the adoption of housing innovations. Interview participants mentioned disability advocates more often than older adults or groups representing their interests. Historically, due to their high voter turnout and the organizational power of groups such as AARP, older adults have successfully pushed policymakers at the federal level to adopt policies (e.g., Medicare) targeted to meet their needs (Elder & Cobb, 1984). At the local level, however, interviews suggest that public advocacy for changes to the physical environment comes from residents with disabilities rather than older adults. Previous research has found that advocacy can lead to the adoption of innovations that are particularly salient to residents, such as those around sex education and gambling (Mooney & Lee, 2000), but plays a smaller role in innovations more removed from people's everyday lives, such

as hazardous waste policies (Daley & Garand, 2005). Some of the innovations examined in this study (e.g., incentives to develop accessible housing) address difficulties associated with functional status rather than age. Disability groups may be more active because individuals who have a disability are more aware of the physical barriers in their communities than older adults who face the possibility of disability in the future. Alternatively, younger individuals with disabilities may be more effective advocates for the adoption of these innovations because the general response to disability varies across age populations. It has been suggested that for younger individuals, disability is more often viewed as a result of problems in the social and physical environment, whereas for older adults disability is more typically attributed to disease (Kane, Priester, & Neumann, 2007). City governments may therefore perceive these innovations as more appropriate for younger adults with disabilities.

The implication is that service providers and advocates should facilitate the involvement of older adults through education and community-building activities. This has proved a successful strategy by the Elder Friendly Communities Project in Calgary, Canada, which has successfully brought about changes, including infrastructure improvements, by training and supporting older adults to plan and carry out actions to change their community (Austin, Des Camp, Flux, McClelland, & Sieppert, 2005). In addition, aging service providers and advocates may also need education about the ways in which the physical environment can affect older adults. Councils on Aging, for example, could broaden their service and advocacy efforts to address community design, transportation, and housing.

Contrary to the second hypothesis and previous research (Berry & Berry, 1999; Shipan & Volden, 2005), there was no significant association with population education or income in any of the four regression models. As discussed in interviews, city government perceptions of the need for many of these innovations may depend on the residents' private economic resources, and city planners in wealthier communities may assume that older residents are wealthy and do not require public assistance. It is possible that older adults with higher education and incomes are less likely to require the public provision of environmental adaptations because of their reduced risk for physical limitations (Freedman & Martin, 1999), lower rates of impairments, and slower deterioration of physical functioning (Mirowsky & Ross, 2000). Higher levels of education have been linked with improved access to care, higher quality of care, and better health behaviors (Goldman & Smith, 2002), and these elders may be able to delay or avoid disability because they can obtain personal care, assistive devices, medical care, healthy foods, and exercise equipment (Schoeni, Freedman, & Martin, 2008). Cities whose residents have a lower socioeconomic status, and are therefore more vulnerable to disease and disability, may be more receptive to advocacy efforts to put these innovations in place.

For the third hypothesis, the positive significant association between the existence of a policy entrepreneur and the total number of innovations indicates that enlisting the support of individuals with a formal role in city government may be an effective strategy to innovation adoption. This is consistent with the proposition of Walker (1973) that "the presence of a single aide on a legislative staff who is enthusiastic about a new program, or the chance reading of an article by a political leader can cause [governments] to adopt new programs more rapidly" (p. 1190). Per capita government spending had an inverse relationship with the total number of innovations. Similar to previous studies (e.g., Boyne & Gould-Williams, 2005), this finding combined with qualitative data suggests that the need for economic revitalization could inspire innovation adoption because it creates a greater need for innovative solutions. For example, because city governments receive much of their revenue from sales taxes, property taxes, and user fees (Warner, 2010), incentives for mixed-use development and the construction of residential buildings that dedicate units for seniors could improve city finances. Another implication of this research is that advocates and residents pushing for these innovations should emphasize the potential economic benefits associated with some of these changes.

Findings from the current study should be interpreted in light of its limitations, and future research should examine whether the results are applicable to other cities. First, this study achieved fairly good response rates but may still have some nonresponse error. Second, future research should address the limitation of self-report data by, for example, soliciting participation from multiple employees in each city. Third, because the nonlinear relationship between the continuous variables and outcome variables indicated problems with functional form, the author used median splits, which in turn affects model precision and could lead to overestimation or underestimation of significant statistical relationships (Maxwell & Delaney, 1993). The small sample size also affects the validity of the quantitative results. For example, the logistic regression model for community design innovations may be overestimating the odds ratios (Nemes, Jonasson, Genell, & Steineck, 2009). Fifth, results may not be generalizable outside of the San Francisco Bay Area because of its unique characteristics, including higher population income and education and rapid population growth at the end of the 20th century (Kawabata & Shen, 2007). Furthermore, the region has a reputation for embracing innovative land use and transportation policies and is often the subject of case studies of these types of innovations (e.g., Bhatia, 2007; Kawabata & Shen).

Additionally, the use of cross-sectional data does not allow for an understanding of the diffusion of innovations over time (Berry & Berry, 1990). Future research should employ techniques such as event history analysis to ascertain which innovations have been in place for years and which have been only recently adopted, uncover if there are particularly influential cities affecting the diffusion process, and further clarify the factors associated with the adoption of these innovations. Other policy researchers (e.g., Downs & Mohr, 1976) have criticized an internal determinants and diffusion framework for the variation in results reported across studies. It is not unusual for factors that are positively associated with one type of policy innovation to be negatively associated, or not associated at all, with other innovations (Downs & Mohr). The researcher selected this framework in part because of its flexibility in the specific characteristics associated with policy adoption, and therefore it is not surprising

that results differed from previous research on, for example, local antismoking policies (see Shipan & Volden, 2005).

The findings and limitations of this study suggest the need for additional research into local government adoption of community design, transportation, and housing innovations that could benefit older adults. Future research should explore modifications to an internal determinants and diffusion framework as it relates to these policies and programs. For example, although per capita government spending has been used as a proxy measure for government resources in earlier research on local government policy adoption (e.g., Shipan & Volden, 2005), other measures (e.g., city revenues) could be used in future studies. Future studies should also explore whether younger individuals with disabilities are more active in advocating for these innovations than older adults. It is possible that this finding reflects the Bay Area, which, as mentioned by interview participants, has a history of supporting disability rights and the independent living movement. It is also possible that older adults are not as engaged in public policy at the local level, and therefore more research is needed to understand how to promote their community involvement. Third, although there is emerging evidence that these innovations can improve elder health, well-being, and ability to age in place, more research is needed to explore the impact of the environment on older adults. Establishing an empirical evidence base for aging in place will ensure that local governments devote their often scarce resources toward effective policies, programs, and infrastructure changes.

Conclusion

This mixed-methods study explored city-level adoption of community design, transportation, and housing innovations that have the potential to improve elder health, well-being, and the ability to age in community. Quantitative and qualitative results indicate that advocacy is an effective strategy to encourage city adoption of innovations that affect the mobility and quality of life of older adults. Successful advocacy efforts should facilitate the involvement of older residents, target key decision makers within government, emphasize potential financial benefits to the city, and focus on cities whose aging residents are particularly vulnerable to disease and disability.

References

AARP Public Policy Institute. (2005). Livable communities: An evaluation guide. Washington, DC: AARP. Retrieved July 8, 2009, from http://assets.aarp.org/rgcenter/il/d18311_communities.pdf

Adler, G., & Rottunda, S. (2006). Older adults' perspectives on driving cessation. *Journal of Aging Studies, 20,* 227–235. doi: 10.1016/j.jaging. 2005.09.003

American Planning Association. (2006). Policy guide on housing. Policy adopted by American Planning Association (APA) Board of Directors. Retrieved January 4, 2010, from http://www.planning.org/policy/guides/pdf/housing.pdf

Austin, C. D., Des Camp, E., Flux, D., McClelland, R. W., & Sieppert, J. (2005). Community development with older adults in their neighborhoods: The Elder Friendly Communities Program. *Families in Society, 86,* 401–409.

City Governments and Aging in Place: Community Design, Transportation, and Housing Innovation Adoption by Amanda J. Lehning

203

Beard, J. R., Cerda, M., Blaney, S., Ahern, J., Vlahov, D., & Galea, S. (2009). Neighborhood characteristics and change in depressive symptoms among older residents of New York City. *American Journal of Public Health, 99,* 1308–1314. doi:10.2105/ AJPH.2007. 125104.

Berke, E. M., Koepsell, T. D., Moudon, A. V., Hoskins, R. E., & Larson, E. B. (2007). Association of the built environment with physical activity and obesity in older persons. *American Journal of Public Health, 97,* 486–492. doi: 10.2105/AJPH.2006.085837

Berry, F. S., & Berry, W. (1999). Innovation and diffusion models in policy research. In P. A. Sabatier (Ed.), *Theories of the policy process* (pp. 169–200). Boulder, CO: Westview Press.

Berry, F. S., & Berry, W. D. (1990). State lottery adoptions as policy innovations: An event history analysis. *The American Political Science Review, 84,* 395–415.

Bhatia, R. (2007). Protecting health using an environmental impact assessment: A case study of San Francisco land use decisionmaking. *American Journal of Public Health, 97,* 406– 413. doi:l0.2105/AJPH.2005. 073817

Boyne, G. A., & Gould-Williams, J. S. (2005). Explaining the adoption of innovation: An empirical analysis of public management reform. *Environment and Planning* C: *Government and Policy, 23,* 419–435. doi:10.1068./c40m

Cameron, A. C, & Trivedi, P. K. (2009). *Microeconometrics using Stata.* College Station, TX: Stata Press.

Colvin, R. A. (2006). Innovation of state-level gay rights laws: The role of Fortune 500 corporations. *Business and Society Review, 111,* 363–386. doi:10.1111/j. 1467–8594.2006.00277.x

Creswell, J. W., & Piano Clark, V. L. (2007). Designing and conducting mixed methods research Thousand Oaks, CA: Sage Publications.

Crimmins, E. M. (2004). Trends in the health of the elderly. *Annual Review Public Health, 25,* 79–98. doi: 10.1146/annurev. publhealth. 25.102802.124401

Cvitkovich, Y., & Wister, A. (2003). Bringing in the life course: A modification to Lawton's ecological model of aging. *Hallym International Journal of Aging, 4,* 15–29.

Daley, D. M., & Garand, J. C. (2005). Horizontal diffusion, vertical diffusion, and internal pressure in state environmental policymaking, 1989–1998. *American Politics Research, 33,* 615–644. doi.l 177/1 532673X04273416

Downs, G.W., & Mohr, L.B. (1976). Conceptual issues in the study of innovation. *Administrative Science Quarterly, 21,* 700–714.

Elder, C. D., & Cobb, R. W. (1984). Agenda-building and the politics of aging. *Policy Studies Journal, 13,* 115–129.

Feldman, P. H., Oberlink, M. R., Simantov, E., & Gursen, M. D. (2004). A tale of two older Americas: Community opportunities and challenges. New York: Center for Home Care Policy and Research.

Feldstein, L.M. (2007). General Plans and Zoning: A Toolkit on Land Use and Health. Sacramento, CA: California Department of Health Services. Retrieved February 26, 2010, from http://www.phlpnet.org/ healthy-planning/products/ general-plans-and-zoning

Freedman, V., & Martin, L. (1999). The role of education in explaining and forecasting trends in functional limitations among older Americans. *Demography, 36,* 461–173. doi: 10.2307/2648084

Freedman, V. A., Grafova, I. B., Schoeni, R. F., & Rogowski, J. (2008). Neighborhoods and disability in later life. *Social Science & Medicine, 66,* 2253–2267. doi:10.1016/j. socscimed.2008.01.013

Frey, W. H. (1999). Beyond social security: The local aspects of an aging America Washington, DC: The Brookings Institution.

Gitlin, L. N., Corcoran, M. A., Winter, L., Boyce, A., & Hauck, W. W. (2001). A randomized controlled trial of a home environmental intervention to enhance self-efficacy and reduce upset in family caregivers of persons with dementia. *The Gerontologist, 41,* 15–30. doi:10.1093/geront/41.1.4

Goldman, D., & Smith, J. P. (2002). Can patient self-management help explain the SES health gradient? *Proceedings of the National Academy of Sciences, 99,* 10929–10934. doi:10.1073/ pnas.l62086599

Handy, S. (2005). Smart growth and the transportation-land use connection: What does the research tell us? *International Regional Science Review, 28,* 146–167. doi:10.1177/0160017604273626

Harrington, C., Ng, T., Kaye, S. H., & Newcomer, R. (2009). Home and community-based services: Public policies to improve access, costs and quality. San Francisco: UCSF Center for Personal Assistance Services.

Kane, R. L., Priester, R., & Neumann, D. (2007). Does disparity in the way disabled older adults are treated imply ageism? *The Gerontologist, 47,* 271–279. doi:10.1093/ geront/47.3.271.

Kawabata, M., & Shen, Q. (2007). Commuting inequality between cars and public transit: The case of the San Francisco Bay Area, 1990–2000. *Urban Studies, 44,* 1759–1780.

Kochera, A. (2002). Accessibility and visitability features in single-family homes: A review of state and local activity. Washington, DC: AARP Public Policy Institute.

Koffman, D., Raphael, D., & Weiner, R. (2004). The impact of federal programs in transportation for older adults. Washington, DC: AARP Public Policy Institute.

Komisar, H. L., & Thompson, L. S. (2007). National spending for long-term care. Washington, DC: Georgetown University. Retrieved July 7, 2009, from http://ltc.georgetown.edu/pdfs/ whopays2006.pdf

Leyden, K. M. (2003). Social capital and the built environment: The importance of walkable neighborhoods. *American Journal of Public Health, 93,* 1546–1551.

Liebig, P. S., Koenig, T., & Pynoos, J. (2006). Zoning, accessory dwelling units, and family caregiving: Issues, trends, and recommendations.

Liu, S. Y., & Lapane, K. L. (2009). Residential modifications and decline in physical function among community-dwelling older adults. *The Gerontologist, 49,* 344–354. doi:10.1093/geront/ gnp033

Lynott, J., Haase, J., Nelson, K., Taylor, A., Twaddell, H., Ulmer, J., et al. (2009). Planning complete streets for an aging America. Washington, DC: AARP Public Policy Institute.

Maisel, J. L., Smith, E., & Steinfeld, E. (2008). Increasing home access: Designing for visitability. Washington, DC: AARP Public Policy Institute.

Martin, L. G., Freedman, V. A., Schoeni, R. F., & Andreski, P. M. (2009). Health and functioning among Baby Boomers approaching 60. *The journal of Gerontology, 64B,* 369–377. doi: 10.1093/geronb/gbn040

Maxwell, S. E., & Delaney, H. D. (1993). Bivariate median splits and spurious statistical significance. *Psychological Bulletin, 113,* 181–190. doi:10.1037/0033-2909.113.1.181

Miles, M. B., & Huberman, M. A. (1984). Qualitative data analysis: An expanded sourcebook. Thousand Oaks, CA: Sage.

Mintrom, M. (1997). Policy entrepreneurs and the diffusion of innovation. *American Journal of Political Science, 41,* 738–770.

Mirowsky, J., & Ross, C. (2000). Socioeconomic status and subjective life expectancy. *Social Psychology Quarterly, 63,* 133–151.

Mooney, C, & Lee, M. H. (2000). The influence of values on consensus and contentious morality policy: US death penalty reform, 1956–82. *The Journal of Politics, 62,* 223–239.

Nemes, S., Jonasson, J. M., Genell, A., &: Steineck, G. (2009). Bias in odds ratios by logistic regression modeling and sample size. *BMC Medical Research Methodology, 9,* 56–60. doi: 10.1186/1471-2288-9-56

Padgett, D. K. (1998). Qualitative methods in social work research: Challenges and rewards. Thousand Oaks, CA: Sage Publications.

Pollack, P. B. (1994). Rethinking zoning to accommodate the elderly in single family housing. *Journal of the American Planning Association, 60,* 521–531. doi:10.1080/01944369408975608

Pynoos, J., Nishita, C., Cicero, C., & Caraviello, R. (2008). Aging in place, housing, and the law. *University of Illinois Elder Law Journal, 16,* 77–107.

Rosenbloom, S. (2009). Meeting transportation needs in an aging-friendly community. *Generations, 33,* 33–43.

Rosenbloom, S., & Herbel, S. (2009). The safety and mobility patterns of older women: Do current patterns foretell the future? *Public Works Management & Policy, 13,* 338–353. doi:10.1177/1087724X09334496

Rosenthal, L. A. (2009). The role of local government: Land use controls and aging-friendliness. *Generations, 33,* 18–23.

Sandelowski, M. (2000). Whatever happened to qualitative description? *Research in Nursing & Health, 23,* 334–340.

Schoeni, R. F., Fteedman, V. A., & Martin, L. G. (2008). Why is late-life disability declining? *The Milbank Quarterly, 86,* 47–89. doi:10.1111/j.1468-0009.2007.00513.x

Shipan, C.R., & Volden, C. (2005). The diffusion of local antismoking policies. Retrieved August 12, 2011, from: http://psweb.sbs.ohio-state.edu/intranet/rap/volden.pdf.

Stearns, S. C., Bernard, S. L., Fasick, S. B., Schwartz, R., Konrad, R., Ory, M. G., et al. (2000). The economic implications of self-care: The effect of lifestyle, functional adaptations, and medical self-care among a national sample of Medicare beneficiaries. *American Journal of Public Health, 90,* 1608–1612.

U.S. Census Bureau. (2008). An older and more diverse nation by midcentury. Retrieved June 19, 2009, from http://www.census.gov/Press-Release/www/releases/archives/population/012496.html

U.S. Census Bureau. (2009). Facts for features: Older Americans month: 2009. Retrieved June 1, 2009, from http://www.census.gov/Press-Release/www/releases/archives/facts_for_features_special_editions/013384.html

U.S. Government Accountability Office. (2004). Transportation-disadvantaged seniors: Efforts to enhance senior mobility could benefit from additional guidance and information. Washington, DC: GAO.

U.S. Government Accountability Office. (2005). Nursing homes: Despite increased oversight, challenges remain in ensuring high-quality care and resident safety. Retrieved June 2, 2009, from http://www.gao.gov/new.items/d06117.pdf

Wahl, H., Fange, A., Oswald, F., Gitlin, L. N., & Iwarsson, S. (2009). The home environment and disability-related outcomes in aging individuals: What is the empirical evidence? *The Gerontologist, 49,* 355–367. doi: 10.1093/geront/gnp056

Walker, J. L. (1969). The diffusion of innovations among the American states. *The American Political Science Revieiv, 63,* 880–899.

Walker, J. L. (1973). Comment: Problems in research on the diffusion of policy innovations. *The American Political Science Review, 67,* 1186–1191.

Warner, M. E. (2010). The future of local government: Twenty-first century challenges. *Public Administration Review,* s1, s145–s147.

Wolman, H. (1986). Innovation in local government and fiscal austerity. *Journal of Public Policy, 6,* 159–180.

Zarit, S. H., Shea, D. G., Berg, S., & Sundstrom, G. (1998). Patterns of formal and informal long term care in the United States and Sweden. AARP Andrus Foundation Final Report. State College, PA: Pennsylvania State University.

Critical Thinking

1. What effect did the percent of the population aged 65 and older have on city governments' willingness to make beneficial community changes for older persons?

2. What effect did the percent of a community's population with disabilities have on city government's willingness to make beneficial changes for older persons?

3. The growing interest in adapting the physical environment of communities to better meet the needs of older adults is a reaction to what factors?

Create Central

www.mhhe.com/createcentral

Internet References

American Association of Homes and Services for the Aging
www.aahsa.org

Center for Demographic Studies
http://cds.duke.edu

Guide to Retirement Living
www.retirement-living.com

The United States Department of Housing and Urban Development
www.hud.gov

Acknowledgments—The author would like to thank Andrew Scharlach, Michael Austin, Fred Collignon, Ruth Dunkle, Letha Chadiha, and two anonymous reviewers for valuable feedback on earlier drafts of this article.

Funding—U.S. Department of Housing and Urban Development's Doctoral Dissertation Research Grant; Society for Social Work Research; Hartford Doctoral Fellows Program; National Institute on Aging (T32-AG000117).

From *The Gerontologist,* June 2012, pp. 345–356. Copyright © 2012 by Gerontological Society of America. Reprinted by permission of Oxford University Press via Rightslink.

Article Prepared by: Elaina F. Osterbur, *Saint Louis University*

The Real Social Network

More than a neighborhood, a village gives older people a better chance to stay in their own home longer.

MARTHA THOMAS

Learning Outcomes

After reading this article, you will be able to:

- Discuss the various services people living in a village can receive from other village members or as part of their village services provided routinely and paid for by service fees.

- Explain how Keystone's health services are better able to coordinate the services for their village patients.

On a bitterly cold morning a few years ago, Eleanor McQueen awoke to what sounded like artillery fire: the ice-covered branches of trees cracking in the wind. A winter storm had knocked out the power in the rural New Hampshire home that Eleanor shared with her husband, Jim. "No heat, no water. Nada," Eleanor recalls.

The outage lasted for nine days; the couple, both 82 at the time, weathered the ordeal in isolation with the help of a camp stove. Their three grown kids were spread out in three different states, and the McQueens weren't very close to their immediate neighbors. "We needed someone to see if we were dead or alive," Eleanor says.

But the McQueens were alone, and it scared them. Maybe, they admitted, it was time to think about leaving their home of 40 years.

Luckily, last year the McQueens found a way to stay. They joined Monadnock at Home, a membership organization for older residents of several small towns near Mount Monadnock, New Hampshire. The group is part of the so-called village movement, which links neighbors together to help one another remain in the homes they love as they grow older.

The concept began in Boston's Beacon Hill neighborhood in 2001, when a group of residents founded a nonprofit called Beacon Hill Village to ease access to the services that often force older Americans to give up their homes and move to a retirement community. More than 56 villages now exist in the United States,

with another 120 or so in development, according to the Village to Village (VtV) Network, a group launched in 2010 that provides assistance to new villages and tracks their growth nationwide.

It works like this: Members pay an annual fee (the average is about $600) in return for services such as transportation, yard work, and bookkeeping. The village itself usually has only one or two paid employees, and most do not provide services directly. Instead, the village serves as a liaison—some even use the word concierge. The help comes from other able-bodied village members, younger neighbors, or youth groups doing community service. Villages also provide lists of approved home-maintenance contractors, many of whom offer discounts to members. By relying on this mix of paid and volunteer help, members hope to cobble together a menu of assistance similar to what they would receive at a retirement community, but without uprooting their household.

The earliest villages, like Beacon Hill, were founded in relatively affluent urban areas, though new villages are now sprouting in suburbs and smaller rural communities, and organizers are adapting Beacon Hill's model to fit economically and ethnically diverse communities. Each is united by a common goal: a determination to age in place. A recent AARP survey found 86 percent of respondents 45 and older plan to stay in their current residence as long as possible. "And as people get older, that percentage increases," says Elinor Ginzler, AARP expert on livable communities.

In its own quiet way, the village movement represents a radical rejection of the postwar American ideal of aging, in which retirees discard homes and careers for lives of leisure amid people their own age. That's the life Eleanor and Jim McQueen turned their backs on when they joined Monadnock at Home.

"To dump 40 years of building a home to move into a condominium doesn't appeal to me at all," Jim says. "The idea of Monadnock at Home is, I won't have to."

You could call it the lightbulb moment—literally: A bulb burns out in that hard-to-reach spot at the top of the stairs, and that's when you realize you're dependent on others for the simplest of household chores. "It's horrible," says Candace Baldwin, codirector of the VtV Network. "I've heard so many stories

What a Village Takes

Want to organize a village of your own? The Village to Village (VtV) Network offers information on helping villages get started. Membership benefits include tools and resources developed by other villages, a peer-to-peer mentoring program, and monthly webinars and discussion forums.

- To find out if a village exists in your region, the VtV website has a searchable online map of all U.S. villages now open or in development.
- The creators of Boston's Beacon Hill Village have written a book on starting a village: *The Village Concept: A Founder's Manual* is a how-to guide that provides tips on fund-raising, marketing, and organizational strategies.
- Existing resources can make your neighborhood more "villagelike," says Candace Baldwin, codirector of the VtV Network. The best place to start is your local agency on aging. The U.S. Department of Health and Human Services offers a searchable index of these services.—M.T.

from people who say they can't get on a ladder and change a lightbulb, so they have to move to a nursing home. A lightbulb can be a disaster."

Especially when the homeowner won't ask for help. Joining a village can ease the resistance, says Christabel Cheung, director of the San Francisco Village. Many members are drawn by the opportunity to give aid as well as receive it. "A lot of people initially get involved because they're active and want to do something," she says. "Then they feel better about asking for help when they need it."

Last winter Blanche and Rudy Hirsch needed that help. The couple, 80 and 82, live in a three-story brick town house in Washington, D.C.; they pay $800 per year in dues to Capitol Hill Village (CHV). During the blizzard-filled February of 2010, Rudy was in the hospital for hip surgery and Blanche stayed with nearby friends as the snow piled up. On the day Rudy came home, Blanche recalls, the driver warned that if their walkways weren't clear "he'd turn around and go back to the hospital." She called CHV executive director Gail Kohn, who summoned the village's volunteer snow brigade. A pair of young architects who lived nearby were quickly dispatched with shovels.

The Hirsches have discussed moving; they've postponed the decision by installing lifts so Rudy can get up and down the stairs. Remembering her visits to a family member who lived in a retirement home, Blanche shudders: "Everyone was so old. It's depressing."

Avoiding "old-age ghettos," says Kohn, is a major draw for villagers. She touts the intergenerational quality of Capitol Hill, full of "people in their 20s and people in their 80s," and CHV organizes a handful of events geared toward people of different ages. One program brings high school freshmen and village members together in the neighborhood's public library, where the kids offer informal computer tutoring to the older folks.

Such social-network building is a natural outgrowth of village life. Indeed, Beacon Hill Village was founded on the idea of forging stronger bonds among members. "There was a program committee in existence before the village even opened its doors," says Stephen Roop, president of the Beacon Hill Village board. "Most of my friends on Beacon Hill I know through the village."

One fall evening in Chicago, Lincoln Park Village members gathered at a neighborhood church for a potluck supper. A group of about 80—village members and college students who volunteer as community service—nibbled sushi and sipped Malbec wine as they chatted with Robert Falls, artistic director of Chicago's Goodman Theatre.

Lincoln Park Village's executive director, Dianne Campbell, 61, doesn't have a background in social work or gerontology; her experience is in fund-raising for charter schools and museums, and she lives in Lincoln Park. To village member Warner Saunders, 76, that's a big plus. "She doesn't see us as elderly clients who need her help," says Saunders, a longtime news anchor for Chicago's NBC affiliate, WMAQ-TV. "I see Dianne as a friend. If she were a social worker, and I viewed my relationship with her as that of a patient, I would probably resent that."

For Saunders, Lincoln Park Village makes his quality of life a lot better. He recently had knee and hip surgeries, and his family—he lives with his wife and sister-in-law—relies on the village for transportation and help in finding contractors. "I'd call the village the best bargain in town," he says.

Others, however, might balk at annual dues that can approach $1,000 for services that might not be needed yet. To expand membership, many villages offer discounts for low-income households.

At 93, Elvina Moen is Lincoln Park Village's oldest, as well as its first "member-plus," or subsidized, resident. She lives in a one-room apartment in an 11-story Chicago Housing Authority building within Lincoln Park. The handful of member-plus residents pay annual dues of $100 and in return receive $200 in credit each year for discounted services from the village's list of vetted providers. Since joining, Moen has enlisted the village to help paint her apartment and install ceiling fans.

But beyond home improvements, Moen doesn't ask a lot from the village yet—she's already created her own village, of a sort. When she cracked her pelvis three years ago, members of her church brought her meals until she got back on her feet; she pays a neighbor to help clean her apartment. Her community-aided self-reliance proves that intergenerational ties and strong social networks help everyone, not just the privileged, age with dignity.

Social scientists call this social capital, and many argue that we don't have enough of it. What the village movement offers is a new way to engineer an old-fashioned kind of connection. "As recently as 100 years ago most everyone lived in a village setting," says Jay Walljasper, author of *All That We Share: A Field Guide to the Commons*, a book about how cooperative movements foster a more livable society. "If you take a few steps back and ask what a village is, you'll realize it's a place where you have face-to-face encounters." He compares the village movement to the local-food movement, which also started with affluent urbanites. Think of a village as a kind of "artisanal retirement," a modern reinterpretation of an older, more enlightened way of life. And just as there's nothing quite like homegrown tomatoes, "there's no replacement for the direct connection with people who live near you," Walljasper says.

Strong, intergenerational communities—just like healthy meals—are good for everyone. Bernice Hutchinson is director of Dupont Circle Village in Washington, D.C., which serves a diverse neighborhood. Many members are well-off; some are getting by on Medicaid. "But at the end of the day," says Hutchinson, "what everyone wants is connectedness."

Connectedness alone, of course, can't ensure healthy aging. What happens next—when villagers' needs grow beyond help with grocery shopping or the name of a reliable plumber?

To meet the growing health demands of members, villages boast a range of wellness services, and many have affiliations with health care institutions. Capitol Hill Village, for example, has a partnership with Washington Hospital Center's Medical House Call Program, which provides at-home primary care visits for elderly patients.

A new village—Pennsylvania's Crozer-Keystone Village—flips the grassroots Beacon Hill model: It's the first village to originate in a health care institution. Barbara Alexis Looby, who oversees the village, works for Keystone, which has five hospitals in the southeastern part of the state. A monthly fee gives members access to a "village navigator," who schedules medical appointments and day-to-day logistics like errands. Members also get discounts on Keystone's health services. Because the village and the hospital system are aligned, says Looby, "the boundaries are flexible. You care for people when they come to the hospital, and you are in a position to coordinate their care when they leave." Keystone hopes this integration will lead to fewer ER visits and hospital readmissions.

How long can a village keep you safe at home? It depends. But Candace Baldwin, of VtV, says that the trust factor between members and the village can help family members and caregivers make choices and find services.

Michal Brown lives about 30 miles outside Chicago, where her 89-year-old mother, Mary Haughey, has lived in a Lincoln Park apartment for more than 20 years. She worries about her mom, who has symptoms of dementia. Brown saw a flyer about Lincoln Park Village in a pharmacy and immediately signed her mother up. Through the village, Brown enrolled her mom in tai chi classes and asked a village member to accompany her as a buddy.

Just before Christmas, Haughey became dizzy at her tai chi class. With her buddy's help, she made it to the hospital, where doctors discovered a blood clot in her lung. Without the village, Brown is convinced, her mother might not have survived.

Through the village, Brown has also learned about counseling services at a local hospital to help plan her mother's next steps. "We can add services bit by bit, whether it's medication management or home health care. The village knows how to get those services."

Nobody knows what Mary Haughey's future holds, but the village has given her options. And it has given her daughter hope that she can delay moving her mother to a nursing home. For now, it helps knowing that her mother is safe, and still in her own apartment, in her own neighborhood.

Critical Thinking

1. In terms of services needed by older persons, what are the advantages of joining and living in a village neighborhood?

2. How does the village movement hope to provide residents a menu of assistance similar to what they would receive in a retirement community?

3. What is the common goal of each village community?

Create Central

www.mhhe.com/createcentral

Internet References

American Association of Homes and Services for the Aging
www.aahsa.org

Center for Demographic Studies
http://cds.duke.edu

Guide to Retirement Living
www.retirement-living.com

The United States Department of Housing and Urban Development
www.hud.gov

MARTHA THOMAS is a Baltimore-based freelance writer.

Unit 8

UNIT

Prepared by: Elaina F. Osterbur, *Saint Louis University*

Social Policies, Programs, and Services for Older Americans

It is a political reality that older Americans will be able to obtain needed assistance from governmental programs only if they are perceived as politically powerful. Political involvement can range from holding and expressing political opinions, voting in elections, participating in voluntary associations to help elect a candidate or party, and holding political office.

Research indicates that older people are just as likely as any other age group to hold political opinions, are more likely than younger people to vote in an election, are about equally divided between Democrats and Republicans, and are more likely than young people to hold political office. Older people, however, have shown little inclination to vote as a bloc on issues affecting their welfare despite encouragement to do so by senior activists, such as Maggie Kuhn and the leaders of the Gray Panthers. Gerontologists have observed that a major factor contributing to the increased push for government services for elderly individuals has been the publicity about their plight generated by such groups as the National Council of Senior Citizens and AARP. The desire of adult children to shift the financial burden of aged parents from themselves onto the government has further contributed to the demand for services for people who are elderly. The resulting widespread support for such programs has almost guaranteed their passage in Congress.

Now, for the first time, groups that oppose increases in spending for services for older Americans are emerging. Requesting generational equity, some politically active groups argue that the federal government is spending so much on older Americans that it is depriving younger age groups of needed services.

The articles in this unit raise a number of problems and issues that result from an ever-larger number and percentage of the population living to age 65 and older.

Article

Prepared by: Elaina F. Osterbur, *Saint Louis University*

End-of-Life Care in the United States: Current Reality and Future Promise: A Policy Review

"Improving end-of-life care should be a national priority, not just from a cost perspective, but from a quality perspective, because we can do much better" (Carlson, 2010, p.17).

Lisa A. Giovanni

Learning Outcomes

After reading this article, you will be able to:

- Identify solutions to end-of-life care as outlined in the article.

- Discuss how these solutions affect the quality of life of patients.

- Discuss the impact of these solutions on the provisions set forth in the Patient Protection and Affordable Care Act.

Caring for individuals at the end of their life has been a topic of conversation for decades, from political, health policy, and quality perspectives. Issues exist in multiple well-defined areas that include access to and disparities in provision of end-of-life care, problems and confusion with financing the care, inadequacies when it comes to professionals' educational preparation related to end-of-life conversations, and the quality of end-of-life care. Additionally, conversations about end-of-life care would not be complete without acknowledging the ethical and legal issues and debate that surround this topic. The purpose of this article is to examine the current reality of end-of-life care and determine what portions of current health care reform will affect end-of-life care practices and policy in the United States. Additionally, hospice, palliative care, and nursing's involvement in end-of-life care and reform are discussed. Research of current literature was conducted and concludes with a discussion of findings to support the author's personal viewpoint that current health care policy fails to recognize and endorse effective reform for end-of-life care.

Hospice and Palliative Care

One solution to end-of-life care, the hospice movement, has seen incredible growth in the United States over the past several decades. It has been over 40 years since hospice care began in the United States. Since that time, "hospice has grown into a business that served over 1 million Medicare beneficiaries, from more than 3,300 providers in 2008, according to the Medicare Payment Advisory Commission" (Zigmond, 2010, p. 6). The history of hospice in the United States dates back to 1963, when Florence Wald, then the dean of the school of nursing at Yale University, invited Dr. Cicely Saunders from London to give a series of lectures on hospice care. "Dr. Cicely Saunders, the matriarch of the worldwide hospice movement, clearly had an impact as shortly after her visit and lecture series, the first hospice in the United States opened in Branford, Connecticut, in 1973" (Connor, 2007, p. 90). Today, hospice focuses on, "caring, not curing and, in most cases: care is provided in a patient's home. Care can also be provided in freestanding hospice centers, hospitals, and nursing homes or other long-term care facilities. Hospice services, which include care management for all aspects of the patient, include family support as well" (National Hospice and Palliative Care Organization [NHPCO], 2011a, ¶ 2)

Palliative care is defined by the World Health Organization (WHO) as, "an approach that improves quality of life for patients and their families facing the problems associated with life-threatening illness, through the prevention and relief of suffering by means of early identification and impeccable assessment and treatment of problems, including physical, psychosocial, and spiritual" (WHO, 2011). NHPCO (2011a) also adds, "palliative care extends the principles of hospice care to a broader population that could benefit from receiving this type of care earlier in their disease process. Palliative care, ideally, would segue into hospice care as the illness progressed" (¶ 3). Certainly both palliative care and hospice have a rightful place and play extremely important roles in end-of-life care. Hospice and palliative care programs exist across the United States, both in for-profit and not-for-profit sectors, as well as in stand-alone organizations or as components of larger health care models. "Palliative care programs are rapidly becoming the norm in American hospitals, with more than 70% of large (more than 200 bed) hospitals reporting the presence of a program in the American Hospital Association's 2006 annual hospital survey" (Weissman, Meier, & Spragens, 2008, p. 1294).

A policy discussion would not be complete or fair without mention of the ways that the hospice and palliative care movements have improved end-of-life care for patients and their families. There is a growing understanding of hospice and palliative care among most people in society, as the realization that hospice is not a place but rather a concept gains momentum, and patients opt for palliative care services earlier in their illness. We must not fail to acknowledge the great work accomplished by hospice and palliative care professionals. This effort must continue to expand in order to reduce access disparities across the nation. "The challenge for hospice and palliative care providers can be boiled down to achieving unfettered access to quality palliative care for all who need it" (Connor, 2007, p. 98).

Problems

While use and advantages of palliative care and hospice are gaining momentum at unprecedented speed, there remains disparity in access geographically. In addition to general access disparities, the type of care patients receive at the end of their life varies according to where they live and what acute care facility they happen to be a patient in. In 2001, Raphael, Ahrens, and Fowler discussed the likelihood of dying in a hospital in the United States as depending on, not patient preference, but rather on number of hospital beds, and physician per patient statistics, which varied greatly across the nation. Medicare beneficiaries in some western and northwestern states had a less than a 20% chance of dying in a hospital, while chances for those in southern and eastern states could be greater than 50% (Raphael et al., 2001).

Research supports the fact this issue is still apparent; geography continues to play a role in end-of-life care today. McKinney (2010) points out that for patients with advanced cancer, the likelihood they will spend their last days in a hospital intensive care unit depends largely on where they live, and which hospital they seek care in. Unfortunately, Goodman and colleagues (2010) found little evidence that treatments are aligned with patient wishes. The report, which examined 235,821 Medicare patients with advanced cancer who died between the years of 2003–2007, found significant variations in end-of-life care from region to region. "Roughly 29% of patients died in a hospital, and that number reached as high as 46.7% in the borough of Manhattan in New York, to as low as 17.8% in Cincinnati, Ohio and 7% in Mason City, Iowa" (McKinney, 2010, p. 6).

Not only is there disparity in whether patients go to and utilize acute care services, but also, once there, there is disparity in what types of care they receive in those acute care organizations. Extensive variation was found in length of stay, number of physician visits, percentage of patients with 10 or more physicians, and transfers to hospice services. Wennberg and associates (2004) found striking variation in all categories.

Medicare, the largest health plan in the United States, is highly influential in end-of-life care because of the large number of beneficiaries who die each year. Numbers vary depending on the source, but according to the Medicare Payment Advisory Commission (MedPAC), "about a quarter of the total Medicare budget is spent on services for beneficiaries in their last year of life, and 40% of that is in the last 30 days of their life" (Raphael, 2001, p. 458). Multiple studies declare that of the total outlay for all Medicare costs, 30%–40% occur in the last year of life for beneficiaries (Hogan, Lunney, Gabel, & Lynn, 2001; Raphael et al., 2001). One key factor involving end-of-life care and financing includes increased numbers of older Americans, which by 2050 is predicted to reach 72.2 million (Raphael et al., 2001). By that time it is also estimated that some 27 million people, most of whom will have multiple chronic diseases, will also need some type of long-term care services (Caffrey, Sengupta, Moss, Harris-Kojetin, & Valverde, 2011).

Chronic disease is an important item to review when discussing end-of-life care, because hospice patients are no longer predominately cancer patients, but also now have diagnoses that include multiple chronic conditions. According to the National Health Statistics Report, in recent years, hospice has become increasingly used by people with noncancerous diagnosis, the rate of which has increased from 25.3% in 2000 to 57.2% in 2007 (Caffrey et al., 2011). Another factor that cannot be overlooked is that many of these future older Americans will originate from ethnic and racial minority groups; therefore, end-of-life care and reform efforts must include an assessment and understanding of the care needs for these culturally diverse groups. Since a large payer of hospice services is Medicare, there is no doubt that political debate exists when discussions about payment for this care are undertaken. However, one thing is certain, discussions regarding quality of care, health policy, and disparity must begin to occur and cannot be dismissed due to the fact these conversations are difficult to have from an ethical and legal perspective. Components of these conversations must include the cost of end-of-life care in acute settings and possible hospice and palliative care contributions as solutions to decrease those costs.

Additional problems exist related to ill-defined quality standards, and decreased numbers of professionals working in hospice or palliative care across geographical pockets, especially in rural areas of the United States. End-of-life care issues remain unsolved as a result of an inability of a nation and its people, including political leaders, to discuss what is inevitable for all—mortality. End-of-life ethical and political policy conversations are difficult and, at times, avoided. There is unwillingness or uneasiness at best, to approach this subject head on.

The Patient Protection and Affordable Care Act

This national avoidance became blatantly evident when misconceptions from a portion of the 2010 Patient Protection and Affordable Care Act (PPACA) that would have enabled physicians to be reimbursed for having advanced care planning discussions with patients, was publicized as something that would result in a "death panel" that would "ration healthcare care in the United States" (Brody, 2011). As a result, the portion of the PPACA dealing with advanced planning conversations was deleted from the final version of the policy. Unfortunately, the true intent of this portion of the proposed act was not realized by the public or policymakers, since it was dismissed too rapidly for consideration. In the end, as with multiple other facets of end-of-life care, the fallout for not addressing this issue results in financial impact to the nation, as well as a quality of life impact for the individuals and families who require end-of-life care for advanced illness in the United States.

Ironically virtually no portion of the PPACA deals with reform, reimbursement, or policy changes related to end-of-life care. There are minor sections of the PPACA that can have an effect on end-of-life care, but no portion relates directly to this vital and hugely important aspect of American health care. Unfortunately, the result is the unique needs of the terminally ill remain poorly addressed in the United States health care system. Perhaps one of the most concerning concepts when it comes to end-of-life care is the fact that so often the care provided is not necessarily the care the patient and family have elected, wanted, or even understood.

Advance Directives

The SUPPORT study, which was funded by the Robert Wood Johnson Foundation and enrolled patients over a 5-year period, was conducted to analyze decision making in patients near the end of life. Other goals of the study included gaining an understanding of communication about end-of-life interactions between patients, their families, nurses, and physicians. Results indicated that a significant number of critically ill patients did not want aggressive life-prolonging care (Celso, & Meenrajan, 2010; Fitzsimmons, Shively, & Verderber, 1995; Smith et al., 2003). Unfortunately, due to multiple reasons, including delayed timeliness in executing advance care planning until patients are terminal and out-of-date or unavailable documents (Tilden et al., 2010), issues remain involving patients advocating for themselves, families advocating for their loved ones, and health care professionals providing care that may or may not be consistent with patient preference. Perhaps the best reason for meaningful discussion and policy reform to occur is a genuine concern for a better patient experience when it comes to end-of-life care. We cannot dismiss the Triple Aim of the Institute for Health Care Improvement, which dictates the pursuit of an improved patient experience, improved health of the population at large, and reduced per capita costs (Berwick, Nolan, & Whittington, 2008). To that end, the United States simply cannot overlook all that hospice, palliative care, and advance directives

have to offer to individuals and families who face serious, life-threatening advanced illness issues.

Expert Opinion

According to NHPCO, a non-profit organization representing over 2,900 hospices in the United States, none of the PPACA that deals with accountable care organizations (ACO) mentions hospice or palliative care programs. ACOs are organizations that will have local accountability for managing populations of people throughout a continuum of lifetime care. ACOs will need to share reimbursement and determine cost-sharing strategies for all providers involved. They will also be required to care for a minimum of 5,000 enrollees and will be paid on a pre-defined outcomes measure basis. NHPCO was so dismayed that there was no mention of end-of-life care in the final ACO regulations that they communicated this fact to the Center for Medicare & Medicaid Services (CMS). In a letter dated June 6, 2011 to Dr. Donald Berwick, CMS administrator, NHPCO President and CEO J. Donald Schumacher stated, "many dying patients in institutions have unmet needs for symptom management, emotional support and being treated with respect." He went on to say, that "it is essential that hospice and palliative care organizations be partners in ACO's in order to contribute to the success of these new care models, and care for patients across the continuum of their life-time" (NHPCO, 2011b).

The American Hospital Association (AHA) recommends multiple items that should be a focus of national quality efforts; one of those recommendations is for greater self-determination related to end-of-life care (Carlson, 2010). The AHA endorses personal tools that allow patients and families to record written advance health care directives, name legally binding health care powers of attorney, and craft physician orders for life sustaining treatment. Providing the right care to the right patient at the right time defines quality. The AHA explains that the right care includes what science suggests would have the best outcomes for the patient, but also considers the patient's wishes about what's important to them (Carlson, 2010).

The Critical Role of Nursing

The Institute of Medicine (2010) in *The Future of Nursing* report calls for the need to transform nursing education, stating that nurses are critical to the success of health care reform, and that nurses need to take their rightful place in leadership endeavors, achieve higher levels of education, practice to the fullest of their ability, and be full partners with other health care professionals.

Multiple studies discuss educational deficiencies and lack of comfort levels that nurses have when it comes to conducting follow up or clarification discussions with patients about end-of-life care or treatment options (Malloy, Virani, Kelly, & Munvevar, 2010; Reinke, et al., 2010; Wittenburg-Lyles, Goldsmith, & Ragan, 2011). Changes in nursing education must occur in order to prepare professional nurses to become advocates and experts in end-of-life care. When assessing the adequacy of skill of health care professionals to initiate and conduct end-of-life conversations there are noted voids and problems.

Reinke and colleagues (2010) identified several skill sets that nurses felt were important but underutilized in end-of-life care conversations. They concluded end-of-life care interventions should address not only system and policy changes, but also improvements in individual nurse's communication skills regarding end-of-life conversations (Reinke et al., 2010). "Nurses can play a pivotal role in patient and family illness and care awareness by facilitating palliative care communication and supporting the conceptual shift to early palliative care" (Wittenberg-Lyles et al., 2011, p. 305). The communication problem exists for physicians as well. Part of this problem originates from poor preparation of professionals in their primary and early health care education programs. While many programs are adapting methods to include didactic training programs, the real experience comes from actual conversations, which of course, is not something a text or video can accomplish. Programs like the End of Life Nursing Education Consortium and continued efforts in physician mentoring and role modeling in end-of-life care conversations will prove very beneficial (Wittenberg-Lyles et al., 2011).

The development and spread of palliative care efforts and hospice education for professionals and the general public will continue to have an impact on growth and acceptance of end-of-life conversations. It is also important for individual professionals, as well as the organizations they work within, to continue to foster and participate in opportunities and experiences that will enhance ability and comfort levels regarding end-of-life conversations. This effort will be of utmost importance for not only physicians, but also for nurses.

"Communication is the cornerstone of basic nursing practice and a fundamental skill across all settings of care is to identify the patient's goals of care. As patients and families continue to face serious illness, transition to palliative care, and make difficult decisions, nurses will play a critical role and remain as the predominant professional at the bedside" (Malloy et al., 2010, p. 172). Physicians most often will champion the initial conversation with patients and families, but nurses have a responsibility and professional ethic to be present for the patient and family after initial conversations takes place. "Nurses accompany patients on their journeys; through such ongoing and intimate encounters, they support patients in confronting the weariness of living and dying" (Ferrell & Coyle, 2008, p. 247). Health care professionals, including nurses, must be vigilant about understanding their communication style and engaging in educational opportunities that enhance their ability to conduct effective end-of-life conversations with patients and families.

Future Promise and Possible Obstacles

The Patient Self-Determination Act of 1991 required all Medicare participating organizations notify patients of their rights to complete an advance directive for health treatments (American Nurses Association, 1991). The overall goal of advance directives is to allow patients to retain control over the life-prolonging treatments they receive. Current health policy sometimes fails patients in this respect, as families can argue patient's choices may change over time, or there can be delays in producing existing documents, or failures in executing the documents all together. While the intent of the federal mandate was well intentioned, it resulted in continued confusion and sporadic compliance by patients and families in completion of advance directives.

At approximately the same time as the passage of the federal Patient Self-Determination Act, another paradigm in advance care planning was initiated that had a goal of turning patient treatment preferences and advance directives into medical orders. The Oregon state legislature introduced a new program to improve adherence to patients' wishes for end-of-life care. The Patient Order for Life Sustaining Care (POLST) paradigm was created to provide a mechanism to communicate patient preference for end-of-life care treatment across care settings. The POLST document turns patient treatment preferences into medical orders, with an overall goal of ensuring that wishes for treatment are honored. "The National Quality Forum and other experts have recommended nationwide implementation of the POLST paradigm" (Hickman, Sabatino, Moss, & Nester, 2008, p. 120).

Some barriers to POLST use do exist. "The most potentially problematic barriers are detailed statutory specifications for out of hospital do-not-resuscitate orders in some states. Other potential barriers include limitations on the authority to forgo life-sustaining treatments in 23 states, medical conditions in 15 states, and witnessing requirements for out of hospital do not resuscitate orders in 12 states" (Hickman et al., 2008, p. 119). Multiple studies regarding use of POLST across care settings have been conducted to determine usefulness in understanding and following patient wishes. Results of studies yield a strong tie between use of POLST forms and adherence to patients' self-determined wishes across care settings (Hickman et al., 2010; Hickman et al., 2009; Meyers, 2004; Schmidt, Hickman, Tolle, & Brooks, 2004). Studies also revealed that patients with POLST medical orders were less likely to receive unwanted care (Hickman et al., 2010; Tilden, Nelson, Dunn, Donius, & Tolle, 2000). Multiple research studies confirm that POLST can have a positive impact on the ability of an individual to self-determine his or her end-of-life preferences.

Access to end-of-life care services is another problem. Access includes awareness of palliative and hospice services, payment and financial coverage for those benefits, and acceptance of benefits from a cultural or religious perspective. Goldsmith, Dietrich, Qingling, and Morrison (2008) concluded that significant disparities in public and educational access to hospital palliative care services exist. "Hospice care is a beneficial, yet underutilized service in advanced dementia. Hospice professionals cite prognostication as the main hindrance to enrolling patients with dementia into hospice" (Mitchell et al., 2012, p. 45).

Current reform and health policy have affected hospice organizations in several ways, the largest of which is decreases in reimbursement related to cuts from Medicare, the largest payer of hospice services. There is also increased scrutiny and regulatory efforts in the form of an additional recertification requirement of face-to-face meetings between patient and physician or nurse practitioner at time of recertification of care, which became effective January 1, 2010 (Morrow, 2010). In an industry with narrow profit margins, reimbursement reductions could worsen the already existing access problems.

Other items involving end-of-life care are present in the historic Patient Protection and Affordable Care Act. Hidden deep and not well publicized are at least two provisions that may have an impact on end-of-life care. They both relate to hospice. One section of the PPACA amends current law to eliminate the requirement for children to elect curative versus hospice care through Medicaid and CHIP programs. A second area deals with adults, "in section 3140, the PPACA authorizes a three year long Medicare Hospice Concurrent Care demonstration project involving a study to determine whether patients benefit when Medicare authorizes payment for receipt of concurrent curative treatment and hospice care" (Cerminara, 2011). The project, which does not have a start date, will begin as soon as the Secretary of Health and Human Services establishes parameters and outcome measurements, and will involve 15 hospice programs nationwide. Astonishingly, other than the previously mentioned items, there are no other portions of the PPACA that directly relate to end of life care. Once more people understand what hospice and palliative care can provide related to quality of life and a peaceful dying process, a major culture shift can begin to occur. The result would be an environment where end-of-life conversations occur prior to a patient's actual end of life. Sometimes awareness occurs because we either experience it ourselves or know someone who has experienced caring for a loved one at the end of his or her life. Despite explosive political debate, the answer really does involve a conversation.

The American Academy of Hospice and Palliative Medicine has multiple recommendations for health care reform. One of those recommendations refers to advance directives and specifically the POLST. The recommendation includes an endorsement to provide reimbursement for physician consultations that would determine goals for medical care. Nothing makes more sense, and seems farther away from death panels than prudent, frank, and transparent conversations about an individual's wishes.

The experience or wishes of the patients cannot be overlooked, especially in end-of-life care when a cure cannot be offered to patients for whatever they are suffering from. From an ethical perspective, shouldn't that be required to be conveyed? Should end-of-life care be recognized as an ethical obligation of health care providers and organizations, and what exactly does that mean? Patients must have a say in what is important to them and ultimately decide their personal wishes. Patients need to determine what defines high-quality dying for them, and decide on how they want to manage their end of life, as it relates to death (Cramer, 2010; Howell & Brazil, 2005).

Conclusion

Paying attention to health care policy, or lack thereof, or the conflicted policy Catch-22s, when it comes to end of life care is a critical responsibility of all health care professionals. In discussing the type and magnitude of changes necessary to implement cost-effective, ethically considerate, culturally acceptable changes in end-of-life care, there will no doubt continue to be difficult and painful conversations, both on individual and political fronts. But, the conversations must occur, and cannot be ignored simply because they are difficult to have. Perhaps, most importantly, the political community, who are often those who write the policy that needs to be executed, must recognize that local, organizational, and state efforts cannot be delayed related to lack of movement on a federal front. There are many examples of great work being done with regard to end-of-life care across America that have nothing to with policy or federal government intervention, and these efforts must increase and continue.

All health care professionals must realize the power they have on two levels, as individuals and as a profession, when it comes to end-of-life reform and improvement efforts. Health care professionals have an ethical responsibility to assist patients to achieve the care and life they want for their last days, and in many cases that may involve assisting them to die with dignity in a surrounding of their choice, and embraced by those they have loved for a lifetime. Hopefully, this article has created a heightened sense of awareness for health care professionals, especially nurses, to pay attention to reform efforts in the United States. Nurses, physicians, and other health care professionals have the ability, knowledge, and power to help shape new regulations and laws when it comes to end-of-life care. Although it is 2012, the insight of Ira Byock, a leading palliative care physician and long-time public advocate for improving end-of-life care, still holds true today. He summarized the current state of end-of-life care and points the way to where we must go by saying:

> A tidal wave of social change is headed our way. For the first time in human history, in the third millennium, there will be more old people than young people on the planet. In addition to the graying of the population, there will be more physical distance between families, smaller families, fewer caregivers, more chronic illness, and increased technological advances. These trends are all converging to create the perfect storm; a social tsunami of care giving that threatens to overwhelm our children's generation and us. We must rise to the challenges and build a model of healthcare that will determine the quality of care we receive tomorrow (2004, pp. 214–215).

Plan for Action

Unless we take personal, professional, and political action today, we will not be able to afford to die with dignity in the future. For multiple reasons that include an aging population, escalating health care spending, and an approach to end-of-life care that often does not conform to the wishes of patients, we cannot delay action. We need to have honest and transparent advance care planning conversations with our families and our physicians. We need to become comfortable talking about dying with those we love and interact with the most, in order to become comfortable talking about end-of-life care publically. All health care professionals should strive to create an environment for patients where the philosophy of palliative care and hospice is understood. Goals of this environment would include increased knowledge about hospice and palliative care, greater symptom control for patients with end-stage diseases, improved advance care planning, better quality of life, and ultimately less money spent on achieving better outcomes for patients facing end-of-life illness and disease.

Interactions between politicians and health care professionals, especially those involved in hospice and palliative care, must accelerate. Professionals in these fields must continue strong advocacy efforts to let the political world know what they do, and what promise their care offers related to improved quality of life and decreased overall spending. Such interactions should include tours of facilities, visits with patients and families, and letters and phone calls to politicians on specific issues that are important to the hospice and palliative care industry. These action items would cost very little, and perhaps only result in an investment of time for those involved.

Opportunities to develop advance care directives are often missed. To that end, we must revisit Medicare reimbursement for physicians participating in voluntary advanced care planning consultations, and end discussions surrounding "death panels" for good. Physicians often have a clear understanding of what defines quality of life for their patients, and this clear understanding, which takes time to develop, involves multiple discussions and explanations that physicians need and want to participate in with their patients. The positive end result would be assurance patients' wishes are understood, documented, and ultimately attainable. While health care professionals can lead the effort aimed at better advanced care planning, politicians play a vital role in assuring that policy makes sense and is not confusing to those who need it. It is simply not prudent of such a smart nation to refuse to pay physicians for this extremely important part of health care planning.

POLST legislation must continue to accelerate and expand to assure acceptance of medical orders that are understood clearly and cross all care continuums in every state. It seems possible that if several states can achieve success in overcoming legal barriers related to POLST implementation, all states can achieve it. The important and expanding work of the POLST paradigm must continue. It is incumbent upon lawmakers to create global policies that enable POLST to be available to those who critically needed it in order to enhance smoother care transitions between providers, and decrease unwanted treatment by clarifying patient's wishes into actual medical orders. The public needs to understand POLST and for whom it is intended. National television and radio commercials addressing POLST and advance care planning could have positive promotional effects, especially if hosted by the next President of the United States of America. It's too important not to consider.

The Medicare Hospice Concurrent Care Demonstration Project (as defined in the PPACA) needs to begin in order to analyze the effects of concurrent care with relation to quality of life and financial outcomes for both rural and urban demographics in the United States. This concurrent approach will address current hospice and palliative care access issues that relate to patients needing to make curative versus palliative decisions independently. A concurrent approach would also address a second population of patients who need end-of-life care but do not have a terminal cancer diagnosis, such as dementia or congestive heart disease. Demonstration results will need to be analyzed by an authoritative body such as CMS or MedPAC for final determinations as to whether quality of life was enhanced and cost savings were realized. If results are positive, then the Medicare hospice regulations that define eligibility will need to be revised. From a nursing perspective, perhaps less money would be spent treating patients who are guided into hospice care through a strong palliative care effort where symptoms are controlled and care is gradually transferred, rather than in a hurry, with short lengths of stay, as exists today for many hospice patients.

Educational voids related to end-of-life care curriculums for both medical and nursing schools should be addressed. It is important curriculums include practice and mentoring in the area of end-of-life conversations since proficiency in this type of communication will not be realized through didactic teaching alone. Conversations are critical to understanding what each patient wishes for end-of-life care.

Efforts focused on medical fraud, waste, and abuse must continue. Monies recovered for these reasons could be used for end-of-life care initiatives and start-up processes for education and advocacy efforts. While most providers are well intentioned and follow all federal and state regulations, those that do not should continue to be identified and removed from the health care service arena.

Hospice and palliative care professionals must ensure their voice is heard when it comes to creation of policy. Local, state, and grassroots end-of-life programs should continue to be developed, financed, and evaluated. While some financing may come from grants or private sources, states should actively assess what they can do to assist financing any initiative that promotes or enhances end-of-life care.

Simply put, we can begin to control the cost of end-of-life care and afford to die with dignity if we act today. We all have a role to play in securing a better means to our end, and creating a nation where quality of life and personal choice are not only a priority but also a responsibility.

References

American Nurses Association. (1991). *ANA position statement: Nursing and the patient self-determination acts.* Washington, DC: Author.

Berwick, D., Nolan, T., & Whittington, J. (2008). The triple aim: Care, health, and cost. *Health Affairs, 27*(3), 759–769.

Brody, J. (2011, January 17). Keep your voice, even at the end of life. *The New York Times.* Retrieved from www.nytimes .com/2011/01/18/health/18brody.html

Byock, I. (2004). *The four things that matter most.* New York, NY. Free Press.

Caffrey, C., Sengupta, M., Moss, A., Harris-Kojetin, L., & Valverde, R. (2011). Home health care discharged and hospice care patients: United States, 2000–2007. *National Health Statistics Report, 38.*

Carlson, J. (2010). Not finished yet: Coalition wants end of life care to be a priority. *Modern Healthcare, 40*(43), 17–18.

Celso, B., & Meenrajan, S. (2010). The triad that matters: Palliative medicine, code status, and health care costs. *American Journal of Hospice & Palliative Medicine, 27*(6), 398–401.

Cerminara, K. (2011). *Health care reform at the end of life: Giving with one hand but taking with the other.* Retrieved from www.aslme.org/print_article.php?aid=460404&bt=ss

Connor, S. (2007). Development of hospice and palliative care in the United States. *Journal of Death & Dying, 56*(1), 89–99.

Cramer, C. (2010). To live until you die. *Clinical Journal of Oncology Nursing, 14*(1), 53–56.

Ferrell, B., & Coyle, N. (2008). The nature of suffering and the goals of nursing. *Oncology Nursing Forum, 35*(2), 241–247.

Fitzsimmons, L., Shively, M., & Verderber, V. (1995). The nurse's role in end of life treatment discussions: Preliminary report from the SUPPORT project. *Journal of Cardiovascular Nursing, 9*(3), 68–77.

Goldsmith, B., Dietrich, J., Qingling, D., & Morrison, S. (2008). Variability in access to hospital palliative care in the United States. *Journal of Palliative Medicine, 11*(8), 1094–1102.

Goodman, D., Fisher, E., Chang, C., Morden, N., Jacobson, J., Murray, K., & Miesfeldt, S. (2010). Quality of end-of-life cancer care for Medicare beneficiaries, regional and hospital-specific analyses. Retrieved from www.dartmouthatlas.org/downloads/reports/Cancer_report_11_16_10.pdf

Hickman, S.E., Nelson, C.A., Perrin, N.A., Moss, A., Hammes, B.J., & Tolle, S. (2010). A comparison of methods to communicate treatment preferences in nursing facilities: Traditional practices versus the physician orders for life sustaining treatment program. *Journal of American Geriatric Society, 58*(7), 1241–1248.

Hickman, S.E., Nelson, C.A., Moss, A., Hammes, B.J., Terwilliger, A., Jackson, A., & Tolle, S. (2009). Use of the physician orders for life sustaining treatment (POLST) paradigm program in the hospice setting. *Journal of Palliative Medicine, 12*(2), 133–140.

Hickman, S., Sabatino, C., Moss, A., & Nester, J. (2008). The POLST paradigm to improve end of life care: Potential state legal barriers to implementation. *Journal of Law, Medicine and Ethics, 36*(1), 119–124.

Hogan, C., Lunney, J., Gabel, J., & Lynn, J. (2001). Medicare beneficiaries' costs in the last years of life. *Health Affairs, 20*(4), 188–195.

Howell, D., & Brazil, K. (2005). Reaching common ground: A patient-family based conceptual framework of quality end of life care. *Journal of Palliative Care, 21*(1), 19–26.

Institute of Medicine (IOM). (2010.) *IOM report brief: The future of nursing—leading change, advancing health.* Retrieved from www.iom.edu/~/media/Files/Report%20Files/2010The-Future-of-Nursing/Future%20of%20Nursing%202010%20Report%20Brief.pdf

Malloy, P., Virani, R., Kelly, K., & Munvevar, C. (2010). Beyond bad news. *Journal of Hospice and Palliative Care, 12*(3), 166–174.

McKinney, M. (2010). Where you live = how you die. *Modern Healthcare, 40*(47), 6–8.

Meyers, J. (2004). Physician orders for life sustaining treatment form. *Journal of Gerontological Nursing, 30*(9), 37–46.

Mitchell, S., Black, B.S., Ersek, M., Hanson, L.C., Miller, S.C., Sachs, G.A., . . . Morrison, R.S. (2012). Advanced dementia: State of the art and priorities for the next decade. *Annals of Internal Medicine, 156*(1), 45–51.

Morrow, A. (2010). *Obama signs health care reform bill— What's next for hospice?* Retrieved from http://dying.about.com/b/2010/03/23/obama-signs-healthcare-reform-bill-whats-next-forhospice.htm

National Hospice and Palliative Care Organization (NHPCO). (2011a). *Definition of hospice.* Retrieved from www.nhpco.org/i4a/pages/index.cfm?pageid$=$4648

National Hospice and Palliative Care Organization (NHPCO). (2011b). *Letter to CMS administrator, Donald Berwick, MD, CMS administrator.* Retrieved from www.nhpco.org/files/public/regulatory/NHPCO_Comments_on_ACO_Proposed_Rule.pdf

Raphael, C., Ahrens, J., & Fowler, N. (2001). Financing end of life care in the USA. *Journal of The Royal Society of Medicine, 94*(9), 458–461.

Reinke, L.F., Shannon, S.E., Engelberg, R., Dotolo, D., Silvestri, G.A., & Curtis, J.R. (2010). Nurses identification of important yet underutilized end of life care: Skills for patients with life limiting or terminal illnesses. *Journal of Palliative Medicine, 13*(6), 753–759.

Schmidt, T., Hickman, S., Tolle, S., & Brooks, H. (2004). The physician orders for life sustaining treatment program: Oregon emergency medical technicians' practical experiences and attitudes. *Journal of American Geriatric Society, 52*(9), 430–434.

Smith, T.J., Coyne, P., Cassel, B., Penberthy, L., Hopson, A., & Hager, M.A. (2003). A high volume specialist palliative care unit and team may reduce in hospital end of life care costs. *Journal of Palliative Medicine, 6*(5), 699–705.

Tilden, V., Corless, I., Dahlin, C., Ferrell, B., Gibson, R., & Lentz, J. (2010). *Advance care planning as an urgent public health concern.* Washington, DC: American Academy of Nursing.

Tilden, V., Nelson, C., Dunn, P., Donius, M., & Tolle, S. (2000). Nursing perspective on improving communication about nursing home residents preferences for medical treatments at end of life. *Nursing Outlook, 48*(3), 109–115.

Weissman, D., Meier, D., & Spragens, L. (2008). Center to advance palliative care consultation service metrics: Consensus recommendation. *Journal of Palliative Medicine, 11*(10), 1294–1298.

Wennberg, J.E., Fisher, E.S., Stukel, T.A., Skinner, J.S., Sharp, S.M., & Bronner, K.K. (2004). Use of hospitals, physician visits, and hospice care during last six months of life among cohorts loyal to highly respected hospitals in the United States. *British Medical Journal, 328*(7440), 607–610.

Wittenberg-Lyles, E., Goldsmith, J., & Ragan, S. (2011). The shift to early palliative care: A typology of illness journeys and the role of nursing. *Clinical Journal of Oncology Nursing, 15*(3), 304–310.

World Health Organization (WHO). (2011). *WHO definition of palliative care.* Retrieved from www.who.int/cancer/palliative/definition/en/

Zigmond, J. (2010). Hospice hot spot: Gentiva-Odyssey pairing bans on inevitability of aging population. *Modern Healthcare, 40*(22), 6–7.

Additional Reading

American Academy of Nursing. (2010). *Advance care planning as an urgent public health concern*. Washington, DC: Author.

Critical Thinking

1. Based on the investigation in this article, does the evidence support increased quality of life as a result of suggested solutions to end-of-life care?
2. What is the role of advance directives in end-of-life decision making and how do these directives influence treatment?

Create Central

www.mhhe.com/createcentral

Internet References

U.S. Department of Health & Human Services
www.hhs.gov/healthcare/rights

U.S. Centers for Medicare & Medicaid Services: Medicaid.gov
www.medicaid.gov/affordablecareact/affordable-care-act.html

U.S. Centers for Medicare & Medicaid Services: Medicare.gov
www.medicare.gov/about-us/affordable-care-act/affordable-care-act.html

LISA A. GIOVANNI, MSN, RN, is Director of Quality, Visiting Nurse Association, St. Luke's University & Health Network, Bethlehem, PA.

Giovanni, Lisa A. From *Nursing Economic$*, GNE Series, May/June 2012, pp. 127–134. Copyright © 2012 by Jannetti Publications, Inc., East Holly Avenue/Box 56, Pitman, NJ 08071-0056; (856) 256-2300, FAX (856) 589-7463; for a sample copy of the journal, please contact the publisher. Used with permission. www.nursingeconomics.net

Article   Prepared by: Elaina F. Osterbur, *Saint Louis University*

Let's Restore the Middle Class

A. BARRY RAND

Learning Outcomes

After reading this article, you will be able to:

- Cite the reasons the author of "Let's Restore the Middle Class" states were responsible for the middle-class falling into poverty.

- Describe the steps the middle class has taken to cope with the challenge of a declining income.

As you read this column, a "super-committee" of the Congress—six Republicans and six Democrats—is hard at work in Washington. Its job is to find ways to reduce the federal deficit by an additional $1.2 trillion between 2012 and 2021.

This is a worthwhile goal. We need to address our nation's long-term fiscal problems. They affect all of us—Republicans, Democrats, independents and, most important, our children and grandchildren. How we address these problems will determine what their future will be.

That future will not be very bright if they are drowning in the red ink of budget deficits and a soaring national debt. But neither their future nor ours will be very bright if health care is unaffordable, or if there is no opportunity to attain long-term financial security.

That's why this is about much more than reducing the deficit. It's about what kind of country we want to be.

Our primary goal must be to restore prosperity to the middle class. A prosperous middle class has been the chief engine of growth in the economy for more than a century. While middle-class families prospered, low-income families were able to move up the economic ladder—to financial security and a better future.

But over the last generation, more and more of the middle class have fallen into poverty—pulled down by a lack of job opportunities, rising health care costs, inadequate savings and stagnant wages. Nor have incomes grown enough to offset increasing family burdens associated with child care and caring for aging parents.

Middle-class families cope by working longer, delaying retirement, relying on double incomes, reducing their standard of living, relying more on government programs to help them make ends meet and accumulating more debt.

This is taking a serious toll. Most Americans are reaching their 60s with so much debt that they can't afford to retire. In fact, working-age adults now make up 56.7 percent of the poor, defined by the Census Bureau as 2010 income under $22,113 for a family of four. In these challenging times, Social Security, Medicare and Medicaid have become increasingly important for middle-class families—especially for security in retirement.

Cutting these benefits—by increasing Medicare's eligibility age, for example, or forcing higher Medicare premiums—is exactly the wrong approach. Imposing these cuts, as many political leaders now propose, would force millions of older Americans out of the middle class and into poverty.

We are fighting—and we must all fight—to make sure that doesn't happen. To restore prosperity to the middle class, we need a four-part strategy:

1. Restore middle-class jobs.
2. Strengthen Social Security and increase retirement savings.

Defining the Pressures

16%	Adults providing unpaid care to a family member or friend 50+
53%	Families that don't think they have enough for comfortable retirement
34%	Head of a family, age 50–64, without retirement savings
75%	Families in 2010 living paycheck to paycheck

From 1989 to 2009

3%	Increase of full-time earnings for men
73%	Increase of average cost of one year of college
182%	Increase of health insurance premiums
292%	Increase of median debt of middle-class families

Sources: "Caregiving in the U.S.," National Alliance for Caregiving/AARP; Gallup: Harris Interactive: AARP Public Policy Institute

3. Slow the growth of health care costs and make Medicare sustainable.
4. Increase revenue for public investments to restore prosperity.

If we focus on restoring prosperity to the middle class, we will get our economy going again, put people back to work, increase the revenue needed to fund the government and reduce the deficit.

This will not happen overnight. It will take time and political courage. But it must be done. Failure to act will only put the American dream of a better life for ourselves, our children and grandchildren further out of reach.

Critical Thinking

1. What current changes being considered by government would force the middle class out of their current standard of living and into poverty?
2. What four steps were proposed to restore prosperity to the middle class?
3. What were presented as the advantages of restoring prosperity to the middle class?

Create Central

www.mhhe.com/createcentral

Internet References

Administration on Aging
www.aoa.dhhs.gov

American Federation for Aging Research
www.afar.org

American Geriatrics Society
www.americangeriatrics.org

Community Transportation Association of America
www.ctaa.org

Community Reports State Inspection Surveys
www.ConsumerReports.org

Medicare Consumer Information from the Health Care Finance Association
cms.hhs.gov/default.asp?fromhcfadotgov_true

National Institutes of Health
www.nih.gov

The United States Senate: Special Committee on Aging
www.senate.gov/~aging

Social Security: Fears vs. Facts: What Social Security Critics Keep Getting Wrong by Liz Weston

221

Article   Prepared by: Elaina F. Osterbur, *Saint Louis University*

Social Security: Fears vs. Facts

What Social Security Critics Keep Getting Wrong

Liz Weston

Learning Outcomes

After reading this article, you will be able to:

- Describe the three myths that the author of "Social Security: Fears vs. Facts" believes exist regarding the future of the Social Security program.

- Identify one of those myths that you think has the greatest credibility and tell why you think that is so.

I've been writing about Social Security for nearly two decades. But even I still have trouble wrapping my brain around some of the system's complexities—from how benefits are calculated to how the trust fund works. So it's not surprising that myths about Social Security persist, often fed by the program's critics. With the debate about Social Security's future once again heating up, these three myths need to be put to rest—so we can focus on the real issues.

Myth #1: By the Time I Retire, Social Security Will Be Broke

If you believe this, you are not alone. More and more Americans have become convinced that the Social Security system won't be there when they need it. In an AARP survey released last year, only 35 percent of adults said they were very or somewhat confident about Social Security's future.

It's true that Social Security's finances need work, because over the long term there will not be enough money to fully cover promised benefits. But radical changes aren't needed. In 2010 a number of different proposals were put forward that, taken in combination, would put the program back on firm financial ground for the future, including changes such as raising the amount of wages subject to the payroll tax (now capped at $106,800) and benefit changes based on longer life expectancy.

Myth #2: The Social Security Trust Fund Assets Are Worthless

Any surplus payroll taxes not used for current benefits are used to purchase special-issue, interest-paying Treasury bonds. In other words, the surplus in the Social Security trust fund has been loaned to the federal government for its general use—the reserve of $2.6 trillion is not a heap of cash sitting in a vault. These bonds are backed by the full faith and credit of the federal government, just as they are for other Treasury bondholders. However, Treasury will soon need to pay back these bonds. This will put pressure on the federal budget, according to Social Security's board of trustees. Even without any changes, Social Security can continue paying full benefits through 2037. After that, the revenue from payroll taxes will still cover about 75 percent of promised benefits.

Myth #3: I Could Invest Better on My Own

Maybe you could, and maybe you couldn't. But the point of Social Security isn't to maximize the return on the payroll taxes you've contributed. Social Security is designed to be the one guaranteed part of your retirement income that can't be outlived or lost in the stock market. It's a secure base of income throughout your working life and retirement. And for many, it's a lifeline. Social Security provides the majority of income for at least half of Americans over age 65; it is 90 percent or more of income for 43 percent of singles and 22 percent of married couples. You can, and should, invest in a retirement fund like a 401(k) or an individual retirement account. Maybe you'll enjoy strong returns and avoid the market turmoil we have seen during the past decade. If not, you'll still have Social Security to fall back on.

Critical Thinking

1. Why do so many young people think Social Security will go broke before they can benefit from the program?

2. Where are Social Security's surplus funds invested to earn money for the program?

3. If the Social Security program went out of existence and people were to invest individually for their own retirement, do you think many of them would do so with adequate investments to assure they had a secure retirement income?

Create Central

www.mhhe.com/createcentral

Internet References

Administration on Aging
www.aoa.dhhs.gov

American Federation for Aging Research
www.afar.org

American Geriatrics Society
www.americangeriatrics.org

Community Transportation Association of America
www.ctaa.org

Community Reports State Inspection Surveys
www.ConsumerReports.org

Medicare Consumer Information from the Health Care Finance Association
cms.hhs.gov/default.asp?fromhcfadotgov_true

National Institutes of Health
www.nih.gov

The United States Senate: Special Committee on Aging
www.senate.gov/~aging

As *AARP The Magazine's* personal finance columnist, LIZ WESTON offers advice on everything from car loans to home sales.

Article

Prepared by: Elaina F. Osterbur, *Saint Louis University*

Social Security Heading for Insolvency Even Faster

Trust Funds Could Run Dry in about 2 Decades

Learning Outcomes

After reading this article, you will be able to:

- Identify the reasons given for the Social Security program heading for insolvency.
- State the time when the Medicare and Social Security trust funds are expected to be insolvent.

Social Security is rushing even faster toward insolvency, driven by retiring baby boomers, a weak economy and politicians' reluctance to take painful action to fix the huge retirement and disability program.

The trust funds that support Social Security will run dry in 2033—three years earlier than previously projected—the government said Monday.

There was no change in the year that Medicare's hospital insurance fund is projected to run out of money. It's still 2024. The program's trustees, however, said the pace of Medicare spending continues to accelerate. Congress enacted a 2 percent cut for Medicare last year, and that is the main reason the trust fund exhaustion date did not advance.

The trustees who oversee both programs say high energy prices are suppressing workers' wages, a trend they see continuing. They also expect people to work fewer hours than previously projected, even after the economy recovers. Both trends would lead to lower payroll tax receipts, which support both programs.

Unless Congress acts—and forcefully—payments to millions of Americans could be cut.

If the Social Security and Medicare funds ever become exhausted, the nation's two biggest benefit programs would collect only enough money in payroll taxes to pay partial benefits. Social Security could cover about 75 percent of benefits, the trustees said in their annual report. Medicare's giant hospital fund could pay 87 percent of costs.

"Lawmakers should not delay addressing the long-run financial challenges facing Social Security and Medicare," the trustees wrote. "If they take action sooner rather than later, more options and more time will be available to phase in changes so that the public has adequate time to prepare."

The trustees project that Social Security benefits will increase next year, though the increase could be small. They project a cost-of-living-adjustment, or COLA, of 1.8 percent for 2013; the actual amount won't be known until October. Beneficiaries got a 3.6 percent increase this year, the first after two years without one.

More than 56 million retirees, disabled workers, spouses and children receive Social Security. The average retirement benefit is $1,232 a month; the average monthly benefit for disabled workers is $1,111.

About 50 million people are covered by Medicare, the medical insurance program for older Americans.

America's aging population—increased by millions of retiring baby boomers—is straining both Social Security and Medicare. Potential options to reduce Social Security costs include raising the full retirement age, which already is being gradually increased to 67, reducing annual benefit increases and limiting benefits for wealthier Americans.

Critical Thinking

1. What do the Social Security and Medicare trustees believe is causing the problems to ultimately run out of funds?
2. What would be the effect of the Social Security and Medicare programs running out of funds?
3. What is the current average retirement benefit coming from Social Security each month?

Create Central

www.mhhe.com/createcentral

Internet References

Administration on Aging
www.aoa.dhhs.gov

American Federation for Aging Research
www.afar.org

American Geriatrics Society
www.americangeriatrics.org

Community Transportation Association of America
www.ctaa.org

Community Reports State Inspection Surveys
www.ConsumerReports.org

Medicare Consumer Information from the Health Care Finance Association
cms.hhs.gov/default.asp?fromhcfadotgov_true

National Institutes of Health
www.nih.gov

The United States Senate: Special Committee on Aging
www.senate.gov/~aging

Article   Prepared by: Elaina F. Osterbur, *Saint Louis University*

Medicare May Soon Take New Shape

Challenge: How to keep program solvent while providing good care.

ROBERT PEAR

Learning Outcomes

After reading this article, you will be able to:

- Explain the different positions of Republicans and Democrats regarding how to utilize future savings in the Medicare program.

- Identify the proposals that have been suggested for reducing the growth and costs of Medicare.

- Describe 3 of the 10 options for shoring up Social Security in the future that you think have the best chance of being adopted by Congress.

- Describe 3 of the 10 options for shoring up Social Security that you think are least likely to be adopted.

President Obama has deep disagreements with House Republicans about how to address Medicare's long-term problems. But in deciding to wade into the fight over entitlements, which he may address in a speech Wednesday afternoon, the president is signaling that he too believes Medicare must change to avert a potentially crippling fiscal crunch.

So the real issue now is not so much whether to re-engineer Medicare to deal with an aging population and rising medical costs, but how.

Even before they debate specific proposals, lawmakers across the ideological spectrum face several fundamental questions:

Will the federal government retain its dominant role in prescribing benefits and other details of the program, like how much doctors and hospitals are paid and which new treatments are covered? Will beneficiaries still have legally enforceable rights to all those services?

Will Medicare spending still increase automatically with health costs, the number of beneficiaries and the amount of care they receive? Or will the government try to limit the costs to taxpayers by paying a fixed amount each year to private health plans to subsidize coverage for older Americans and those who are disabled?

Public concern about the federal deficit and debt has revived interest in proposals to slow the growth of Medicare, including ideas from Mr. Obama's deficit reduction commission. Here are some leading proposals:

- Increase the age of eligibility for Medicare to 67, from 65.
- Charge co-payments for home health care services and laboratory tests.
- Require beneficiaries to pay higher premiums.
- Pay a lump sum to doctors and hospitals for all services in a course of treatment or an episode of care. The new health care law establishes a pilot program to test such "bundled payments," starting in 2013.
- Reduce Medicare payments to health care providers in parts of the country where spending per beneficiary is much higher than the national average. (Payments could be adjusted to reflect local prices and the "health status" of beneficiaries.)
- Require drug companies to provide additional discounts, or rebates, to Medicare for brand-name drugs bought by low-income beneficiaries.
- Reduce Medicare payments to teaching hospitals for the cost of training doctors.

In debate last year over Mr. Obama's health plan, Republicans said repeatedly that he was "raiding Medicare" to pay for a new entitlement providing insurance for people under 65. The Senate Republican leader, Mitch McConnell of Kentucky, said the Democrats were using Medicare as a piggy bank. Senator Jim Risch of Idaho said, "We are talking about a half-trillion dollars that is being stolen from Medicare." Senator Charles E. Grassley of Iowa said the cuts "threaten seniors' access to care."

Now it is Republicans, especially House Republicans, proposing to cut the growth of Medicare, with a difference.

"Any potential savings would be used to shore up Medicare, not to pay for new entitlements," said Representative Paul D. Ryan, Republican of Wisconsin and chairman of the House Budget Committee.

The House is expected to vote this week on his budget blueprint for the next 10 years.

Mr. Ryan points to Medicare's prescription drug coverage as a model. That benefit, added to Medicare under a 2003 law, is delivered entirely by private insurers competing for business, and competition has been intense. Premiums for beneficiaries and costs to the government have been much lower than projected.

Republicans rarely mention one secret to the success of Medicare's drug program. Under presidents of both parties, Medicare officials have regulated the prescription drug plans to protect consumers and to make sure the sickest patients have access to the drugs they need.

Many Democrats like Medicare as it is: an entitlement program in which three-fourths of the 47 million beneficiaries choose their doctors and other health care providers, and one-fourth have elected to enroll in managed-care plans. These Democrats acknowledge that care could be better coordinated, but say that could be done in the traditional fee-for-service Medicare program, without forcing beneficiaries into private health plans offered by insurance companies.

Marilyn Moon, a health economist and former Democratic trustee of the Medicare trust fund, said serious discussion of changes in Medicare was warranted, and she noted that the government spent more than a half-trillion dollars a year on the program. Still, Ms. Moon said, it would be preferable to shore up Medicare without "the philosophical sea change" sought by Republicans, who would give private insurers more latitude to decide what benefits are available and what services are covered.

Obama administration officials said Tuesday that Medicare could save $50 billion over 10 years by reducing medical errors, injuries, infections and complications that prolong hospital stays or require readmission of patients.

In any program as big as Medicare, which accounts for one-fifth of all health spending, even decisions about small, seemingly technical questions can have vast consequences for beneficiaries, the health care industry and the economy as a whole.

Gradually raising the eligibility age, for example, would save $125 billion over 10 years, the Congressional Budget Office says.

But it would increase costs for people who would otherwise have Medicare. Some of those 65- and 66-year-olds would obtain insurance from Medicaid or from employers, as active workers or retirees, thus increasing costs for Medicaid and for employer-sponsored health plans.

If Congress decided to make a fixed contribution to a private health plan on behalf of each Medicare beneficiary, lawmakers and lobbyists could spend years debating how to set payment rates and how to adjust them, based on increases in consumer prices or medical costs or the growth of the economy.

Those decisions would directly affect beneficiaries. Under the House Republican proposal, the Congressional Budget Office said, beneficiaries "would bear a much larger share of their health care costs," requiring them to "reduce their use of health care services, spend less on other goods and services, or save more in advance of retirement."

The history of Medicare is filled with unsuccessful efforts to rein in costs. Private health plans entered Medicare with a promise to shave 5 percent off costs, but ended up costing more than the traditional Medicare program. For two decades, Congress has tried to limit Medicare spending on doctors' services, but the limits have proved so unrealistic that Congress has repeatedly intervened to increase them.

Critical Thinking

1. How do the Republicans and Democrats differ in terms of possible new entitlements to the Medicare program?

2. How do the Republicans and Democrats differ in terms of whether the Medicare beneficiaries should be forced into private health plans offered by insurance companies?

3. Has the cost of current Medicare prescription drug coverage handled by private insurance companies been higher or lower than expected?

Create Central

www.mhhe.com/createcentral

Internet References

Administration on Aging
www.aoa.dhhs.gov

American Federation for Aging Research
www.afar.org

American Geriatrics Society
www.americangeriatrics.org

Community Transportation Association of America
www.ctaa.org

Community Reports State Inspection Surveys
www.ConsumerReports.org

Medicare Consumer Information from the Health Care Finance Association
cms.hhs.gov/default.asp?fromhcfadotgov_true

National Institutes of Health
www.nih.gov

The United States Senate: Special Committee on Aging
www.senate.gov/~aging

Article   Prepared by: Elaina F. Osterbur, *Saint Louis University*

Time for a Tune-Up

Social Security faces challenges. Retirement for future generations is at stake. Here are 10 options on the table.

JONATHAN PETERSON

Learning Outcomes

After reading this article, you will be able to:

- Discuss the 10 options that would help to shore up Social Security funds.

- Determine the probability that Congress will establish private accounts with regard to payroll taxes.

- Determine the probability that there will be a Social Security program when you reach retirement.

In just 21 years, Social Security will be able to pay only three-fourths of its promised benefits, an outlook that guarantees debate about the future of—and the meaning of—Social Security in American life. Yet the projected shortfall is not the only challenge facing the program and those who depend on it. Changes in lifestyle, demographics and the economy are bringing *insecurity* to many older Americans.

Experts have put forth a number of proposals that in some combination could sustain Social Security for the long haul, while making it more helpful and fair. Here are 10 options now on the policy table in Washington:

1. Increase the Cap

You make payroll tax contributions to Social Security on your earnings up to a limit ($110,100 in 2012). If you're like most workers, you earn less than the cap. Increasing the cap to $215,400—so that 90 percent of U.S. earnings are covered—would reduce Social Security's shortfall by about 36 percent. Eliminating it altogether would end almost all of the shortfall in one stroke. Supporters say that raising the cap would be fair and that the amount would not be onerous. The main argument against such a rise is that high earners already get less of a return on contributions than lower-income workers, because benefits are progressive by design. Also, raising the earnings base would amount to a big tax hike on high earners.

2. Raise the Payroll Tax Rate

In recent years, wage earners have paid a Social Security tax of 6.2 percent on earnings up to the income cap, as have their employers. (Congress temporarily cut the employee share to 4.2 percent in 2011 and 2012 as a way to boost the economy.)

Raising the tax rate to 6.45 percent for both employees and employers would eliminate 22 percent of the shortfall and could be phased in. Critics voice concerns about the economic impact and say employers might respond by cutting other payroll costs, such as jobs.

Other ways to raise revenues include increasing income taxes on benefits. Taxing the money that goes into "salary reduction plans," which let you divert pretax income to health care, transit and other uses, could reduce the shortfall by 10 percent. But such a move would hit consumers who may rely on such accounts.

3. Consider Women's Work Patterns

Women workers—single or married—tend to get lower benefits because they're paid less over the course of their careers and because they are more likely than men to take time off from paid employment for caregiving or child-rearing. One proposal would give workers credit for at least some of the time spent caregiving or child-rearing. At the same time, a non-married woman potentially gets a much smaller benefit (depending on her earnings history) than a nonworking wife because she can't rely on a higher-earning spouse for benefits. Measures addressing these issues would be gender-neutral, so they could also help some men. The cost of such a proposal would have to be offset, however, or it could increase the shortfall.

4. Adjust Benefits

Benefit cuts are nothing to cheer about, but they would save money. They could be structured in a way that doesn't hurt current or near-retirees and low-income individuals. Any changes could be phased in after a long lead time, giving younger workers years to adjust their financial plans.

Still, reducing benefits for modest-income people could affect their standard of living in retirement. Reducing benefits for higher earners could undermine the broad public support for Social Security as a program in which everyone pays in and everyone gets benefits.

5. Set a Minimum Benefit

People who had low incomes during their working lives—perhaps one in five earners—now may end up with benefits that are still below the poverty line. A minimum benefit might be set at 125 percent of the poverty line, indexed to wage increases to keep it adequate over time.

6. Modify the COLA Formula

Social Security benefits generally rise to keep up with the cost of living. This cost-of-living adjustment, known as the COLA, is currently based on the Consumer Price Index for Urban Wage Earners and Clerical Workers (known as CPI-W).

One proposal would switch to a different measure, the "chained CPI," which assumes consumers alter their buying patterns if a price goes up too much. Say the price of beef soars—people may switch to chicken. The chained CPI rises about 0.3 percentage point more slowly each year than the CPI-W, meaning benefits would grow more slowly, too—about 6 percent less over the course of 20 years. Adopting a chained CPI would reduce the shortfall by about 23 percent.

Another approach would substitute a formula known as CPI-E. It takes into special account the type of spending that is more common among people 62 and older, such as medical care, which continues to rise faster than other costs. This could increase benefits, expanding the shortfall by about 16 percent.

7. Raise the Full Retirement Age

The age at which you can get full Social Security benefits is gradually rising to 67 for people born in 1960 and later. Pushing it up even further would save money and provide an incentive for people to keep working.

A full retirement age of 68 could reduce the shortfall by about 18 percent. Raising it to 70 would close 44 percent. Such increases could be phased in, and proponents say this approach makes sense in an era of increased life expectancy. A healthy 65-year-old man, for example, is expected to live beyond 82. But not everyone has benefited equally from increases in longevity—lower-income, less educated workers have not gained as much as their more affluent, more educated counterparts. And a later full retirement age could be onerous for workers with health problems or physically demanding jobs. A

related proposal—longevity indexing—would link benefits to increased life expectancy.

8. Give the Oldest a Boost

Americans are living longer, and the oldest often are the poorest. They may have little savings left; usually they no longer work and any pensions they have are likely eroded by inflation. A longevity bonus, for example, a 5 percent benefit increase for people above a certain age, say 85, could help them.

9. Establish Private Accounts

Free-market advocates have long pushed to make Social Security more of a private program, in which some of your payroll taxes would go into a personal account that would rise and fall with the financial markets. Supporters believe that stock market returns could make up for benefit cuts. You would own the assets in your personal account and could pass them on to your heirs. Personal accounts could be introduced gradually and become a choice for younger workers, while retirees and near retirees could remain in the current system. Opponents worry that they would replace a guaranteed, inflation-protected benefit for workers and, potentially, family members, with more limited protections. Private accounts only pay out the amount in the account. Also, diverting money to private accounts means additional funding could be needed to pay currently promised benefits.

10. Cover More Workers

Not all workers take part in Social Security. The largest uncovered group is about 25 percent of state and local government employees who rely on state pension systems. Bringing new hires into Social Security would raise enough new revenue to trim about 8 percent of the long-term shortfall (though down the road, when these people claim benefits, costs would rise). State and local governments may oppose such a measure because it would divert dollars from public pensions that are already underfunded.

Critical Thinking

1. Why do you think that at the present time the United States Congress has not discussed adopting any of the ten options that would help to shore up the Social Security funds?

2. Do you think that it is likely that Congress will establish private accounts in which some of a person's payroll taxes paid would go into an individual's account whose earnings would rise and fall with the financial markets?

3. What do you think is the probability that there will be a Social Security program when you reach retirement age and that you will receive a monthly check from the program?

Create Central

www.mhhe.com/createcentral

Internet References

Administration on Aging
www.aoa.dhhs.gov

American Federation for Aging Research
www.afar.org

American Geriatrics Society
www.americangeriatrics.org

Community Transportation Association of America
www.ctaa.org

Community Reports State Inspection Surveys
www.ConsumerReports.org

Medicare Consumer Information from the Health Care Finance Association
cms.hhs.gov/default.asp?fromhcfadotgov_true

National Institutes of Health
www.nih.gov

The United States Senate: Special Committee on Aging
www.senate.gov/~aging

Article

Prepared by: Elaina F. Osterbur, *Saint Louis University*

Protect Social Security

A. BARRY RAND

Learning Outcomes

After reading this article, you will be able to:

- Identify the different groups of people who depend on Social Security to provide a large part of their income.

- Explain why, at age 65 and older, Social Security provides a higher percentage of income for a woman than it does for a man.

In August, we celebrate the 75th anniversary of Social Security. Ever since Ida Mae Fuller received the first Social Security check in January 1940, Social Security has provided the foundation of retirement security and helped people to live their lives with independence and dignity.

At AARP, we are committed to protecting and fighting for Social Security so that people 75 years from now will still enjoy the peace of mind it provides today. We also know that Social Security needs to be strengthened for future generations, and we will work diligently toward that goal.

We understand that Social Security is much more than just a public policy. It is a guaranteed pension that, on average, replaces 40 percent of a retiree's wages. And because it is risk-free—the only part of the retirement system that is—it is the lifeline that many older Americans, their families, people with disabilities, widows and other survivors count on for their day-to-day lives.

Fighting for, protecting and strengthening Social Security won't be easy. The president's bipartisan fiscal commission—co-chaired by Alan Simpson and Erskine Bowles—and others in Washington are targeting Social Security to help close the growing federal budget deficit. More than most, we understand the importance of balanced budgets, but it's essential that the deficit not be closed by cutting benefits that today's seniors and future generations have earned over a lifetime of hard work.

If Washington wants to restore confidence in our nation's budget, lawmakers should deal with what's really caused our federal deficit. The fact is, Americans pay for Social Security, and it hasn't added one dime to the deficit. It's a sacred promise we make to seniors, our children and our grandchildren—one that must not be broken. We believe that.

As we look ahead, we are guided by some basic principles:

- Any changes to Social Security should be discussed as part of a broader conversation about how to help Americans prepare for a secure retirement, especially as other sources of retirement income—such as pensions, savings and home equity—have been crumbling over the past decade.
- If you pay into Social Security, you should receive the full benefits you've earned over a lifetime of hard work.
- Your Social Security benefits should keep up with inflation for as long as you live.
- You should continue to be covered in case you become disabled and can no longer work, and your family should continue to be protected if you die.
- We will provide educational support and advocate policies to help people save. And we will encourage better pensions and more private savings in addition to—not at the expense of—Social Security.

So as we celebrate Social Security's 75th anniversary in August, we need to protect and strengthen Social Security so future generations will continue

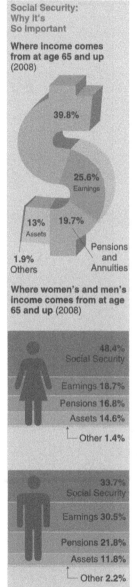

Social Security: Why It's So Important

Where income comes from at age 65 and up (2008)

39.8%

25.6% Earnings

13% Assets

19.7%

1.9% Others

Pensions and Annuities

Where women's and men's income comes from at age 65 and up (2008)

48.4% Social Security
Earnings 18.7%
Pensions 16.8%
Assets 14.6%
Other 1.4%

33.7% Social Security
Earnings 30.5%
Pensions 21.8%
Assets 11.8%
Other 2.2%

to have a strong foundation of income they can count on in retirement for the next 75 years. You can count on AARP to lead this fight.

Critical Thinking

1. What percentage of a 65 or older person's income is provided by Social Security?

2. Why should a 65 or older person expect to be able to draw a Social Security check for the rest of their life?

3. What factor causes Social Security payments to be increased from time to time?

Create Central

www.mhhe.com/createcentral

Internet References

Administration on Aging
www.aoa.dhhs.gov

American Federation for Aging Research
www.afar.org

American Geriatrics Society
www.americangeriatrics.org

Community Transportation Association of America
www.ctaa.org

Community Reports State Inspection Surveys
www.ConsumerReports.org

Medicare Consumer Information from the Health Care Finance Association
cms.hhs.gov/default.asp?fromhcfadotgov_true

National Institutes of Health
www.nih.gov

The United States Senate: Special Committee on Aging
www.senate.gov/~aging

Article   Prepared by: Elaina F. Osterbur, *Saint Louis University*

Retooling Medicare?

Medicare faces challenges. Retirement for future generations is at stake. Here are 7 options on the table.

PATRICIA BARRY

Learning Outcomes

After reading this article, you will be able to:

- Describe the proposed changes in Medicare that Rep. Paul Ryan, a Wisconsin Republican, is proposing.

- Identify the specific changes in Medicare payments and benefits that Ryan's plan, known as "premium support" to its proponents, is proposing.

Politicians are eyeing Medicare as a spending program ripe for cuts to help reduce the nation's deficit. And so it follows that the future of Medicare looms as a key battleground issue in the 2012 general election. But proposals to change the popular program tend to alarm older Americans, who see Medicare as part of their retirement security. And these same older Americans vote in large numbers. So stand by to hear all candidates claim that they want to "save" Medicare for future generations—but often in very different ways.

Proposed changes to the program include raising the eligibility age to 67, raising payroll taxes and requiring better-off beneficiaries to pay more. The most politically contentious plan, devised by Rep. Paul Ryan (R-Wis.), chairman of the House Budget Committee, would limit federal spending on Medicare and alter the way the government pays for benefits. Republicans say this plan is a fiscally responsible way of extending Medicare's viability as millions of boomers enter the program. Democrats call it "the end of Medicare as we know it" and a way to shift more costs to beneficiaries.

The future of Medicare looms as a key battleground issue in the 2012 election, and older Americans vote in large numbers.

Polls show that most Americans prefer to keep Medicare as it is. "Ryan's plan is a fundamental change in the structure of the program," so it makes older voters more nervous than lesser proposals do, says Robert Blendon, professor of health policy at Harvard's School of Public Health. But whoever gains the upper political hand in November, he adds, will have to wrestle with the budget deficit—and some of those decisions will likely affect Medicare.

With that in mind, AARP asked policy experts from across the political spectrum—Henry Aaron, senior fellow of the economic studies program at the Brookings Institution; Stuart Butler, director of the Center for Policy Innovation at the Heritage Foundation; and experts at Avalere Health, a Washington health care policy and research company—to give arguments for and against some Medicare proposals. (Read these in full and contact the experts at earnedasay.org.) Here are summaries of their opposing positions on seven options that most directly affect beneficiaries:

Changing the Way Medicare Pays for Benefits

Medicare now offers two ways to receive benefits. If you're in traditional Medicare, the government pays directly for each covered medical service you use. If you're in a Medicare Advantage private plan, the government pays a set annual amount to the plan for your care. Under the Ryan plan—known as "premium support" to its proponents and as a "voucher system" to its critics—the government would allow you a certain sum of money to buy coverage from competing private plans or from a revised version of traditional Medicare.

For

This would put Medicare on a budget to hold down spending and reduce the tax burden on future generations. You'd receive a share of this budget to help you purchase your health care and have more flexibility to make choices. For example, if you wanted more generous coverage (such as seeing any doctor of your choice), you'd pay the premium difference out of your own pocket, and if the difference became too high, you could switch to a less expensive plan.

Against

The value of the voucher would be tied to some economic index—not to actual health costs, which generally rise faster than other costs. So there is a high risk that benefits would become increasingly inadequate and more out-of-pocket costs would be shifted to the consumer. Medicare already has competing private plans, through the Medicare Advantage and Part D drug programs, yet the hoped-for savings from them have not yet materialized.

Raising Medicare Eligibility Age to 67

Eligibility for Medicare has always been at age 65, except for younger people with disabilities. This proposal aims to gradually bring Medicare in line with Social Security, where full retirement age is now 66 and set to rise to 67 by 2027.

For

With more Americans living longer, and health spending on older people rising, we can't afford Medicare at age 65. Raising the eligibility age would reduce federal spending on Medicare by about 5 percent over the next 20 years.

Against

This proposal would increase other health care spending—especially costs for employer health plans and Medicaid—and uninsured people would pay full costs for a longer time. Medicare premiums would rise due to fewer people in the program to share costs.

Raising the Medicare Payroll Tax

This tax, which funds Medicare Part A hospital insurance, is currently 2.9 percent of all earnings (1.45 percent each for employers and employees; 2.9 percent for the self-employed). People who have paid this tax for a sufficient time do not pay monthly premiums for Part A.

For

Part A currently faces a small long-term deficit after 2024, when it's estimated that available funds will not fully pay for all services. Increasing the payroll tax by just 0.5 percent each for employers and employees would more than fix that problem, leaving a small surplus to act as a cushion against future shortfalls or fund extra benefits in Medicare.

Against

Raising the payroll tax would mean a higher rate of tax for each dollar earned by working Americans, slowing economic growth and increasing the tax burden on future generations.

Even workers not earning enough to pay income taxes would pay this bigger tax.

Raising Medicare Premiums for Higher-Income People

Most people pay monthly premiums for Part B, which covers doctors' services and outpatient care, and for Part D prescription drug coverage. The standard premiums pay for about 25 percent of the costs of these services, while Medicare pays the remaining 75 percent out of general tax revenues. People with incomes over a certain level—those whose tax returns show a modified adjusted gross income of $85,000 for a single person or $170,000 for a married couple—pay higher premiums.

For

The easiest way to bring in more money for Medicare would be to raise the premiums even more for higher income people—so that the wealthiest older people pay the full cost and receive no taxpayer-funded subsidy. Another option is to lower the income level at which the higher premium charge kicks in, so that more people have to pay it.

Against

Higher-income earners already have paid more into the Medicare program through higher payroll and income taxes, and now pay up to three times more for the same Part B and D coverage. If increased taxes make healthier and wealthier people drop out of the program, standard premiums would eventually become more expensive for everyone.

Changing Medigap Supplemental Insurance

About one in six people with Medicare buys private supplemental insurance, also known as medigap. It covers some of their out-of-pocket expenses under traditional Medicare, such as the 20 percent copayments typically required for Part B services. This option would limit medigap coverage, requiring people to bear more out-of-pocket costs.

For

People buy medigap to limit their out-of-pocket spending in Medicare. But because they pay less, they tend to use more Medicare services, increasing the burden for taxpayers.

Against

There is no evidence that raising medigap premiums or reducing benefits would deter people from using health services unnecessarily, and most patients can't tell whether a service is necessary or not. But there is evidence that postponing needed services leads to greater health problems that cost Medicare more to fix.

Redesigning Copays and Deductibles

Currently, Parts A and B in traditional Medicare have different copays and deductibles. Some proposals would combine the programs to have only one deductible—for example, $550 annually, and uniform copays for Part A and Part B services, plus an annual out-of-pocket expense limit, similar to employer insurance plans.

For

Simplifying Medicare benefits to make them less confusing could save Medicare up to $110 billion over 10 years. An out-of-pocket cap would provide great financial protection, especially for sicker beneficiaries, and reduce the need for medigap supplemental insurance.

Against

Some beneficiaries might pay less, but others—especially those who use few services or spend longer periods in the hospital—would pay more out of pocket than they do now, unless they have additional insurance.

Adding Copays for Some Services

Medicare does not charge copays for home health care, the first 20 days in a skilled nursing facility—rehab after surgery, for example—or for laboratory services such as blood work and diagnostic tests. Several proposals would require copays for one or all of these.

For

Added copays would discourage unnecessary use of these services. Over 10 years, copays could save Medicare up to $40 billion for home health, $21 billion for stays in skilled nursing facilities and $16 billion for lab tests.

Against

Patients without supplemental insurance could pay significantly more for these services, or might not be able to afford them. This could end up harming patients and costing Medicare even more money if postponing treatment worsened patients' health, leading to expensive emergency room visits and hospital admissions. Also, patients generally follow doctors' orders and do not know which services are medically necessary and which are not.

Critical Thinking

1. What two proposed financial changes would bring in money directly to the Medicare funds?
2. What is the benefit to people who buy Medigap supplemental insurance?
3. What could be done to assure that Medicare would have adequate funds to pay for all services in the future?

Create Central

www.mhhe.com/createcentral

Internet References

Administration on Aging
www.aoa.dhhs.gov

American Federation for Aging Research
www.afar.org

American Geriatrics Society
www.americangeriatrics.org

Community Transportation Association of America
www.ctaa.org

Community Reports State Inspection Surveys
www.ConsumerReports.org

Medicare Consumer Information from the Health Care Finance Association
cms.hhs.gov/default.asp?fromhcfadotgov_true

National Institutes of Health
www.nih.gov

The United States Senate: Special Committee on Aging
www.senate.gov/~aging